W9-ARC-601

# EUROPEAN MORALS

## VOL. I

# HISTORY OF
# EUROPEAN MORALS

## FROM AUGUSTUS
## TO CHARLEMAGNE

ST. JOSEPH'S UNIVERSITY    STX
1.L46              v. 1
istory of European morals from Augustus

9353 00122 1090

59726

BY

WILLIAM EDWARD HARTPOLE LECKY, M. A.

*THIRD EDITION, REVISED*

BJ71
.L46
V. I

IN TWO VOLUMES

VOL. I

ST. JOSEPH'S COLLEGE
HOUSE LIBRARY

NEW YORK
D. APPLETON AND COMPANY
1903

*Authorized Edition.*

# ADVERTISEMENT
## TO THE THIRD EDITION.

---

I HAVE availed myself of the interval since the last
edition, to subject this book to a minute and careful
revision, removing such inaccuracies as I have been able
myself to discover, as well as those which have been
brought under my notice by reviewers or correspondents.
I must especially acknowledge the great assistance I
have derived in this task from my German translator,
Dr. H. Jolowicz—now, unhappily, no more—one of the
most conscientious and accurate scholars with whom I
have ever been in communication.  In the controversial part of the first chapter, which has given rise to a
good deal of angry discussion, four or five lines which
stood in the former editions have been omitted, and
three or four short passages have been inserted, eluci-
dating or supporting positions which had been misun-
derstood or contested.

*January 1877.*

# PREFACE.

THE questions with which an historian of Morals is chiefly concerned are the changes that have taken place in the moral standard and in the moral type. By the first, I understand the degrees in which, in different ages, recognised virtues have been enjoined and practised. By the second, I understand the relative importance that in different ages has been attached to different virtues. Thus, for example, a Roman of the age of Pliny, an Englishman of the age of Henry VIII., and an Englishman of our own day, would all agree in regarding humanity as a virtue, and its opposite as a vice; but their judgments of the acts which are compatible with a humane disposition would be widely different. A humane man of the first period might derive a keen enjoyment from those gladiatorial games, which an Englishman, even in the days of the Tudors, would regard as atrociously barbarous; and this last would, in his turn, acquiesce in many sports which would now be emphatically condemned. And, in addition to this change of standard, there is a continual change in the order of precedence which is given to virtues. Patriotism, chastity, charity, and humility are examples of virtues, each of which has in some ages been brought forward as of the most supreme and transcendent importance, and the very basis of a virtuous character, and in other ages been thrown into the background, and reckoned among the minor graces of a noble life. The heroic virtues, the amiable virtues, and what are called more especially the religious virtues, form distinct groups, to which, in different periods, different degrees of prominence have been assigned; and the nature, causes, and consequences of these changes in the moral type are among the most important branches of history.

In estimating, however, the moral condition of an age, it is not sufficient to examine the ideal of moralists. It is necessary also to enquire how far that ideal has been realised among the people. The corruption of a nation is often reflected in the indulgent and selfish ethics of its teachers; but it sometimes produces a reaction, and impels the moralist to an asceticism which is the extreme opposite of the prevailing spirit of society. The means which moral teachers possess of acting upon their fellows, vary greatly in their nature and efficacy, and the age of the highest moral teaching is often not that of the highest general level of practice. Sometimes we find a kind of aristocracy of virtue, exhibiting the most refined excellence in their teaching and in their actions, but exercising scarcely any appreciable influence upon the mass of the community. Sometimes we find moralists of a much less heroic order, whose influence has permeated every section of society. In addition, therefore, to the type and standard of morals inculcated by the teachers, an historian must investigate the realised morals of the people.

The three questions I have now briefly indicated are those which I have especially regarded in examining the moral history of Europe between Augustus and Charlemagne. As a preliminary to this enquiry, I have discussed at some length the rival theories concerning the nature and obligations of morals, and have also endeavoured to show what virtues are especially appropriate to each successive stage of civilisation, in order that we may afterwards ascertain to what extent the natural evolution has been affected by special agencies. I have then followed the moral history of the Pagan Empire, reviewing the Stoical, the Eclectic, and the Egyptian philosophies, that in turn flourished, showing in what respects they were the products or expressions of the general condition of society, tracing their influence in many departments of legislation and literature, and investigating the causes of the deepseated corruption which baffled all the efforts of

emperors and philosophers. The triumph of the
Christian religion in Europe next demands our attention. In treating this subject, I have endeavoured, for
the most part, to exclude all considerations of a purely
theological or controversial character, all discussions
concerning the origin of the faith in Palestine, and
concerning the first type of its doctrine, and to regard
the Church simply as a moral agent, exercising its influence in Europe. Confining myself within these
limits, I have examined the manner in which the circumstances of the Pagan Empire impeded or assisted
its growth, the nature of the opposition it had to
encounter, the transformations it underwent under the
influence of prosperity, of the ascetic enthusiasm, and
of the barbarian invasions, and the many ways in
which it determined the moral condition of society.
The growing sense of the sanctity of human life, the
history of charity, the formation of the legends of the
hagiology, the effects of asceticism upon civic and
domestic virtues, the moral influence of monasteries,
the ethics of the intellect, the virtues and vices of the
decaying Christian Empire and of the barbarian king-
doms that replaced it, the gradual apotheosis of secular
rank, and the first stages of that military Christianity
which attained its climax at the Crusades, have been
all discussed with more or less detail; and I have
concluded my work by reviewing the changes that
have taken place in the position of women, and in

the moral questions connected with the relations of the sexes.

In investigating these numerous subjects, it has occasionally, though rarely, happened that my path has intersected that which I had pursued in a former work, and in two or three instances I have not hesitated to repeat facts to which I had there briefly referred. I have thought that such a course was preferable to presenting the subject shorn of some material incident, or to falling into what has always the appearance of an unpleasing egotism, by appealing unnecessarily to my own writings. Although the history of the period I have traced has never, so far as I am aware, been written from exactly the point of view which I have adopted, I have, of course, been for the most part moving over familiar ground, which has been often and ably investigated; and any originality that may be found in this work must lie, not so much in the facts which have been exhumed, as in the manner in which they have been grouped, and in the significance that has been ascribed to them. I have endeavoured to acknowledge the more important works from which I have derived assistance; and if I have not always done so, I trust the reader will ascribe it to the great multitude of the special histories relating to the subjects I have treated, to my unwillingness to overload my pages with too numerous references, and perhaps, in some cases, to the difficulty that all who

nave been much occupied with a single department
of history must sometimes have, in distinguishing
the ideas which have sprung from their own reflections, from those which have been derived from
books.

There is one writer, however, whom I must especially mention, for his name occurs continually in the
following pages, and his memory has been more frequently, and in these latter months more sadly, present
to my mind than any other.  Brilliant and numerous
as are the works of the late Dean Milman, it was those
only who had the great privilege of his friendship, who
could fully realise the amazing extent and variety of
his knowledge ; the calm, luminous, and delicate judgment which he carried into so many spheres ; the
inimitable grace and tact of his conversation, corus-
cating with the happiest anecdotes, and the brightest
and yet the gentlest humour ; and, what was perhaps more remarkable than any single faculty, the
admirable harmony and symmetry of his mind and
character, so free from all the disproportion, and ec-
centricity, and exaggeration that sometimes make
even genius assume the form of a splendid disease.
They can never forget those yet higher attributes,
which rendered him so unspeakably reverend to all
who knew him well—his fervent love of truth, his wide
tolerance, his large, generous, and masculine judg-

ments of men and things; his almost instinctive perception of the good that is latent in each opposing party, his disdain for the noisy triumphs and the fleeting popularity of mere sectarian strife, the fond and touching affection with which he dwelt upon the images of the past, combining, even in extreme old age, with the keenest and most hopeful insight into the progressive movements of his time, and with a rare power of winning the confidence and reading the thoughts of the youngest about him. That such a writer should have devoted himself to the department of history, which more than any other has been distorted by ignorance, puerility, and dishonesty, I conceive to be one of the happiest facts in English literature, and (though sometimes diverging from his views) in many parts of the following work I have largely availed myself of his researches.

I cannot conceal from myself that this book is likely to encounter much, and probably angry, contradiction from different quarters and on different grounds. It is strongly opposed to a school of moral philosophy which is at present extremely influential in England; and, in addition to the many faults that may be found in its execution, its very plan must make it displeasing to many. Its subject necessarily includes questions on which it is exceedingly difficult for an English writer to touch, and the portion of history with which it is concerned has been obscured by no common measure of misrepresentation and passion. I have endeavoured to carry into it a judicial impartiality, and I trust that the attempt, however imperfect, may not be wholly useless to my readers.

LONDON: *March* 1869.

# CONTENTS

# OF THE FIRST VOLUME.

---

## CHAPTER I.

### THE NATURAL HISTORY OF MORALS.

                                                      PAGE

Fundamental division of moral theories . . . . . 1
Necessity of imputing immoral consequences to false theories . . 2

*The Utilitarian School*
    Mandeville . . . . . . . . . . 6
    Hobbes and his followers . . . . . . . . 7
    Theological Utilitarians . . . . . . . 14
    Enlargement of the school by the recognition of benevolence . 21
    And by Hartley's doctrine of association . . . . 22
    How far selfish . . . . . . . . . 30

*Objections to the School*
    From the common language and feelings of men . . 33
    From the impossibility of virtue bringing pleasure if practised
        only with that end . . . . . . . 35
    From the separation of morals from all other means to enjoy-
        ment . . . . . . . . . . 37
    Intuitive moralists do not deny the utility of virtue . . 39
    The degrees of virtue and vice do not correspond to the degrees
        of utility or the reverse . . . . . . 40

                                                                PAGE
*Consequence of Acting on Utilitarian Principles*
    Weakness of the doctrine of remote consequences    .    .    42
    Secret sins    .    .    .    .    .    .    .    .    .    .    43
    Sins of imagination    .    .    .    .    .    .    .    .    44
    Infanticide    .    .    .    .    .    .    .    .    .    .    45
    Cruelty to animals    .    .    .    .    .    .    .    .    46
    Chastity    .    .    .    .    .    .    .    .    .    .    49
    Love of truth    .    .    .    .    .    .    .    .    .    50

*Utilitarian Sanctions*
    Theological Utilitarianism makes the 'goodness of God' an un
        meaning term    .    .    .    .    .    .    .    .    .    54
    Destroys a chief argument for a future life    .    .    .    54
    Subverts natural religion .    .    .    .    .    .    54–55
    How far Supreme excellence is conducive to happiness    .    57
    The suffering caused by vice not proportioned to its criminality    61
    The rewards and punishments of conscience    .    .    .    62
    Nature of obligations    .    .    .    .    .    .    .    .    64
    The best men seldom the happiest    .    .    .    .    .    69
    Summary of objections    .    .    .    .    .    .    .    69
    Cause of the attraction of Utilitarianism    .    .    .    .    71
    Ambiguity of the term inductive as applied to morals    .    .    73

*Intuitive School*
    Doctrines of Butler, Adam Smith, Cudworth, Clarke, Wollaston,
        Hutcheson, Henry More, Reid, Hume, and Lord Kames    76–77
    The analogies of beauty and virtue    .    .    .    .    .    .    77
    Their differences .    .    .    .    .    .    .    .    .    82
    Illustrations of the distinction between the higher and lower
        parts of our nature    .    .    .    .    .    .    .    .    83
    Ethical importance of this distinction    .    .    .    .    91

*Alleged Diversities of Moral Judgment*
    Are frequently due to intellectual causes.—Usury and abortion    92
    Distinction between natural duties and those resting on posi-
        tive law    .    .    .    .    .    .    .    .    .    .    93
    Ancient customs canonised by time.—On women drinking wine    93
    Confused association of ideas.—Admiration for conquerors. .    94
    Calvinistic ethics .    .    .    .    .    .    .    .    .    96
    Persecution    .    .    .    .    .    .    .    .    .    .    98
    Antipathy to free enquiry    .    .    .    .    .    .    .    98

| | PAGE |
|---|---|
| General moral principles alone revealed by intuition . . | 99 |
| The moral unity of different ages is therefore a unity not of standard, but of tendency . . . . . . . | 100 |
| Application of this to the history of benevolence . . . | 100 |
| Utilitarian objections which it answers . . . . . | 101 |
| Intuitive morals not unprogressive . . . . . | 102 |
| Sketch of the history of chastity . . . . . . | 108 |
| Answers to miscellaneous objections . . . . . . | 108 |
| The standard, though not the essence, of virtue determined by the condition of society . . . . . . | 109 |
| Occasional duty of sacrificing higher principles to lower ones . | 110 |
| The difficulty of finding a fixed rule for these cases applies to the Utilitarian as well as his opponent. . . . . | 116 |
| Summary of the relations of virtue and interest . . . | 117 |
| Two senses of the word natural . . . . . . | 119 |
| The ethics of savages . . . . . . . | 120 |

*Each of the Two Schools of Morals related to the General Condition of Society*

| | |
|---|---|
| Their relations to metaphysical schools . . . . | 122 |
| To the Baconian philosophy.—Contrast between ancient and modern civilisation . . . . . . . | 125 |
| Practical consequences of each school . . . . . | 127 |

*The Order in which Moral Feelings are developed*

| | |
|---|---|
| Decline of ascetic and saintly qualities . . . . | 130 |
| Growth of the gentler virtues.—Relation of the imagination to benevolence . . . . . . . . | 132 |
| Callous and vindictive cruelty . . . . . . | 134 |
| Indulgent judgments towards criminals . . . . | 135 |
| Moral enthusiasms appropriate to different stages of civilisation | 136 |
| Growth of veracity—industrial, political, and philosophical | 137–140 |
| Theological influences have retarded the last . . . | 139 |
| The thrifty and the speculating character . . . | 140 |
| Forethought . . . . . . . . . | 140 |
| Decline of reverence . . . . . . . . | 141 |
| Female virtue . . . . . . . . . | 143 |
| Influenced by climate . . . . . . . . | 144 |
| By large towns . . . . . . . . . | 145 |
| By tardy marriages . . . . . . . . | 146 |

                                                                   PAGE
Each stage of civilisation is specially appropriate to some
    virtues . . . . . . . . . . . . . . 147
Relations of intellectual to moral progress . . . 149
The moral standard of most men lower in political than in
    private judgments . . . . . . . . . . 150
National vices . . . . . . . . . . 151
Qualities of corporations . . . . . . . . . . 152
French and English types . . . . . . . . 153
The manner in which virtues are grouped . . . . . 153
Rudimentary virtues . . . . . . . . . 154
All characters cannot be moulded into one type . . . . 155
Concluding remarks on moral types. . . . . . 155–160

# CHAPTER II.

## THE PAGAN EMPIRE.

Pagan religion had little influence on morals . . . . 161
Greek scepticism . . . . . . . . . . 161
Its extension to Rome—Opinions of the philosophers . 162–167
Roman religion never a source of moral enthusiasm . . . 167
Inroad of luxury . . . . . . . . . . 168
Growth of astrological fatalism . . . . . . . 171
Philosophers the true moral teachers . . . . . 171
Epicureanism and Stoicism the expression of different types of
    character . . . . . . . . . . . . 172
Military and patriotic enthusiasm formed in Rome the Stoical
    type . . . . . . . . . . . . . 172
The predisposition strengthened by the prominence of bio-
    graphy in moral teaching . . . . . . . 174
Epicureanism never became a school of virtue in Rome . . 175
Its function destructive . . . . . . . . 176–177

*Stoicism*
Its two essentials.—The unselfish ideal, and the subjugation of
    the affections to the reason . . . . . . . 17,
The first due to patriotism, the most unselfish of enthusiasms 178
Four possible motives of virtue . . . . . . . 178
Stoicism the best example of the perfect severance of virtue
    and interest . . . . . . . . . . . 181

                                                                    PAGE
Stoics disregarded or disbelieved in a future world  .  . 181–183
Taught men to sacrifice reputation  .  .  .  .  .  .   185
Distinguished the obligation from the attraction of virtue  .  186
The second characteristic, the repression of the desires  .  .  187
Deliberate virtue the most estimable—impulsive virtue the
    most attractive  .  .  .  .  .  .  .  .  .  .  188
Doctrine of Seneca concerning Pity  .  .  .  .  .  189
Evil consequences resulting from the suppression of the emotions  191
Hardness of character  .  .  .  .  .  .  .  .  192
Love of paradox  .  .  .  .  .  .  .  .  .  192
Many noted Stoics whose lives were very imperfect  .  .  193
Stoicism unfitted for common characters  .  .  .  .  194
Its high sense of the natural virtue of man and of the power
    of his will  .  .  .  .  .  .  .  .  .  .  195
Recognition of Providence  .  .  .  .  .  .  .  198
The habits of public life saved Stoics from quietism  .  .  199
Contemplation of death.—Bacon's objection to the Stoics  .  202
The literature of 'Consolations'  .  .  .  .  .  .  204
Death not regarded as penal  .  .  .  .  .  .  .  205
Pagan death-beds  .  .  .  .  .  .  .  .  .  205
Distinction between the Pagan and Christian conceptions of
    death  .  .  .  .  .  .  .  .  .  .  .  208
Suicide .  .  .  .  .  .  .  .  .  .  .  212
Grandeur of the Stoical ideal  .  .  .  .  .  .  222
Recapitulation  .  .  .  .  .  .  .  .  .  223
Contrast between the austerity of Roman Stoicism and the
    luxury of Roman society  .  .  .  .  .  .  .  225

Growth of a Gentler and more Cosmopolitan Spirit in Rome
Due first of all to the union of the Greek and Roman civilisa-
    tions.—Gentleness of the Greek character  .  .  .  227
Greek cosmopolitanism due to philosophical criticism and to
    the career of Alexander  .  .  .  .  .  .  .  229
Extent of Greek influence at Rome  .  .  .  .  .  230
A cosmopolitan spirit strengthened by the destruction of the
    power of the aristocracy  .  .  .  .  .  .  .  231
And by the aggrandisement of the colonies, the attraction of
    many foreigners to Rome, and the increased facilities for
    travelling  .  .  .  .  .  .  .  .  .  .  233
Foreigners among the most prominent of Latin writers  .  .  234

  PAGE

Multitude of emancipated slaves . . . . . 235
Roman legislators endeavoured to consolidate the Empire by
    admitting the conquered to the privileges of the conquerors 237
Stoicism proved quite capable of representing the cosmopolitan
    spirit . . . . . . . . . . . 239
But not equally so of representing the softening spirit of the age 241

*Rise of Eclectic Moralists*

Comparison of Plutarch and Seneca . . . . . 243
Influence of the new spirit on the Stoics . . . 244
Stoicism became more religious . . . . . 245
And more introspective.—History of the practice of self-
    examination . . . . . . . . . 247
Marcus Aurelius the best example of later Stoicism.—His
    life and character . . . . . . . . 249

*The People still very corrupt.—Causes of the Corruption*

Decadence of all the conditions of republican virtue . 256
Effects of the Imperial system on morals—the apotheosis of
    emperors . . . . . . . . . . 257
Moral consequences of slavery.—Increase of idleness and de-
    moralising employments . . . . . . 262
And of sensuality . . . . . . . . . 263
Decline of public spirit . . . . . . . 264
Universal empire prevented the political interaction which in
    modern nations sustains national life . . . . 264
History of the decline of agricultural pursuits and habits . 265
And of military virtue . . . . . . . 268
The gladiatorial shows—their origin and history . . 271
Their effects upon the theatre . . . . . . 277
Nature of their attraction . . . . . . . 278
Horrible excesses they attained . . . . . . 280
The manner in which their influence pervaded Roman life . 282
How they were regarded by moralists and historians . 284
The passion for them not inconsistent with humanity in other
    spheres . . . . . . . . . . 288

*Effects of Stoicism on the Corruption of Society*

It raised up many good emperors . . . . . 292
It produced a noble opposition under the worst emperors . 292

PAGE

It greatly extended Roman law . . . . . . 294
Roman law adopted the stoical conception of a law of nature
    to which it must conform . . . . . . 294
Its principles of equity derived from Stoicism . . . 295
Change in the relation of Romans to provincials . . . 297
Changes in domestic legislation . . . . . . 297
Slavery—its three stages at Rome.—Review of the condition
    of slaves . . . . . . . . . 300
Opinions of philosophers about slavery . . . . . 305
Laws in favour of slaves . . . . . . . 306
Stoics as consolers of the suffering, advisers of the young,
    and popular preachers . . . . . . . 308
The later Cynics an offshoot of Stoicism . . . . 309
Stoical Rhetoricians . . . . . . . . 310
Maximus of Tyre . . . . . . . . . 312
Dion Chrysostom . . . . . . . . . 312
Aulus Gellius, the best chronicler of the Rhetoricians . . 313
Rapid decadence of Stoicism . . . . . . 317

*Passion for Oriental Religions*
Mysticism partly a reaction against the disputations of the
    Rhetoricians.— Modern parallels . . . . . 318
Partly due to the increasing prominence given by moralists to
    the emotions . . . . . . . . . 318
And partly to the influx of Oriental slaves and the increasing
    importance of Alexandria . . . . . . . 319
But chiefly to a natural longing for belief . . . . 319
The Platonic and Pythagorean schools . . . . . 320
Plutarch's defence of the ancient creeds . . . . 321
Maximus of Tyre pursues the same course . . . . 322
Apuleius . . . . . . . . . . 323
Contrast of the Greek and Egyptian spirits . . . . 324
Difference between the stoical and the Egyptian pantheism . 325

*Neoplatonism*
Destroys active virtue and a critical spirit . . . . 329
The doctrine of dæmons supersedes the stoical naturalism . 330
New doctrine concerning suicide . . . . . . 331
Increasing belief in another life . . . . . . 331
Fusion of philosophy with religion . . . . . 332
Summary of the whole chapter . . . . . 332–335

# CHAPTER III.

### THE CONVERSION OF ROME.

                                                                    PAGE
Unconsciousness of the moral importance of Christianity mani-
        fested by Pagan writers . . . . . . . . . . 336
Due to the separation in antiquity of religion and morals . 338
Three popular errors concerning the conversion of Rome . . 339

*Examination of the Theory which ascribes Part of the Teaching
        of the later Pagan Moralists to Christian Influence*
Two opinions in the early Church concerning the Pagan
        writings . . . . . . . . . . . 343
The 'seminal logos' . . . . . . . . . 344
Pagan writings supposed to be plagiarisms from the Old Testa-
        ment, or to be receptacles of demoniacal traditions . . 345
But these theories were applied only to the ancient Greek
        writers, and not to contemporary moralists . . . . 346

*Theory which attributes the Conversion of the Empire to the
        Evidences of Miracles*
To estimate this it is necessary to review the causes of the
        belief in miracles . . . . . . . . . . 346
Rapid decline of the belief . . . . . . . . 347
Miracles not impossible . . . . . . . . 348
Established by much evidence . . . . . . . 348
The histories of them naturally fade with education . . . 349
Illustrated by the belief in fairies . . . . . . 349
The savage regards the whole world as governed by isolated
        acts of intervention . . . . . . . . . 350
Latent fetishism . . . . . . . . . . 350
Feebleness of the imagination a source of legends—myths . . 350
Miraculous stories the natural expression of a certain theory
        of the universe . . . . . . . . . . 351
Education destroys these stories by teaching men to exact
        greater severity of proof . . . . . . . . 351
By strengthening their power of abstraction, and thus closing
        the age of myths . . . . . . . . . . 353
By physical science, which establishes the reign of law . 353

PAGE

Three ways in which physical science affects the belief in
   miracles . . . . . . . . . . 354
Theological notions about rain and epidemics . . . 356
Sphere of inductive reasoning in theology . . . . 357
Common error in reasoning about miracles . . . . 361
In some states of society this predisposition towards the mi-
   raculous is so strong as to accumulate round legends more
   evidence than is required to establish even improbable na-
   tural facts . . . . . . . . . . 362
Illustrations of this from divination, witchcraft, and the king's
   touch . . . . . . . . . . 363
State of opinion on this subject in the Roman Empire . . 365
Extreme credulity even in matters of natural history . . 369
Great increase of credulity through the influence of Egyptian
   philosophy—miracles of the Pythagorean school . . . 373
Attitude of Christians towards the Pagan miracles . . 374
Incapacity of the Christians of the third century for judging
   historic miracles . . . . . . . . 375
Or for judging prophecies—the Sibylline books . . . 376
Contemporary Christian miracles—exorcism . . . 377
Much despised by the Pagans . . . . . . 383
On the whole, neither past nor contemporary Christian miracles
   had much weight with the Pagans . . . . . 385
The progress of Christianity due to the disintegration of old
   religions, and the thirst for belief which was general . . 386
Singular adaptation of Christianity to the wants of the time . 387
Heroism it inspired . . . . . . . . 390
The conversion of the Roman Empire easily explicable . . 393

*The Persecution the Church underwent not of a Nature to Crush it*
Persecution may have many causes . . . . . 395
Review of the religious policy of Rome . . . . . 398
Reasons why the Christians were more persecuted than the
   Jews . . . . . . . . . . 407
The religious motive of persecution was the belief that cala-
   mities were a consequence of the neglect of the gods . 407
History of this belief . . . . . . . . 408
Political persecutions . . . . . . . . 412
Charges of immorality brought against Christians . . . 414
Due in a great measure to the Jews and heretics . . . 416

PAGE

The disturbance of domestic life caused by female conversions    418
Antipathy of the Romans to every system which employed
  religious terrorism    .    .    .    .    .    .    .    . 420
Christian intolerance of Pagan worship .    .    .    .    . 422
And of diversity of belief .    .    .    .    .    .    . 427
These causes fully explain the persecution of the Christians  . 428

*History of the Persecutions*

Persecution by Nero .    .    .    .    .    .    .    . 429
By Domitian    .    .    .    .    .    .    .    .    . 432
Condition of the Christians under the Antonines    .    .    . 434
After Marcus Aurelius, Christianity became a great political
  power    .    .    .    .    .    .    .    .    .    . 442
Attitude of the rulers towards it, from M. Aurelius to Decius  442
Condition of the Church at the eve of the Decian persecution  449
Horrors of the persecution    .    .    .    .    .    .    . 449
The catacombs    .    .    .    .    .    .    .    .    . 453
Troubles under Gallus and Valerian.—Gallienus proclaims tole-
  ration    .    .    .    .    .    .    .    .    .    . 454
Cyprian to Demetrianus    .    .    .    .    .    .    . 455
Almost unbroken peace till Diocletian    .    .    .    .    . 458
His character and persecution    .    .    .    .    .    . 458
Galerius    .    .    .    .    .    .    .    .    .    . 459
Close of the persecutions    .    .    .    .    .    .    . 463
General considerations on their history    .    .    .    .    . 464

# HISTORY OF
# EUROPEAN MORALS.

## CHAPTER I.

### THE NATURAL HISTORY OF MORALS.

A BRIEF ENQUIRY into the nature and foundations of morals appears an obvious, and, indeed, almost an indispensable preliminary, to any examination of the moral progress of Europe. Unfortunately, however, such an enquiry is beset with serious difficulties, arising in part from the extreme multiplicity of detail which systems of moral philosophy present, and in part from a fundamental antagonism of principles, dividing them into two opposing groups. The great controversy, springing from the rival claims of intuition and utility to be regarded as the supreme regulator of moral distinctions, may be dimly traced in the division between Plato and Aristotle; it appeared more clearly in the division between the Stoics and the Epicureans; but it has only acquired its full distinctness of definition, and the importance of the questions depending on it has only been fully appreciated, in modern times, under the influence of such writers as Cudworth, Clarke, and Butler upon the one side, and Hobbes, Helvétius, and Bentham on the other

Independently of the broad intellectual difficulties which must be encountered in treating this question, there is a difficulty of a personal kind, which it may be advisable at once to meet. There is a disposition in some moralists to resent, as an imputation against their own characters, any charge of immoral consequences that may be brought against the principles they advocate. Now it is a peculiarity of this controversy that every moralist is compelled, by the very nature of the case, to bring such charges against the opinions of his opponents. The business of a moral philosophy is to account for and to justify our moral sentiments, or in other words, to show how we come to have our notions of duty, and to supply us with a reason for acting upon them. If it does this adequately, it is impregnable, and therefore a moralist who repudiates one system is called upon to show that, according to its principles, the notion of duty, or the motives for performing it, could never have been generated. The Utilitarian accuses his opponent of basing the entire system of morals on a faculty that has no existence, of adopting a principle that would make moral duty vary with the latitude and the epoch, of resolving all ethics into an idle sentiment. The intuitive moralist, for reasons I shall hereafter explain, believes that the Utilitarian theory is profoundly immoral. But to suppose that either of these charges extends to the character of the moralist is altogether to misconceive the position which moral theories actually hold in life. Our moral sentiments do not flow from, but long precede our ethical systems; and it is usually only after our characters have been fully formed that we begin to reason about them. It is both possible and very common for the reasoning to be very defective, without any corresponding imperfection in the disposition of the man.

The two rival theories of morals are known by many names, and are subdivided into many groups. One of them is generally described as the stoical, the intuitive, the independent or the sentimental; the other as the epicurean, the inductive, the utilitarian, or the selfish. The moralists of the former school, to state their opinions in the broadest form, believe that we have a natural power of perceiving that some qualities, such as benevolence, chastity, or veracity, are better than others, and that we ought to cultivate them, and to repress their opposites. In other words, they contend, that by the constitution of our nature, the notion of right carries with it a feeling of obligation; that to say a course of conduct is our duty, is in itself, and apart from all consequences, an intelligible and sufficient reason for practising it; and that we derive the first principles of our duties from intuition. The moralist of the opposite school denies that we have any such natural perception. He maintains that we have by nature absolutely no knowledge of merit and demerit, of the comparative excellence of our feelings and actions, and that we derive these notions solely from an observation of the course of life which is conducive to human happiness. That which makes actions good is, that they increase the happiness or diminish the pains of mankind. That which constitutes their demerit is their opposite tendency. To procure 'the greatest happiness for the greatest number,' is therefore the highest aim of the moralist, the supreme type and expression of virtue.

It is manifest, however, that this last school, if it proceeded no further than I have stated, would have failed to accomplish the task which every moralist must undertake. It is easy to understand that experience may show that certain actions are conducive to the happiness of mankind, and that these actions may in consequence be regarded as supremely excellent. The question still remains, why we are bound to perform them. If men, who believe that virtuous actions are those which experience shows to be useful to society, believe also that they are under a natural obligation to seek the happiness of others, rather than their

own, when the two interests conflict, they have certainly no
claim to the title of inductive moralists. They recognise a
moral faculty, or natural sense of moral obligation or duty
as truly as Butler or as Cudworth. And, indeed, a position
very similar to this has been adopted by several intuitive
moralists. Thus Hutcheson, who is the very founder in
modern times of the doctrine of 'a moral sense,' and who
has defended the disinterested character of virtue more
powerfully than perhaps any other moralist, resolved all
virtue into benevolence, or the pursuit of the happiness of
others; but he maintained that the excellence and obligation of benevolence are revealed to us by a 'moral sense.'
Hume, in like manner, pronounced utility to be the criterion
and essential element of all virtue, and is so far undoubtedly
a Utilitarian; but he asserted also that our pursuit of virtue
is unselfish, and that it springs from a natural feeling of
approbation or disapprobation distinct from reason, and produced by a peculiar sense, or taste, which rises up within us
at the contemplation of virtue or of vice.[1]  A similar
doctrine has more recently been advocated by Mackintosh.

---

[1] The opinions of Hume on
moral questions are grossly misrepresented by many writers, who
persist in describing them as substantially identical with those of
Bentham. How far Hume was
from denying the existence of a
moral sense, the following passages
will show:—'The final sentence, it
is probable, which pronounces
characters and actions amiable or
odious, praiseworthy or blame-
able . . . depends on some internal
sense or feeling which nature has
made universal in the whole
species.' — *Enquiry Concerning
Morals*, § 1. 'The hypothesis we
embrace . . . defines virtue to be
whatever mental action or quality
gives to the spectator the pleasing
sentiment of approbation.'—Ibid.
Append. I. 'The crime or immorality is no particular fact or relation which can be the object of the
understanding, but arises entirely
from the sentiment of disapprobation, which, by the structure of
human nature, we unavoidably feel
on the apprehension of barbarity or
treachery.' — Ibid.   'Reason in-
structs us in the several tendencies
of actions, and humanity makes a
distinction in favour of those which
are useful and beneficial.'—Ibid.
'As virtue is an end, and is desirable on its own account without
fee or reward, merely for the immediate satisfaction it conveys, it
is requisite that there should be
some sentiment which it touches,

It is supposed by many that it is a complete description of the Utilitarian system of morals, that it judges all actions and dispositions by their consequences, pronouncing them moral in proportion to their tendency to promote, immoral in proportion to their tendency to diminish, the happiness of man. But such a summary is clearly inadequate, for it deals only with one of the two questions which every moralist must answer. A theory of morals must explain not only what constitutes a duty, but also how we obtain the notion of there being such a thing as duty. It must tell us not merely what is the course of conduct we *ought* to pursue, but also what is the meaning of this word ' ought,' and from what source we derive the idea it expresses.

Those who have undertaken to prove that all our morality is a product of experience, have not shrunk from this task, and have boldly entered upon the one path that was open to them. The notion of there being any such feeling as an original sense of obligation distinct from the anticipation of pleasure or pain, they treat as a mere illusion of the imagination. All that is meant by saying we ought to do an action is, that if we do not do it, we shall suffer. A desire to obtain happiness and to avoid pain is the only possible motive to action. The reason, and the only reason, why we should perform virtuous actions, or in other words, seek the good of others, is that on the whole such a course will bring us the greatest amount of happiness.

We have here then a general statement of the doctrine which bases morals upon experience. If we ask what constitutes virtuous, and what vicious actions, we are told that the first are those which increase the happiness or diminish the

---

some internal taste or feeling, or whatever you please to call it, which distinguishes moral good and evil, and which embraces the one and rejects the other.'—Ibid. The two writers to whom Hume was most indebted were Hutcheson and Butler. In some interesting letters to the former (Burton's *Life of Hume*, vol. i.), he discusses the points on which he differed from them.

pains of mankind; and the second are those which have the opposite effect. If we ask what is the motive to virtue, we are told that it is an enlightened self-interest. The words happiness, utility, and interest include, however, many different kinds of enjoyment, and have given rise to many different modifications of the theory.

Perhaps the lowest and most repulsive form of this theory is that which was propounded by Mandeville, in his 'Enquiry into the Origin of Moral Virtue.'[1] According to this writer, virtue sprang in the first instance from the cunning of rulers. These, in order to govern men, found it necessary to persuade them that it was a noble thing to restrain, instead of indulging their passions, and to devote themselves entirely to the good of the community. The manner in which they attained this end was by acting upon the feeling of vanity. They persuaded men that human nature was something nobler than the nature of animals, and that devotion to the community rendered a man pre-eminently great. By statues, and titles, and honours; by continually extolling such men as Regulus or Decius; by representing those who were addicted to useless enjoyments as a low and despicable class, they at last so inflamed the vanity of men as to kindle an intense emulation, and inspire

---

- 'The chief thing therefore which lawgivers and other wise men that have laboured for the establishment of society have endeavoured, has been to make the people they were to govern believe that it was more beneficial for everybody to conquer than to indulge his appetites, and much better to mind the public than what seemed his private interest . . . observing that none were either so savage as not to be charmed with praise, or so despicable as patiently to bear contempt, they justly concluded that flattery must be the most powerful argument that could be used to human creatures. Making use of this bewitching engine, they extolled the excellency of our nature above other animals . . . by the help of which we were capable of performing the most noble achievements. Having, by this artful flattery, insinuated themselves into the hearts of men, they began to instruct them in the notions of honour and shame, &c.' —*Enquiry into the Origin of Moral Virtue.*

the most heroic actions. And soon new influences came into play. Men who began by restraining their passions, in order to acquire the pleasure of the esteem of others, found that this restraint saved them from many painful consequences that would have naturally ensued from over-indulgence, and this discovery became a new motive to virtue. Each member of the community moreover found that he himself derived benefit from the self-sacrifice of others, and also that when he was seeking his own interest, without regard to others, no persons stood so much in his way as those who were similarly employed, and he had thus a double reason for diffusing abroad the notion of the excellence of self-sacrifice. The result of all this was that men agreed to stigmatise under the term 'vice' whatever was injurious, and to eulogise as 'virtue' whatever was beneficial to society.

The opinions of Mandeville attracted, when they were published, an attention greatly beyond their intrinsic merit, but they are now sinking rapidly into deserved oblivion. The author, in a poem called the 'Fable of the Bees,' and in comments attached to it, himself advocated a thesis altogether inconsistent with that I have described, maintaining that 'private vices were public benefits,' and endeavouring, in a long series of very feeble and sometimes very grotesque arguments, to prove that vice was in the highest degree beneficial to mankind. A far greater writer had however already framed a scheme of morals which, if somewhat less repulsive, was in no degree less selfish than that of Mandeville; and the opinions of Hobbes concerning the essence and origin of virtue, have, with no very great variations, been adopted by what may be termed the narrower school of Utilitarians.

According to these writers we are governed exclusively by our own interest.[1] Pleasure, they assure us, is the only

---

[1] 'I conceive that when a man deliberates whether he shall do a thing or not do it, he does nothing else but consider whether it be better for himself to do it or not to do it.'—Hobbes *On Liberty and*

good,[1] and moral good and moral evil mean nothing more than our voluntary conformity to a law that will bring it to us.[2] To love good simply as good, is impossible.[3] When we speak of the goodness of God, we mean only His goodness to

---

*Necessity.* 'Good and evil are names that signify our appetites and aversions.'—Ibid. *Leviathan*, part i. ch. xvi. 'Obligation is the necessity of doing or omitting any action in order to be happy.'—Gay's dissertation prefixed to King's *Origin of Evil*, p. 36. 'The only reason or motive by which individuals can possibly be induced to the practice of virtue, must be the feeling immediate or the prospect of future private happiness.'—Brown *On the Characteristics*, p. 159. 'En tout temps, en tout lieu, tant en matière de morale qu'en matière d'esprit, c'est l'intérêt personnel qui dicte le jugement des particuliers, et l'intérêt général qui dicte celui des nations. . . . Tout homme ne prend dans ses jugements conseil que de son intérêt.'—Helvétius *De l'Esprit*, discours ii. 'Nature has placed mankind under the governance of two sovereign masters, pain and pleasure. It is for them alone to point out what we ought to do, as well as to determine what we shall do. . . . The principle of utility recognises this subjection, and assumes it for the foundation of that system, the object of which is to rear the fabric of felicity by the hands of reason and of law. Systems which attempt to question it, deal in sounds instead of sense, in caprice instead of reason, in darkness instead of light.'—Bentham's *Principles of Morals and Legislation*, ch. i. 'By the principle of utility is meant that principle which approves or disapproves of every action whatsoever, according to the tendency

which it appears to have to augment or diminish the happiness of the party whose interest is in question. —Ibid. 'Je regarde l'amour éclairé de nous-mêmes comme le principe de tout sacrifice moral.'—D'Alembert quoted by D. Stewart, *Active and Moral Powers*, vol. i. p. 220.

[1] 'Pleasure is in itself a good; nay, even setting aside immunity from pain, the only good; pain is in itself an evil, and, indeed, without exception, the only evil, or else the words good and evil have no meaning.'—Bentham's *Principles of Morals and Legislation*, ch. x.

[2] 'Good and evil are nothing but pleasure and pain, or that which occasions or procures pleasure or pain to us. Moral good and evil then is only the conformity or disagreement of our voluntary actions to some law whereby good or evil is drawn on us by the will and power of the law maker, which good and evil, pleasure or pain, attending our observance or breach of the law by the decree of the law maker, is that we call reward or punishment.'—Locke's *Essay*, book ii. ch. xxviii. 'Take away pleasures and pains, not only happiness, but justice, and duty, and obligation, and virtue, all of which have been so elaborately held up to view as independent of them, are so many empty sounds.'—Bentham's *Springs of Action*, ch. i. § 15.

[3] 'Il lui est aussi impossible d'aimer le bien pour le bien, que d'aimer le mal pour le mal.'—Helvétius *De l'Esprit*, disc. ii. ch. v.

us.[1] Reverence is nothing more than our conviction, that one who has power to do us both good and harm, will only do us good.[2] The pleasures of piety arise from the belief that we are about to receive pleasure, and the pains of piety from the belief that we are about to suffer pain from the Deity.[3] Our very affections, according to some of these writers, are all forms of self-love. Thus charity springs partly from our desire to obtain the esteem of others, partly from the expectation that the favours we have bestowed will be reciprocated, and partly, too, from the gratification of the sense of power, by the proof that we can satisfy not only our own desires but also the desires of others.[4] Pity is an emotion arising from a vivid realisation of sorrow that may befall ourselves, suggested by the sight of the sorrows of others. We pity especially those who have not

---

[1] ' Even the goodness which we apprehend in God Almighty, is his goodness to us.'—Hobbes *On Human Nature*, ch. vii. § 3. So Waterland, 'To love God is in effect the same thing as to love happiness, eternal happiness; and the love of happiness is still the love of ourselves.'—*Third Sermon on Self-love*.

[2] ' Reverence is the conception we have concerning another, that he hath the power to do unto us both good and hurt, but not the will to do us hurt.'—Hobbes *On Human Nature*, ch. viii. § 7.

[3] ' The pleasures of piety are the pleasures that accompany the belief of a man's being in the acquisition, or in possession of the good-will or favour of the Supreme Being; and as a fruit of it, of his being in the way of enjoying pleasures to be received by God's special appointment either in this life or in a life to come.'—Bentham's *Principles of Morals and Legislation*, ch. v. 'The pains of piety are the pains that accompany the belief of a man's

being obnoxious to the displeasure of the Supreme Being, and in consequence to certain pains to be inflicted by His especial appointment, either in this life or in a life to come. These may be also called the pains of religion.'—Ibid.

[4] ' There can be no greater argument to a man of his own power, than to find himself able not only to accomplish his own desires, but also to assist other men in theirs; and this is that conception wherein consisteth charity.'—Hobbes *On Hum. Nat.* ch. ix. § 17. 'No man giveth but with intention of good to himself, because gift is voluntary; and of all voluntary acts, the object to every man is his own good.'—Hobbes' *Leviathan*, part i. ch. xv. 'Dream not that men will move their little finger to serve you, unless their advantage in so doing be obvious to them. Men never did so, and never will while human nature is made of its present materials.'—Bentham's *Deontology*, vol. ii. p. 133

deserved calamity, because we consider ourselves to belong to
that category ; and the spectacle of suffering against which no
forethought could provide, reminds us most forcibly of what
may happen to ourselves.[1]  Friendship is the sense of the
need of the person befriended.[2]

From such a conception of human nature it is easy to
divine what system of morals must flow.  No character,
feeling, or action is naturally better than others, and as long
as men are in a savage condition, morality has no existence.
Fortunately, however, we are all dependent for many of our
pleasures upon others.  Co-operation and organisation are
essential to our happiness, and these are impossible without

---

[1] ' Pity is imagination or fiction
of future calamity to ourselves, proceeding from the sense of another
man's calamity.  But when it light-
eth on such as we think have not
deserved the same, the compassion
is greater, because there then ap-
peareth more probability that the
same may happen to us ; for the
evil that happeneth to an innocent
man may happen to every man.'—
Hobbes On Hum. Nat. ch. ix. § 10.
' La pitié est souvent un sentiment
de nos propres maux dans les maux
d'autrui.  C'est une habile prévoy-
ance des malheurs où nous pouvons
tomber.  Nous donnons des secours
aux autres pour les engager à nous
en donner en de semblables occasions, et ces services que nous leur
rendons sont, à proprement parler,
des biens que nous nous faisons
à nous-mêmes par avance.'—La
Rochefoucauld, Maximes, 264.  Butler has remarked that if Hobbes'
account were true, the most fearful
would be the most compassionate
nature ; but this is perhaps not
quite just, for Hobbes' notion of
pity implies the union of two not
absolutely identical, though nearly
allied, influences, timidity and ima-

gination.  The theory of Adam
Smith, though closely connected
with, differs totally in consequences
from that of Hobbes on this point.
He says, ' When I condole with you
for the loss of your son, in order to
enter into your grief, I do not consider what I, a person of such a
character and profession, should
suffer if I had a son, and if that son
should die — I consider what I
should suffer if I was really you.
I not only change circumstances
with you, but I change persons and
characters.  My grief, therefore, is
entirely upon your account. . . .
A man may sympathise with a
woman in child-bed, though it is
impossible he should conceive himself suffering her pains in his own
proper person and character.'—
Moral Sentiments, part vii. ch. i.
§ 3.

[2] ' Ce que les hommes ont nommé
amitié n'est qu'une société, qu'un
ménagement réciproque d'intérêts
et qu'un échange de bons offices.
Ce n'est enfin qu'un commerce où
l'amour-propre se propose toujours
quelque chose à gagner.'—La
Rochefoucauld, Max. 83.  See this
idea developed at large in Helvétius.

some restraint being placed upon our appetites.  Laws are enacted to secure this restraint, and being sustained by rewards and punishments, they make it the interest of the individual to regard that of the community.  According to Hobbes, the disposition of man is so anarchical, and the importance of restraining it so transcendent, that absolute government alone is good; the commands of the sovereign are supreme, and must therefore constitute the law of morals. The other moralists of the school, though repudiating this notion, have given a very great and distinguished place to legislation in their schemes of ethics; for all our conduct being determined by our interests, virtue being simply the conformity of our own interests with those of the community, and a judicious legislation being the chief way of securing this conformity, the functions of the moralist and of the .egislator are almost identical.[1]  But in addition to the rewards and punishments of the penal code, those arising from public opinion—fame or infamy, the friendship or hostility of those about us—are enlisted on the side of virtue. The educating influence of laws, and the growing perception of the identity of interests of the different members of the community, create a public opinion favourable to all the qualities which are 'the means of peaceable, sociable, and comfortable living.'[2]  Such are justice, gratitude, modesty,

---

[1] 'La science de la morale n'est autre chose que la science même de la législation.'—Helvétius *De l'Esprit*, ii. 17.

[2] This doctrine is expounded at length in all the moral works of Hobbes and his school. The following passage is a fair specimen of their meaning:—'Moral philosophy is nothing else but the science of what is good and evil in the conversation and society of mankind. Good and evil are names that signify our appetites and aver-

sions, which in different tempers, customs, and doctrines of men are different . . . from whence arise disputes, controversies, and at last war. And therefore, so long as man is in this condition of mere nature (which is a condition of war), his private appetite is the measure of good and evil. And consequently all men agree in this, that peace is good, and therefore also that the ways or means of peace, (which, as I have showed before) are justice, gratitude, modesty, equity, and mercy; and such, too, are purity and chastity, which, considered in themselves alone, are in no degree more excellent than the coarsest and most indiscriminate lust, but which can be shown to be conducive to the happiness of society, and become in consequence virtues.[1] This education of public opinion grows continually stronger with civilisation, and gradually moulds the characters of men, making them more and more disinterested, heroic, and unselfish. A disinterested, unselfish, and heroic man, it is explained, is one who is strictly engrossed in the pursuit of his own pleasure, but who pursues it in such a manner as to include in its gratification the happiness of others.[2]

It is a very old assertion, that a man who prudently sought his own interest would live a life of perfect virtue. This opinion is adopted by most of those Utilitarians who are least inclined to lay great stress upon religious motives; and as they maintain that every man necessarily pursues exclusively his own happiness, we return by another path to the old Platonic doctrine, that all vice is ignorance. Virtue is a judicious, and vice an injudicious, pursuit of pleasure. Virtue is a branch of prudence, vice is nothing more than

---

equity, mercy, and the rest of the laws of nature are good . . . and their contrary vices evil.'—Hobbes' *Leviathan*, part i. ch. xvi. See, too, a striking passage in Bentham's *Deontology*, vol. ii. p. 132.

[1] As an ingenious writer in the *Saturday Review* (Aug. 10, 1867) expresses it: 'Chastity is merely a social law created to encourage the alliances that most promote the permanent welfare of the race, and to maintain woman in a social position which it is thought advisable she should hold.' See, too, on this view, Hume's *Inquiry concerning Morals*, § 4, and also *note* x.: 'To what other purpose do all

the ideas of chastity and modesty serve? Nisi utile est quod facimus, frustra est gloria.'

[2] 'All pleasure is necessarily self-regarding, for it is impossible to have any feelings out of our own mind. But there are modes of delight that bring also satisfaction to others, from the round that they take in their course. Such are the pleasures of benevolence. Others imply no participation by any second party, as, for example, eating, drinking, bodily warmth, property, and power; while a third class are fed by the pains and privations of fellow-beings, as the delights of sport and tyranny. The

imprudence or miscalculation.[1]  He who seeks to improve the moral condition of mankind has two, and only two, ways of accomplishing his end.  The first is, to make it more and more the interest of each to conform to that of the others ; the second is, to dispel the ignorance which prevents men from seeing their true interest.[2]  If chastity or truth, or any other of what we regard as virtues, could be shown to produce on the whole more pain than they destroy, or to deprive men of more pleasure than they afford, they would not be virtues, but vices.[3]  If it could be shown that

condemnatory phrase, selfishness, applies with especial emphasis to the last-mentioned class, and, in a qualified degree, to the second group; while such terms as unselfishness, disinterestedness, self-devotion, are applied to the vicarious position wherein we seek our own satisfaction in that of others.'—Bain *On the Emotions and Will*, p. 113.

[1] 'Vice may be defined to be a miscalculation of chances, a mistake in estimating the value of pleasures and pains.  It is false moral arithmetic.' — Bentham's *Deontology*, vol. i. p. 131.

[2] 'La récompense, la punition, la gloire et l'infamie soumises à ses volontés sont quatre espèces de divinités avec lesquelles le législateur peut toujours opérer le bien public et créer des hommes illustres en tous les genres.  Toute l'étude des moralistes consiste à déterminer l'usage qu'on doit faire de ces récompenses et de ces punitions et les secours qu'on peut tirer pour lier l'intérêt personnel à l'intérêt général'—Helvétius *De l'Esprit*, i. 22.  'La justice de nos jugements et de nos actions n'est jamais que la rencontre heureuse de notre intérêt avec l'intérêt pub-

lic.'—Ibid. ii. 7.  'To prove that the immoral action is a miscalculation of self-interest, to show how erroneous an estimate the vicious man makes of pains and pleasures, is the purpose of the intelligent moralist.  Unless he can do this he does nothing; for, as has been stated above, for a man not to pursue what he deems likely to produce to him the greatest sum of enjoyment, is, in the very nature of things, impossible.'—Bentham's *Deontology*.

[3] 'If the effect of virtue were to prevent or destroy more pleasure than it produced, or to produce more pain than it prevented, its more appropriate name would be wickedness and folly ; wickedness as it affected others, folly as respected him who practised it.'—Bentham's *Deontology*, vol. i. p. 142.  'Weigh pains, weigh pleasures, and as the balance stands will stand the question of right and wrong.' — Ibid. vol. i. p. 137.  'Moralis philosophiæ caput est, Faustine fili, ut scias quibus ad beatam vitam perveniri rationibus possit.'—Apuleius, *Ad Doct. Platonis*, ii.  'Atque ipsa utilitas, justi prope mater et æqui.' — Horace, *Sat.* I. iii. 98.

it is not for our own interest to practise any of what are
admitted to be virtues, all obligation to practise them would
immediately cease.[1] The whole scheme of ethics may be
evolved from the four canons of Epicurus. The pleasure
which produces no pain is to be embraced. The pain which
produces no pleasure is to be avoided. The pleasure is to be
avoided which prevents a greater pleasure, or produces a
greater pain. The pain is to be endured which averts a
greater pain, or secures a greater pleasure.[2]

So far I have barely alluded to any but terrestrial motives. These, in the opinion of many of the most illustrious
of the school, are sufficient, but others—as we shall see, I
think, with great reason—are of a different opinion. Their
obvious resource is in the rewards and punishments of
another world, and these they accordingly present as the
motive to virtue. Of all the modifications of the selfish
theory, this alone can be said to furnish interested motives
for virtue which are invariably and incontestably adequate.
If men introduce the notion of infinite punishments and
infinite rewards distributed by an omniscient Judge, they can
undoubtedly supply stronger reasons for practising virtue
than can ever be found for practising vice. While admitting
therefore in emphatic terms, that any sacrifice of our pleasure,
without the prospect of an equivalent reward, is a simple
act of madness, and unworthy of a rational being,[3] these

---

[1] 'We can be obliged to nothing
but what we ourselves are to gain
or lose something by; for nothing
else can be "violent motive" to us.
As we should not be obliged to
obey the laws or the magistrate
unless rewards or punishments,
pleasure or pain, somehow or other,
depended upon our obedience; so
neither should we, without the
same reason, be obliged to do what
is right, to practise virtue, or to
obey the commands of God.'—

Paley's *Moral Philosophy*, book ii.
ch. ii.

[2] See Gassendi *Philosophiæ
Epicuri Syntagma*. These four
canons are a skilful condensation
of the argument of Torquatus in
Cicero, *De Fin.* i. 2. See, too, a
very striking letter by Epicurus
himself, given in his life by Diogenes Laërtius.

[3] 'Sanus igitur non est, qui
nulla spe majore proposita, iis bonis
quibus cæteri utuntur in vita, la-

writers maintain that we may reasonably sacrifice the enjoyments of this life, because we shall be rewarded by far greater enjoyment in the next. To gain heaven and avoid hell should be the spring of all our actions,[1] and virtue is simply prudence extending its calculations beyond the grave.[2]

---

bores et cruciatus et miserias anteponat. . . . . Non aliter his bonis præsentibus abstinendum est quam si sint aliqua majora, propter quæ tanti sit et voluptates omittere et mala omnia sustinere.'—Lactantius, *Div. Inst.* vi. 9. Macaulay, in some youthful essays against the Utilitarian theory (which he characteristically described as 'Not much more laughable than phrenology, and immeasurably more humane than cock-fighting'), maintains the theological form of selfishness in very strong terms. 'What proposition is there respecting human nature which is absolutely and universally true? We know of only one, and that is not only true but identical, that men always act from self-interest.'—Review of Mill's *Essay on Government.* 'Of this we may be sure, that the words "greatest happiness" will never in any man's mouth mean more than the greatest happiness of others, which is consistent with what he thinks his own. . . . This direction (Do as you would be done by) would be utterly unmeaning, as it actually is in Mr. Bentham's philosophy, unless it were accompanied by a sanction. In the Christian scheme accordingly it is accompanied by a sanction of immense force. To a man whose greatest happiness in this world is inconsistent with the greatest happiness of the greatest number, is held out the prospect of an infinite happiness hereafter, from

which he excludes himself by wronging his fellow-creatures here.'—*Answer to the Westminster Review's Defence of Mill.*

[1] 'All virtue and piety are thus resolvable into a principle of self-love. It is what Scripture itself resolves them into by founding them upon faith in God's promises, and hope in things unseen. In this way it may be rightly said that there is no such thing as disinterested virtue. It is with reference to ourselves and for our own sakes that we love even God Himself.'—Waterland, *Third Sermon on Self-love.* 'To risk the happiness of the whole duration of our being in any case whatever, were it possible, would be foolish.'—Robert Hall's *Sermon on Modern Infidelity.* 'In the moral system the means are virtuous practice; the end, happiness.'—Warburton's *Divine Legation,* book ii. Appendix.

[2] 'There is always understood to be a difference between an act of prudence and an act of duty. Thus, if I distrusted a man who owed me a sum of money, I should reckon it an act of prudence to get another person bound with him; but I should hardly call it an act of duty. . . . Now in what, you will ask, does the difference consist, inasmuch as, according to our account of the matter, both in the one case and the other, in acts of duty as well as acts of prudence, we consider solely what we our-

This calculation is what we mean by the 'religious motive.'[1] The belief that the nobility and excellence of virtue could incite us, was a mere delusion of the Pagans.[2]

Considered simply in the light of a prudential scheme, there are only two possible objections that could be brought against this theory. It might be said that the amount of virtue required for entering heaven was not defined, and that therefore it would be possible to enjoy some vices on earth with impunity. To this, however, it is answered that the very indefiniteness of the requirement renders zealous piety a matter of prudence, and also that there is probably a graduated scale of rewards and punishments adapted to every variety of merit and demerit.[3] It might be said too that present pleasures are at least certain, and that those of another world are not equally so. It is answered that the rewards and punishments offered in another world are so transcendently great, that according to the rules of ordinary

---

selves shall gain or lose by the act? The difference, and the only difference, is this: that in the one case we consider what we shall gain or lose in the present world; in the other case, we consider also what we shall gain or lose in the world to come.'—Paley's *Moral Philosophy*, ii. 3.

[1] 'Hence we may see the weakness and mistake of those falsely religious . . . who are scandalised at our being determined to the pursuit of virtue through any degree of regard to its happy consequences in this life. . . . For it is evident that the religious motive is precisely of the same kind, only stronger, as the happiness expected is greater and more lasting.'— Brown's *Essays on the Characteristics*, p. 220.

[2] 'If a Christian, who has the view of happiness and misery in

another life, be asked why a man must keep his word, he will give this as a reason, because God, who has the power of eternal life and death, requires it of us. But if an Hobbist be asked why, he will answer, because the public requires it, and the Leviathan will punish you if you do not. And if one of the old heathen philosophers had been asked, he would have answered, because it was dishonest, below the dignity of man, and opposite to virtue, the highest perfection of human nature, to do otherwise.' —Locke's *Essay*, i. 3.

[3] Thus Paley remarks that— 'The Christian religion hath not ascertained the precise quantity of virtue necessary to salvation,' and he then proceeds to urge the probability of graduated scales of rewards and punishments. (*Moral Philosophy*, book i. ch. vii.)

prudence, if there were only a probability, or even a bare possibility, of their being real, a wise man should regulate his course with a view to them.[1]

Among these writers, however, some have diverged to a certain degree from the broad stream of utilitarianism, declaring that the foundation of the moral law is not utility, but the will or arbitrary decree of God. This opinion, which was propounded by the schoolman Ockham, and by several other writers of his age,[2] has in modern times found many adherents,[3] and been defended through a variety of motives. Some have upheld it on the philosophical ground that a law can be nothing but the sentence of a lawgiver; others from a desire to place morals in permanent subordination to theology; others in order to answer objections to Christianity derived from apparently immoral acts said to have been sanctioned by the Divinity; and others because having adopted strong Calvinistic sentiments, they were at once profoundly opposed to utilitarian morals, and at the

---

[1] This view was developed by Locke (*Essay on the Human Understanding*, book ii. ch. xxi.) Pascal, in a well-known passage, applied the same argument to Christianity, urging that the rewards and punishments it promises are so great, that it is the part of a wise man to embrace the creed, even though he believes it improbable, if there be but a possibility in its favour.

[2] Cudworth, in his *Immutable Morals*, has collected the names of a number of the schoolmen who held this view. See, too, an interesting note in Miss Cobbe's very learned *Essay on Intuitive Morals*, pp. 18, 19.

[3] E. g. Soame Jenyns, Dr. Johnson, Crusius, Pascal, Paley, and Austin. Warburton is generally quoted in the list, but not I think

quite fairly. See his theory, which is rather complicated (*Divine Legation*, i. 4). Waterland appears to have held this view, and also Condillac. See a very remarkable chapter on morals, in his *Traité des Animaux*, part ii. ch. vii. Closely connected with this doctrine is the notion that the morality of God is generically different from the morality of men, which having been held with more or less distinctness by many theologians (Archbishop King being perhaps the most prominent), has found in our own day an able defender in Dr. Mansel. Much information on the history of this doctrine will be found in Dr. Mansel's *Second Letter to Professor Goldwin Smith* (Oxford, 1862).

same time too firmly convinced of the total depravity of
human nature to admit the existence of any trustworthy
moral sense.[1]

In the majority of cases, however, these writers have
proved substantially utilitarians. When asked how we can
know the will of God, they answer that in as far as it is not
included in express revelation, it must be discovered by the
rule of utility; for nature proves that the Deity is supremely
benevolent, and desires the welfare of men, and therefore
any conduct that leads to that end is in conformity with
His will.[2] To the question why the Divine will should be
obeyed, there are but two answers. The first, which is that
of the intuitive moralist, is that we are under a natural
obligation of gratitude to our Creator. The second, which
is that of the selfish moralist, is that the Creator has infinite
rewards and punishments at His disposal. The latter answer
appears usually to have been adopted, and the most eminent
member has summed up with great succinctness the opinion
of his school. 'The good of mankind,' he says, 'is the subject, the will of God the rule, and everlasting happiness the
motive and end of all virtue.'[3]

---

[1] Leibnitz noticed the frequency
with which Supralapsarian Calvin-
ists adopt this doctrine. (*Théo-
dicée*, part ii. § 176.) Archbishop
Whately, who from his connection
with the Irish Clergy had admirable opportunities of studying the
tendencies of Calvinism, makes a
similar remark as the result of his
own experience. (*Whately's Life*,
vol. ii. p. 339.)

[2] 'God designs the happiness of
all His sentient creatures. . . .
Knowing the tendencies of our actions, and knowing His benevolent
purpose, we know His tacit commands.'—Austin's *Lectures on Jurisprudence*, vol. i. p. 31. 'The

commands which He has revealed
we must gather from the terms
wherein they are promulgated.
The commands which He has not
revealed we must construe by the
principle of utility.'—Ibid. p. 96.
So Paley's *Moral Philosophy*, book
ii. ch. iv. v.

[3] Paley's *Moral Philosophy*,
book i. ch. vii. The question of
the disinterestedness of the love we
should bear to God was agitated in
the Catholic Church, Bossuet taking the selfish, and Fénelon the unselfish side. The opinions of Fénelon and Molinos on the subject
were authoritatively condemned.
In England, the less dogmatic cha-

We have seen that the distinctive characteristic of the
inductive school of moralists is an absolute denial of the
existence of any natural or innate moral sense or faculty
enabling us to distinguish between the higher and lower
parts of our nature, revealing to us either the existence of a
law of duty or the conduct that it prescribes. We have
seen that the only postulate of these writers is that happiness being universally desired is a desirable thing, that the
only merit they recognise in actions or feelings is their tendency to promote human happiness, and that the only motive
to a virtuous act they conceive possible is the real or supposed
happiness of the agent. The sanctions of morality thus constitute its obligation, and apart from them the word 'ought'
is absolutely unmeaning. Those sanctions, as we have
considered them, are of different kinds and degrees of magnitude. Paley, though elsewhere acknowledging the others,
regarded the religious one as so immeasurably the first, that
he represented it as the one motive of virtue.[1] Locke
divided them into Divine rewards and punishments, legal
penalties and social penalties;[2] Bentham into physical,
political, moral or popular, and religious—the first being
the bodily evils that result from vice, the second the enactments of legislators, the third the pleasures and pains
arising from social intercourse, the fourth the rewards and
punishments of another world.[3]

---

racter of the national faith, and
also the fact that the great anti-
Christian writer, Hobbes, was the
advocate of extreme selfishness in
morals, had, I think, a favourable
influence upon the ethics of the
church. Hobbes gave the first
great impulse to moral philosophy
in England, and his opponents
were naturally impelled to an unselfish theory. Bishop Cumber-
land led the way, resolving virtue
(like Hutcheson) into benevolence.

The majority of divines, however,
till the present century, have, I
think, been on the selfish side.

[1] *Moral Philosophy*, ii. 3.
[2] *Essay on the Human Understanding*, ii. 28.
[3] *Principles of Morals and Legislation*, ch. iii. Mr. Mill observes that, 'Bentham's idea of the
world is that of a collection of
persons pursuing each his separate
interest or pleasure, and the prevention of whom from jostling one

During the greater part of the sixteenth and seventeenth centuries the controversy in England between those who derived the moral code from experience, and those who derived it from intuitions of the reason, or from a special faculty, or from a moral sense, or from the power of sympathy, turned mainly upon the existence of an unselfish element in our nature. The reality of this existence having been maintained by Shaftesbury, was established with an unprecedented, and I believe an irresistible force, by Hutcheson, and the same question occupies a considerable place in the writings of Butler, Hume, and Adam Smith. The selfishness of the school of Hobbes, though in some degree mitigated, may be traced in every page of the writings of Bentham; but some of his disciples have in this respect deviated very widely from their master, and in their hands the whole tone and complexion of utilitarianism have been changed.[1] The two means by which this transformation

---

another more than is unavoidable, may be attempted by hopes and fears derived from three sources—the law, religion, and public opinion. To these three powers, considered as binding human conduct, he gave the name of sanctions; the political sanction operating by the rewards and penalties of the law; the religious sanction by those expected from the ruler of the universe; and the popular, which he characteristically calls also the moral sanction, operating through the pains and pleasures arising from the favour or disfavour of our fellow-creatures.'—*Dissertations*, vol. i. pp. 362–363.

[1] Hume on this, as on most other points, was emphatically opposed to the school of Hobbes, and even declared that no one could honestly and in good faith deny the reality of an unselfish element

in man. Following in the steps of Butler, he explained it in the following passage :—' Hunger and thirst have eating and drinking for their end, and from the gratification of these primary appetites arises a pleasure which may become the object of another species of desire or inclination that is secondary and interested. In the same manner there are mental passions by which we are impelled immediately to seek particular objects, such as fame or power or vengeance, without any regard to interest, and when these objects are attained a pleasing enjoyment ensues. . . . Now where is the difficulty of conceiving that this may likewise be the case with benevolence and friendship, and that from the original frame of our temper we may feel a desire of another's happiness or good, which by means of

has been effected are the recognition of our unselfish or sympathetic feelings, and the doctrine of the association of ideas.

That human nature is so constituted that we naturally take a pleasure in the sight of the joy of others is one of those facts which to an ordinary observer might well appear among the most patent that can be conceived. We have seen, however, that it was emphatically denied by Hobbes, and during the greater part of the last century it was fashionable among writers of the school of Helvétius to endeavour to prove that all domestic or social affections were dictated simply by a need of the person who was beloved. The reality of the pleasures and pains of sympathy was admitted by Bentham;[1] but in accordance with the whole spirit of his philosophy, he threw them as much as possible into the background, and, as I have already noticed, gave them no place in his summary of the sanctions of virtue. The tendency, however, of the later members of the school has been to recognise them fully,[2] though they

that affection becomes our own good, and is afterwards pursued, from the combined motives of benevolence and self-enjoyment?'— Hume's *Enquiry concerning Morals*, Appendix II. Compare Butler, 'If there be any appetite or any inward principle besides self-love, why may there not be an affection towards the good of our fellow-creatures, and delight from that affection's being gratified and uneasiness from things going contrary to it?'—*Sermon on Compassion*.

[1] 'By sympathetic sensibility is to be understood the propensity that a man has to derive pleasure from the happiness, and pain from the unhappiness, of other sensitive beings.'—Bentham's *Principles of Morals and Legislation*, ch. vi.

'The sense of sympathy is universal. Perhaps there never existed a human being who had reached full age without the experience of pleasure at another's pleasure, of uneasiness at another's pain. . . . Community of interests, similarity of opinion, are sources from whence it springs.'—*Deontology*, vol. i. pp. 169–170.

[2] 'The idea of the pain of another is naturally painful. The idea of the pleasure of another is naturally pleasurable. . . . In this, the unselfish part of our nature, lies a foundation, even independently of inculcation from without, for the generation of moral feelings'—Mill's *Dissertations*, vol. i. p. 137. See, too, Bain's *Emotions and the Will*, pp. 289, 313 ; and es-

differ as to the source from which they spring. According to one section our benevolent affections are derived from our selfish feelings by an association of ideas in a manner which I shall presently describe. According to the other they are an original part of the constitution of our nature. However they be generated, their existence is admitted, their cultivation is a main object of morals, and the pleasure derived from their exercise a leading motive to virtue. The differences between the intuitive moralists and their rivals on this point are of two kinds. Both acknowledge the existence in human nature of both benevolent and malevolent feelings, and that we have a natural power of distinguishing one from the other; but the first maintain and the second deny that we have a natural power of perceiving that one is better than the other. Both admit that we enjoy a pleasure in acts of benevolence to others, but most writers of the first school maintain that that pleasure follows unsought for, while writers of the other school contend that the desire of obtaining it is the motive of the action.

But by far the most ingenious and at the same time most influential system of utilitarian morals is that which owes its distinctive feature to the doctrine of association of Hartley. This doctrine, which among the modern achievements of ethics occupies on the utilitarian side a position corresponding in importance to the doctrine of innate moral faculties as distinguished from innate moral ideas on the intuitive side, was not absolutely unknown to the ancients, though they never perceived either the extent to which it may be carried or the important consequences that might be deduced from it. Some traces of it may be found in Aris-

pecially Austin's *Lectures on Jurisprudence.* The first volume of this brilliant work contains, I think without exception, the best modern statement of the utilitarian theory in its most plausible form—a statement equally remarkable for its ability, its candour, and its uniform courtesy to opponents.

totle,[1] and some of the Epicureans applied it to friendship, maintaining that, although we first of all love our friend on account of the pleasure he can give us, we come soon to love him for his own sake, and apart from all considerations of utility.[2]   Among moderns Locke has the merit of having devised the phrase, 'association of ideas;'[3] but he applied it only to some cases of apparently eccentric sympathies or antipathies.  Hutcheson, however, closely anticipated both the doctrine of Hartley and the favourite illustration of the school; observing that we desire some things as themselves pleasurable and others only as means to obtain pleasurable things, and that these latter, which he terms 'secondary desires,' may become as powerful as the former.   'Thus, as soon as we come to apprehend the use of wealth or power to gratify any of our original desires we must also desire them. Hence arises the universality of these desires of wealth and power, since they are the means of gratifying all our desires.'[4] The same principles were carried much farther by a clergyman named Gay in a short dissertation which is now almost forgotten, but to which Hartley ascribed the first suggestion of his theory,[5] and in which indeed the most valuable part of it is clearly laid down.  Differing altogether from Hutcheson as to the existence of any innate moral sense or principle

---

[1] See a collection of passages from Aristotle, bearing on the subject, in Mackintosh's *Dissertation*.

[2] Cic. *De Finibus*, i. 5.  This view is adopted in Tucker's *Light of Nature* (ed. 1842), vol. i. p. 167. See, too, Mill's *Analysis of the Human Mind*, vol. ii. p. 174.

[3] *Essay*, book ii. ch. xxxiii.

[4] Hutcheson *On the Passions*, § 1.  The 'secondary desires' of Hutcheson are closely related to the 'reflex affections' of Shaftesbury. ' Not only the outward beings which offer themselves to the sense are

the objects of the affection; but the very actions themselves, and the affections of pity, kindness, gratitude, and their contraries, being brought into the mind by reflection become objects.  So that by means of this reflected sense, there arises another kind of affection towards those very affections themselves.'— Shaftesbury's *Enquiry concerning Virtue*, book i. part ii. § 3.

[5] See the preface to Hartley *On Man*.  Gay's essay is prefixed to Law's translation of Archbishop King *On the Origin of Evil*.

of benevolence in man, Gay admitted that the arguments of
Hutcheson to prove that the adult man possesses a moral
sense were irresistible, and he attempted to reconcile this fact
with the teaching of Locke by the doctrine of 'secondary
desires.' He remarks that in our reasonings we do not always fall back upon first principles or axioms, but sometimes
start from propositions which though not self-evident we
know to be capable of proof. In the same way in justifying
our actions we do not always appeal to the tendency to
produce happiness which is their one ultimate justification,
but content ourselves by showing that they produce some of
the known 'means to happiness.' These 'means to happiness' being continually appealed to as justifying motives
come insensibly to be regarded as ends, possessing an intrinsic
value irrespective of their tendency; and in this manner it is
that we love and admire virtue even when unconnected with
our interests.[1]

The great work of Hartley expanding and elaborating
these views was published in 1747. It was encumbered by
much physiological speculation into which it is needless for
us now to enter, about the manner in which emotions act
upon the nerves, and although accepted enthusiastically by
Priestley and Belsham, and in some degree by Tucker, I do not
think that its purely ethical speculations had much influence
until they were adopted by some leading utilitarians in the

---

[1] 'The case is this. We first
perceive or imagine some real good;
i.e. fitness to promote our happiness
in those things which we love or approve of. . . . . Hence those things
and pleasures are so tied together
and associated in our minds, that
one cannot present itself, but the
other will also occur. And the association remains even after that
which at first gave them the connection is quite forgotten, or perhaps
does not exist, but the contrary.'—
Gay's *Essay,* p. lii. 'All affections
whatsoever are finally resolvable
into reason, pointing out private
happiness, and are conversant only
about things apprehended to be
means tending to this end; and
whenever this end is not perceived,
they are to be accounted for from
the association of ideas, and may
properly enough be called habits.
—Ibid. p. xxxi.

present century.[1] Whatever may be thought of the truth, it is impossible to withhold some admiration from the intellectual grandeur of a system which starting from a conception of human nature as low and as base as that of Mandeville or Hobbes professes without the introduction of a single new or nobler element, by a strange process of philosophic alchemy, to evolve out of this original selfishness the most heroic and most sensitive virtue. The manner in which this achievement is effected is commonly illustrated by the passion of avarice. Money in itself possesses absolutely nothing that is admirable or pleasurable, but being the means of procuring us many of the objects of our desire, it becomes associated in our minds with the idea of pleasure; it is therefore itself loved; and it is possible for the love of money so completely to eclipse or supersede the love of all those things which money procures, that the miser will forego them all, rather than part with a fraction of his gold.[2]

---

[1] Principally by Mr. James Mill, whose chapter on association, in his *Analysis of the Human Mind*, may probably rank with Paley's beautiful chapter on happiness, at the head of all modern writings on the utilitarian side,—either of them, I think, being far more valuable than anything Bentham ever wrote on morals. This last writer—whose contempt for his predecessors was only equalled by his ignorance of their works, and who has added surprisingly little to moral science (considering the reputation he attained), except a barbarous nomenclature and an interminable series of classifications evincing no real subtlety of thought—makes, as far as I am aware, no use of the doctrine of association. Paley states it with his usual admirable clearness. 'Having experienced in some instances a particular conduct to be beneficial to ourselves, or observed that it would be so, a sentiment of approbation rises up in our minds, which sentiment afterwards accompanies the idea or mention of the same conduct, although the private advantage which first existed no longer exist.'—Paley, *Moral Philos.* i. 5. Paley, however, made less use of this doctrine than might have been expected from so enthusiastic an admirer of Tucker. In our own day it has been much used by Mr. J. S. Mill.

[2] This illustration, which was first employed by Hutcheson, is very happily developed by Gay (p. lii.). It was then used by Hartley, and finally Tucker reproduced the whole theory with the usual illustration without any acknowledgment of the works of his predecessors, employing however, the term 'translation' instead of 'associa-

The same phenomenon may be traced, it is said, in a multitude of other forms.[1] Thus we seek power, because it gives us the means of gratifying many desires. It becomes associated with those desires, and is, at last, itself passionately loved. Praise indicates the affection of the eulogist, and marks us out for the affection of others. Valued at first as a means, it is soon desired as an end, and to such a pitch can our enthusiasm rise, that we may sacrifice all earthly things for posthumous praise which can never reach our ear. And the force of association may extend even farther. We love praise, because it procures us certain advantages. We then love it more than these advantages. We proceed by the same process to transfer our affections to those things which naturally or generally procure praise. We at last love what is praiseworthy more than praise, and will endure perpetual obloquy rather than abandon it.[2] To this process, it is said, all our moral sentiments must be ascribed. Man has no natural benevolent feelings. He is at first governed solely by his interest, but the infant learns to associate its pleasures with the idea of its mother, the boy with the idea of his family, the man with those of his class, his church, his country, and at last of all mankind, and in each case an independent affection is at length formed.[3] The sight of suffering in others awakens in the child a painful recollection of his own sufferings, which parents, by appealing to the infant imagination, still further strengthen, and besides, ' when several children are educated together, the pains, the

---

tion' of ideas. See his curious chapter on the subject, *Light of Nature*, book i. ch. xviii.

[1] 'It is the nature of translation to throw desire from the end upon the means, which thenceforward become an end capable of exciting an appetite without prospect of the consequences whereto they lead. Our habits and most of the

desires that occupy human life are of this translated kind.'—Tucker's *Light of Nature*, vol. ii. (ed. 1842), p. 281.

[2] Mill's *Analysis of the Human Mind*. The desire for posthumous fame is usually cited by intuitive moralists as a proof of a naturally disinterested element in man.

[3] Mill's *Analysis*.

denials of pleasure, and the sorrows which affect one gradu ally extend in some degree to all;' and thus the suffering of others becomes associated with the idea of our own, and the feeling of compassion is engendered.[1] Benevolence and justice are associated in our minds with the esteem of our fellow-men, with reciprocity of favours, and with the hope of future reward. They are loved at first for these, and finally for themselves, while opposite trains of association produce opposite feelings towards malevolence and injustice.[2] And thus virtue, considered as a whole, becomes the supreme object of our affections. Of all our pleasures, more are derived from those acts which are called virtuous, than from any other source. The virtuous acts of others procure us countless advantages. Our own virtue obtains for us the esteem of men and return of favours. All the epithets of praise are appropriated to virtue, and all the epithets of blame to vice. Religion teaches us to connect hopes of infinite joy with the one, and fears of infinite suffering with the other. Virtue becomes therefore peculiarly associated with the idea of pleasurable things. It is soon loved, independently of and

---

[1] Hartley *On Man*, vol. i. pp. 474-475.

[2] 'Benevolence . . . has also a high degree of honour and esteem annexed to it, procures us many advantages and returns of kindness, both from the person obliged and others, and is most closely connected with the hopes of reward in a future state, and of self-approbation or the moral sense; and the same things hold with respect to generosity in a much higher degree. It is easy therefore to see how such associations may be formed as to engage us to forego great pleasure, or endure great pain for the sake of others, how these associations may be attended with so great a degree of pleasure as to overrule the positive pain endured or the negative one from the foregoing of a pleasure, and yet how there may be no direct explicit expectation of reward either from God or man, by natural consequence or express appointment, not even of the concomitant pleasure that engages the agent to undertake the benevolent and generous action; and this I take to be a proof from the doctrine of association that there is and must be such a thing as pure disinterested benevolence; also a just account of the origin and nature of it.'—Hartley *On Man*, vol. i. pp. 473-474. See too Mill's *Analysis*, vol. ii. p. 252.

more than these; we feel a glow of pleasure in practising it, and an intense pain in violating it. Conscience, which is thus generated, becomes the ruling principle of our lives,[1] and having learnt to sacrifice all earthly things rather than disobey it, we rise, by an association of ideas, into the loftiest region of heroism.[2]

The influence of this ingenious, though I think in some respect fanciful, theory depends less upon the number than upon the ability of its adherents. Though little known, I believe, beyond England, it has in England exercised a great fascination over exceedingly dissimilar minds,[3] and it does undoubtedly evade some of the objections to the other forms of the inductive theory. Thus, when intuitive moralists contend that our moral judgments, being instantaneous and effected under the manifest impulse of an emotion of sympathy or repulsion, are as far as possible removed from that cold calculation of interests to which the utilitarian reduces them, it is answered, that the association of ideas is

---

[1] Mill's *Analysis*, vol. ii. pp. 244–247.

[2] 'With self-interest,' said Hartley, 'man must begin; he may end in self-annihilation;' or as Coleridge happily puts it, 'Legality precedes morality in every individual, even as the Jewish dispensation preceded the Christian in the world at large.'—*Notes Theological and Political*, p. 340. It might be retorted with much truth, that we begin by practising morality as a duty—we end by practising it as a pleasure, without any reference to duty. Coleridge, who expressed for the Benthamite theories a very cordial detestation, sometimes glided into them himself. 'The happiness of man,' he says, 'is the end of virtue, and truth is the knowledge of the means.' (*The Friend*,

ed. 1850, vol. ii. p. 192 ) 'What can be the object of human virtue but the happiness of sentient, still more of moral beings ?' (*Notes Theol. and Polit.* p. 351.) Leibnitz says, 'Quand on aura appris à faire des actions louables par ambition, on les fera après par inclination.' (*Sur l'Art de connaître les Hommes*.)

[3] E.g. Mackintosh and James Mill. Coleridge in his younger days was an enthusiastic admirer of Hartley; but chiefly, I believe, on account of his theory of vibrations. He named his son after him, and described him in one of his poems as :—

' He of mortal kind
Wisest, the first who marked the ideal tribes
Up the fine fibres through the sentient brain.' *Religious Musings*

sufficient to engender a feeling which is the proximate cause of our decision.[1] Alone, of all the moralists of this school, the disciple of Hartley recognises conscience as a real and important element of our nature,[2] and maintains that it is possible to love virtue for itself as a form of happiness without any thought of ulterior consequences.[3] The immense value this theory ascribes to education, gives it an unusual practical importance. When we are balancing between a crime and a virtue, our wills, it is said, are necessarily determined by the greater pleasure. If we find more pleasure in the vice than in the virtue, we inevitably gravitate to evil. If we find more pleasure in the virtue than in the vice, we are as irresistibly attracted towards good. But the strength of such motives may be immeasurably enhanced by an early association of ideas. If we have been accustomed from childhood to associate our ideas of praise and pleasure with

---

[1] This position is elaborated in a passage too long for quotation by Mr. Austin. (*Lectures on Jurisprudence*, vol. i. p. 44.)

[2] Hobbes defines conscience as 'the opinion of evidence' (*On Human Nature*, ch. vi. § 8). Locke as 'our own opinion or judgment of the moral rectitude or pravity of our own actions' (*Essay*, book i. ch. iii. § 8). In Bentham there is very little on the subject; but in one place he informs us that 'conscience is a thing of fictitious existence, supposed to occupy a seat in the mind' (*Deontology*, vol. i. p. 137); and in another he ranks 'love of duty' (which he describes as an 'impossible motive, in so far as duty is synonymous to obligation') as a variety of the 'love of power' (*Springs of Action*, ii.) Mr. Bain says, 'conscience is an imitation within ourselves of the government without us.' (*Emotions and Will*, p. 313.)

[3] 'However much they [utilitarians] may believe (as they do) that actions and dispositions are only virtuous because they promote another end than virtue, yet this being granted . . . they not only place virtue at the very head of the things which are good as means to the ultimate end, but they also recognise as a psychological fact the possibility of its being to the individual a good in itself. . . . Virtue, according to the utilitarian doctrine, is not naturally and originally part of the end, but it is capable of becoming so. . . . What was once desired as an instrument for the attainment of happiness has come to be desired . . . as part of happiness. . . . Human nature is so constituted as to desire nothing which is not either a part of happiness or a means of happiness.'—J. S. Mill's *Utilitarianism*, pp. 54, 55. 56, 58.

virtue, we shall readily yield to virtuous motives; if with vice, to vicious ones. This readiness to yield to one or other set of motives, constitutes disposition, which is thus, according to these moralists, altogether an artificial thing, the product of education, and effected by association of ideas.[1]

It will be observed, however, that this theory, refined and imposing as it may appear, is still essentially a selfish one. Even when sacrificing all earthly objects through love of virtue, the good man is simply seeking his greatest enjoyment, indulging a kind of mental luxury which gives him more pleasure than what he foregoes, just as the miser finds more pleasure in accumulation than in any form of expenditure.[2] There has been, indeed, one attempt to emancipate the

---

[1] 'A man is tempted to commit adultery with the wife of his friend. The composition of the motive is obvious. He does not obey the motive. Why? He obeys other motives which are stronger. Though pleasures are associated with the immoral act, pains are associated with it also—the pains of the injured husband, the pains of the wife, the moral indignation of mankind, the future reproaches of his own mind. Some men obey the first rather than the second motive. The reason is obvious. In these the association of the act with the pleasure is from habit unduly strong, the association of the act with pains is from want of habit unduly weak. This is the case of a bad education. . . . Among the different classes of motives, there are men who are more easily and strongly operated on by some, others by others. We have also seen that this is entirely owing to habits of association. This facility of being acted upon by motives of a particular description, is that which we call disposition.'—Mill's *Analysis*, vol. ii. pp. 212, 213, &c. Adam Smith says, I think with much wisdom, that 'the great secret of education is to direct vanity to proper objects.'—*Moral Sentiments*, part vi. § 3.

[2] 'Goodness in ourselves is the prospect of satisfaction annexed to the welfare of others, so that we please them for the pleasure we receive ourselves in so doing, or to avoid the uneasiness we should feel in omitting it. But God is completely happy in Himself, nor can His happiness receive increase or diminution from anything befalling His creatures; wherefore His goodness is pure, disinterested bounty, without any return of joy or satisfaction to Himself. Therefore it is no wonder we have imperfect notions of a quality whereof we have no experience in our own nature.'—Tucker's *Light of Nature*, vol. i. p. 355. 'It is the privilege of God alone to act upon pure, disinterested bounty, without the least addition thereby to His own enjoy-

theory from this condition, but it appears to me altogether
futile. It has been said that men in the first instance indulge in baneful excesses, on account of the pleasure they
afford, but the habit being contracted, continue to practise
them after they have ceased to afford pleasure, and that a
similar law may operate in the case of the habit of virtue.[1]
But the reason why men who have contracted a habit continue to practise it after it has ceased to give them positive
enjoyment, is because to desist, creates a restlessness and
uneasiness which amounts to acute mental pain. To avoid
that pain is the motive of the action.

The reader who has perused the passages I have accumu-
lated in the notes, will be able to judge with what degree of
justice utilitarian writers denounce with indignation the
imputation of selfishness, as a calumny against their system.
It is not, I think, a strained or unnatural use of language
to describe as selfish or interested, all actions which a man
performs, in order himself to avoid suffering or acquire the

---

ment.'—Ibid. vol. ii. p. 279. On
the other hand, Hutcheson asks,
'If there be such disposition in
the Deity, where is the impossibility of some small degree of this
public love in His creatures, and
why must they be supposed incapable of acting but from self-
love?'—Enquiry concerning Moral
Good, § 2.

[1] 'We gradually, through the
influence of association, come to
desire the means without thinking
of the end; the action itself becomes an object of desire, and is
performed without reference to any
motive beyond itself. Thus far, it
may still be objected that the action
having, through association, become pleasurable, we are as much
as before moved to act by the anticipation of pleasure, namely, the
pleasure of the action itself. But
granting this, the matter does not
end here. As we proceed in the
formation of habits, and become
accustomed to will a particular act
. . . because it is pleasurable, we
at last continue to will it without
any reference to its being pleasurable. . . . In this manner it is that
habits of hurtful excess continue to
be practised, although they have
ceased to be pleasurable, and in
this manner also it is that the
habit of willing to persevere in the
course which he has chosen, does
not desert the moral hero, even
when the reward . . . is anything
but an equivalent for the suffering
he undergoes, or the wishes he may
have to renounce.'—Mill's Logic
(4th edition), vol. ii. pp. 416, 417.

greatest possible enjoyment. If this be so, the term selfish is strictly applicable to all the branches of this system.[1] At the same time it must be acknowledged, that there is a broad difference between the refined hedonism of the utilitarians we have last noticed, and the writings of Hobbes, of Mandeville, or of Paley. It must be acknowledged, also, that not a few intuitive or stoical moralists have spoken of the pleasure to be derived from virtue in language little if at all different from these writers.[2] The main object of the earlier members of the inductive school, was to depress human nature to their standard, by resolving all the noblest actions into coarse and selfish elements. The main object of some of the more influential of the later members of this school,

---

[1] 'In regard to interest in the most extended, which is the original and only strictly proper sense of the word disinterested, no human act has ever been or ever can be disinterested. . . . In the only sense in which disinterestedness can with truth be predicated of human actions, it is employed . . . to denote, not the absence of all interest . . . but only the absence of all interest of the self-regarding class. Not but that it is very frequently predicated of human action in cases in which divers interests, to no one of which the appellation of self-regarding can with propriety be denied, have been exercising their influence, and in particular fear of God, or hope from God, and fear of ill-repute, or hope of good repute. If what is above be correct, the most disinterested of men is not less under the dominion of interest than the most interested. The only cause of his being styled disinterested, is its not having been observed that the sort of motive (suppose it sympathy for an individual or class) has as truly a corresponding interest belonging to it as any other species of motive has. Of this contradiction between the truth of the case and the language employed in speaking of it, the cause is that in the one case men have not been in the habit of making—as in point of consistency they ought to have made—of the word interest that use which in the other case they have been in the habit of making of it.'—Bentham's *Springs of Action*, ii. § 2.

[2] Among others Bishop Butler, who draws some very subtle distinctions on the subject in his first sermon 'on the love of our neighbour.' Dugald Stewart remarks that 'although we apply the epithet selfish to avarice and to low and private sensuality, we never apply it to the desire of knowledge or to the pursuits of virtue, which are certainly sources of more exquisite pleasure than riches or sensuality can bestow.'—*Active and Moral Powers*, vol. i. p. 19.

has been to sublimate their conceptions of happiness and interest in such a manner, as to include the highest displays of heroism.  As we have seen, they fully admit that conscience is a real thing, and should be the supreme guide of our lives, though they contend that it springs originally from selfishness, transformed under the influence of the association of ideas.  They acknowledge the reality of the sympathetic feelings, though they usually trace them to the same source. They cannot, it is true, consistently with their principles, recognise the possibility of conduct which is in the strictest sense of the word unselfish, but they contend that it is quite possible for a man to find his highest pleasure in sacrificing himself for the good of others, that the association of virtue and pleasure is only perfect when it leads habitually to spontaneous and uncalculating action, and that no man is in a healthy moral condition who does not find more pain in committing a crime than he could derive pleasure from any of its consequences.  The theory in its principle remains unchanged, but in the hands of some of these writers the spirit has wholly altered.

Having thus given a brief, but, I trust, clear and faithful account of the different modifications of the inductive theory, I shall proceed to state some of the principal objections that have been and may be brought against it.  I shall then endeavour to define and defend the opinions of those who believe that our moral feelings are an essential part of our constitution, developed by, but not derived from education, and I shall conclude this chapter by an enquiry into the order of their evolution; so that having obtained some notion of the natural history of morals, we may be able, in the ensuing chapters, to judge, how far their normal progress has been accelerated or retarded by religious or political agencies.

'Psychology,' it has been truly said, 'is but developed

consciousness.'[1]  When moralists assert, that what we call
virtue derives its reputation solely from its utility, and that
the interest or pleasure of the agent is the one motive to
practise it, our first question is naturally how far this theory
agrees with the feelings and with the language of mankind.
But if tested by this criterion, there never was a doctrine
more emphatically condemned than utilitarianism.  In all
its stages, and in all its assertions, it is in direct opposition
to common language and to common sentiments.  In all
nations and in all ages, the ideas of interest and utility on
the one hand and of virtue on the other, have been regarded
by the multitude as perfectly distinct, and all languages recognise the distinction.  The terms honour, justice, rectitude
or virtue, and their equivalents in every language, present to
the mind ideas essentially and broadly differing from the
terms prudence, sagacity, or interest.  The two lines of conduct may coincide, but they are never confused, and we have
not the slightest difficulty in imagining them antagonistic.
When we say a man is governed by a high sense of honour,
or by strong moral feeling, we do not mean that he is prudently pursuing either his own interests or the interests of
society.  The universal sentiment of mankind represents
self-sacrifice as an essential element of a meritorious act, and
means by self-sacrifice the deliberate adoption of the least
pleasurable course without the prospect of any pleasure in
return.  A selfish act may be innocent, but cannot be virtuous, and to ascribe all good deeds to selfish motives, is not
the distortion but the negation of virtue.  No Epicurean
could avow before a popular audience that the one end of his
life was the pursuit of his own happiness without an outburst
of indignation and contempt.[2]  No man could consciously
make this—which according to the selfish theory is the only
rational and indeed possible motive of action—the deliberate

---

[1] Sir W. Hamilton.        [2] Cic. *De Fin.* lib. ii.

object of all his undertakings, without his character becoming despicable and degraded.    Whether we look within ourselves or examine the conduct either of our enemies or of our friends, or adjudicate upon the characters in history or in fiction, our feelings on these matters are the same.    In exact proportion as we believe a desire for personal enjoyment to be the motive of a good act is the merit of the agent diminished.    If we believe the motive to be wholly selfish the merit is altogether destroyed.    If we believe it to be wholly disinterested the merit is altogether unalloyed.    Hence, the admiration bestowed upon Prometheus, or suffering virtue constant beneath the blows of Almighty malice, or on the atheist who with no prospect of future reward suffered a fearful death, rather than abjure an opinion which could be of no benefit to society, because he believed it to be the truth. Selfish moralists deny the possibility of that which all ages, all nations, all popular judgments pronounce to have been the characteristic of every noble act that has ever been performed.    Now, when a philosophy which seeks by the light of consciousness to decipher the laws of our moral being proves so diametrically opposed to the conclusions arrived at by the great mass of mankind, who merely follow their consciousness without endeavouring to frame systems of philosophy, that it makes most of the distinctions of common ethical language absolutely unmeaning, this is, to say the least, a strong presumption against its truth.    If Molière's hero had been speaking prose all his life without knowing it, this was simply because he did not understand what prose was.    In the present case we are asked to believe that men have been under a total delusion about the leading principles of their lives which they had distinguished by a whole vocabulary of terms.

It is said that the case becomes different when the pleasure sought is not a gross or material enjoyment, but the satisfaction of performed virtue.    I suspect that if men could persuade themselves that the one motive of a virtuous man was the certainty that the act he accomplished would be followed by a glow of satisfaction so intense as more than to compensate for any sacrifice he might have made, the difference would not be as great as is supposed. In fact, however—and the consciousness of this lies, I conceive, at the root of the opinions of men upon the subject—the pleasure of virtue is one which can only be obtained on the express condition of its not being the object sought. Phenomena of this kind are familiar to us all. Thus, for example, it has often been observed that prayer, by a law of our nature and apart from all supernatural intervention, exercises a reflex influence of a very beneficial character upon the minds of the worshippers. The man who offers up his petitions with passionate earnestness, with unfaltering faith, and with a vivid realisation of the presence of an Unseen Being has risen to a condition of mind which is itself eminently favourable both to his own happiness and to the expansion of his moral qualities. But he who expects nothing more will never attain this. To him who neither believes nor hopes that his petitions will receive a response such a mental state is impossible. No Protestant before an image of the Virgin, no Christian before a pagan idol, could possibly attain it. If prayers were offered up solely with a view to this benefit, they would be absolutely sterile and would speedily cease. Thus again, certain political economists have contended that to give money in charity is worse than useless, that it is positively noxious to society, but they have added that the gratification of our benevolent affections is pleasing to ourselves, and that the pleasure we derive from this source may be so much greater than the evil resulting from our gift, that we may justly, according to the 'greatest happiness principle,' purchase this large amount of gratification to ourselves by a slight injury to our neighbours. The political economy involved in this very characteristic specimen of utilitarian ethics I shall hereafter examine. At present it is sufficient to observe that no one who consciously practised benevolence solely from this motive could obtain the pleasure in question. We receive enjoyment from the thought that we have done good. We never could receive that enjoyment if we believed and realised that we were doing harm. The same thing is pre-eminently true of the satisfaction of conscience. A feeling of satisfaction follows the accomplishment of duty for itself, but if the duty be performed solely through the expectation of a mental pleasure conscience refuses to ratify the bargain.

There is no fact more conspicuous in human nature than the broad distinction, both in kind and degree, drawn between the moral and the other parts of our nature. But this on utilitarian principles is altogether unaccountable. If the excellence of virtue consists solely in its utility or tendency to promote the happiness of men, we should be compelled to canonise a crowd of acts which are utterly remote from all our ordinary notions of morality. The whole tendency of political economy and philosophical history which reveal the physiology of societies, is to show that the happiness and welfare of mankind are evolved much more from our selfish than from what are termed our virtuous acts. The prosperity of nations and the progress of civilisation are mainly due to the exertions of men who while pursuing strictly their own interests, were unconsciously promoting the interests of the community. The selfish instinct that leads men to accumulate, confers ultimately more advantage upon the world than the generous instinct that leads men to give. A great historian has contended with some force that intellectual development is more important to societies than moral development. Yet who ever seriously questioned the reality of the distinction that separates these things? The reader will probably exclaim that the key to that distinction is to be found in the motive; but it is one of the paradoxes of the

utilitarian school that the motive of the agent has absolutely
no influence on the morality of the act. According to Bentham, there is but one motive possible, the pursuit of our own
enjoyment. The most virtuous, the most vicious, and the
most indifferent of actions, if measured by this test, would
be exactly the same, and an investigation of motives should
therefore be altogether excluded from our moral judgments.[1]
Whatever test we adopt, the difficulty of accounting for the
unique and pre-eminent position mankind have assigned to
virtue will remain. If we judge by tendencies, a crowd of
objects and of acts to which no mortal ever dreamed of ascribing virtue, contribute largely to the happiness of man.
If we judge by motives, the moralists we are reviewing have
denied all generic difference between prudential and virtuous

---

[1] 'As there is not any sort of
pleasure that is not itself a good,
nor any sort of pain the exemption
from which is not a good, and as
nothing but the expectation of the
eventual enjoyment of pleasure in
some shape, or of exemption from
pain in some shape, can operate in
the character of a motive, a necessary consequence is that if by motive be meant *sort* of motive, there
is not any such thing as a bad
motive.'—Bentham's *Springs of
Action*, ii. § 4. The first clauses
of the following passage I have already quoted: 'Pleasure is itself a
good, nay, setting aside immunity
from pain, the only good. Pain is
in itself an evil, and indeed, without exception, the only evil, or else
the words good and evil have no
meaning. And this is alike true of
every sort of pain, and of every sort
of pleasure. It follows therefore
immediately and incontestably that
there is no such thing as any sort
of motive that is in itself a bad
one.'—*Principles of Morals and
Legislation*, ch. ix. 'The search
after motive is one of the prominent
causes of men's bewilderment in
the investigation of questions of
morals. . . . But this is a pursuit
in which every moment employed
is a moment wasted. All motives
are abstractedly good. No man
has ever had, can, or could have a
motive different from the pursuit of
pleasure or of shunning pain.'—
*Deontology*, vol. i. p. 126. Mr.
Mill's doctrine appears somewhat
different from this, but the difference is I think only apparent. He
says: 'The motive has nothing to
do with the morality of the action,
though much with the worth of the
agent,' and he afterwards explains
this last statement by saying that
the 'motive makes a great difference in our moral estimation of the
agent, especially if it indicates a
good or a bad habitual disposition,
a bent of character from which useful or from which hurtful actions
are likely to arise.'—*Utilitarianism*, 2nd ed. pp. 26–27.

motives. If we judge by intentions, it is certain that however much truth or chastity may contribute to the happiness
of mankind, it is not with philanthropic intentions that those
virtues are cultivated.

It is often said that intuitive moralists in their reasonings
are guilty of continually abandoning their principles by themselves appealing to the tendency of certain acts to promote
human happiness as a justification, and the charge is usually
accompanied by a challenge to show any confessed virtue that
has not that tendency. To the first objection it may be
shortly answered that no intuitive moralist ever dreamed of
doubting that benevolence or charity, or in other words, the
promotion of the happiness of man, is a duty. He maintains
that it not only is so, but that we arrive at this fact by direct
intuition, and not by the discovery that such a course is
conducive to our own interest. But while he cordially
recognises this branch of virtue, and while he has therefore a
perfect right to allege the beneficial effects of a virtue in its
defence, he refuses to admit that all virtue can be reduced to
this single principle. With the general sentiment of mankind
he regards charity as a good thing only because it is of use
to the world. With the same general sentiment of mankind
he believes that chastity and truth have an independent value,
distinct from their influence upon happiness. To the question
whether every confessed virtue is conducive to human happiness, it is less easy to reply, for it is usually extremely difficult to calculate the remote tendencies of acts, and in cases
where, in the common apprehension of mankind, the morality
is very clear, the consequences are often very obscure. Notwithstanding the claim of great precision which utilitarian
writers so boastfully make, the standard by which they profess to measure morals is itself absolutely incapable of defini
tion or accurate explanation. Happiness is one of the most
indeterminate and undefinable words in the language, and
what are the conditions of ' the greatest possible happiness

no one can precisely say. No two nations, perhaps no two individuals, would find them the same.[1] And even if every virtuous act were incontestably useful, it by no means follows that its virtue is derived from its utility.

It may be readily granted, that as a general rule those acts which we call virtuous, are unquestionably productive of happiness, if not to the agent, at least to mankind in general, but we have already seen that they have by no means that monopoly or pre-eminence of utility which on utilitarian principles, the unique position assigned to them would appear to imply. It may be added, that if we were to proceed in detail to estimate acts by their consequences, we should soon be led to very startling conclusions. In the first place, it is obvious that if virtues are only good because they promote, and vices only evil because they impair the happiness of mankind, the degrees of excellence or criminality must be strictly proportioned to the degrees of utility or the reverse.[2] Every action, every disposition, every class, every condition of society must take its place on the moral scale precisely in accordance with the degree in which it promotes or diminishes human happiness. Now it is extremely questionable, whether some of the most monstrous forms of sensuality which it is scarcely possible to name, cause as much unhappiness as some infirmities of temper, or procrastination or hastiness of judgment. It is scarcely doubtful that a modest, diffident, and retiring nature, distrustful of its own abilities, and shrinking with humility from conflict, produces on the whole less benefit to the world than the self-assertion of an audacious and arrogant nature, which is impelled to every struggle, and de-

---

[1] This truth has been admirably illustrated by Mr. Herbert Spencer (*Social Statics*, pp. 1–8).

[2] 'On évalue la grandeur de la vertu en comparant les biens obtenus aux maux au prix desquels on les achète : l'excédant en bien mesure la valeur de la vertu, comme l'excédant en mal mesure le degré de haine que doit inspirer le vice —Ch. Comte, *Traité de Legislation*, liv. ii. ch. xii.

velopes every capacity. Gratitude has no doubt done much to soften and sweeten the intercourse of life, but the corresponding feeling of revenge was for centuries the one bulwark against social anarchy, and is even now one of the chief restraints to crime.[1] On the great theatre of public life, especially in periods of great convulsions when passions are fiercely roused, it is neither the man of delicate scrupulosity and sincere impartiality, nor yet the single-minded religious enthusiast, incapable of dissimulation or procrastination, who confers most benefit upon the world. It is much rather the astute statesman earnest about his ends but unscrupulous about his means, equally free from the trammels of conscience and from the blindness of zeal, who governs because he partly yields to the passions and the prejudices of his time. But however much some modern writers may idolize the heroes of success, however much they may despise and ridicule those far nobler men, whose wide tolerance and scrupulous honour

---

[1] M. Dumont, the translator of Bentham, has elaborated in a rather famous passage the utilitarian notions about vengeance. ‘Toute espèce de satisfaction entraînant une peine pour le délinquant produit naturellement un plaisir de vengeance pour la partie lésée. Ce plaisir est un gain. Il rappelle la parabole de Samson. C'est le doux qui sort du terrible. C'est le miel recueilli dans la gueule du lion. Produit sans frais, résultat net d'une opération nécessaire à d'autres titres, c'est une jouissance à cultiver comme toute autre ; car le plaisir de la vengeance considérée abstraitement n'est comme tout autre plaisir qu'un bien en lui-même.'— Principes du Code pénal, 2me partie, ch. xvi. According to a very acute living writer of this school, ‘The criminal law stands to the passion of revenge in much the same relation as marriage to the sexual appetite' (J. F. Stephen On the Criminal Law of England, p. 99). Mr Mill observes that, ‘In the golden rule of Jesus of Nazareth, we read the complete spirit of the ethics of utility' (Utilitarianism, p. 24). It is but fair to give a specimen of the opposite order of extravagance. ‘So well convinced was Father Claver of the eternal happiness of almost all whom he assisted,' says this saintly missionary's biographer, ‘that speaking once of some persons who had delivered a criminal into the hands of justice, he said, God forgive them; but they have secured the salvation of this man at the probable risk of their own.'—Newman's Anglican Difficulties, p. 205.

rendered them unfit leaders in the fray, it has scarcely yet
been contended that the delicate conscientiousness which in
these cases impairs utility constitutes vice.   If utility is the
sole measure of virtue, it is difficult to understand how we
could look with moral disapprobation on any class who prevent greater evils than they cause.   But with such a principle we might find strange priestesses at the utilitarian shrine.
'Aufer meretrices de rebus humanis,' said St. Augustine,
'turbaveris omnia libidinibus.'[1]

Let us suppose an enquirer who intended to regulate his
life consistently by the utilitarian principle; let us suppose
him to have overcome the first great difficulty of his school,
arising from the apparent divergence of his own interests from
his duty, to have convinced himself that that divergence does
not exist, and to have accordingly made the pursuit of duty his
single object, it remains to consider what kind of course he
would pursue.  He is informed that it is a pure illusion to suppose that human actions have any other end or rule than happiness, that nothing is intrinsically good or intrinsically bad
apart from its consequences, that no act which is useful can
possibly be vicious, and that the utility of an act constitutes
and measures its value.   One of his first observations will be
that in very many special cases acts such as murder, theft,
or falsehood, which the world calls criminal, and which in
the majority of instances would undoubtedly be hurtful,
appear eminently productive of good.   Why then, he may
ask, should they not in these cases be performed?   The
answer he receives is that they would not really be useful,
because we must consider the remote as well as the immediate consequences of actions, and although in particular
instances a falsehood or even a murder might appear beneficial, it is one of the most important interests of mankind

---

[1] *De Ordine*, ii. 4.  The experiment has more than once been tried
at Venice, Pisa, &c., and always
with the results St. Augustine pre
dicted.

that the sanctity of life and property should be preserved, and that a high standard of veracity should be maintained. But this answer is obviously insufficient. It is necessary to show that the extent to which a single act of what the world calls crime would weaken these great bulwarks of society is such as to counterbalance the immediate good which it produces. If it does not, the balance will be on the side of happiness, the murder or theft or falsehood will be useful, and therefore, on utilitarian principles, will be virtuous. Now even in the case of public acts, the effect of the example of an obscure individual is usually small, but if the act be accomplished in perfect secrecy, the evil effects resulting from the example will be entirely absent. It has been said that it would be dangerous to give men permission to perpetrate what men call crimes in secret. This may be a very good reason why the utilitarian should not proclaim such a principle, but it is no reason why he should not act upon it. If a man be convinced that no act which is useful can possibly be criminal, if it be in his power by perpetrating what is called a crime to obtain an end of great immediate utility, and if he is able to secure such absolute secrecy as to render it perfectly certain that his act cannot become an example, and cannot in consequence exercise any influence on the general standard of morals, it appears demonstrably certain that on utilitarian principles he would be justified in performing it. If what we call virtue be only virtuous *because* it is useful, it can only be virtuous *when* it is useful. The question of the morality of a large number of acts must therefore depend upon the probability of their detection,[1]

---

[1] The reader will here observe the very transparent sophistry of an assertion which is repeated ad nauseam by utilitarians. They tell us that a regard to the remote consequences of our actions would lead us to the conclusion that we should never perform an act which would not be conducive to human happiness if it were universally performed, or, as Mr. Austin expresses it, that 'the question is if acts of this class were generally done or generally forborne or omit-

and a little adroit hypocrisy must often, not merely in appearance but in reality, convert a vice into a virtue. The only way by which it has been attempted with any plausibility to evade this conclusion has been by asserting that the act would impair the disposition of the agent, or in other words predispose him on other occasions to perform acts which are generally hurtful to society. But in the first place a single act has no such effect upon disposition as to counteract a great immediate good, especially when, as we have supposed, that act is not a revolt against what is believed to be right, but is performed under the full belief that it is in accordance with the one rational rule of morals, and in the next place, as far as the act would form a habit it would appear to be the habit of in all cases regulating actions by a precise and minute calculation of their utility, which is the very ideal of utilitarian virtue.

If our enquirer happens to be a man of strong imagination and of solitary habits, it is very probable that he will be accustomed to live much in a world of imagination, a world peopled with beings that are to him as real as those of

---

ted, what would be the probable effect on the general happiness or good?' (*Lectures on Jurisprudence*, vol. i. p. 32.) The question is nothing of the kind. If I am convinced that utility alone constitutes virtue, and if I am meditating any particular act, the sole question of morality must be whether that act is on the whole useful, produces a net result of happiness. To determine this question I must consider both the immediate and the remote consequences of the act; but the latter are not ascertained by asking what would be the result if every one did as I do, but by asking how far, as a matter of fact, my act is likely to produce imi-

tators, or affect the conduct and future acts of others. It may no doubt be convenient and useful to form classifications based on the general tendency of different courses to promote or diminish happiness, but such classification cannot alter the morality of particular acts. It is quite clear that no act which produces on the whole more pleasure than pain can on utilitarian principles be vicious. It is, I think, equally clear that no one could act consistently on such a principle without being led to consequences which in the common judgment of mankind are grossly and scandalously immoral.

flesh, with its joys and sorrows, its temptations and its sins. In obedience to the common feelings of our nature he may have struggled long and painfully against sins of the imagination, which he was never seriously tempted to convert into sins of action. But his new philosophy will be admirably fitted to console his mind. If remorse be absent the indulgence of the most vicious imagination is a pleasure, and if this indulgence does not lead to action it is a clear gain, and therefore to be applauded. That a course may be continually pursued in imagination without leading to corresponding actions he will speedily discover, and indeed it has always been one of the chief objections brought against fiction that the constant exercise of the sympathies in favour of imaginary beings is found positively to indispose men to practical benevolence.[1]

Proceeding farther in his course, our moralist will soon find reason to qualify the doctrine of remote consequences, which plays so large a part in the calculations of utilitarianism. It is said that it is criminal to destroy human beings, even when the crime would appear productive of great utility, for every instance of murder weakens the sanctity of life. But experience shows that it is possible for men to be perfectly indifferent to one particular section of human life, without this indifference extending to others. Thus among the ancient Greeks, the murder or exposition of the children of poor parents was continually practised with the most absolute callousness, without exercising any appreciable influence upon the respect for adult life. In the same manner what may be termed religious unveracity, or the habit of propagating what are deemed useful superstitions, with the consciousness of their being false, or at least suppressing or misrepresenting the facts that might invalidate

---

[1] There are some very good remarks on the possibility of living a life of imagination wholly distinct from the life of action in Mr. Bain's *Emotions and Will*, p. 246.

them, does not in any degree imply industrial unveracity. Nothing is more common than to find extreme dishonesty in speculation coexisting with scrupulous veracity in business. If any vice might be expected to conform strictly to the utilitarian theory, it would be cruelty; but cruelty to animals may exist without leading to cruelty to men, and even where spectacles in which animal suffering forms a leading element exercise an injurious influence on character, it is more than doubtful whether the measure of human unhappiness they may ultimately produce is at all equivalent to the passionate enjoyment they immediately afford.

This last consideration, however, makes it necessary to notice a new, and as it appears to me, almost grotesque development of the utilitarian theory. The duty of humanity to animals, though for a long period too much neglected, may, on the principles of the intuitive moralist, be easily explained and justified. Our circumstances and characters produce in us many and various affections towards all with whom we come in contact, and our consciences pronounce these affections to be good or bad. We feel that humanity or benevolence is a good affection, and also that it is due in different degrees to different classes. Thus it is not only natural but right that a man should care for his own family more than for the world at large, and this obligation applies not only to parents who are responsible for having brought their children into existence, and to children who owe a debt of gratitude to their parents, but also to brothers who have no such special tie. So too we feel it to be both unnatural and wrong to feel no stronger interest in our fellow-countrymen than in other men. In the same way we feel that there is a wide interval between the humanity it is both natural and right to exhibit towards animals, and that which is due to our own species. Strong philanthropy could hardly coexist with cannibalism, and a man who had no hesitation in destroying human life for the sake of obtaining the skins of the victims, or of freeing himself from some trifling inconvenience, would scarcely be eulogised for his benevolence. Yet a man may be regarded as very humane to animals who has no scruple in sacrificing their lives for his food, his pleasures, or his convenience.

Towards the close of the last century an energetic agitation in favour of humanity to animals arose in England, and the utilitarian moralists, who were then rising into influence, caught the spirit of their time and made very creditable efforts to extend it.[1] It is manifest, however, that a theory which recognised no other end in virtue than the promotion of human happiness, could supply no adequate basis for the movement. Some of the recent members of the school have accordingly enlarged their theory, maintaining that acts are virtuous when they produce a net result of happiness, and vicious when they produce a net result of suffering, altogether irrespective of the question whether this enjoyment or suffering is of men or animals. In other words, they place the duty of man to animals on exactly the same basis as the duty of man to his fellow-men, maintaining that no suffering can be rightly inflicted on brutes, which does not produce a larger amount of happiness to man.[2]

The first reflection suggested by this theory is, that it

---

[1] Bentham especially recurs to this subject frequently. See Sir J. Bowring's edition of his works (Edinburgh, 1843), vol. i. pp. 142, 143, 562 ; vol. x. pp. 549–550.

[2] 'Granted that any practice causes more pain to animals than it gives pleasure to man; is that practice moral or immoral? And if exactly in proportion as human beings raise their heads out of the slough of selfishness they do not with one voice answer "immoral," let the morality of the principle of utility be for ever condemned.'—Mill's *Dissert.* vol. ii. p. 485. 'We

deprive them [animals] of life, and this is justifiable—their pains do not equal our enjoyments. There is a balance of good.'—Bentham's *Deontology*, vol. i. p. 14. Mr. Mill accordingly defines the principle of utility, without any special reference to man. 'The creed which accepts as the foundation of morals, utility or the great happiness principle, holds that actions are right in proportion as they tend to promote happiness, wrong as they tend to produce the reverse of happiness.'—*Utilitarianism*, pp. 9–10.

appears difficult to understand how, on the principles of the inductive school, it could be arrived at. Benevolence, as we have seen, according to these writers begins in interest. We first of all do good to men, because it is for our advantage, though the force of the habit may at last act irrespective of interest. But in the case of animals which cannot resent barbarity, this foundation of self-interest does not for the most part[1] exist. Probably, however, an association of ideas might help to solve the difficulty, and the habit of benevolence generated originally from the social relations of men might at last be extended to the animal world; but that it should be so to the extent of placing the duty to animals on the same basis as the duty to men, I do not anticipate, or (at the risk of being accused of great inhumanity), I must add, desire. I cannot look forward to a time when no one will wear any article of dress formed out of the skin of an animal, or feed upon animal flesh, till he has ascertained that the pleasure he derives from doing so, exceeds the pain inflicted upon the animal, as well as the pleasure of which by abridging its life he has deprived it.[2] And supposing that

---

[1] The exception of course being domestic animals, which may be injured by ill-treatment, but even this exception is a very partial one. No selfish reason could prevent any amount of cruelty to animals that were about to be killed, and even in the case of previous ill-usage the calculations of selfishness will depend greatly upon the price of the animal. I have been told that on some parts of the continent diligence horses are systematically under-fed, and worked to a speedy death, their cheapness rendering such a course the most economical.

[2] Bentham, as we have seen, is of opinion that the gastronomic pleasure would produce the requisite excess of enjoyment. Hartley, who has some amiable and beautiful remarks on the duty of kindness to animals, without absolutely condemning, speaks with much aversion of the custom of eating 'our brothers and sisters,' the animals. (*On Man*, vol. ii. pp. 222–223.) Paley, observing that it is quite possible for men to live without flesh-diet, concludes that the only sufficient justification for eating meat is an express divine revelation in the Book of Genesis. (*Moral Philos.* book ii. ch. 11.) Some reasoners evade the main issue by contending that they kill animals because they would otherwise overrun the earth; but this, as Windham said, 'is an indifferent reason for killing fish.'

with such a calculation before him, the utilitarian should continue to feed on the flesh of animals, his principle might carry him to further conclusions, from which I confess I should recoil. If, when Swift was writing his famous essay in favour of employing for food the redundant babies of a half-starving population, he had been informed that, according to the more advanced moralists, to eat a child, and to eat a sheep, rest upon exactly the same ground; that in the one case as in the other, the single question for the moralist is, whether the repast on the whole produces more pleasure than pain, it must be owned that the discovery would have greatly facilitated his task.

The considerations I have adduced will, I think, be sufficient to show that the utilitarian principle if pushed to its full logical consequences would be by no means as accordant with ordinary moral notions as is sometimes alleged; that it would, on the contrary, lead to conclusions utterly and outrageously repugnant to the moral feelings it is intended to explain. I will conclude this part of my argument by very briefly adverting to two great fields in which, as I believe, it would prove especially revolutionary.

The first of these is the field of chastity. It will be necessary for me in the course of the present work to dwell at greater length than I should desire upon questions connected with this virtue. At present, I will merely ask the reader to conceive a mind from which all notion of the intrinsic excellence or nobility of purity was banished, and to suppose such a mind comparing, by a utilitarian standard, a period in which sensuality was almost unbridled, such as the age of Athenian glory or the English restoration, with a period of austere virtue. The question which of these societies was morally the best would thus resolve itself solely into the question in which there was produced the greatest amount of enjoyment and the smallest amount of suffering. The pleasures of domestic life, the pleasures resulting from a

freer social intercourse,[1] the different degrees of suffering
inflicted on those who violated the law of chastity, the
ulterior consequences of each mode of life upon well-being
and upon population, would be the chief elements of the
comparison.   Can any one believe that the balance of enjoyment would be so unquestionably and so largely on the side
of the more austere society as to justify the degree of superiority which is assigned to it ?[2]

The second sphere is that of speculative truth.   No class
of men have more highly valued an unflinching hostility to
superstition than utilitarians.   Yet it is more than doubtful
whether upon their principles it can be justified.   Many
superstitions do undoubtedly answer to the Greek conception

---

[1] In commenting upon the
French licentiousness of the eighteenth century, Hume says, in a
passage which has excited a great
deal of animadversion :—' Our
neighbours, it seems, have resolved
to sacrifice some of the domestic to
the social pleasures ; and to prefer
ease, freedom, and an open commerce, to strict fidelity and constancy.   These ends are both good,
and are somewhat difficult to reconcile ; nor must we be surprised
if the customs of nations incline too
much sometimes to the one side,
and sometimes to the other.'—
Dialogue.

[2] There are few things more
pitiable than the blunders into
which writers have fallen when
trying to base the plain virtue of
chastity on utilitarian calculations.
Thus since the writings of Malthus
it has been generally recognised
that one of the very first conditions
of all material prosperity is to
check early marriages, to restrain
the tendency of population to multiply more rapidly than the means

of subsistence.   Knowing this,
what can be more deplorable than
to find moralists making such ar
guments as these the very foundation of morals?—' The first and
great mischief, and by consequence
the guilt, of promiscuous concubi-
nage consists in its tendency to
diminish marriages.'   (Paley's
Moral Philosophy, book iii. part
iii. ch. ii.)   'That is always the
most happy condition of a nation,
and that nation is most accurately
obeying the laws of our constitution, in which the number of the
human race is most rapidly increasing.   Now it is certain that
under the law of chastity, that is,
when individuals are exclusively
united to each other, the increase
of population will be more rapid
than under any other circumstances.'   (Wayland's Elements of
Moral Science, p. 298, 11th ed.,
Boston, 1839.)   I am sorry to
bring such subjects before the
reader, but it is impossible to
write a history of morals without
doing so.

of slavish ' fear of the gods, and have been productive of
unspeakable misery to mankind, but there are very many
others of a different tendency. Superstitions appeal to our
hopes as well as to our fears. They often meet and gratify
the inmost longings of the heart. They offer certainties
when reason can only afford possibilities or probabilities.
They supply conceptions on which the imagination loves
to dwell. They sometimes even impart a new sanction
to moral truths. Creating wants which they alone can
satisfy, and fears which they alone can quell, they often
become essential elements of happiness, and their consoling
efficacy is most felt in the languid or troubled hours when
it is most needed. We owe more to our illusions than to
our knowledge. The imagination, which is altogether constructive, probably contributes more to our happiness than
the reason, which in the sphere of speculation is mainly
critical and destructive. The rude charm which in the hour
of danger or distress the savage clasps so confidently to his
breast, the sacred picture which is believed to shed a hallowing and protecting influence over the poor man's cottage,
can bestow a more real consolation in the darkest hour of
human suffering than can be afforded by the grandest theories
of philosophy. The first desire of the heart is to find something on which to lean. Happiness is a condition of feeling,
not a condition of circumstances, and to common minds one
of its first essentials is the exclusion of painful and harassing
doubt. A system of belief may be false, superstitious, and
reactionary, and may yet be conducive to human happiness if
it furnishes great multitudes of men with what they believe
to be a key to the universe, if it consoles them in those
seasons of agonizing bereavement when the consolations of enlightened reason are but empty words, if it supports their feeble
and tottering minds in the gloomy hours of sickness and of
approaching death. A credulous and superstitious nature
may be degraded, but in the many cases where superstition

does not assume a persecuting or appalling form it is not
unhappy, and degradation, apart from unhappiness, can have
no place in utilitarian ethics.  No error can be more grave
than to imagine that when a critical spirit is abroad the
pleasant beliefs will all remain, and the painful ones alone
will perish.  To introduce into the mind the consciousness
of ignorance and the pangs of doubt is to inflict or endure
much suffering, which may even survive the period of transition.  'Why is it,' said Luther's wife, looking sadly back
upon the sensuous creed which she had left, ' that in our old
faith we prayed so often and so warmly, and that our
prayers are now so few and so cold?'[1]  It is related of an
old monk named Serapion, who had embraced the heresy of
the anthropomorphites, that he was convinced by a brother
monk of the folly of attributing to the Almighty a human
form.  He bowed his reason humbly to the Catholic creed ;
but when he knelt down to pray, the image which his imagination had conceived, and on which for so many years his
affections had been concentrated, had disappeared, and the
old man burst into tears, exclaiming, ' You have deprived me
of my God.'[2]

These are indeed facts which must be deeply painful to
all who are concerned with the history of opinion.  The
possibility of often adding to the happiness of men by diffusing abroad, or at least sustaining pleasing falsehoods, and
the suffering that must commonly result from their dissolution, can hardly reasonably be denied.  There is one, and
but one, adequate reason that can always justify men in
critically reviewing what they have been taught.  It is, the
conviction that opinions should not be regarded as mere
mental luxuries, that truth should be deemed an end distinct
from and superior to utility, and that it is a moral duty to

---

[1] See Luther's *Table Talk*.          *à l'Hist. ecclésiastique*, tcme x. p. 57
[2] Tillemont, *Mém. pour servir*

pursue it, whether it leads to pleasure or whether it leads to pain. Among the many wise sayings which antiquity ascribed to Pythagoras, few are more remarkable than his division of virtue into two distinct branches—to be truthful and to do good.[1]

Of the sanctions which, according to the utilitarians, constitute the sole motives to virtue, there is one, as I have said, unexceptionably adequate. Those who adopt the religious sanction, can always appeal to a balance of interest in favour of virtue; but as the great majority of modern utilitarians confidently sever their theory from all theological considerations, I will dismiss this sanction with two or three remarks.

In the first place, it is obvious that those who regard the arbitrary will of the Deity as the sole rule of morals, render it perfectly idle to represent the Divine attributes as deserving of our admiration. To speak of the goodness of God, either implies that there is such a quality as goodness, to which the Divine acts conform, or it is an unmeaning tautology. Why should we extol, or how can we admire, the perfect goodness of a Being whose will and acts constitute the sole standard or definition of perfection?[2] The theory which teaches that the arbitrary will of the Deity is the one rule of morals, and the anticipation of future rewards and punishments the one reason for conforming to it, consists of two parts. The first annihilates the goodness of God; the second, the virtue of man.

---

[1] Τό τε ἀληθεύειν καὶ τὸ εὐεργετεῖν. (Ælian, Var. Hist. xii. 59.) Longinus in like manner divides virtue into εὐεργεσία καὶ ἀλήθεια. (De Sublim. § 1.) The opposite view in England is continually expressed in the saying, 'You should never pull down an opinion until you have something to put in its place,' which can only mean, if you are convinced that some religious or other hypothesis is false, you are morally bound to repress or conceal your conviction until you have discovered positive affirmations or explanations as unqualified and consolatory as those you have destroyed.

[2] See this powerfully stated by Shaftesbury. (Inquiry concerning Virtue, book i. part iii.) The same objection applies to Dr. Mansel's modification of the theological doctrine—viz. that the origin of morals is not the will but the nature of God.

Another and equally obvious remark is, that while these theologians represent the hope of future rewards, and the fear of future punishments, as the only reason for doing right, one of our strongest reasons for believing in the existence of these rewards and punishments, is our deep-seated feeling of merit and demerit. That the present disposition of affairs is in many respects unjust, that suffering often attends a course which deserves reward, and happiness a course which deserves punishment, leads men to infer a future state of retribution. Take away the consciousness of desert, and the inference would no longer be made.

A third remark, which I believe to be equally true, but which may not be acquiesced in with equal readiness, is that without the concurrence of a moral faculty, it is wholly impossible to prove from nature that supreme goodness of the Creator, which utilitarian theologians assume. We speak of the benevolence shown in the joy of the insect glittering in the sunbeam, in the protecting instincts so liberally bestowed among the animal world, in the kindness of the parent to its young, in the happiness of little children, in the beauty and the bounty of nature, but is there not another side to the picture? The hideous disease, the countless forms of rapine and of suffering, the entozoa that live within the bodies, and feed upon the anguish of sentient beings, the ferocious instinct of the cat, that prolongs with delight the agonies of its victim, all the multitudinous forms of misery that are manifested among the innocent portion of creation, are not these also the works of nature? We speak of the Divine veracity. What is the whole history of the intellectual progress of the world but one long struggle of the intellect of man to emancipate itself from the deceptions of nature? Every object that meets the eye of the savage awakens his curiosity only to lure him into some deadly error. The sun that seems a diminutive light revolving around his world; the moon and the stars that appear formed only to light his path; the strange fantastic diseases that suggest irresistibly the notion of present dæmons; the terrific phenomena of nature which appear the results, not of blind forces, but of isolated spiritual agencies— all these things fatally, inevitably, invincibly impel him into superstition. Through long centuries the superstitions thus generated have deluged the world with blood. Millions of prayers have been vainly breathed to what we now know were inexorable laws of nature. Only after ages of toil did the mind of man emancipate itself from those deadly errors to which by the deceptive appearances of nature the long infancy of humanity is universally doomed.

And in the laws of wealth how different are the appearances from the realities of things! Who can estimate the wars that have been kindled, the bitterness and the wretchedness that have been caused, by errors relating to the apparent antagonism of the interests of nations which were so natural that for centuries they entangled the very strongest intellects, and it was scarcely till our own day that a tardy science came to dispel them?

What shall we say to these things? If induction alone were our guide, if we possessed absolutely no knowledge of some things being in their own nature good, and others in their own nature evil, how could we rise from this spectacle of nature to the conception of an all-perfect Author? Even if we could discover a predominance of benevolence in the creation, we should still regard the mingled attributes of nature as a reflex of the mingled attributes of its Contriver. Our knowledge of the Supreme Excellence, our best evidence even of the existence of the Creator, is derived not from the material universe but from our own moral nature.[1]  It is

---

[1] 'The one great and binding ground of the belief of God and a hereafter is the law of conscience.' —Coleridge, *Notes Theological and Political*, p. 367. That our moral faculty is our one reason for maintaining the supreme benevolence of the Deity was a favourite position of Kant.

not of reason but of faith. In other words it springs from that instinctive or moral nature which is as truly a part of our being as is our reason, which teaches us what reason could never teach, the supreme and transcendent excellence of moral good, which rising dissatisfied above this world of sense, proves itself by the very intensity of its aspiration to be adapted for another sphere, and which constitutes at once the evidence of a Divine element within us, and the augury of the future that is before us.[1]

These things belong rather to the sphere of feeling than of reasoning. Those who are most deeply persuaded of their truth, will probably feel that they are unable by argument to express adequately the intensity of their conviction, but they may point to the recorded experience of the best and greatest men in all ages, to the incapacity of terrestrial things to satisfy our nature, to the manifest tendency, both in individuals and nations, of a pure and heroic life to kindle, and of a selfish and corrupt life to cloud, these aspirations, to the historical fact that no philosophy and no scepticism have been able permanently to repress them. The lines of our moral nature tend upwards. In it we have the common root of religion and of ethics, for the same consciousness that tells us that, even when it is in fact the weakest element of our constitution, it is by right supreme, commanding and authoritative, teaches us also that it is Divine. All the nobler religions that have governed mankind, have done so by virtue of the affinity of their teaching with this nature, by speaking, as common religious language correctly describes it, 'to the heart,' by appealing not to self-interest, but to that Divine element of self-sacrifice which is latent in every soul.[2] The reality of this moral nature is the one great

---

[1] 'Nescio quomodo inhæret in mentibus quasi sæculorum quoddam augurium futurorum; idque in maximis ingeniis altissimisque animis et exsistit maxime et apparet facillime.'—Cic. *Tusc. Disp.* i. 14.

[2] 'It is a calumny to say that men are roused to heroic actions

question of natural theology, for it involves that connection between our own and a higher nature, without which the existence of a First Cause were a mere question of archæology, and religion but an exercise of the imagination.

I return gladly to the secular sanctions of utilitarianism. The majority of its disciples assure us that these are sufficient to establish their theory, or in other words, that our duty coincides so strictly with our interest when rightly understood, that a perfectly prudent would necessarily become a perfectly virtuous man.[1] Bodily vice they tell us ultimately brings bodily weakness and suffering. Extravagance is followed by ruin; unbridled passions by the loss of domestic peace; disregard for the interests of others by social or legal penalties; while on the other hand, the most moral is also the most tranquil disposition; benevolence is one of the truest of our pleasures, and virtue may become by habit, an essential of enjoyment. As the shopkeeper who has made his fortune, still sometimes continues at the counter, because the daily routine has become necessary to his happiness, so the 'moral hero' may continue to practise that virtue which was at first the mere instrument of his pleasures, as being in itself more precious than all besides.[2]

---

by ease, hope of pleasure, recompense—sugar-plums of any kind in this world or the next. In the meanest mortal there lies something nobler. The poor swearing soldier hired to be shot has his "honour of a soldier," different from drill, regulations, and the shilling a day. It is not to taste sweet things, but to do noble and true things, and vindicate himself under God's heaven as a God-made man, that the poorest son of Adam dimly longs. Show him the way of doing that, the dullest daydrudge kindles into a hero. They wrong man greatly who say he is

to be seduced by ease. Difficulty, abnegation, martyrdom, death, are the allurements that act on the heart of man. Kindle the inner genial life of him, you have a flame that burns up all lower considerations.'—Carlyle's *Hero-worship*, p. 237 (ed. 1858).

[1] 'Clamat Epicurus, is quem vos nimis voluptatibus esse deditum dicitis, non posse jucunde vivi nisi sapienter, honeste, justeque vivatur, nec sapienter, honeste, juste nisi jucunde.'—Cicero, *De Fin.* i. 18.

[2] 'The virtues to be complete must have fixed their residence in the heart and become appetites

This theory of the perfect coincidence of virtue and interest rightly understood, which has always been a commonplace of moralists, and has been advocated by many who were far from wishing to resolve virtue into prudence, contains no doubt a certain amount of truth, but only of the most general kind. It does not apply to nations as wholes, for although luxurious and effeminate vices do undoubtedly corrode and enervate national character, the histories of ancient Rome and of not a few modern monarchies abundantly prove that a career of consistent rapacity, ambition, selfishness, and fraud may be eminently conducive to national prosperity.[1] It does not apply to imperfectly organised societies, where the restraints of public opinion are unfelt and where force is the one measure of right. It does not apply except in a very partial degree even to the most civilised of mankind. It is, indeed, easy to show that in a polished community a certain low standard of virtue is essential to prosperity, to paint the evils of unrestrained passions, and to prove that it is better to obey than to violate the laws of society. But if turning from the criminal or the drunkard we were to compare the man who simply falls in with or slightly surpasses the average morals of those about

impelling to actions without further thought than the gratification of them; so that after their expedience ceases they still continue to operate by the desire they raise. .... I knew a mercer who having gotten a competency of fortune, thought to retire and enjoy himself in quiet; but finding he could not be easy without business was forced to return to the shop and assist his former partners gratis, in the nature of a journeyman. Why then should it be thought strange that a man long inured to the practice of moral duties should persevere in them out of liking,

when they can yield him no further advantage?'—Tucker's *Light of Nature*, vol. i. p. 269. Mr. J. S. Mill in his *Utilitarianism* dwells much on the heroism which he thinks this view of morals may produce.

[1] See Lactantius, *Inst. Div.* vi. 9. Montesquieu, in his *Décadence de l'Empire romain*, has shown in detail the manner in which the crimes of Roman politicians contributed to the greatness of their nation. Modern history furnishes only too many illustrations of the same truth.

THE NATURAL HISTORY OF MORALS.        59

him, and indulges in a little vice which is neither injurious
to his own health nor to his reputation, with the man who
earnestly and painfully adopts a much higher standard than
that of his time or of his class, we should be driven to another
conclusion. Honesty it is said is the best policy—a fact,
however, which depends very much upon the condition of
the police force—but heroic virtue must rest upon a different
basis. If happiness in any of its forms be the supreme object
of life, moderation is the most emphatic counsel of our being,
but moderation is as opposed to heroism as to vice. There
is no form of intellectual or moral excellence which has not
a general tendency to produce happiness if cultivated in
moderation. There are very few which if cultivated to great
perfection have not a tendency directly the reverse. Thus a
mind that is sufficiently enlarged to range abroad amid the
pleasures of intellect has no doubt secured a fund of inex-
haustible enjoyment; but he who inferred from this that the
highest intellectual eminence was the condition most favourable to happiness would be lamentably deceived. The diseased nervous sensibility that accompanies intense mental
exertion, the weary, wasting sense of ignorance and vanity,
the disenchantment and disintegration that commonly follow
a profound research, have filled literature with mournful
echoes of the words of the royal sage, ' In much wisdom is
much grief, and he that increaseth knowledge increaseth
sorrow.' The lives of men of genius have been for the
most part a conscious and deliberate realisation of the
ancient myth—the tree of knowledge and the tree of life
stood side by side, and they chose the tree of knowledge
rather than the tree of life.

Nor is it otherwise in the realm of morals.[1] The virtue
which is most conducive to happiness is plainly that which

---

[1] 'That quick sensibility which
is the groundwork of all advances
towards perfection increases the
pungency of pains and vexations.'—
Tucker's *Light of Nature*, ii. 16,
§ 4.

can be realised without much suffering, and sustained without
much effort.   Legal and physical penalties apply only to the
grosser and more extreme forms of vice.   Social penalties
may strike the very highest forms of virtue.[1]   That very
sentiment of unity with mankind which utilitarians assure
us is one day to become so strong as to overpower all unsocial feelings, would make it more and more impossible for
men consistently with their happiness to adopt any course,
whether very virtuous or very vicious, that would place
them out of harmony with the general sentiment of society.   It
may be said that the tranquillity of a perfectly virtuous mind
is the highest form of happiness, and may be reasonably
preferred not only to material advantages, but also to the
approbation of society ; but no man can fully attain, and few
can even approximate, to such a condition.   When vicious
passions and impulses are very strong, it is idle to tell the
sufferer that he would be more happy if his nature were
radically different from what it is.   If happiness be his object,
he must regulate his course with a view to the actual condition of his being, and there can be little doubt that his peace
would be most promoted by a compromise with vice.   The
selfish theory of morals applies only to the virtues of temperament, and not to that much higher form of virtue which
is sustained in defiance of temperament.[2]   We have no doubt
a certain pleasure in cultivating our good tendencies, but we
have by no means the same pleasure in repressing our bad
ones.   There are men whose whole lives are spent in willing
one thing, and desiring the opposite.   In such cases as these

---

[1] This position is forcibly illustrated by Mr. Maurice in his fourth
lecture *On Conscience* (1868).   It
is manifest that a tradesman resisting a dishonest or illegal trade
custom, an Irish peasant in a disturbed district revolting against
the agrarian conspiracy of his class,
or a soldier in many countries conscientiously refusing in obedience
to the law to fight a duel, would
incur the full force of social penalties, because he failed to do that
which was illegal or criminal.

[2] See Brown *On the Characteristics,* pp. 206–209.

virtue clearly involves a sacrifice of happiness; for the suffering caused by resisting natural tendencies is much greater than would ensue from their moderate gratification.

The plain truth is that no proposition can be more palpably and egregiously false than the assertion that as far as this world is concerned, it is invariably conducive to the happiness of a man to pursue the most virtuous career. Circumstances and disposition will make one man find his highest happiness in the happiness, and another man in the misery, of his kind; and if the second man acts according to his interest, the utilitarian, however much he may deplore the result, has no right to blame or condemn the agent. For that agent is following his greatest happiness, and this, in the eyes of utilitarians, in one form or another, is the highest, or to speak more accurately, the only motive by which human nature can be actuated.

We may remark too that the disturbance or pain which does undoubtedly usually accompany what is evil, bears no kind of proportion to the enormity of the guilt. An irritability of temper, which is chiefly due to a derangement of the nervous system, or a habit of procrastination or indecision, will often cause more suffering than some of the worst vices that can corrupt the heart.[1]

But it may be said this calculation of pains and pleasures is defective through the omission of one element. Although a man who had a very strong natural impulse towards some vice would appear more likely to promote the tranquillity of his nature by a moderate and circumspect gratification of that

---

[1] 'A toothache produces more violent convulsions of pain than a phthisis or a dropsy. A gloomy disposition . . . may be found in very worthy characters, though it is sufficient alone to embitter life. . . . A selfish villain may possess a spring and alacrity of temper, which is indeed a good quality, but which is rewarded much beyond its merit, and when attended with good fortune will compensate for the uneasiness and remorse arising from all the other vices.'—Hume's *Essays: The Sceptic.*

vice, than by endeavouring painfully to repress his natural tendencies, yet he possesses a conscience which adjudicates upon his conduct, and its sting or its approval constitutes a pain or pleasure so intense, as more than to redress the balance. Now of course, no intuitive moralist will deny, what for a long time his school may be almost said to have been alone in asserting, the reality of conscience, or the pleasures and pains it may afford. He simply denies, and he appeals to consciousness in attestation of his position, that those pains and pleasures are so powerful or so proportioned to our acts as to become an adequate basis for virtue. Conscience, whether we regard it as an original faculty, or as a product of the association of ideas, exercises two distinct functions. It points out a difference between right and wrong, and when its commands are violated, it inflicts a certain measure of suffering and disturbance. The first function it exercises persistently through life. The second it only exercises under certain special circumstances. It is scarcely conceivable that a man in the possession of his faculties should pass a life of gross depravity and crime without being conscious that he was doing wrong; but it is extremely possible for him to do so without this consciousness having any appreciable influence upon his tranquillity. The condition of their consciences, as Mr. Carlyle observes, has less influence on the happiness of men than the condition of their livers. Considered as a source of pain, conscience bears a striking resemblance to the feeling of disgust. Notwithstanding the assertion of Dr. Johnson, I venture to maintain that there are multitudes to whom the necessity of discharging the duties of a butcher would be so inexpressibly painful and revolting, that if they could obtain flesh diet on no other condition, they would relinquish it for ever. But to those who are inured to the trade, this repugnance has simply ceased. It has no place in their emotions or calculations. Nor can it be reasonably questioned that most men by an assiduous attendance at the slaughter-house could acquire a similar indifference. In like manner, the reproaches of conscience are doubtless a very real and important form of suffering to a sensitive, scrupulous, and virtuous girl who has committed some trivial act of levity or disobedience ; but to an old and hardened criminal they are a matter of the most absolute indifference.

Now it is undoubtedly conceivable, that by an association of ideas men might acquire a feeling that would cause that which would naturally be painful to them to be pleasurable, and that which would naturally be pleasurable to be painful.[1] But the question will immediately arise, why should they respect this feeling ? We have seen that, according to the inductive theory, there is no such thing as natural duty. Men enter into life solely desirous of seeking their own happiness. The whole edifice of virtue arises from the observed fact, that owing to the constitution of our nature, and the intimacy of our social relations, it is necessary for our happiness to abstain from some courses that would be immediately pleasurable and to pursue others that are immediately the reverse. Self-interest is the one ultimate reason for virtue, however much

---

[1] At the same time, the following passage contains, I think, a great deal of wisdom and of a kind peculiarly needed in England at the present day :—' The nature of the subject furnishes the strongest presumption that no better system will ever, for the future, be invented, in order to account for the origin of the benevolent from the selfish affections, and reduce all the various emotions of the human mind to a perfect simplicity. The case is not the same in this species of philosophy as in physics. Many an hypothesis in nature, contrary to first appearances, has been found, on more accurate scrutiny, solid and satisfactory. . . . But the presumption always lies on the other side in all enquiries concerning the origin of our passions, and of the internal operations of the human mind. The simplest and most obvious cause which can there be assigned for any phenomenon, is probably the true one. . . . The affections are not susceptible of any impression from the refinements of reason or imagination ; and it is always found that a vigorous exertion of the latter faculties, necessarily, from the narrow capacity of the human mind, destroys all activity in the former.'—Hume's *Enquiry Concerning Morals*, Append. II.

the moral chemistry of Hartley may disguise and transform it. Ought or ought not, means nothing more than the prospect of acquiring or of losing pleasure. The fact that one line of conduct promotes, and another impairs the happiness of others is, according to these moralists, in the last analysis, no reason whatever for pursuing the former or avoiding the latter, unless such a course is that which brings us the greatest happiness. The happiness may arise from the action of society upon ourselves, or from our own naturally benevolent disposition, or, again, from an association of ideas, which means the force of a habit we have formed, but in any case our own happiness is the one possible or conceivable motive of action. If this be a true picture of human nature, the reasonable course for every man is to modify his disposition in such a manner that he may attain the greatest possible amount of enjoyment. If he has formed an association of ideas, or contracted a habit which inflicts more pain than it prevents, or prevents more pleasure than it affords, his reasonable course is to dissolve that association, to destroy that habit. This is what he 'ought' to do according to the only meaning that word can possess in the utilitarian vocabulary. If he does not, he will justly incur the charge of imprudence, which is the only charge utilitarianism can consistently bring against vice.

That it would be for the happiness as it would certainly be in the power of a man of a temperament such as I have lately described, to quench that conscientious feeling, which by its painful reproaches prevents him from pursuing the course that would be most conducive to his tranquillity, I conceive to be self-evident. And, indeed, on the whole, it is more than doubtful whether conscience, considered apart from the course of action it prescribes, is not the cause of more pain than pleasure. Its reproaches are more felt than its approval. The self-complacency of a virtuous man reflecting with delight upon his own exceeding merit, is frequently spoken of in the writings of moral philosophers,[1] but is rarely found in actual life where the most tranquil is seldom the most perfect nature, where the sensitiveness of conscience increases at least in proportion to moral growth, and where in the best men a feeling of modesty and humility is always present to check the exuberance of self-gratulation.

In every sound system of morals and religion the motives of virtue become more powerful the more the mind is concentrated upon them. It is when they are lost sight of, when they are obscured by passion, unrealised or forgotten, that

---

[1] 'The pleasing consciousness and self-approbation that rise up in the mind of a virtuous man, exclusively of any direct, explicit, consideration of advantage likely to accrue to himself from his possession of those good qualities' (Hartley *On Man*, vol. i. p. 493), form a theme upon which moralists of both schools are fond of dilating, in a strain that reminds one irresistibly of the self-complacency of a famous nursery hero, while reflecting upon his own merits over a Christmas-pie. Thus Adam Smith says, 'The man who, not from frivolous fancy, but from proper motives, has performed a generous action, when he looks forward to those whom he has served, feels himself to be the natural object of their love and gratitude, and by sympathy with them, of the esteem and approbation of all mankind. And when he looks backward to the motive from which he acted, and surveys it in the light in which the indifferent spectator will survey it, he still continues to enter into it, and applauds himself by sympathy with the approbation of this supposed impartial judge. In both these points of view his conduct appears to him every way agreeable. . . . Misery and wretchedness can never enter the breast in which dwells complete self-satisfaction.'—*Theory of Moral Sentiments*, part ii. ch. ii. § 2 ; part iii. ch. iii. I suspect that many moralists confuse the self-gratulation which they suppose a virtuous man to feel, with the delight a religious man experiences from the sense of the protection and favour of the Deity. But these two feelings are clearly distinct, and it will, I believe, be found that the latter is most strongly experienced by the very men who most sincerely disclaim all sense of merit. 'Were the perfect man to exist,' said that good and great writer, Archer Butler, 'he himself would be the last to know it; for the highest stage of advancement is the lowest descent in humility.' At all events, the reader will observe, that on utilitarian principles nothing could be more pernicious or criminal than that modest, humble, and diffident spirit, which diminishes the pleasure of self-gratulation, one of the highest utilitarian motives to virtue.

they cease to operate. But it is a peculiarity of the utilitarian conception of virtue that it is wholly unable to resist
the solvent of analysis, and that the more the mind realises
its origin and its nature, the more its influence on character
must decline. The pleasures of the senses will always defy
the force of analysis, for they have a real foundation in
our being. They have their basis in the eternal nature of
things. But the pleasure we derive from the practice of
virtue rests, according to this school, on a wholly different
basis. It is the result of casual and artificial association, of
habit, of a confusion by the imagination of means with ends,
of a certain dignity with which society invests qualities or
actions that are useful to itself. Just in proportion as this
is felt, just in proportion as the mind separates the idea of
virtue from that of natural excellence and obligation, and
realises the purely artificial character of the connection, just
in that proportion will the coercive power of the moral motive
be destroyed. The utilitarian rule of judging actions and
dispositions by their tendency to promote or diminish happiness, or the maxim of Kant that man should always
act so that the rule of his conduct might be adopted as a
law by all rational beings may be very useful as a guide in
life; but in order that they should acquire moral weight,
it is necessary to presuppose the sense of moral obligation,
the consciousness that duty, when discovered, has a legitimate claim to be the guiding principle of our lives. And it
is this element which, in the eye of reason, the mere artificial association of ideas can never furnish.

If the patience of the reader has enabled him to accompany me through this long train of tedious arguments, he
will, I think, have concluded that the utilitarian theory,
though undoubtedly held by many men of the purest, and
by some men of almost heroic virtue, would if carried to
its logical conclusions prove subversive of morality, and
especially, and in the very highest degree, unfavourable to

self-denial and to heroism. Even if it explains these, it fails to justify them, and conscience being traced to a mere confusion of the means of happiness with its end, would be wholly unable to resist the solvent of criticism. That this theory of conscience gives a true or adequate description of the phenomenon it seeks to explain, no intuitive moralist will admit. It is a complete though common mistake to suppose that the business of the moralist is merely to explain the genesis of certain feelings we possess. At the root of all morals lies an intellectual judgment which is clearly distinct from liking or disliking, from pleasure or from pain. A man who has injured his position by some foolish but perfectly innocent act, or who has inadvertently violated some social rule, may experience an emotion of self-reproach or of shame quite as acute as if he had committed a crime. But he is at the same time clearly conscious that his conduct is not a fit subject for moral reprobation, that the grounds on which it may be condemned are of a different and of a lower kind. The sense of obligation and of legitimate supremacy, which is the essential and characteristic feature of conscience, and which distinguishes it from all the other parts of our nature, is wholly unaccounted for by the association of ideas. To say that a certain course of conduct is pleasing, and that a certain amount of pain results from the weakening of feelings that impel men towards it, is plainly different from what men mean when they say we ought to pursue it. The virtue of Hartley is, in its last analysis, but a disease of the imagination. It may be more advantageous to society than avarice; but it is formed in the same manner, and has exactly the same degree of binding force.[1]

---

[1] Hartley has tried in one place to evade this conclusion by an appeal to the doctrine of final causes. He says that the fact that conscience is not an original principle of our nature, but is formed mechanically in the manner I have described, does not invalidate the fact that it is intended for our guide, 'for all the things which have evident final causes, are plainly brought about by mechanical

These considerations will help to supply an answer to the common utilitarian objection that to speak of duty as distinct from self-interest is unmeaning, because it is absurd to say that we are under an obligation to do any thing when no evil consequences would result to us from not doing it. Rewards and punishments it may be answered are undoubtedly necessary to enforce, but they are not necessary to constitute, duty. This distinction, whether it be real or not, has at all events the advantage of appearing self-evident to all who are not philosophers. Thus when a party of colonists occupy a new territory they divide the unoccupied land among themselves, and they murder, or employ for the gratification of their lusts, the savage inhabitants. Both acts are done with perfect impunity, but one is felt to be innocent and the other wrong. A lawful government appropriates the land and protects the aboriginals, supporting its enactments by penalties. In the one case the law both creates and enforces a duty, in the other it only enforces it. The intuitive moralist simply asserts that we have the power of perceiving that certain courses of action are higher, nobler.

---

means;' and he appeals to the milk in the breast, which is intended for the sustenance of the young, but which is nevertheless mechanically produced. (*On Man*, vol. ii. pp. 338–339.) But it is plain that this mode of reasoning would justify us in attributing an authoritative character to any habit—e.g. to that of avarice—which these writers assure us is in the manner of its formation an exact parallel to conscience. The later followers of Hartley certainly cannot be accused of any excessive predilection for the doctrine of final causes, yet we sometimes find them asking what great difference it can make whether (when conscience is admitted by both parties to be real) it is

regarded as an original principle of our nature, or as a product of association? Simply this. If by the constitution of our nature we are subject to a law of duty which is different from and higher than our interest, a man who violates this law through interested motives, is deserving of reprobation. If on the other hand there is no natural law of duty, and if the pursuit of our interest is the one original principle of our being, no one can be censured who pursues it, and the first criterion of a wise man will be his determination to eradicate every habit (conscientious or otherwise) which impedes him in doing so.

and better than others, and that by the constitution of our
being, this fact, which is generically distinct from the prospect
of pleasure or the reverse, may and ought to be and continually is a motive of action. It is no doubt possible for a
man to prefer the lower course, and in this case we say he
is deserving of punishment, and if he remains unpunished
we say that it is unjust. But if there were no power to
reward or punish him, his acts would not be indifferent.
They would still be intelligibly described as essentially base
or noble, shameful though there were none to censure, admirable though there were none to admire.

That men have the power of preferring other objects
than happiness is a proposition which must ultimately be
left to the attestation of consciousness. That the pursuit of
virtue, however much happiness may eventually follow in
its train, is in the first instance an example of this preference,
must be established by that common voice of mankind which
has invariably regarded a virtuous motive as generically
different from an interested one. And indeed even when
the conflict between strong passions and a strong sense of
duty does not exist it is impossible to measure the degrees
of virtue by the scale of enjoyment. The highest nature is
rarely the happiest. Petronius Arbiter was, very probably,
a happier man than Marcus Aurelius. For eighteen centuries
the religious instinct of Christendom has recognised its ideal
in the form of a ' Man of Sorrows.'

Considerations such as I have now urged lead the intuitive moralists to reject the principles of the utilitarian.
They acknowledge indeed that the effect of actions upon the
happiness of mankind forms a most important element in
determining their moral quality, but they maintain that
without natural moral perceptions we never should have
known that it was our duty to seek the happiness of mankind when it diverged from our own, and they deny that
virtue was either originally evolved from or is necessarily

proportioned to utility. They acknowledge that in the existing condition of society there is at least a general coincidence between the paths of virtue and of prosperity, but they contend that the obligation of virtue is of such a nature that no conceivable convulsion of affairs could destroy it, and that it would continue even if the government of the world belonged to supreme malice instead of supreme benevolence. Virtue, they believe, is something more than a calculation or a habit. It is impossible to conceive its fundamental principles reversed. Notwithstanding the strong tendency to confuse cognate feelings, the sense of duty and the sense of utility remain perfectly distinct in the apprehension of mankind, and we are quite capable of recognising each separate ingredient in the same act. Our respect for a gallant but dangerous enemy, our contempt for a useful traitor, our care in the last moments of life for the interests of those who survive us, our clear distinction between intentional and unintentional injuries, and between the consciousness of imprudence and the consciousness of guilt, our conviction that the pursuit of interest should always be checked by a sense of duty, and that selfish and moral motives are so essentially opposed, that the presence of the former necessarily weakens the latter, our indignation at those who when honour or gratitude call them to sacrifice their interests pause to calculate remote consequences, the feeling of remorse which differs from every other emotion of our nature—in a word, the universal, unstudied sentiments of mankind all concur in leading us to separate widely our virtuous affections from our selfish ones. Just as pleasure and pain are ultimate grounds of action, and no reason can be given why we should seek the former and avoid the latter, except that it is the constitution of our nature that we should do so, so we are conscious that the words right and wrong express ultimate intelligible motives, that these motives are generically different from the others, that they are of a higher order, and that they carry with them a sense of obligation. Any scheme of morals that omits these facts fails to give an accurate and adequate description of the states of feeling which consciousness reveals. The consciences of men in every age would have echoed the assertion of Cicero that to sacrifice pleasure with a view of obtaining any form or modification of pleasure in return, no more answers to our idea of virtue, than to lend money at interest to our idea of charity. The conception of pure disinterestedness is presupposed in our estimates of virtue. It is the root of all the emotions with which we contemplate acts of heroism. We feel that man is capable of pursuing what he believes to be right although pain and disaster and mental suffering and an early death be the consequence, and although no prospect of future reward lighten upon his tomb. This is the highest prerogative of our being, the point of contact between the human nature and the divine.

In addition to the direct arguments in its support, the utilitarian school owes much of its influence to some very powerful moral and intellectual predispositions in its favour—the first, which we shall hereafter examine, consisting of the tendency manifested in certain conditions of society towards the qualities it is most calculated to produce, and the second of the almost irresistible attraction which unity and precision exercise on many minds. It was this desire to simplify human nature, by reducing its various faculties and complex operations to a single principle or process, that gave its great popularity to the sensational school of the last century. It led most metaphysicians of that school to deny the duality of human nature. It led Bonnet and Condillac to propose an animated statue, endowed with the five senses as channels of ideas, and with faculties exclusively employed in transforming the products of sensation, as a perfect representative of humanity. It led Helvétius to assert that the original faculties of all men were precisely the same, all the difference between what we call genius and what we call stupidity arising from differences of circumstances, and all the difference between men and animals arising mainly from the structure of the human hand. In morals, theories of unification are peculiarly plausible, and I think peculiarly dangerous, because, owing to the interaction of our moral sentiments, and the many transformations that each can undergo, there are few affections that might not under some conceivable circumstances become the parents of every other. When Hobbes, in the name of the philosophy of self-interest, contended that 'Pity is but the imagination of future calamity to ourselves, produced by the sense of another man's calamity;'[1] when Hutcheson, in the name of the philosophy of benevolence, argued that the vice of intemperance is that it impels us to violence towards others, and weakens our capacity for doing them good;[2] when other moralists defending the excellence of our nature maintained that compassion is so emphatically the highest of our pleasures that a desire of gratifying it is the cause of our acts of barbarity;[3] each of these theories,

---

[1] *On Human Nature*, chap. ix. § 10.

[2] *Enquiry concerning Good and Evil.*

[3] This theory is noticed by Hutcheson, and a writer in the *Spectator* (No. 436) suggests that it may explain the attraction of prize-fights. The case of the pleasure derived from fictitious sorrow is a distinct question, and has been admirably treated in Lord Kames' *Essays on Morality*. Bishop Butler notices (*Second Sermon on Compassion*), that it is possible for the very intensity of a feeling of compassion to divert men from charity by making them 'industriously turn away from the miserable;' and it is well known that Goethe, on account of this very susceptibility, made it one of the rules of his life to avoid everything that could suggest painful ideas. Hobbes makes the following very characteristic comments on some famous lines of Lucretius : 'From what passion proceedeth it that men take pleasure to behold from the shore the danger of those that are at sea in a tempest or in fight, or from a safe castle to behold two armies charge one another in the field? It is certainly in the whole sum joy, else men would never flock to such a spectacle. Nevertheless, there is both joy and grief, for as there is novelty and remembrance of our own security present, which is delight, so there is also pity, which is grief. But the delight is so far predominant that men usually are

extravagant as it is, contains a germ of undoubted psychological truth. It is true that a mind intensely apprehensive
of future calamities would on that account receive a shock at
the sight of the calamities of others. It is true that a very
keen and absorbing sentiment of benevolence would be in
itself sufficient to divert men from any habit that impaired
their power of gratifying it. It is true that compassion involves a certain amount of pleasure, and conceivable that
this pleasure might be so intensified that we might seek it
by a crime. The error in these theories is not that they
exaggerate the possible efficacy of the motives, but that
they exaggerate their actual intensity in human nature and
describe falsely the process by which the results they seek to
explain have been arrived at. The function of observation
in moral philosophy is not simply to attest the moral sentiments we possess, leaving it to the reason to determine
deductively how they may have been formed; it is rather to
follow them through all the stages of their formation.

And here I may observe that the term inductive, like
most others that are employed in moral philosophy, may give

---

content in such a case to be spectators of the misery of their
friends.' (*On Human Nature*, ch. ix.
§ 19.) Good Christians, according
to some theologians, are expected
to enjoy this pleasure in great
perfection in heaven. 'We may
believe in the next world also the
goodness as well as the happiness
of the blest will be confirmed and
advanced by reflections naturally
arising from the view of the misery
which some shall undergo, which
seems to be a good reason for the
creation of those beings who shall
be finally miserable, and for the
continuation of them in their miserable existence . . . . though in
one respect the view of the misery

which the damned undergo might
seem to detract from the happiness
of the blessed through pity and
commiseration, yet under another,
a nearer and much more affecting
consideration, viz. that all this is
the misery they themselves were
often exposed to and in danger of
incurring, why may not the sense
of their own escape so far overcome
the sense of another's ruin as quite
to extinguish the pain that usually
attends the idea of it, and even
render it productive of some real
happiness? To this purpose, Lucretius' *Suave mari*,' etc. (*Law's
notes to his Translation of King's
Origin of Evil*, pp. 477, 479.)

7

rise to serious misconception. It is properly applied to those moralists who, disbelieving the existence of any moral sense or faculty revealing to us what is right and wrong, maintain that the origin of those ideas is simply our experience of the tendency of different lines of conduct to promote or impair true happiness. It appears, however, to be sometimes imagined that inductive moralists alone think that it is by induction or experience that we ought to ascertain what is the origin of our moral ideas. But this I conceive to be a complete mistake. The basis of morals is a distinct question from the basis of theories of morals. Those who maintain the existence of a moral faculty do not, as is sometimes said, assume this proposition as a first principle of their arguments, but they arrive at it by a process of induction quite as severe as any that can be employed by their opponents.[1] They examine, analyse, and classify their existing moral feelings, ascertain in what respects those feelings agree with or differ from others, trace them through their various phases, and only assign them to a special faculty when they think they have shown them to be incapable of resolution, and generically different from all others.[2]

---

[1] See e.g. *Reid's Essays on the Active Powers*, essay iii. ch. v.

[2] The error I have traced in this paragraph will be found running through a great part of what Mr. Buckle has written upon morals—I think the weakest portion of his great work. See, for example, an elaborate confusion on the subject, *History of Civilisation*, vol. ii. p. 429. Mr. Buckle maintains that all the philosophers of what is commonly called 'the Scotch school' (a school founded by the Irishman Hutcheson, and to which Hume does not belong), were incapable of inductive reasoning, because they maintained the existence of a moral sense or faculty, or of first principles, incapable of resolution; and he enters into a learned enquiry into the causes which made it impossible for Scotch writers to pursue or appreciate the inductive method. It is curious to contrast this view with the language of one, who, whatever may be the value of his original speculations, is, I conceive, among the very ablest philosophical critics of the present century. 'Les philosophes écossais adoptèrent les procédés que Bacon avait recommandé d'appliquer à l'étude du monde physique, et les transportèrent dans l'étude du monde

This separation is all that is meant by a moral faculty. We are apt to regard the term as implying a distinct and well defined organ, bearing to the mind the same kind of relation as a limb to the body. But of the existence of such organs, and of the propriety of such material imagery, we know nothing. Perceiving in ourselves a will, and a crowd of intellectual and emotional phenomena that seem wholly different from the properties of matter, we infer the existence of an immaterial substance which wills, thinks, and feels, and can classify its own operations with considerable precision. The term faculty is simply an expression of classification. If we say that the moral faculty differs from the æsthetic faculty, we can only mean that the mind forms certain judgments of moral excellence, and also certain judgments of beauty, and that these two mental processes are clearly distinct. To ask to what part of our nature moral perceptions should be attributed, is only to ask to what train of mental phenomena they bear the closest resemblance.

If this simple, but often neglected, consideration be borne

---

moral. Ils firent voir que l'induction baconienne, c'est-à-dire, l'induction précédée d'une observation scrupuleuse des phénomènes, est en philosophie comme en physique la seule méthode légitime. C'est un de leurs titres les plus honorables d'avoir insisté sur cette démonstration, et d'avoir en même temps joint l'exemple au précepte. . . . Il est vrai que le zèle des philosophes écossais en faveur de la méthode d'observation leur a presque fait dépasser le but. Ils ont incliné à renfermer la psychologie dans la description minutieuse et continuelle de phénomènes de l'âme sans réfléchir assez que cette description doit faire place à l'induction et au raisonnement déductif, et qu'une philosophie qui se borne-

rait à l'observation serait aussi stérile que celle qui s'amuserait à construire des hypothèses sans avoir préalablement observé.'— Cousin, Hist. de la Philos. Morale au xviii^me Siècle, Tome 4, p. 14–16. Dugald Stewart had said much the same thing, but he was a Scotchman, and therefore, according to Mr. Buckle (*Hist. of Civ.* ii. pp. 485–86), incapable of understanding what induction was. I may add that one of the principal objections M. Cousin makes against Locke is, that he investigated the origin of our ideas before analysing minutely their nature, and the propriety of this method is one of the points on which Mr. Mill (*Examination of Sir W. Hamilton*) is at issue with M. Cousin.

in mind, the apparent discordance of intuitive moralists will appear less profound than might at first sight be supposed, for each section merely elucidates some one characteristic of moral judgments. Thus Butler insists upon the sense of obligation that is involved in them, contends that this separates them from all other sentiments, and assigns them in consequence to a special faculty of supreme authority called conscience. Adam Smith and many other writers were especially struck by their sympathetic character. We are naturally attracted by humanity, and repelled by cruelty, and this instinctive, unreasoning sentiment constitutes, according to these moralists, the difference between right and wrong. Cudworth, however, the English precursor of Kant, had already anticipated, and later metaphysicians have more fully exhibited, the inadequacy of such an analysis. Justice, humanity, veracity, and kindred virtues not merely have the power of attracting us, we have also an intellectual perception that they are essentially and immutably good, that their nature does not depend upon, and is not relative to, our constitutions; that it is impossible and inconceivable they should ever be vices, and their opposites, virtues. They are, therefore, it is said, intuitions of the reason. Clarke, developing the same rational school, and following in the steps of those moralists who regard our nature as a hierarchy of powers or faculties, with different degrees of dignity, and an appropriate order of supremacy and subordination, maintained that virtue consisted in harmony with the nature of things. Wollaston endeavoured to reduce it to truth, and Hutcheson to benevolence, which he maintained is recognised and approved by what his respect for the philosophy of Locke induced him to call 'a moral sense,' but what Shaftesbury had regarded as a moral 'taste.' The pleasure attending the gratification of this taste, according to Shaftesbury and Henry More, is the motive to virtue. The doctrine of a moral sense or faculty was the basis of the ethics of Reid. Hume maintained that the peculiar quality of virtue is its utility, but that our affections are purely disinterested, and that we arrive at our knowledge of what is virtuous by a moral sense implanted in our nature, which leads us instinctively to approve of all acts that are beneficial to others. Expanding a pregnant hint which had been thrown out by Butler, he laid the foun dation for a union of the schools of Clarke and Shaftesbury, by urging that our moral decisions are not simple, but complex, containing both a judgment of the reason, and an emotion of the heart. This fact has been elucidated still further by later writers, who have observed that these two elements apply in varying degrees to different kinds of virtue. According to Lord Kames, our intellectual perception of right and wrong applies most strictly to virtues like justice or veracity, which are of what is called 'perfect obligation,' or, in other words, are of such a nature, that their violation is a distinct crime, while the emotion of attraction or affection is shown most strongly towards virtues of imperfect obligation, like benevolence or charity. Like Hutcheson and Shaftesbury, Lord Kames notices the analogies between our moral and æsthetical judgments.

These last analogies open out a region of thought widely different from that we have been traversing. The close connection between the good and the beautiful has been always felt, so much so, that both were in Greek expressed by the same word, and in the philosophy of Plato, moral beauty was regarded as the archetype of which all visible beauty is only the shadow or the image. We all feel that there is a strict propriety in the term moral beauty. We feel that there are different forms of beauty which have a natural correspondence to different moral qualities, and much of the charm of poetry and eloquence rests upon this harmony. We feel that we have a direct, immediate, intuitive perception that some objects, such as the sky above us, are beautiful, that this perception of beauty is totally different, and could not possibly be derived, from a perception of their utility, and that it bears a very striking resemblance to the instantaneous and unreasoning admiration elicited by a generous or heroic action. We perceive too, if we examine with care the operations of our own mind, that an æsthetical judgment includes an intuition or intellectual perception, and an emotion of attraction or admiration, very similar to those which compose a moral judgment. The very idea of beauty again implies that it should be admired, as the idea of happiness implies that it should be desired, and the idea of duty that it should be performed. There is also a striking correspondence between the degree and kind of uniformity we can in each case discover. That there is a difference between right and wrong, and between beauty and ugliness, are both propositions which are universally felt. That right is better than wrong, and beauty than ugliness, are equally unquestioned. When we go further, and attempt to define the nature of these qualities, we are met indeed by great diversities of detail, but by a far larger amount of substantial unity. Poems like the Iliad or the Psalms, springing in the most dissimilar quarters, have commanded the admiration of men, through all the changes of some 3,000 years. The charm of music, the harmony of the female countenance, the majesty of the starry sky, of the ocean or of the mountain, the gentler beauties of the murmuring stream or of the twilight shades, were felt, as they are felt now, when the imagination of the infant world first embodied itself in written words. And in the same way types of heroism, and of virtue, descending from the remotest ages, command the admiration of mankind. We can sympathise with the emotions of praise or blame revealed in the earliest historians, and the most ancient moralists strike a responsive chord in every heart. The broad lines remain unchanged. No one ever contended that justice was a vice or injustice a virtue; or that a summer sunset was a repulsive object, or that the sores upon a human body were beautiful. Always, too, the objects of æsthetical admiration were divided into two great classes, the sublime and the beautiful, which in ethics have their manifest counterparts in the heroic and the amiable.

If, again, we examine the undoubted diversities that exist in judgments of virtue and of beauty, we soon discover that in each case a large proportion of them are to be ascribed to the different degrees of civilisation. The moral standard changes within certain limits, and according to a regular process with the evolutions of society. There are virtues very highly estimated in a rude civilisation which sink into comparative insignificance in an organised society, while conversely, virtues that were deemed secondary in the first become primary in the other. There are even virtues that it is impossible for any but highly cultivated minds to recognise. Questions of virtue and vice, such as the difference between humanity and barbarity, or between temperance and intemperance, are sometimes merely questions of degree, and the standard at one stage of civilisation may be much higher than at another. Just in the same way a steady modification of tastes, while a recognition of the broad features of beauty remains unchanged, accompanies advancing civilisation. The preference of gaudy to subdued tints, of colour to form, of a florid to a chaste style, of convulsive attitudes, gigantic figures, and strong emotions, may be looked for with considerable confidence in an uninstructed people. The refining influence of cultivation is in no sphere more remarkable than in the canons of taste it produces, and there are few better measures of the civilisation of a people than the conceptions of beauty it forms, the type or ideal it endeavours to realise.

Many diversities, however, both of moral and æsthetical judgments, may be traced to accidental causes. Some one who is greatly admired, or who possesses great influence, is distinguished by some peculiarity of appearance, or introduces some peculiarity of dress. He will soon find countless imitators. Gradually the natural sense of beauty will be come vitiated; the eye and the taste will adjust themselves to a false and artificial standard, and men will at last judge according to it with the most absolute spontaneity. In the same way, if any accidental circumstance has elevated an indifferent action to peculiar honour, if a religious system enforces it as a virtue or brands it as a vice, the consciences of men will after a time accommodate themselves to the sentence, and an appeal to a wider than a local tribunal is necessary to correct the error. Every nation, again, from its peculiar circumstances and position, tends to some particular type, both of beauty and of virtue, and it naturally extols its national type beyond all others. The virtues of a small poor nation, living among barren mountains, surrounded by powerful enemies, and maintaining its independence only by the most inflexible discipline, watchfulness, and courage, will be in some degree different from those of a rich people removed from all fear of invasion and placed in the centre of commerce. The former will look with a very lenient eye on acts of barbarity or treachery, which to the latter would appear unspeakably horrible, and will value very highly certain virtues of discipline which the other will comparatively neglect. So, too, the conceptions of beauty formed by a nation of negroes will be different from those formed by a nation of whites;[1] the splendour of a tropical sky or the savage grandeur of a northern ocean, the aspect of great mountains or of wide plains, will not only supply nations with present images of sublimity or beauty, but will also contribute to form their standard and affect their judgments. Local customs or observances become so interwoven with our earliest recollections, that we at last regard them as es-

---

[1] M. Ch. Comte, in his very learned *Traité de Législation*, liv. iii. ch. iv., has made an extremely curious collection of instances in which different nations have made their own distinctive peculiarities of colour and form the ideal of beauty.

sentially venerable, and even in the most trivial matters it requires a certain effort to dissolve the association. There was much wisdom as well as much wit in the picture of the novelist who described the English footman's contempt for the uniforms of the French, 'blue being altogether ridiculous for regimentals, except in the blue guards and artillery;' and I suppose there are few Englishmen into whose first confused impression of France there does not enter a half-instinctive feeling of repugnance caused by the ferocious appearance of a peasantry who are all dressed like butchers.[1]

It has been said [2] that 'the feelings of beauty, grandeur, and whatever else is comprehended under the name of taste, do not lead to action, but terminate in delightful contemplation, which constitutes the essential distinction between them and the moral sentiments to which in some points of view they may doubtless be likened.' This position I conceive to be altogether untenable. Our æsthetical judgment is of the nature of a preference. It leads us to prefer one class of objects to another, and whenever other things are equal, becomes a ground for action. In choosing the persons with whom we live, the neighbourhood we inhabit, the objects that surround us, we prefer that which is beautiful to that which is the reverse, and in every case in which a choice between beauty and deformity is in question, and no counteracting motive intervenes, we choose the former, and avoid the latter. There are no doubt innumerable events in life in which this question does not arise, but there are also very many in which we are not called upon to make a moral judgment. We say a man is actuated by strong moral principle who chooses according to its dictates in every case involving a moral judgment that comes naturally before him,

---

[1] 'How particularly fine the hard theta is in our English terminations, as in that grand word death, for which the Germans gutturise a sound that *puts you in mind of nothing but a loathsome toad.*'— Coleridge's *Table Talk*, p. 181.

[2] Mackintosh, *Dissert.* p. 238.

and who in obedience to its impulse pursues special courses
of action.   Corresponding propositions may be maintained
with perfect truth concerning our sense of beauty.   In proportion to its strength does it guide our course in ordinary
life, and determine our peculiar pursuits.   We may indeed
sacrifice our sense of material beauty to considerations of
utility with much more alacrity than our sense of moral
beauty ; we may consent to build a shapeless house sooner
than to commit a dishonourable action, but we cannot voluntarily choose that which is simply deformed, rather than that
which is beautiful, without a certain feeling of pain, and a
pain of this kind, according to the school of Hartley, is the
precise definition of conscience.   Nor is it at all difficult to
conceive men with a sense of beauty so strong that they
would die rather than outrage it.

Considering all these things, it is not surprising that many
moralists should have regarded moral excellence as simply
the highest form of beauty, and moral cultivation as the
supreme refinement of taste.   But although this manner of
regarding it is, as I think, far more plausible than the theory
which resolves virtue into utility, although the Greek moralists and the school of Shaftesbury have abundantly proved
that there is an extremely close connection between these
orders of ideas, there are two considerations which appear to
show the inadequacy of this theory.   We are clearly conscious
of the propriety of applying the epithet ' beautiful ' to virtues
such as charity, reverence, or devotion, but we cannot apply
it with the same propriety to duties of perfect obligation,
such as veracity or integrity.   The sense of beauty and the
affection that follows it attach themselves rather to modes of
enthusiasm and feeling than to the course of simple duty
which constitutes a merely truthful and upright man.[1]   Besides this, as the Stoics and Butler have shown, the position

---

[1] Lord Kames' *Essays on Morality* (1st edition), pp. 55-56.

of conscience in our nature is wholly unique, and clearly separates morals from a study of the beautiful.   While each of our senses or appetites has a restricted sphere of operation, it is the function of conscience to survey the whole constitution of our being, and assign limits to the gratification of all our various passions and desires.   Differing not in degree, but in kind from the other principles of our nature, we feel that a course of conduct which is opposed to it may be intelligibly described as unnatural, even when in accordance with our most natural appetites, for to conscience is assigned the prerogative of both judging and restraining them all.   Its power may be insignificant, but its title is undisputed, and ' if it had might as it has right, it would govern the world.'[1] It is this faculty, distinct from, and superior to, all appetites, passions, and tastes, that makes virtue the supreme law of life, and adds an imperative character to the feeling of attraction it inspires.   It is this which was described by Cicero as the God ruling within us ; by the Stoics as the sovereignty of reason ; by St. Paul as the law of nature ; by Butler as the supremacy of conscience.

The distinction of different parts of our nature, as higher or lower, which appears in the foregoing reasoning, and which occupies so important a place in the intuitive system of morals, is one that can only be defended by the way of illustrations.   A writer can only select cases in which such distinctions seem most apparent, and leave them to the feelings of his reader.   A few examples will, I hope, be sufficient to show that even in our pleasures, we are not simply determined by the amount of enjoyment, but that there is a difference of kind, which may be reasonably described by the epithets, higher or lower.

If we suppose a being from another sphere, who derived his conceptions from a purely rational process, without the

---

[1] See Butler's *Three Sermons on Human Nature*, and the preface

intervention of the senses, to descend to our world, and to enquire into the principles of human nature, I imagine there are few points that would strike him as more anomalous, or which he would be more absolutely unable to realise, than the different estimates in which men hold the pleasures derived from the two senses of tasting and hearing. Under the first is comprised the enjoyment resulting from the action of certain kinds of food upon the palate. Under the second the charm of music. Each of these forms of pleasure is natural, each can be greatly heightened by cultivation, in each case the pleasure may be vivid, but is very transient, and in neither case do evil consequences necessarily ensue. Yet with so many undoubted points of resemblance, when we turn to the actual world, we find the difference between these two orders of pleasure of such a nature, that a comparison seems absolutely ludicrous. In what then does this difference consist? Not, surely, in the greater intensity of the enjoyment derived from music, for in many cases this superiority does not exist.[1] We are all conscious that in our comparison of these pleasures, there is an element distinct from any consideration of their intensity, duration, or consequences. We naturally attach a faint notion of shame to the one, while we as naturally glory in the other. A very keen sense of the pleasures of the palate is looked upon as in a certain degree discreditable. A man will hardly boast that he is very fond of eating, but he has no hesitation in acknowledging that he is very fond of music. The first

---

[1] Speaking of the animated statue which he regarded as a representative of man, Condillac says, 'Le goût peut ordinairement contribuer plus que l'odorat à son bonheur et à son malheur. . . . Il y contribue même encore plus que les sons harmonieux, parce que le besoin de nourriture lui rend les saveurs plus nécessaires, et par conséquent les lui fait goûter avec plus de vivacité. La faim pourra la rendre malheureuse, mais dès qu'elle aura remarqué les sensations propres à l'apaiser, elle y déterminera davantage son attention, les désirera avec plus de violence et en jouira avec plus de délire.'—*Traité des Sensations*, 1re partie, ch. x.

taste lowers, and the second elevates him in his own eyes, and in those of his neighbours.

Again, let a man of cheerful disposition, and of a cultivated but not very fastidious taste, observe his own emotions and the countenances of those around him during the representation of a clever tragedy and of a clever farce, and it is probable that he will come to the conclusion that his enjoyment in the latter case has been both more unmingled and more intense than in the former. He has felt no lassitude, he has not endured the amount of pain that necessarily accompanies the pleasure of pathos, he has experienced a vivid, absorbing pleasure, and he has traced similar emotions in the violent demonstrations of his neighbours. Yet he will readily admit that the pleasure derived from the tragedy is of a higher order than that derived from the farce. Sometimes he will find himself hesitating which of the two he will choose. The love of mere enjoyment leads him to the one. A sense of its *nobler* character inclines him to the other.

A similar distinction may be observed in other departments. Except in the relation of the sexes, it is probable that a more intense pleasure is usually obtained from the grotesque and the eccentric, than from the perfections of beauty. The pleasure derived from beauty is not violent in its nature, and it is in most cases peculiarly mixed with melancholy. The feelings of a man who is deeply moved by a lovely landscape are rarely those of extreme elation. A shade of melancholy steals over his mind. His eyes fill with tears. A vague and unsatisfied longing fills his soul. Yet, troubled and broken as is this form of enjoyment, few persons would hesitate to pronounce it of a higher kind than any that can be derived from the exhibitions of oddity.

If pleasures were the sole objects of our pursuit, and if their excellence were measured only by the quantity of enjoyment they afford, nothing could appear more obvious than that the man would be esteemed most wise who attained his object at least cost. Yet the whole course of civilisation is in a precisely opposite direction. A child derives the keenest and most exquisite enjoyment from the simplest objects. A flower, a doll, a rude game, the least artistic tale, is sufficient to enchant it. An uneducated peasant is enraptured with the wildest story and the coarsest wit. Increased cultivation almost always produces a fastidiousness which renders necessary the increased elaboration of our pleasures. We attach a certain discredit to a man who has retained those of childhood. The very fact of our deriving pleasure from certain amusements creates a kind of humiliation, for we feel that they are not in harmony with the nobility of our nature.[1]

Our judgments of societies resemble in this respect our judgments of individuals. Few persons, I think, who have compared the modes of popular life in stagnant and undeveloped countries like Spain with those in the great centres of industrial civilisation, will venture to pronounce with any confidence that the quantum or average of actual realised enjoyment is greater in the civilised than in the semi-civilised society. An undeveloped nature is by no means necessarily an unhappy nature, and although we possess no accurate gauge of happiness, we may, at least, be certain that its degrees do not coincide with the degrees of prosperity. The tastes and habits of men in a backward society accommodate themselves to the narrow circle of a few pleasures, and pro-

---

[1] This is one of the favourite thoughts of Pascal, who, however, in his usual fashion dwells upon it in a somewhat morbid and exaggerated strain. ' C'est une bien grande misère que de pouvoir prendre plaisir à des choses si basses et si méprisables . . . l'homme est encore plus à plaindre de ce qu'il peut se divertir à ces choses si frivoles et si basses, que de ce qu'il s'afflige de ses misères effectives. . . . D'où vient que cet homme, qui a perdu depuis peu son fils unique, et qui, accablé de procès et de querelles, était ce matin si troublé, n'y pense plus maintenant ? Ne vous en étonnez pas ; il est tout occupé à voir par où passera un cerf que ses chiens poursuivent. . . . C'est une joie de malade et de frénétique.'— Pensées (Misère de l'homme).

bably find in these as complete satisfaction as more civilised men in a wider range; and if there is in the first condition somewhat more of the weariness of monotony, there is in the second much more of the anxiety of discontent. The superiority of a highly civilised man lies chiefly in the fact that he belongs to a higher order of being, for he has approached more nearly to the end of his existence, and has called into action a larger number of his capacities. And this is in itself an end. Even if, as is not improbable, the lower animals are happier than man,[1] and semi-barbarians than civilised men, still it is better to be a man than a brute, better to be born amid the fierce struggles of civilisation than in some stranded nation apart from all the flow of enterprise and knowledge. Even in that material civilisation which utilitarianism delights to glorify, there is an element which the philosophy of mere enjoyment cannot explain.

Again, if we ask the reason of the vast and indisputable superiority which the general voice of mankind gives to mental pleasures, considered as pleasures, over physical ones, we shall find, I think, no adequate or satisfactory answer on the supposition that pleasures owe all their value to the quantity of enjoyment they afford. The former, it is truly said, are more varied and more prolonged than the latter but on the other hand, they are attained with more effort, and they are diffused over a far narrower circle. No one who compares the class of men who derive their pleasure chiefly from field sports or other forms of physical enjoyment with those who derive their pleasure from the highest intellectual sources; no one who compares the period of boyhood when enjoyments are chiefly animal with early

---

[1] 'Quæ singula improvidam mortalitatem involvunt, solum ut inter ista certum sit, nihil esse certi, nec miserius quidquam homine, aut superbius. Cæteris quippe animantium sola victus cura est, in quo sponte naturæ benignitas sufficit: uno quidem vel præferenda cunctis bonis, quod de gloria, de pecunia, ambitione, superque de morte, non cogitant.'— Plin. Hist. Nat. ii. 5.

manhood when they are chiefly intellectual, will be able to discover in the different levels of happiness any justification of the great interval the world places between these pleasures. No painter or novelist, who wished to depict an ideal of perfect happiness, would seek it in a profound student. Without entering into any doubtful questions concerning the relations of the body to all mental states, it may be maintained that bodily conditions have in general more influence upon our enjoyment than mental ones. The happiness of the great majority of men is far more affected by health and by temperament,[1] resulting from physical conditions, which again physical enjoyments are often calculated to produce, than by any mental or moral causes, and acute physical sufferings paralyse all the energies of our nature to a greater extent than any mental distress. It is probable that the American inventor of the first anæsthetic has done more for the real happiness of mankind than all the moral philosophers from Socrates to Mill. Moral causes may teach men patience, and the endurance of felt suffering, or may even alleviate its pangs, but there are temperaments due to phy-

---

[1] Paley, in his very ingenious, and in some respects admirable, chapter on happiness tries to prove the inferiority of animal pleasures, by showing the short time their enjoyment actually lasts, the extent to which they are dulled by repetition, and the cases in which they incapacitate men for other pleasures. But this calculation omits the influence of some animal enjoyments upon health and temperament. The fact, however, that health, which is a condition of body, is the chief source of happiness, Paley fully admits. 'Health,' he says, 'is the one thing needful . . . . when we are in perfect health and spirits, we feel in ourselves a happiness indepen-dent of any particular outward gratification. . . . This is an enjoyment which the Deity has annexed to life, and probably constitutes in a great measure the happiness of infants and brutes . . . of oysters, periwinkles, and the like; for which I have sometimes been at a loss to find out amusement.' On the test of happiness he very fairly says, 'All that can be said is that there remains a presumption in favour of those conditions of life in which men generally appear most cheerful and contented; for though the apparent happiness of mankind be not always a true measure of their real happiness, it is the best measure we have.'—*Moral Philoso phy*, i. 6.

sical causes from which most sufferings glance almost unfelt. It is said that when an ancient was asked 'what use is philosophy?' he answered, 'it teaches men how to die,' and he verified his words by a noble death; but it has been proved on a thousand battle-fields, it has been proved on a thousand scaffolds, it is proved through all the wide regions of China and India, that the dull and animal nature which feels little and realises faintly, can meet death with a calm that philosophy can barely rival.[1] The truth is, that the mental part of our nature is not regarded as superior to the physical part, because it contributes most to our happiness. The superiority is of a different kind, and may be intelligibly expressed by the epithets higher and lower.

And, once more, there is a class of pleasures resulting from the gratification of our moral feelings which we naturally place in the foremost rank. To the great majority of mankind it will probably appear, in spite of the doctrine of Paley, that no multiple of the pleasure of eating pastry can be an equivalent to the pleasure derived from a generous action. It is not that the latter is so inconceivably intense. It is that it is of a higher order.

This distinction of kind has been neglected or denied by most utilitarian writers;[2] and although an attempt has re-

---

[1] A writer who devoted a great part of his life to studying the deaths of men in different countries, classes, and churches, and to collecting from other physicians information on the subject, says: 'À mesure qu'on s'éloigne des grands foyers de civilisation, qu'on se rapproche des plaines et des montagnes, le caractère de la mort prend de plus en plus l'aspect calme du ciel par un beau crépuscule du soir. . . . En général la mort s'accomplit d'une manière d'autant plus simple et naturelle qu'on est plus libre des innombrables liens de la civilisation.' Lauvergne, *De l'agonie de la Mort*, tome i. pp. 131–132.

[2] 'I will omit much usual declamation upon the dignity and capacity of our nature, the superiority of the soul to the body, of the rational to the animal part of our constitution, upon the worthiness, refinement, and delicacy of some satisfactions, or the meanness, grossness, and sensuality of others; because I hold that pleasures differ in nothing but in continuance and

cently been made to introduce it into the system, it appears
manifestly incompatible with its principle. If the reality of
the distinction be admitted, it shows that our wills are so far
from tending necessarily to that which produces most enjoyment that we have the power even in our pleasures of recognising a higher and a wholly different quali`y, and of making
that quality rather than enjoyment the object of our choice.
If it be possible for a man in choosing between two pleasures
deliberately to se'ect as preferable, apart from all consideration
of consequences, that which he is conscious gives least enjoy-

---

intensity.'—Paley's *Moral Philosophy*, book i. ch. vi. Bentham in
like manner said, 'Quantity of
pleasure being equal, pushpin is as
good as poetry,' and he maintained
that the value of a pleasure depends on—its (1) intensity, (2)
duration, (3) certainty, (4) propin-
quity, (5) purity, (6) fecundity, (7)
extent (*Springs of Action*). The
recognition of the 'purity' of a
pleasure might seem to imply the
distinction for which I have contended in the text, but this is not
so. The purity of a pleasure or
pain, according to Bentham, is 'the
chance it has of not being followed
by sensations of the opposite kind :
that is pain if it be a pleasure,
pleasure if it be a pain.'—*Morals
and Legislation*, i. § 8. Mr. Buckle
(*Hist. of Civilisation*, vol. ii. pp. 399
–400) writes in a somewhat similar
strain, but less unequivocally, for
he admits that mental pleasures
are 'more ennobling' than physical
ones. The older utilitarians, as far
as I have observed, did not even
advert to the question. This being
the case, it must have been a matter of surprise as well as of gratification to most intuitive moralists
to find Mr. Mill fully recognising
the existence of different kinds of

pleasure, and admitting that the
superiority of the higher kinds
does not spring from their being
greater in amount.—*Utilitarianism*, pp. 11–12. If it be meant by
this that we have the power of
recognising some pleasures as
superior to others in kind, irrespective of all consideration of
their intensity, their cost, and
their consequences, I submit that
the admission is completely incompatible with the utilitarian theory,
and that Mr. Mill has only succeeded in introducing Stoical elements into his system by loosening
its very foundation. The impossibility of establishing an aristocracy
of enjoyments in which, apart from
all considerations of consequences,
some which give less pleasure and
are less widely diffused are regarded as intrinsically superior to
others which give more pleasure
and are more general, without
admitting into our estimate a moral
element, which on utilitarian principles is wholly illegitimate, has
been powerfully shown since the
first edition of this book by Professor Grote, in his *Examination
of the Utilitarian Philosophy*, chap.
iii.

ment because he recognises in it a greater worthiness, or elevation, it is certain that his conduct is either wholly irrational, or that he is acting on a principle of judgment for which 'the greatest happiness' philosophy is unable to account. Consistently with that philosophy, the terms higher and lower as applied to different parts of our nature, to different regions of thought or feeling, can have no other meaning than that of productive of more or less enjoyment. But if once we admit a distinction of quality as well as a distinction of quantity in our estimate of pleasure, all is changed. It then appears evident that the different parts of our nature to which these pleasures refer, bear to each other a relation of another kind, which may be clearly and justly described by the terms higher and lower; and the assertion that our reason reveals to us intuitively and directly this hierarchy of our being, is a fundamental position of the greatest schools of intuitive moralists. According to these writers, when we say that our moral and intellectual is superior to our animal nature, that the benevolent affections are superior to the selfish ones, that conscience has a legitimate supremacy over the other parts of our being; this language is not arbitrary, or fantastic, or capricious, because it is intelligible. When such a subordination is announced, it corresponds with feelings we all possess, falls in with the natural course of our judgments, with our habitual and unstudied language.

The arguments that have been directed against the theory of natural moral perceptions are of two kinds, the first, which I have already noticed, being designed to show that all our moral judgments may be resolved into considerations of utility; the second resting upon the diversity of these judgments in different nations and stages of civilisation, which, it is said, is altogether inexplicable upon the supposition of a moral faculty. As these variations form the great stumbling-block in the way of the doctrine I am maintaining, and as they

constitute a very important part of the history of morals, I
shall make no apology for noticing them in some detail.

In the first place, there are many cases in which diversities of moral judgment arise from causes that are not
moral, but purely intellectual. Thus, for example, when
theologians pronounced loans at interest contrary to the law
of nature and plainly extortionate, this error obviously arose
from a false notion of the uses of money. They believed
that it was a sterile thing, and that he who has restored
what he borrowed, has cancelled all the benefit he received
from the transaction. At the time when the first Christian
moralists treated the subject, special circumstances had rendered the rate of interest extremely high, and consequently
extremely oppressive to the poor, and this fact, no doubt,
strengthened the prejudice; but the root of the condemnation of usury was simply an error in political economy.
When men came to understand that money is a productive
thing, and that the sum lent enables the borrower to create
sources of wealth that will continue when the loan has been
returned, they perceived that there was no natural injustice
in exacting payment for this advantage, and usury either
ceased to be assailed, or was assailed only upon the ground
of positive commands.

Thus again the question of the criminality of abortion
has been considerably affected by physiological speculations
as to the time when the foetus in the womb acquires the
nature, and therefore the rights, of a separate being. The
general opinion among the ancients seems to have been that
it was but a part of the mother, and that she had the same
right to destroy it as to cauterise a tumour upon her body.
Plato and Aristotle both admitted the practice. The Roman
law contained no enactment against voluntary abortion till the
time of Ulpian. The Stoics thought that the infant received
its soul when respiration began. The Justinian code fixed
its animation at forty days after conception. In modern

legislations it is treated as a distinct being from the moment of conception.[1] It is obvious that the solution of such questions, though affecting our moral judgments, must be sought entirely outside the range of moral feelings.

In the next place, there is a broad distinction to be drawn between duties which rest immediately on the dictates of conscience, and those which are based upon positive commands. The iniquity of theft, murder, falsehood, or adultery rests upon grounds generically distinct from those on which men pronounce it to be sinful to eat meat on Friday, or to work on Sunday, or to abstain from religious assemblies. The reproaches conscience directs against those who are guilty of these last acts are purely hypothetical, conscience enjoining obedience to the Divine commands, but leaving it to reason to determine what those commands may be. The distinction between these two classes of duties becomes apparent on the slightest reflection, and the variations in their relative prominence form one of the most important branches of religious history.

Closely connected with the preceding are the diversities which result from an ancient custom becoming at last, through its very antiquity, or through the confusion of means with ends, an object of religious reverence. Among the many safeguards of female purity in the Roman republic was an enactment forbidding women even to taste wine, and this very intelligible law being enforced with the earliest education, became at last, by habit and traditionary reverence, so incorporated with the moral feelings of the people, that its violation was spoken of as a monstrous crime. Aulus Gellius has preserved a passage in which Cato observes, 'that the husband has an absolute authority over his wife; it is for him to condemn and punish her, if she has been

---

[1] Büchner, *Force et Matière*, pp. 163-164. There is a very curious collection of the speculations of the ancient philosophers on this subject in Plutarch's treatise, *De Placitis Philos.*

guilty of any shameful act, such as drinking wine or com
mitting adultery.'[1]  As soon as the reverence for tradition
was diminished, and men ventured to judge old customs upon
their own merits, they were able, by steadily reflecting upon
this belief, to reduce it to its primitive elements, to separate
the act from the ideas with which it had been associated
and thus to perceive that it was not necessarily opposed to
any of those great moral laws or feelings which their consciences revealed, and which were the basis of all their
reasonings on morals.

A confused association of ideas, which is easily exposed
by a patient analysis, lies at the root of more serious anomalies.  Thus to those who reflect deeply upon moral history,
few things, I suppose, are more humiliating than to contrast
the admiration and profoundly reverential attachment excited
by a conqueror, who through the promptings of simple
vanity, through love of fame, or through greed of territory,
has wantonly caused the deaths, the sufferings, or the be-

---

[1] Aulus Gellius, *Noctes*, x. 23.
The law is given by Dion. Halicarn.
Valerius Maximus says, ' Vini usus
olim Romanis feminis ignotus fuit,
ne scilicet in aliquod dedecus pro-
laberentur : quia proximus a Libero
patre intemperantiæ gradus ad
inconcessam Venerem esse consue-
vit' (Val. Max. ii. 1, § 5). This is
also noticed by Pliny (*Hist. Nat.*
xiv. 14), who ascribes the law to
Romulus, and who mentions two
cases in which women were said to
have been put to death for this
offence, and a third in which the
offender was deprived of her dowry.
Cato said that the ancient Romans
were accustomed to kiss their wives
for the purpose of discovering
whether they had been drinking
wine.  The Bona Dea, it is said,
was originally a woman named
Fatua, who was famous for her
modesty and fidelity to her husband, but who, unfortunately, having once found a cask of wine in the
house, got drunk, and was in consequence scourged to death by her
husband.  He afterwards repented
of his act, and paid divine honours
to her memory, and as a memorial
of her death, a cask of wine was
always placed upon the altar
during the rites. (Lactantius, *Div.
Inst.* i. 22.)  The Milesians, also,
and the inhabitants of Marseilles
are said to have had laws forbidding women to drink wine (Ælian,
*Hist. Var.* ii. 38).  Tertullian describes the prohibition of wine
among the Roman women as in his
time obsolete, and a taste for it
was one of the great trials of St.
Monica (*Aug. Conf.* x. 8).

reavements of thousands, with the abhorrence produced by a single act of murder or robbery committed by a poor and ignorant man, perhaps under the pressure of extreme want or intolerable wrong. The attraction of genius and power, which the vulgar usually measure by their material fruits, the advantages acquired by the nation to which he belongs, the belief that battles are decided by providential interference, and that military success is therefore a proof of Divine favour, and the sanctity ascribed to the regal office, have all no doubt conspired to veil the atrocity of the conqueror's career; but there is probably another and a deeper influence behind. That which invests war, in spite of all the evils that attend it, with a certain moral grandeur, is the heroic self-sacrifice it elicits. With perhaps the single exception of the Church, it is the sphere in which mercenary motives have least sway, in which performance is least weighed and measured by strict obligation, in which a disinterested enthusiasm has most scope. A battle-field is the scene of deeds of self-sacrifice so transcendent, and at the same time so dramatic, that in spite of all its horrors and crimes, it awakens the most passionate moral enthusiasm. But this feeling produced by the thought of so many who have sacrificed their life-blood for their flag or for their chief, needs some definite object on which to rest. The multitude of nameless combatants do not strike the imagination. They do not stand out, and are not realised, as distinct and living figures conspicuous to the view. Hence it is that the chief, as the most prominent, becomes the representative warrior; the martyr's aureole descends upon his brow, and thus by a confusion that seems the very irony of fate, the enthusiasm evoked by the self-sacrifice of thousands sheds a sacred glow around the very man whose prodigious egotism had rendered that sacrifice necessary.

Another form of moral paradox is derived from the fact that positive religions may override our moral perceptions in

such a manner, that we may consciously admit a moral con
tradiction.    In this respect there is a strict parallelism
between our intellectual and our moral faculties.    It is at
present the professed belief of at least three-fourths of the
Christian Church, and was for some centuries the firm belief
of the entire Church, that on a certain night the Founder of
the Christian faith, being seated at a supper table, held His
own body in His own hand, broke that body, distributed it
to His disciples, who proceeded to eat it, the same body remaining at the same moment seated intact at the table, and
soon afterwards proceeding to the garden of Gethsemane.
The fact of such a doctrine being believed, does not imply
that the faculties of those who hold it are of such a nature
that they perceive no contradiction or natural absurdity in
these statements.    The well-known argument derived from
the obscurity of the metaphysical notion of substance is
intended only in some slight degree to soften the difficulty.
The contradiction is clearly perceived, but it is accepted by
faith as part of the teaching of the Church.

What transubstantiation is in the order of reason the
Augustinian doctrine of the damnation of unbaptised infants,
and the Calvinistic doctrine of reprobation, are in the order
of morals.    Of these doctrines it is not too much to say, that
in the form in which they have often been stated, they surpass in atrocity any tenets that have ever been admitted into
any pagan creed, and would, if they formed an essential part
of Christianity, amply justify the term 'pernicious superstition,' which Tacitus applied to the faith.    That a little
child who lives but a few moments after birth and dies
before it has been sprinkled with the sacred water is in such
a sense responsible for its ancestors having 6,000 years before
eaten some forbidden fruit  that it may with perfect justice be
resuscitated and cast into an abyss of eternal fire in expiation
of this ancestral crime, that an all-righteous and all-merciful
Creator in the full exercise of those attributes deliberately

calls into existence sentient beings whom He has from eternity irrevocably destined to endless, unspeakable, unmitigated torture, are propositions which are at once so extravagantly absurd and so ineffably atrocious that their adoption might well lead men to doubt the universality of moral perceptions. Such teaching is in fact simply dæmonism, and dæmonism in its most extreme form. It attributes to the Creator acts of injustice and of barbarity, which it would be absolutely impossible for the imagination to surpass, acts before which the most monstrous excesses of human cruelty dwindle into insignificance, acts which are in fact considerably worse than any that theologians have attributed to the devil. If there were men who while vividly realising the nature of these acts naturally turned to them as the exhibitions of perfect goodness, all systems of ethics founded upon innate moral perceptions would be false. But happily this is not so. Those who embrace these doctrines do so only because they believe that some inspired Church or writer has taught them, and because they are still in that stage in which men consider it more irreligious to question the infallibility of an apostle than to disfigure by any conceivable imputation the character of the Deity. They accordingly esteem it a matter of duty, and a commendable exercise of humility, to stifle the moral feelings of their nature, and they at last succeed in persuading themselves that their Divinity would be extremely offended if they hesitated to ascribe to him the attributes of a fiend. But their moral feelings, though not unimpaired by such conceptions, are not on ordinary subjects generically different from those of their neighbours. With an amiable inconsistency they can even find something to revolt them in the lives of a Caligula or a Nero. Their theological estimate of justice and mercy is isolated. Their doctrine is accepted as a kind of moral miracle, and as is customary with a certain school of theologians, when they enunciate a proposition which is palpably self-contradictory they call it a mystery and an occasion for faith.

In this instance a distinct moral contradiction is consciously admitted. In the case of persecution, a strictly moral and logical inference is drawn from a very immoral proposition which is accepted as part of a system of dogmatic theology. The two elements that should be considered in punishing a criminal are the heinousness of his guilt and the injury he inflicts. When the greatest guilt and the greatest injury are combined, the greatest punishment naturally follows. No one would argue against the existence of a moral faculty, on the ground that men put murderers to death. When therefore theologians believed that a man was intensely guilty who held certain opinions, and that he was causing the damnation of his fellows if he propagated them, there was no moral difficulty in concluding that the heretic should be put to death. Selfish considerations may have directed persecution against heresy rather than against vice, but the Catholic doctrines of the guilt of error, and of the infallibility of the Church, were amply sufficient to justify it.

It appears then that a dogmatic system which is accepted on rational or other grounds, and supported by prospects of rewards and punishments, may teach a code of ethics differing from that of conscience; and that in this case the voice of conscience may be either disregarded or stifled. It is however also true, that it may be perverted. When, for example, theologians during a long period have inculcated habits of credulity, rather than habits of enquiry; when they have persuaded men that it is better to cherish prejudice than to analyse it; better to stifle every doubt of what they have been taught than honestly to investigate its value, they will at last succeed in forming habits of mind that will instinctively and habitually recoil from all impartiality and intellectual honesty. If men continually violate a duty they may at last cease to feel its obligation. But this, though it forms a great difficulty in ethical enquiries, is no argument against the reality of moral perceptions, for it is simply a law to which all our powers are subject. A bad intellectual education will produce not only erroneous or imperfect information but also a false ply or habit of judgment. A bad æsthetical education will produce false canons of taste. Systematic abuse will pervert and vitiate even some of our physical perceptions. In each case the experience of many minds under many conditions must be appealed to, to determine the standard of right and wrong, and long and difficult discipline is required to restore the diseased organ to sanity. We may decide particular moral questions by reasoning, but our reasoning is an appeal to certain moral principles which are revealed to us by intuition.

The principal difficulty I imagine which most men have in admitting that we possess certain natural moral perceptions arises from the supposition that it implies the existence of some mysterious agent like the dæmon of Socrates, which gives us specific and infallible information in particular cases. But this I conceive to be a complete mistake. All that is necessarily meant by the adherents of this school is comprised in two propositions. The first is that our will is not governed exclusively by the law of pleasure and pain, but also by the law of duty, which we feel to be distinct from the former, and to carry with it the sense of obligation. The second is that the basis of our conception of duty is an intuitive perception that among the various feelings, tendencies, and impulses that constitute our emotional being, there are some which are essentially good, and ought to be encouraged, and some which are essentially bad, and ought to be repressed. They contend that it is a psychological fact that we are intuitively conscious that our benevolent affections are superior to our malevolent ones, truth to falsehood, justice to injustice, gratitude to ingratitude, chastity to sensuality, and that in all ages and countries the path of virtue has been towards the higher and not towards the lower feelings. It may be that the sense of duty is so weak as to be scarcely perceptible, and then the lower part of our nature will be supreme. It may happen that certain conditions of society lead men to direct their anxiety for moral improvement altogether in one or two channels, as was the case in ancient Greece, where civic and intellectual virtues were very highly cultivated, and the virtue of chastity was almost neglected. It may happen that different parts of our higher nature in a measure conflict, as when a very strong sense of justice checks our benevolent feelings. Dogmatic systems may enjoin men to propitiate certain unseen beings by acts which are not in accordance with the moral law. Special circumstances may influence, and the intermingling of many different motives may obscure and complicate, the moral evolution; but above all these one great truth appears. No one who desires to become holier and better imagines that he does so by becoming more malevolent, or more untruthful, or more unchaste. Every one who desires to attain perfection in these departments of feeling is impelled towards benevolence, towards veracity, towards chastity.[1]

Now it is manifest that according to this theory the moral unity to be expected in different ages is not a unity of standard, or of acts, but a unity of tendency. Men come into the world with their benevolent affections very inferior in power to their selfish ones, and the function of morals is to invert this order. The extinction of all selfish feeling is impossible for an individual, and if it were general, it would result in the dissolution of society. The question of morals must always be a question of proportion or of degree. At

---

[1] 'La loi fondamentale de la morale agit sur toutes les nations bien connues. Il y a mille différences dans les interprétations de cette loi en mille circonstances; mais le fond subsiste toujours le même, et ce fond est l'idée du juste et de l'injuste.'—Voltaire, *Le Philosophe ignorant.*

one time the benevolent affections embrace merely the family, soon the circle expanding includes first a class, then a nation, then a coalition of nations, then all humanity, and finally, its influence is felt in the dealings of man with the animal world. In each of these stages a standard is formed, different from that of the preceding stage, but in each case the same tendency is recognised as virtue.

We have in this fact a simple, and as it appears to me a conclusive, answer to the overwhelming majority of the objections that are continually and confidently urged against the intuitive school. That some savages kill their old parents, that infanticide has been practised without compunction by even civilised nations, that the best Romans saw nothing wrong in the gladiatorial shows, that political or revengeful assassinations have been for centuries admitted, that slavery has been sometimes honoured and sometimes condemned, are unquestionable proofs that the same act may be regarded in one age as innocent, and in another as criminal. Now it is undoubtedly true that in many cases an historical examination will reveal special circumstances, explaining or palliating the apparent anomaly. It has been often shown that the gladiatorial shows were originally a form of human sacrifice adopted through religious motives; that the rude nomadic life of savages rendering impossible the preservation of aged and helpless members of the tribe, the murder of parents was regarded as an act of mercy both by the murderer and the victim; that before an effective administration of justice was organised, private vengeance was the sole preservative against crime,[1] and political assassination against usurpation; that the insensibility of some savages to the criminality of theft arises from the fact that they were accustomed to

---

[1] The feeling in its favour being often intensified by filial affection. 'What is the most beautiful thing on the earth?' said Osiris to Horus. 'To avenge a parent's wrongs,' was the reply.— Plutarch *De Iside et Osiride.*

have all things in common; that the Spartan law, legalising theft, arose partly from a desire to foster military dexterity among the people, but chiefly from a desire to discourage wealth; that slavery was introduced through motives of mercy, to prevent conquerors from killing their prisoners.[1] All this is true, but there is another and a more general answer. It is not to be expected, and it is not maintained, that men in all ages should have agreed about the application of their moral principles. All that is contended for is that these principles are themselves the same. Some of what appear to us monstrous acts of cruelty, were dictated by that very feeling of humanity, the universal perception of the merit of which they are cited to disprove,[2] and even when this is not the case, all that can be inferred is, that the standard of humanity was very low. But still humanity was recognised as a virtue, and cruelty as a vice.

At this point, I may observe how completely fallacious is the assertion that a progressive morality is impossible upon the supposition of an original moral faculty.[3]    To such

---

[1] Hence the Justinian code and also St. Augustine (De Civ. Dei, xix. 15) derived servus from 'servare,' to preserve, because the victor preserved his prisoners alive.

[2] 'Les habitants du Congo tuent les malades qu'ils imaginent ne pouvoir en revenir; c'est, disent-ils, pour leur épargner les douleurs de l'agonie. Dans l'île Formose, lorsqu'un homme est dangereusement malade, on lui passe un nœud coulant au col et on l'étrangle, pour l'arracher à la douleur.'— Helvétius, De l'Esprit, ii. 13. A similar explanation may be often found for customs which are quoted to prove that the nations where they existed had no sense of chastity. 'C'est pareillement sous la sauvegarde des lois que les

Siamoises, la gorge et les cuisses à moitié découvertes, portées dans les rues sur les palanquins, s'y présentent dans des attitudes très-lascives. Cette loi fut établie par une de leurs reines nommée Tirada, qui, pour dégoûter les hommes d'un amour plus déshonnête, crut devoir employer toute la puissance de la beauté.'—De l'Esprit, ii. 14.

[3] 'The contest between the morality which appeals to an external standard, and that which grounds itself on internal conviction, is the contest of progressive morality against stationary, of reason and argument against the deification of mere opinion and habit.' (Mill's Dissertations, vol. ii. p. 472); a passage with a true Bentham ring. See, too, vol. i. p.

statements there are two very simple answers. In the first place, although the intuitive moralist asserts that certain qualities are necessarily virtuous, he fully admits that the degree in which they are acted upon, or in other words, the standard of duty, may become progressively higher. In the next place, although he refuses to resolve all virtue into utility, he admits as fully as his opponents, that benevolence, or the promotion of the happiness of man, is a virtue, and that therefore discoveries which exhibit more clearly the true interests of our kind, may throw new light upon the nature of our duty.

The considerations I have urged with reference to humanity, apply with equal force to the various relations of the sexes. When the passions of men are altogether unrestrained, community of wives and all eccentric forms of sensuality will be admitted. When men seek to improve their nature in this respect, their object will be to abridge and confine the empire of sensuality. But to this process of improvement there are obvious limits. In the first place the continuance of the species is only possible by a sensual act. In the next place the strength of this passion and the weakness of humanity are so great, that the moralist must take into account the fact that in all societies, and especially in those in which free scope had long been given to the passions, a large amount of indulgence will arise which is not due to a simple desire of propagating the species. If then incest is prohibited, and community of wives replaced by ordinary polygamy, a moral improvement will have been effected, and a standard of virtue formed. But this standard soon becomes the starting-point of new progress. If we examine the Jewish law, we find the legislator prohibiting adultery, regulating the degrees

---

158. There is, however, a schism on this point in the utilitarian camp. The views which Mr. Buckle has expressed in his most eloquent chapter on the comparative influence of intellectual and moral agencies in civilisation diverge widely from those of Mr. Mill.

of marriage, but at the same time authorising polygamy, though with a caution against the excessive multiplication of wives. In Greece monogamy, though not without exceptions, had been enforced, but a concurrence of unfavourable influences prevented any high standard being attained among the men, and in their case almost every form of indulgence beyond the limits of marriage was permitted. In Rome the standard was far higher. Monogamy was firmly established. The ideal of female morality was placed as high as among Christian nations. Among men, however, while unnatural love and adultery were regarded as wrong, simple unchastity before marriage was scarcely considered a fault. In Catholicism marriage is regarded in a twofold light, as a means for the propagation of the species, and as a concession to the weakness of humanity, and all other sensual enjoyment is stringently prohibited.

In these cases there is a great difference between the degrees of earnestness with which men exert themselves in the repression of their passions, and in the amount of indulgence which is conceded to their lower nature; [1] but there is no difference in the direction of the virtuous impulse. While, too, in the case of adultery, and in the production of children, questions of interest and utility do undoubtedly intervene, we are conscious that the general progress turns upon a totally different order of ideas. The feeling of all men and the language of all nations, the sentiment which though often weakened is never wholly effaced, that this appetite, even in its most legitimate gratification, is a thing to be veiled and withdrawn from sight, all that is known under the names of decency and indecency, concur in proving that we have an innate, intuitive, instinctive perception that there is something degrading in the sensual part of our nature, something

---

[1] 'Est enim sensualitas quædam    vis animæ est superior.'— Peter
vis animæ inferior. . . . Ratio vero    Lombard, *Sent*. ii. 24.

to which a feeling of shame is naturally attached, something that jars with our conception of perfect purity, something we could not with any propriety ascribe to an all-holy being. It may be questioned whether anyone was ever altogether destitute of this perception, and nothing but the most inveterate passion for system could induce men to resolve it into a mere calculation of interests. It is this feeling or instinct which lies at the root of the whole movement I have described, and it is this too that produced that sense of the sanctity of perfect continence which the Catholic church has so warmly encouraged, but which may be traced through the most distant ages, and the most various creeds. We find it among the Nazarenes and Essenes of Judæa, among the priests of Egypt and India, in the monasteries of Tartary, in the histories of miraculous virgins that are so numerous in the mythologies of Asia. Such, for example, was the Chinese legend that tells how when there was but one man with one woman upon earth, the woman refused to sacrifice her virginity even in order to people the globe, and the gods honouring her purity granted that she should conceive beneath the gaze of her lover's eyes, and a virgin-mother became the parent of humanity.[1] In the midst of the sensuality of ancient Greece, chastity was the pre-eminent attribute of sanctity ascribed to Athene and Artemis. 'Chaste daughter of Zeus,' prayed the suppliants in Æschylus, 'thou whose calm eye is never troubled, look down upon us! Virgin, defend the virgins.' The Parthenon, or virgin's temple, was the noblest religious edifice of Athens. Celibacy was an essential condition in a few of the orders of priests, and in several orders of priestesses. Plato based his moral system upon the distinction between the bodily or sensual, and the spiritual or rational part of our nature, the first being the sign of our degradation, and the second of our dignity. The

[1] Helvétius, *De l'Esprit*, discours iv. See too, Dr. Draper's extremely remarkable *History of Intellectual Development in Europe* (New York, 1864), pp. 48, 53.

9

whole school of Pythagoras made chastity one of its leading
virtues, and even laboured for the creation of a monastic
system.  The conception of the celestial Aphrodite, the uniter
of souls, unsullied by the taint of matter, lingered side by
side with that of the earthly Aphrodite or patroness of lust,
and if there was a time when the sculptors sought to pander
to the excesses of passion there was another in which all their
art was displayed in refining and idealising it.  Strabo mentions the existence in Thrace of societies of men aspiring to
perfection by celibacy and austere lives.  Plutarch applauds
certain philosophers who vowed to abstain for a year from
wine and women in order 'to honour God by their continence.'[1]  In Rome the religious reverence was concentrated
more especially upon married life.  The great prominence accorded to the Penates was the religious sanction of domesticity.
So too, at first, was the worship so popular among the Roman
women of the Bona Dea—the ideal wife who according to the
legend had, when on earth, never looked in the face or known
the name of any man but her husband.[2]  'For altar and
hearth' was the rallying cry of the Roman soldier.  But
above all this we find the traces of a higher ideal.  We find
it in the intense sanctity attributed to the vestal virgins
whose continence was guarded by such fearful penalties, and
supposed to be so closely linked with the prosperity of the
state, whose prayer was believed to possess a miraculous
power, and who were permitted to drive through the streets
of Rome at a time when that privilege was refused even to
the Empress.[3]  We find it in the legend of Claudia, who,

---

[1] Plutarch, *De Cohibenda Ira.*
[2] Lactantius, *Div. Inst.* i. 22.
The mysteries of the Bona Dea
became, however, after a time, the
occasion of great disorders.  See
Juvenal, *Sat.* vi.  M. Magnin has
examined the nature of these rites
(*Origines du Théâtre*, pp. 257-259).

[3] The history of the vestals,
which forms one of the most curious
pages in the moral history of Rome,
has been fully treated by the Abbé
Nadal, in an extremely interesting
and well-written memoir, read before the Académie des Belles-
lettres, and republished in 1725.

when the ship bearing the image of the mother of the gods
had been stranded in the Tiber, attached her girdle to its
prow, and vindicated her challenged chastity by drawing with
her virgin hand, the ponderous mass which strong men had
sought in vain to move.   We find it in the prophetic gift so
often attributed to virgins,[1] in the law which sheltered them
from the degradation of an execution,[2] in the language of
Statius, who described marriage itself as a fault.[3]   In Christianity one great source of the attraction of the faith has
been the ascription of virginity to its female ideal.   The
Catholic monastic system has been so constructed as to draw
many thousands from the sphere of active duty; its irrevoc-
able vows have doubtless led to much suffering and not a little
crime; its opposition to the normal development of our
mingled nature has often resulted in grave aberrations of the
imagination, and it has placed its ban upon domestic affections and sympathies which have a very high moral value;
but in its central conception that the purely animal side

---

It was believed that the prayer of
a vestal could arrest a fugitive
slave in his flight, provided he had
not got past the city walls.   Pliny
mentions this belief as general in
his time.   The records of the order
contained many miracles wrought
at different times to save the vestals or to vindicate their questioned
purity, and also one miracle which
is very remarkable as furnishing a
precise parallel to that of the Jew
who was struck dead for touching
the ark to prevent its falling.

[1] As for example the Sibyls
and Cassandra.   The same prophetic power was attributed in
India to virgins.—Clem. Alexan-
drin. *Strom.* iii. 7.

[2] This custom continued to the
worst period of the empire, though
it was shamefully and characteris-

tically evaded.   After the fall of
Sejanus the senate had no compunction in putting his innocent
daughter to death, but their religious feelings were shocked at the
idea of a virgin falling beneath the
axe.   So by way of improving matters 'filia constuprata est prius a
carnifice, quasi impium esset vir-
ginem in carcere perire.'—Dion
Cassius, lviii. 11. See too, Tacitus,
*Annal.* v. 9. If a vestal met a
prisoner going to execution the
prisoner was spared, provided the
vestal declared that the encounter
was accidental.   On the reverence
the ancients paid to virgins, see
Justus Lipsius, *De Vesta et Ves-
talibus.*

[3] See his picture of the first
night of marriage :—

of our being is a low and a degraded side, it reflects, I believe, with perfect fidelity the feelings of our nature.[1]

To these considerations some others of a different nature may be added. It is not true that some ancient nations regarded polygamy as good in the same sense as others regarded chastity. There is a great difference between deeming a state permissible and proposing it as a condition of sanctity. If Mohammedans people paradise with images of sensuality, it is not because these form their ideal of holiness. It is because they regard earth as the sphere of virtue, heaven as that of simple enjoyment. If some pagan nations deified sensuality, this was simply because the deification of the forces of nature, of which the prolific energy is one of the most conspicuous, is among the earliest forms of religion, and long precedes the identification of the Deity with a moral ideal.[2] If there have

'Tacitè subit ille supremus
Virginitatis amor, primæque modestia culpæ
Confundit    vultus.    Tunc    ora
rigantur honestis
Imbribus.'
       *Thebaidos*, lib. ii. 232–34.

[1] Bees (which Virgil said had in them something of the divine nature) were supposed by the ancients to be the special emblems or models of chastity. It was a common belief that the bee mother begot her young without losing her virginity. Thus in a fragment ascribed to Petronius we read,

Sic sine concubitu textis apis
   excita ceris
Fervet, et audaci milite castra
replet.'
       Petron. *De Varia Animalium
                Generatione.*

So too Virgil:—
'Quod neque concubitu indulgent
nec corpora segnes

In Venerem solvunt aut fœtus nixibus edunt.'—*Georg.* iv. 198–99.

Plutarch says that an unchaste person cannot approach bees, for they immediately attack him and cover him with stings. Fire was also regarded as a type of virginity. Thus Ovid, speaking of the vestals, says:—

'Nataque de flamma corpora
   nulla vides:
Jure igitur virgo est, quæ semina
   nulla remittit
Nec capit, et comites virginitatis
   amat.'

'The Egyptians believed that there are no males among vultures, and they accordingly made that bird an emblem of nature.'—Ammianus Marcellinus, xvii. 4.

[2] 'La divinité étant considérée comme renfermant en elle toutes les qualités, toutes les forces intellectuelles et morales de l'homme, chacune de ces forces ou de ces

been nations who attached a certain stigma to virginity, this has not been because they esteemed sensuality intrinsically holier than chastity ; but because a scanty, warlike people whose position in the world depends chiefly on the number of its warriors, will naturally make it its main object to encourage population. This was especially the case with the ancient Jews, who always regarded extreme populousness as indissolubly connected with national prosperity, whose religion was essentially patriotic, and among whom the possibility of becoming an ancestor of the Messiah had imparted a peculiar dignity to childbirth. Yet even among the Jews the Essenes regarded virginity as the ideal of sanctity.

The reader will now be in a position to perceive the utter futility of the objections which from the time of Locke have been continually brought against the theory of natural moral perceptions, upon the ground that some actions which were admitted as lawful in one age, have been regarded as immoral in another. All these become absolutely worthless when it is perceived that in every age virtue has consisted in the cultivation of the same feelings, though the standards of excellence attained have been different. The terms higher and lower, nobler or less noble, purer or less pure, represent moral facts with much greater fidelity than the terms right or wrong, or virtue or vice. There is a certain sense in which moral distinctions are absolute and immutable. There is another sense in which they are altogether relative and transient. There are some acts which are so manifestly and grossly opposed to our moral feelings, that they are regarded as wrong in the very earliest stages of the cultivation of these feelings. There are distinctions, such as that between truth and falsehood, which from their nature assume at once a sharpness of definition that separates them from mere

qualités, conçue séparément, s'offrait comme un Être divin. . . . De-là aussi les contradictions les plus choquantes dans les notions que les anciens avaient des attributs divins.'—Maury, *Hist. des Religions de la Grèce antique*, tome i. pp. 578–579.

virtues of degree, though even in these cases there are wide
variations in the amount of scrupulosity that is in different
periods required. But apart from positive commands, the
sole external rule enabling men to designate acts, not simply
as better or worse, but as positively right or wrong, is, I
conceive, the standard of society; not an arbitrary standard
like that which Mandeville imagined, but the level which
society has attained in the cultivation of what our moral
faculty tells us is the higher or virtuous part of our nature.
He who falls below this is obstructing the tendency which is
the essence of virtue. He who merely attains this, may not
be justified in his own conscience, or in other words, by the
standard of his own moral development, but as far as any
external rule is concerned, he has done his duty. He who
rises above this has entered into the region of things which
it is virtuous to do, but not vicious to neglect—a region
known among Catholic theologians by the name of 'counsels
of perfection.' No discussions, I conceive, can be more idle
than whether slavery, or the slaughter of prisoners in war,
or gladiatorial shows, or polygamy, are essentially wrong.
They may be wrong now—they were not so once—and when
an ancient countenanced by his example one or other of these,
he was not committing a crime. The unchangeable proposition for which we contend is this—that benevolence is always
a virtuous disposition—that the sensual part of our nature is
always the lower part.

At this point, however, a very difficult problem naturally
arises. Admitting that our moral nature is superior to
our intellectual or physical nature, admitting, too, that by
the constitution of our being we perceive ourselves to be
under an obligation to develope our nature to its perfection,
establishing the supreme ascendency of moral motives, the
question still remains whether the disparity between the
different parts of our being is such that no material or intellectual advantage, however great, may be rightly purchased

by any sacrifice of our moral nature, however small. This is the great question of casuistry, the question which divines express by asking whether the end ever justifies the means; and on this subject there exists among theologians a doctrine which is absolutely unrealised, which no one ever dreams of applying to actual life, but of which it may be truly said that though propounded with the best intentions, it would, if acted upon, be utterly incompatible with the very rudiments of civilisation. It is said that an undoubted sin, even the most trivial, is a thing in its essence and in its consequences so unspeakably dreadful, that no conceivable material or intellectual advantage can counterbalance it; that rather than it should be committed, it would be better that any amount of calamity which did not bring with it sin should be endured, even that the whole human race should perish in agonies.[1] If this be the case, it is manifest that the supreme object of humanity should be sinlessness, and it is equally manifest that the means to this end is the absolute suppression of the desires. To expand the circle of wants is necessarily to multiply temptations, and therefore to increase the number of sins. It may indeed elevate the moral standard, for a torpid sinlessness is not a high moral condition; but if every sin be what these theologians assert, if it be a thing deserving eternal agony, and so inconceivably frightful that the ruin of a world is a less evil than its commission, even moral advantages are utterly incommensurate with it. No heightening of the moral tone, no depth or ecstasy of devotion, can for a moment be placed in the balance. The consequences of this doctrine, if applied to actual life, would be

---

[1] 'The Church holds that it were better for sun and moon to drop from heaven, for the earth to fail, and for all the many millions who are upon it to die of starvation in extremest agony, so far as temporal affliction goes, than that one soul, I will not say should be lost, but should commit one single venial sin, should tell one wilful untruth, though it harmed no one, or steal one poor farthing without excuse.'—Newman's *Anglican Difficulties*, p. 190.

so extravagant, that their simple statement is a refutation. A sovereign, when calculating the consequences of a war, should reflect that a single sin occasioned by that war, a single blasphemy of a wounded soldier, the robbery of a single hencoop, the violation of the purity of a single woman, is a greater calamity than the ruin of the entire commerce of his nation, the loss of her most precious provinces, the destruction of all her power. He must believe that the evil of the increase of unchastity, which invariably results from the formation of an army, is an immeasurably greater calamity than any material or political disasters that army can possibly avert. He must believe that the most fearful plague or famine that desolates his land should be regarded as a matter of rejoicing, if it has but the feeblest and most transient influence in repressing vice. He must believe that if the agglomeration of his people in great cities adds but one to the number of their sins, no possible intellectual or material advantages can prevent the construction of cities being a fearful calamity. According to this principle, every elaboration of life, every amusement that brings multitudes together, almost every art, every accession of wealth that awakens or stimulates desires, is an evil, for all these become the sources of some sins, and their advantages are for the most part purely terrestrial. The entire structure of civilisation is founded upon the belief that it is a good thing to cultivate intellectual and material capacities, even at the cost of certain moral evils which we are often able accurately to foresee.[1] The time may come when the man who lays the foundation-stone of a manufacture will be able to predict with assurance in what proportion the drunkenness and the unchastity of his city will be increased by his enterprise.

---

[1] There is a remarkable dissertation on this subject, called 'The Limitations of Morality,' in a very ingenious and suggestive little work of the Benthamite school, called *Essays by a Barrister* (reprinted from the *Saturday Review*)

Yet he will still pursue that enterprise, and mankind will pronounce it to be good.

The theological doctrine on the subject, considered in its full stringency, though professed by many, is, as I have said, realised and consistently acted on by no one; but the practical judgments of mankind concerning the extent of the superiority of moral over all other interests vary greatly, and this variation supplies one of the most serious objections to intuitive moralists. The nearest practical approach to the theological estimate of a sin may be found in the ranks of the ascetics. Their whole system rests upon the belief that it is a thing so transcendently dreadful as to bear no proportion or appreciable relation to any earthly interests. Starting from this belief, the ascetic makes it the exclusive object of his life to avoid sinning. He accordingly abstains from all the active business of society, relinquishes all worldly aims and ambitions, dulls by continued discipline his natural desires, and endeavours to pass a life of complete absorption in religious exercises. And in all this his conduct is reasonable and consistent. The natural course of every man who adopts this estimate of the enormity of sin is at every cost to avoid all external influences that can prove temptations, and to attenuate as far as possible his own appetites and emotions. It is in this respect that the exaggerations of theologians paralyse our moral being. For the diminution of sins, however important, is but one part of moral progress. Whenever it is forced into a disproportionate prominence, we find tame, languid, and mutilated natures, destitute of all fire and energy, and this tendency has been still further aggravated by the extreme prominence usually given to the virtue of gentleness, which may indeed be attained by men of strong natures and vehement emotions, but is evidently more congenial to a somewhat feeble and passionless character.

Ascetic practices are manifestly and rapidly disappearing, and their decline is a striking proof of the evanescence of the moral notions of which they were the expression, but in many existing questions relating to the same matter, we find perplexing diversity of judgment. We find it in the contrast between the system of education usually adopted by the Catholic priesthood, which has for its pre-eminent object to prevent sins, and for its means a constant and minute supervision, and the English system of public schools, which is certainly not the most fitted to guard against the possibility of sin, or to foster any very delicate scrupulosity of feeling; but is intended, and popularly supposed, to secure the healthy expansion of every variety of capacity. We find it in the widely different attitudes which good men in different periods have adopted towards religious opinions they believe to be false; some, like the reformers, refusing to participate in any superstitious service, or to withhold on any occasion, or at any cost, their protest against what they regarded as a lie; others, like most ancient, and some modern philosophers and politicians, combining the most absolute personal incredulity with an assiduous observance of superstitious rites, and strongly censuring those who disturbed delusions which are useful or consolatory to the people; while a third class silently, but without protest, withdraw themselves from the observances, and desire that their opinions should have a free expression in literature, but at the same time discourage all proselytising efforts to force them rudely on unprepared minds. We find it in the frequent conflicts between the political economist and the Catholic priest on the subject of early marriages, the former opposing them on the ground that it is an essential condition of material well-being that the standard of comfort should not be depressed, the latter advocating them on the ground that the postponement of marriages, through prudential motives, by any large body of men, is the fertile mother of sin. We find it most conspicuously in the marked diversities of tolerance manifested in different communities towards amusements which may in themselves be perfectly innocent, but which prove the sources or the occasions of vice. The Scotch Puritans probably represent one extreme, the Parisian society of the empire the other, while the position of average Englishmen is perhaps equidistant between them. Yet this difference, great as it is, is a difference not of principle, but of degree. No Puritan seriously desires to suppress every clan-gathering, every highland game which may have occasioned an isolated fit of drunkenness, though he may be unable to show that it has prevented any sin that would otherwise have been committed. No Frenchman will question that there is a certain amount of demoralisation which should not be tolerated, however great the enjoyment that accompanies it. Yet the one dwells almost exclusively upon the moral, the other upon the attractive, nature of a spectacle. Between these there are numerous gradations, which are shown in frequent disputes about the merits and demerits of the racecourse, the ball, the theatre, and the concert. Where then, it may be asked, is the line to be drawn ? By what rule can the point be determined at which an amusement becomes vitiated by the evil of its consequences?

To these questions the intuitive moralist is obliged to answer, that such a line cannot be drawn, that such a rule does not exist. The colours of our moral nature are rarely separated by the sharp lines of our vocabulary. They fade and blend into one another so imperceptibly, that it is impossible to mark a precise point of transition. The end of man is the full development of his being in that symmetry and proportion which nature has assigned it, and such a development implies that the supreme, the predominant motive of his life, should be moral. If in any society or individual this ascendency does not exist, that society or that individual is in a diseased and abnormal condition. But the superiority of the moral part of our nature, though unquestionable, is indefinite not infinite, and the prevailing standard is not at all times the same. The moralist can only lay down general principles. Individual feeling or the general sentiment of society must draw the application.

The vagueness that on such questions confessedly hangs over the intuitive theory, has always been insisted upon by members of the opposite school, who 'in the greatest happiness principle' claim to possess a definite formulary, enabling them to draw boldly the frontier line between the lawful and the illicit, and to remove moral disputes from the domain of feeling to that of demonstration. But this claim, which forms the great attraction of the utilitarian school, is, if I mistake not, one of the grossest of impostures. We compare with accuracy and confidence the value of the most various material commodities, for we mean by this term, exchangeable value, and we have a common measure of exchange. But we seek in vain for such a measure enabling us to compare different kinds of utility or happiness. Thus, to take a very familiar example, the question may be proposed, whether excursion trains from a country district to a seaport town produce more good than evil, whether a man governed by moral principles should encourage or oppose them. They give innocent and healthy enjoyment to many thousands, they enlarge in some degree the range of their ideas, they can hardly be said to prevent any sin that would otherwise have been committed, they give rise to many cases of drunkenness, each of which, according to the theological doctrine we have reviewed, should be deemed a more dreadful calamity than the earthquake of Lisbon, or a visitation of the cholera, but which have not usually any lasting terrestrial effects; they also often produce a measure, and sometimes no small measure, of more serious vice, and it is probable that hundreds of women may trace their first fall to the excursion train. We have here a number of advantages and disadvantages, the first being intellectual and physical, and the second moral. Nearly all moralists would acknowledge that a few instances of immorality would not prevent the excursion train being, on the whole, a good thing. All would acknowledge that very numerous instances would more than counterbalance its advantages. The intuitive moralist confesses that he is unable to draw a precise line, showing where the moral evils outweigh the physical benefits. In what possible respect the introduction of Benthamite formularies improves the matter, I am unable to understand. No utilitarian would reduce the question to one of simple majority, or would have the cynicism to balance the ruin of one woman by the day's enjoyment of another. The impossibility of drawing, in such cases, a distinct line of division, is no argument against the intuitive moralist, for that impossibility is shared to the full extent by his rival.

There are, as we have seen, two kinds of interest with which utilitarian moralists are concerned—the private interest which they believe to be the ultimate motive, and the public interest which they believe to be the end, of all virtue. With reference to the first, the intuitive moralist denies that a selfish act can be a virtuous or meritorious one. If a man when about to commit a theft, became suddenly conscious of the presence of a policeman, and through fear of arrest and punishment were to abstain from the act he would otherwise have committed, this abstinence would not appear in the eyes of mankind to possess any moral value; and if he were determined partly by conscientious motives, and partly by fear, the presence of the latter element would, in proportion to its strength, detract from his merit. But although selfish considerations are distinctly opposed to virtuous ones, it would be a mistake to imagine they can never ultimately have a purely moral influence. In the first place, a well-ordered system of threats and punishments marks out the path of virtue with a distinctness of definition it could scarcely have otherwise attained. In the next place, it often happens that when the mind is swayed by a conflict of motives, the expectation of reward or punishment will so reinforce or support

the virtuous motives, as to secure their victory; and, as
every triumph of these motives increases their strength and
weakens the opposing principles, a step will thus have been
made towards moral perfection, which will render more probable the future triumph of unassisted virtue.

With reference to the interests of society, there are two
distinct assertions to be made. The first is, that although
the pursuit of the welfare of others is undoubtedly one form
of virtue, it does not include all virtue, or, in other words,
that there are forms of virtue which, even if beneficial to
mankind, do not become virtuous on that account, but have
an intrinsic excellence which is not proportioned to or dependent on their utility. The second is, that there may occasionally arise considerations of extreme and overwhelming utility
that may justify a sacrifice of these virtues. This sacrifice
may be made in various ways—as, when a man undertakes
an enterprise which is in itself perfectly innocent, but which
in addition to its great material advantages will, as he well
knows, produce a certain measure of crime; or when, abstaining from a protest, he tacitly countenances beliefs which
he considers untrue, because he regards them as transcendently useful; or again, when, for the benefit of others, and
under circumstances of great urgency, he utters a direct falsehood, as, for example, when by such means alone he can
save the life of an innocent man.[1] But the fact, that in these
cases considerations of extreme utility are suffered to over-

[1] The following passage, though
rather vague and rhetorical, is not
unimpressive: 'Oui, dit Jacobi,
je mentirais comme Desdemona
mourante je tromperais comme
Oreste quand il veut mourir à la
place de Pylade, j'assassinerais
comme Timoléon, je serais parjure
comme Épaminondas et Jean de
Witt, je me déterminerais au sui-
side comme Caton, je serais sacri-
lége comme David; car j'ai la
certitude en moi-même qu'en par-
donnant à ces fautes suivant la
lettre l'homme exerce le droit
souverain que la majesté de son
être lui confère; il appose le sceau
de sa divine nature sur la grâce
qu'il accorde.'—Barchou de Pen-
hoen, *Hist. de la Philos. allemande,*
tome i. p. 295.

ride considerations of morality, is in no degree inconsistent with the facts, that the latter differ in kind from the former, that they are of a higher nature, and that they may supply adequate and legitimate motives of action not only distinct from, but even in opposition to utility. Gold and silver are different metals. Gold is more valuable than silver; yet a very small quantity of gold may be advantageously exchanged for a very large quantity of silver.

The last class of objections to the theory of natural moral perceptions which it is necessary for me to notice, arises from a very mischievous equivocation in the word natural.[1] The term natural man is sometimes regarded as synonymous with man in his primitive or barbarous condition, and sometimes as expressing all in a civilised man that is due to nature as distinguished from artificial habits or acquirements. This equivocation is especially dangerous, because it implies one of the most extravagant excesses to which the sensational philosophy could be pushed—the notion that the difference between a savage and a civilised man is simply a difference of acquisition, and not at all a difference of development. In accordance with this notion, those who deny original moral distinctions have ransacked the accounts of travellers for examples of savages who appeared destitute of moral sentiments, and have adduced them as conclusive evidence of their position. Now it is, I think, abundantly evident that these narratives are usually exceedingly untrustworthy.[2] They

---

[1] This equivocation seems to me to lie at the root of the famous dispute whether man is by nature a social being, or whether, as Hobbes averred, the state of nature is a state of war. Few persons who have observed the recent light thrown on the subject will question that the primitive condition of man was that of savage life, and fewer still will question that savage life is a state of war. On the other hand, it is, I think, equally certain that man necessarily becomes a social being in exact proportion to the development of the capacities of his nature.

[2] One of the best living authorities on this question writes: 'The asserted existence of savages so low as to have no moral standard is too groundless to be discussed. Every human tribe has its general views as to what conduct is right and what

have been in most cases collected by uncritical and unphilo-sophical travellers, who knew little of the language and still less of the inner life of the people they described, whose means of information were acquired in simply traversing the country, who were more struck by moral paradox, than by unostenta-tious virtue, who were proverbially addicted to embellishing and exaggerating the singularities they witnessed, and who very rarely investigated their origin. It should not be for-gotten that the French moralists of the last century, who in-sisted most strongly on this species of evidence, were also the dupes of one of the most curious delusions in the whole com-pass of literary history. Those unflinching sceptics who claimed to be the true disciples of the apostle who believed nothing that he had not touched, and whose relentless criti-cism played with withering effect on all the holiest feelings of our nature, and on all the tenets of traditional creeds, had discovered one happy land where the ideal had ceased to be a dream. They could point to one people whose pure and rational morality, purged from all the clouds of bigotry and enthusiasm, shone with an almost dazzling splendour above the ignorance and superstition of Europe. Voltaire forgot to gibe, and Helvétius kindled into enthusiasm, when China and the Chinese rose before their minds, and to this semi-barbarous nation they habitually attributed maxims of conduct that neither Roman nor Christian virtue had ever realised.

But putting aside these considerations, and assuming the fidelity of the pictures of savage life upon which these writers rely, they fail to prove the point for which they are adduced. The moralists I am defending, assert that we possess a natural power of distinguishing between the higher and lower parts of our nature. But the eye of the mind, like

wrong, and each generation hands the standard on to the next. Even in the details of their moral stand-ards, wide as their differences are, there is yet wider agreement throughout the human race.'—Tylor on Primitive Society, *Contem-porary Review*, April 1873, **p. 702.**

the eye of the body, may be closed. Moral and rational faculties may be alike dormant, and they will certainly be so if men are wholly immersed in the gratification of their senses. Man is like a plant, which requires a favourable soil for the full expansion of its natural or innate powers.[1] Yet those powers both rational and moral are there, and when quickened into action, each will discharge its appointed functions. If it could be proved that there are savages who are absolutely destitute of the progressive energy which distinguishes reason from instinct and of the moral aspiration which constitutes virtue, this would not prove that rational or moral faculties form no part of their nature. If it could be shown that there is a stage of barbarism in which man knows, feels and does nothing that might not be known, felt and done by an ape, this would not be sufficient to reduce him to the level of the brute. There would still be this broad distinction between them—the one possesses a capacity for development which the other does not possess. Under favourable circumstances the savage will become a reasoning;

---

[1] The distinction between innate faculties evolved by experience and innate ideas independent of experience, and the analogy between the expansion of the former and that of the bud into the flower has been very happily treated by Reid. (*On the Active Powers*, essay iii. chap. viii. p. 4.) Professor Sedgwick, criticising Locke's notion of the soul being originally like a sheet of white paper, beautifully says: 'Naked man comes from his mother's womb, endowed with limbs and senses indeed well fitted to the material world, yet powerless from want of use; and as for knowledge, his soul is one unvaried blank; yet has this blank been already touched by a celestial hand, and when plunged in the colours which surround it, it takes not its tinge from accident but design, and comes forth covered with a glorious pattern.' (*On the Studies of the University,* p. 54.) Leibnitz says: 'L'esprit n'est point une table rase. Il est tout plein de caractères que la sensation ne peut que découvrir et mettre en lumière au lieu de les y imprimer. Je me suis servi de la comparaison d'une pierre de marbre qui a des veines plutôt que d'une pierre de marbre tout unie. . . . S'il y avait dans la pierre des veines qui marquassent la figure d'Hercule préférablement à d'autres figures, . . . . Hercule y serait comme inné en quelque façon, quoiqu'il fallût du travail pour découvrir ces veines.' —*Critique de l'Essai sur l'Entendement.*

progressive, and moral man : under no circumstances can a similar transformation be effected in the ape. It may be as difficult to detect the oakleaf in the acorn as in the stone ; yet the acorn may be converted into an oak : the stone will always continue to be a stone.[1]

The foregoing pages will, I trust, have exhibited with sufficient clearness the nature of the two great divisions of moral philosophy—the school which proceeds from the primitive truth that all men desire happiness, and endeavours out of this fact to evolve all ethical doctrines, and the school which traces our moral systems to an intuitive perception that certain parts of our nature are higher or better than others. It is obvious that this difference concerning the origin of our moral conceptions forms part of the very much wider metaphysical question, whether our ideas are derived exclusively from sensation or whether they spring in part from the mind itself. The latter theory in antiquity was chiefly represented by the Platonic doctrine of pre-existence, which rested on the conviction that the mind has the power of drawing from its own depths certain conceptions or ideas which cannot be explained by any post-natal experience, and must therefore, it was said, have been acquired in a previous

---

[1] The argument against the intuitive moralists derived from savage life was employed at some length by Locke. Paley then adopted it, taking a history of base ingratitude related by Valerius Maximus, and asking whether a savage would view it with disapprobation. (*Moral Phil.* book i. ch. 5.) Dugald Stewart (*Active and Moral Powers,* vol. i. pp. 230–231) and other writers have very fully answered this, but the same objection has been revived in another form by Mr. Austin, who supposes (*Lectures on Jurisprudence,* vol. i. pp. 82 83) a savage who first meets a hunter carrying a dead deer, kills the hunter and steals the deer, and is afterwards himself assailed by another hunter whom he kills. Mr. Austin asks whether the savage would perceive a moral difference between these two acts of homicide? Certainly not. In this early stage of development, the savage recognises a duty of justice and humanity to the members of his tribe, but to no one beyond this circle. He is in a 'state of war' with the foreign hunter. He has a right to kill the hunter and the hunter an equal right to kill him.

existence. In the seventeenth century it took the orm of a doctrine of innate ideas. But though this theory in the form in which it was professed by Lord Herbert of Cherbury and assailed by Locke has almost disappeared, the doctrine that we possess certain faculties which by their own expansion, and not by the reception of notions from without, are not only capable of, but must necessarily attain, certain ideas, as the bud must necessarily expand into its own specific flower, still occupies a distinguished place in the world of speculation, and its probability has been greatly strengthened by recent observations of the range and potency of instinct in animals. From some passages in his Essay, it appears that Locke himself had a confused perception of this distinction,[1] which was by no means unknown to previous writers; and after the publication of the philosophy of Locke it was clearly exhibited by Shaftesbury and Leibnitz, and incidentally noticed by Berkeley long before Kant established his distinction between the form and the matter of our knowledge, between ideas which are received *a priori* and ideas which are received *a posteriori*. The existence or non-existence of this source of ideas forms the basis of the opposition between the inductive philosophy of England and the French philosophy of the eighteenth century on the one hand, and the German and

---

[1] Everyone who is acquainted with metaphysics knows that there has been an almost endless controversy about Locke's meaning on this point. The fact seems to be that Locke, like most great originators of thought, and indeed more than most, often failed to perceive the ultimate consequences of his principles, and partly through some confusion of thought, and partly through unhappiness of expression, has left passages involving the conclusions of both schools. As a matter of history the sensual school of Condillac grew professedly out of his philosophy. In defence of the legitimacy of the process by which these writers evolved their conclusions from the premisses of Locke, the reader may consult the very able lectures of M. Cousin on Locke. The other side has been treated, among others, by Dugald Stewart in his *Dissertation*, by Professor Webb in his *Intellectualism of Locke*, and by Mr. Rogers in an essay reprinted from the *Edinburgh Review*.

Scotch philosophies, as well as the French eclecticism of the nineteenth century upon the other. The tendency of the first school is to restrict as far as possible the active powers of the human mind, and to aggrandise as far as possible the empire of external circumstances. The other school dwells especially on the instinctive side of our nature, and maintains the existence of certain intuitions of the reason, certain categories or original conceptions, which are presupposed in all our reasonings and cannot be resolved into sensations. The boast of the first school is that its searching analysis leaves no mental phenomenon unresolved, and its attraction is the extreme simplicity it can attain. The second school multiplies faculties or original principles, concentrates its attention mainly upon the nature of our understanding, and asserts very strongly the initiative force both of our will and of our intellect.

We find this connection between a philosophy based upon the senses, and a morality founded upon utility from the earliest times. Aristotle was distinguished among the ancients for the emphasis with which he dwelt upon the utility of virtue, and it was from the writings of Aristotle that the schoolmen derived the famous formulary which has become the motto of the school of Locke. Locke himself devoted especial research to the refutation of the doctrine of a natural moral sense, which he endeavoured to overthrow by a catalogue of immoral practices that exist among savages, and the hesitation he occasionally exhibited in his moral doctrine corresponds not unfaithfully to the obscurity thrown over his metaphysics by the admission of reflection as a source of ideas. If his opponent Leibnitz made pleasure the object of moral action, it was only that refined pleasure which is produced by the contemplation of the happiness of others. When, however, Condillac and his followers, removing reflection from the position Locke had assigned it, reduced the philosophy of sensation to its simplest expression, and when the Scotch and German writers elaborated the principles of the opposite school, the moral tendencies of both were indisputably manifested. Everywhere the philosophy of sensation was accompanied by the morals of interest, and the ideal philosophy, by an assertion of the existence of a moral faculty, and every influence that has affected the prevailing theory concerning the origin of our ideas, has exercised a corresponding influence upon the theories of ethics.

The great movement of modern thought, of which Bacon was at once the highest representative and one of the chief agents, has been truly said to exhibit a striking resemblance, and at the same time a striking contrast, to the movement of ancient thought, which was effected chiefly by the genius of Socrates. In the name of utility, Socrates diverted the intellect of antiquity from the fantastic cosmogonies with which it had long been occupied, to the study of the moral nature of man. In the name of the same utility Bacon laboured to divert the modern intellect from the idle metaphysical speculations of the schoolmen to natural science, to which newly discovered instruments of research, his own sounder method, and a cluster of splendid intellects, soon gave an unprecedented impulse. To the indirect influence of this movement, perhaps, even more than to the direct teaching of Gassendi and Locke, may be ascribed the great ascendency of sensational philosophy among modern nations, and it is also connected with some of the most important differences between ancient and modern history. Among the ancients the human mind was chiefly directed to philosophical speculations, in which the law seems to be perpetual oscillation, while among the moderns it has rather tended towards physical science, and towards inventions, in which the law is perpetual progress. National power, and in most cases even national independence, implied among the ancients the constant energy of high intellectual or moral qualities. When the heroism or the genius of the people had relaxed, when an enervating philosophy or the lassitude that often accompanies civilisation arrived, the whole edifice speedily tottered, the sceptre was transferred to another state, and the same history was elsewhere reproduced. A great nation bequeathed indeed to its successors works of transcendent beauty in art and literature, philosophies that could avail only when the mind had risen to their level, examples that might stimulate the heroism of an aspiring people, warnings that might sometimes arrest it on the path to ruin. But all these acted only through the mind. In modern times, on the other hand, if we put aside religious influences, the principal causes of the superiority of civilised men are to be found in inventions which when once discovered can never pass away, and the effects of which are in consequence in a great measure removed from the fluctuations of moral life. The causes which most disturbed or accelerated the normal progress of society in antiquity were the appearance of great men, in modern times they have been the appearance of great inventions. Printing has secured the intellectual achievements of the past, and furnished a sure guarantee of future progress. Gunpowder and military machinery have rendered the triumph of barbarians impossible. Steam has united nations in the closest bonds. Innumerable mechanical contrivances have given a decisive preponderance to that industrial element which has coloured all the developments of our civilisation. The leading characteristics of modern societies are in consequence marked out much more by the triumphs of inventive skill than by the sustained energy of moral causes.

Now it will appear evident, I think, to those who reflect carefully upon their own minds, and upon the course of history, that these three things, the study of physical science, inventive skill, and industrial enterprise, are connected in such a manner, that when in any nation there is a long-sustained tendency towards one, the others will naturally follow. This connection is partly that of cause and effect, for success in either of these branches facilitates success in the others, a knowledge of natural laws being the basis of many of the most important inventions, and being itself acquired by the aid of instruments of research, while industry is manifestly indebted to both. But besides this connection, there is a connection of congruity. The same cast or habit of thought developes itself in these three forms. They all represent the natural tendencies of what is commonly called the practical as opposed to the theoretical mind, of the inductive or experimental as opposed to the deductive or ideal, of the cautious and the plodding as opposed to the imaginative and the ambitious, of the mind that tends naturally to matter as opposed to that which dwells naturally on ideas. Among the ancients, the distaste for physical science, which the belief in the capricious divine government of all natural phenomena, and the distaste for industrial enterprise which slavery produced, conspired to favour the philosophical tendency, while among the moderns physical science and the habits of industrial life continually react upon one another.

There can be no question that the intellectual tendencies of modern times are far superior to those of antiquity, both in respect to the material prosperity they effect, and to the uninterrupted progress they secure. Upon the other hand, it is, I think, equally unquestionable that this superiority is purchased by the sacrifice of something of dignity and elevation of character. It is when the cultivation of mental and moral qualities is deemed the primary object, when the mind and its interests are most removed from the things of sense, that great characters are most frequent, and the standard of heroism is most high. In this, as in other cases, the law of congruity is supreme. The mind that is concentrated most on the properties of matter, is predisposed to derive all ideas from the senses, while that which dwells naturally upon its own operations inclines to an ideal philosophy, and the prevailing system of morals depends largely upon the distinction.

In the next place, we may observe that the practical

consequences, so far as ethics are concerned,[1] of the opposition between the two great schools of morals, are less than might be inferred from the intellectual chasm that separates them. Moralists grow up in the atmosphere of society, and experience all the common feelings of other men. Whatever theory of the genesis of morals they may form, they commonly recognise as right the broad moral principles of the world, and they endeavour—though I have attempted to show not always successfully—to prove that these principles may be accounted for and justified by their system. The great practical difference between the schools lies, not in the difference of the virtues they inculcate, but in the different degrees of prominence they assign to each, in the different casts of mind they represent and promote. As Adam Smith observed, a system like that of the Stoics, which makes self-control the ideal of excellence, is especially favourable to the heroic qualities, a system like that of Hutcheson, which resolves virtue into benevolence, to the amiable qualities, and utilitarian systems to the industrial virtues. A society in which any one of these three forms of moral excellence is especially prominent, has a natural tendency towards the corresponding theory of ethics; but, on the other hand, this theory, when formed, reacts upon and strengthens the moral tendency that elicited it. The Epicureans and the Stoics can each claim a great historical fact in their favour. When every other Greek school modified or abandoned the teaching of its founder, the disciples of Epicurus at Athens preserved their hereditary faith unsullied and unchanged.[2]     On the other hand, in the

---

[1] I make this qualification, because I believe that the denial of a moral nature in man capable of perceiving the distinction between duty and interest and the rightful supremacy of the former, is both philosophically and actually subversive of natural theology.

[2] See the forcible passage in the life of Epicurus by Diogenes Laërtius. So Mackintosh: 'It is remarkable that, while, of the three professors who sat in the Porch from Zeno to Posidonius, every one either softened or exaggerated the doctrines of his predecessor, and

Roman empire, almost every great character, almost every effort in the cause of liberty, emanated from the ranks of Stoicism, while Epicureanism was continually identified with corruption and with tyranny. The intuitive school, not having a clear and simple external standard, has often proved somewhat liable to assimilate with superstition and mysticism, to become fantastic, unreasoning, and unpractical, while the prominence accorded to interest, and the constant intervention of calculation in utilitarian systems, have a tendency to depress the ideal, and give a sordid and unheroic ply to the character. The first, dwelling on the moral initiative, elevates the tone and standard of life. The second, revealing the influence of surrounding circumstances upon character, leads to the most important practical reforms.[1] Each school has thus proved in some sense at once the corrective and the complement of the other. Each when pushed to its extreme results, produces evils which lead to the reappearance of its rival.

Having now considered at some length the nature and

---

while the beautiful and reverend philosophy of Plato had in his own Academy degenerated into a scepticism which did not spare morality itself, the system of Epicurus remained without change; his disciples continued for ages to show personal honour to his memory in a manner which may seem unaccountable among those who were taught to measure propriety by a calculation of palpable and outward usefulness.'—*Dissertation on Ethical Philosophy*, p. 85, ed. 1836. See, too, Tennemann (*Manuel de la Philosophie*, ed. Cousin, tome i. p. 211).

[1] Thus e.g. the magnificent chapters of Helvétius on the moral effects of despotism, form one of the best modern contributions to political ethics. We have a curious illustration of the emphasis with which this school dwells on the moral importance of institutions in a memoir of M. De Tracy, *On the best Plan of National Education*, which appeared first towards the close of the French Revolution, and was reprinted during the Restoration. The author, who was one of the most distinguished of the disciples of Condillac, argued that the most efficient of all ways of educating a people is, the establishment of a good system of police, for the constant association of the ideas of crime and punishment in the minds of the masses is the one effectual method of creating moral habits, which will continue to act when the fear of punishment is removed.

tendencies of the theories according to which men test and
classify their moral feelings, we may pass to an examination
of the process according to which these feelings are developed,
or, in other words, of the causes that lead societies to elevate
their moral standard and determine their preference of some
particular kinds of virtue. The observations I have to offer
on this subject will be of a somewhat miscellaneous character,
but they will all, I trust, tend to show the nature of the
changes that constitute moral history, and to furnish us with
some general principles which may be applied in detail in the
succeeding chapters.

It is sufficiently evident, that, in proportion to the high
organisation of society, the amiable and the social virtues
will be cultivated at the expense of the heroic and the ascetic.
A courageous endurance of suffering is probably the first
form of human virtue, the one conspicuous instance in savage
life of a course of conduct opposed to natural impulses, and
pursued through a belief that it is higher or nobler than the
opposite. In a disturbed, disorganised, and warlike society,
acts of great courage and great endurance are very frequent,
and determine to a very large extent the course of events;
but in proportion to the organisation of communities the
occasions for their display, and their influence when displayed,
are alike restricted. Besides this the tastes and habits of
civilisation, the innumerable inventions designed to promote
comfort and diminish pain, set the current of society in a
direction altogether different from heroism, and somewhat
emasculate, though they refine and soften, the character.
Asceticism again—including under this term, not merely the
monastic system, but also all efforts to withdraw from the
world in order to cultivate a high degree of sanctity—belongs
naturally to a society which is somewhat rude, and in which
isolation is frequent and easy. When men become united in
very close bonds of co-operation, when industrial enterprise
becomes very ardent, and the prevailing impulse is strongly

towards material wealth and luxurious enjoyments, virtue is regarded chiefly or solely in the light of the interests of society, and this tendency is still further strengthened by the educational influence of legislation, which imprints moral distinctions very deeply on the mind, but at the same time accustoms men to measure them solely by an external and utilitarian standard.[1] The first table of the law gives way to the second. Good is not loved for itself, but as the means to an end. All that virtue which is required to form upright and benevolent men is in the highest degree useful to society, but the qualities which constitute a saintly or spiritual character as distinguished from one that is simply moral and amiable, have not the same direct, uniform and manifest tendency to the promotion of happiness, and they are accordingly little valued.[2] In savage life the animal

---

[1] An important intellectual revolution is at present taking place in England. The ascendency in literary and philosophical questions which belonged to the writers of books is manifestly passing in a very great degree to weekly and even daily papers, which have long been supreme in politics, and have begun within the last ten years systematically to treat ethical and philosophical questions. From their immense circulation, their incontestable ability and the power they possess of continually reiterating their distinctive doctrines, from the impatience, too, of long and elaborate writings, which newspapers generate in the public, it has come to pass that these periodicals exercise probably a greater influence than any other productions of the day, in forming the ways of thinking of ordinary educated Englishmen. The many consequences, good and evil, of this change it will be the duty of future literary historians to trace, but there is one which is, I think, much felt in the sphere of ethics. An important effect of these journals has been to evoke a large amount of literary talent in the lawyer class. Men whose professional duties would render it impossible for them to write long books, are quite capable of treating philosophical subjects in the form of short essays, and have in fact become conspicuous in these periodicals. There has seldom, I think, before, been a time when lawyers occupied such an important literary position as at present, or when legal ways of thinking had so great an influence over English philosophy; and this fact has been eminently favourable to the progress of utilitarianism.

[2] There are some good remarks on this point in the very striking chapter on the present condition of Christianity in Wilberforce's *Practical View*.

nature being supreme, these higher qualities are unknown
In a very elaborate material civilisation the prevailing atmosphere is not favourable either to their production or their
appreciation. Their place has usually been in an intermediate stage.

On the other hand, there are certain virtues that are the
natural product of a cultivated society. Independently of
all local and special circumstances, the transition of men
from a barbarous or semi-civilised to a highly organised state
necessarily brings with it the destruction or abridgment of
the legitimate sphere of revenge, by transferring the office of
punishment from the wronged person to a passionless tribunal
appointed by society; [1] a growing substitution of pacific for
warlike occupations, the introduction of refined and intellectual tastes which gradually displace amusements that
derive their zest from their barbarity, the rapid multiplication of ties of connection between all classes and nations,
and also the strengthening of the imagination by intellectual
culture. This last faculty, considered as the power of realisation, forms the chief tie between our moral and intellectual
natures. In order to pity suffering we must realise it, and
the intensity of our compassion is usually proportioned to
the vividness of our realisation. [2] The most frightful catastrophe in South America, an earthquake, a shipwreck, or a
battle, will elicit less compassion than the death of a single
individual who has been brought prominently before our eyes.
To this cause must be chiefly ascribed the extraordinary
measure of compassion usually bestowed upon a conspicuous

---

[1] See Reid's *Essays on the Active
Powers*, iii. 4.

[2] I say usually proportioned,
because it is, I believe, possible
for men to realise intensely suffering, and to derive pleasure from
that very fact. This is especially
the case with vindictive cruelty,
but it is not, I think, altogether
confined to that sphere. This question we shall have occasion to
examine when discussing the gladiatorial shows. Most cruelty,
however, springs from callousness,
which is simply dulness of imagination.

condemned criminal, the affection and enthusiasm that centre upon sovereigns, and many of the glaring inconsistencies of our historical judgments. The recollection of some isolated act of magnanimity displayed by Alexander or Cæsar moves us more than the thought of the 30,000 Thebans whom the Macedonian sold as slaves, of the 2,000 prisoners he crucified at Tyre, of the 1,100,000 men on whose corpses the Roman rose to fame. Wrapt in the pale winding-sheet of general terms the greatest tragedies of history evoke no vivid images in our minds, and it is only by a great effort of genius that an historian can galvanise them into life. The irritation displayed by the captive of St. Helena in his bickerings with his gaoler affects most men more than the thought of the nameless thousands whom his insatiable egotism had hurried to the grave. Such is the frailty of our nature that we are more moved by the tears of some captive princess, by some trifling biographical incident that has floated down the stream of history, than by the sorrows of all the countless multitudes who perished beneath the sword of a Tamerlane, a Bajazet, or a Zenghis Khan.

If our benevolent feelings are thus the slaves of our imaginations, if an act of realisation is a necessary antecedent and condition of compassion, it is obvious that any influence that augments the range and power of this realising faculty is favourable to the amiable virtues, and it is equally evident that education has in the highest degree this effect. To an uneducated man all classes, nations, modes of thought and existence foreign to his own are unrealised, while every increase of knowledge brings with it an increase of insight, and therefore of sympathy. But the addition to his knowledge is the smallest part of this change. The realising faculty is itself intensified. Every book he reads, every intellectual exercise in which he engages, accustoms him to rise above the objects immediately present to his senses, to extend his realisations into new spheres, and reproduce in his imagination

the thoughts, feelings, and characters of others, with a vividness inconceivable to the savage.   Hence, in a great degree,
the tact with which a refined mind learns to discriminate
and adapt itself to the most delicate shades of feeling, and
hence too the sensitive humanity with which, in proportion
to their civilisation, men realise and recoil from cruelty.

We have here, however, an important distinction to
draw.   Under the name of cruelty are comprised two kinds
of vice, altogether different in their causes and in most of
their consequences.   There is the cruelty which springs from
callousness and brutality, and there is the cruelty of vindictiveness.   The first belongs chiefly to hard, dull, and somewhat lethargic characters, it appears most frequently in
strong and conquering nations and in temperate climates,
and it is due in a very great degree to defective realisation.
The second is rather a feminine attribute, it is usually displayed in oppressed and suffering communities, in passionate
natures, and in hot climates.   Great vindictiveness is often
united with great tenderness, and great callousness with
great magnanimity, but a vindictive nature is rarely magnanimous, and a brutal nature is still more rarely tender.   The
ancient Romans exhibited a remarkable combination of great
callousness and great magnanimity, while by a curious
contrast the modern Italian character verges manifestly
towards the opposite combination.   Both forms of cruelty
are, if I mistake not, diminished with advancing civilisation,
but by different causes and in different degrees.   Callous
cruelty disappears before the sensitiveness of a cultivated
imagination.   Vindictive cruelty is diminished by the substitution of a penal system for private revenge.

The same intellectual culture that facilitates the realisation of suffering, and therefore produces compassion, facilitates also the realisation of character and opinions, and
therefore produces charity.   The great majority of uncharit-
able judgments in the world may be traced to a deficiency of

imagination. The chief cause of sectarian animosity, is the incapacity of most men to conceive hostile systems in the light in which they appear to their adherents, and to enter into the enthusiasm they inspire. The acquisition of this power of intellectual sympathy is a common accompaniment of a large and cultivated mind, and wherever it exists, it assuages the rancour of controversy. The severity of our judgment of criminals is also often excessive, because the imagination finds it more easy to realise an action than a state of mind. Any one can conceive a fit of drunkenness or a deed of violence, but few persons who are by nature very sober or very calm can conceive the natural disposition that predisposes to it. A good man brought up among all the associations of virtue reads of some horrible crime, his imagination exhausts itself in depicting its circumstances, and he then estimates the guilt of the criminal, by asking himself, 'How guilty should *I* be, were I to perpetrate such an act?' To realise with any adequacy the force of a passion we have never experienced, to conceive a type of character radically different from our own, above all, to form any just appreciation of the lawlessness and obtuseness of moral temperament, inevitably generated by a vicious education, requires a power of imagination which is among the rarest of human endowments. Even in judging our own conduct, this feebleness of imagination is sometimes shown, and an old man recalling the foolish actions, but having lost the power of realising the feelings, of his youth, may be very unjust to his own past. That which makes it so difficult for a man of strong vicious passions to unbosom himself to a naturally virtuous man, is not so much the virtue as the ignorance of the latter. It is the conviction that he cannot possibly understand the force of a passion he has never felt. That which alone renders tolerable to the mind the thought of judgment by an all-pure Being, is the union of the attribute of omniscience with that of purity, for perfect knowledge implies a perfect power of realisation. The further our analysis extends, and the more our realising faculties are cultivated, the more sensible we become of the influence of circumstances both upon character and upon opinions, and of the exaggerations of our first estimates of moral inequalities. Strong antipathies are thus gradually softened down. Men gain much in charity, but they lose something in zeal.

We may push, I think, this vein of thought one step farther. Our imagination, which governs our affections, has in its earlier and feebler stages little power of grasping ideas, except in a personified and concrete form, and the power of rising to abstractions is one of the best measures of intellectual progress. The beginning of writing is the hieroglyphic or symbolical picture; the beginning of worship is fetishism or idolatry; the beginning of eloquence is pictorial, sensuous, and metaphorical; the beginning of philosophy is the myth. The imagination in its first stages concentrates itself on individuals; gradually by an effort of abstraction it rises to an institution or well-defined organisation; it is only at a very advanced stage that it can grasp a moral and intellectual principle. Loyalty, patriotism, and attachment to a cosmopolitan cause are therefore three forms of moral enthusiasm respectively appropriate to three successive stages of mental progress, and they have, I think, a certain analogy to idolatrous worship, church feeling, and moral culture, which are the central ideas of three stages of religious history.

The reader will readily understand that generalisations of this kind can pretend to nothing more than an approximate truth. Our knowledge of the laws of moral progress is like that of the laws of climate. We lay down general rules about the temperature to be expected as we approach or recede from the equator, and experience shows that they are substantially correct; but yet an elevated plain, or a chain of mountains, or the neighbourhood of the sea, will often in some degree derange our calculations. So, too, in the history of moral changes, innumerable special agencies, such as religious or political institutions, geographical conditions, traditions, antipathies, and affinities, exercise a certain retarding, accelerating, or deflecting influence, and somewhat modify the normal progress. The proposition for which I am contending is simply that there is such a thing as a natural history of morals, a defined and regular order, in which our moral feelings are unfolded ; or, in other words, that there are certain groups of virtues which spring spontaneously out of the circumstances and mental conditions of an uncivilised people, and that there are others which are the normal and appropriate products of civilisation. The virtues of uncivilised men are recognised as virtues by civilised men, but they are neither exhibited in the same perfection, nor given the same position in the scale of duties. Of these moral changes none are more obvious than the gradual decadence of heroism both active and passive, the increase of compassion and of charity, and the transition from the enthusiasm of loyalty to those of patriotism and liberty.

Another form of virtue which usually increases with civilisation is veracity, a term which must be regarded as including something more than the simple avoidance of direct falsehood. In the ordinary intercourse of life it is readily understood that a man is offending against truth, not only when he utters a deliberate falsehood, but also when in his statement of a case he suppresses or endeavours to conceal essential facts, or makes positive assertions without having conscientiously verified their grounds. The earliest form in which the duty of veracity is enforced is probably the observance of vows, which occupy a position of much prominence in youthful religions. With the subsequent progress of civilisation, we find the successive inculcation of three forms of veracity, which may be termed respectively industrial, political, and philosophical. By the first I understand that

11

accuracy of statement or fidelity to engagements which is commonly meant when we speak of a truthful man.  Though in some cases sustained by the strong sense of honour which accompanies a military spirit, this form of veracity is usually the special virtue of an industrial nation, for although industrial enterprise affords great temptations to deception, mutual confidence, and therefore strict truthfulness, are in these occupations so transcendently important that they acquire in the minds of men a value they had never before possessed. Veracity becomes the first virtue in the moral type, and no character is regarded with any kind of approbation in which it is wanting.  It is made more than any other the test distinguishing a good from a bad man.  We accordingly find that even where the impositions of trade are very numerous, the supreme excellence of veracity is cordially admitted in theory, and it is one of the first virtues that every man aspiring to moral excellence endeavours to cultivate.  This constitutes probably the chief moral superiority of nations pervaded by a strong industrial spirit over nations like the Italians, the Spaniards, or the Irish, among whom that spirit is wanting.  The usual characteristic of the latter nations is a certain laxity or instability of character, a proneness to exaggeration, a want of truthfulness in little things, an infidelity to engagements from which an Englishman, educated in the habits of industrial life, readily infers a complete absence of moral principle.  But a larger philosophy and a deeper experience dispel his error.  He finds that where the industrial spirit has not penetrated, truthfulness rarely occupies in the popular mind the same prominent position in the catalogue of virtues.  It is not reckoned among the fundamentals of morality, and it is possible and even common to find in these nations—what would be scarcely possible in an industrial society—men who are habitually dishonest and untruthful in small things, and whose lives are nevertheless influenced by a deep religious feeling, and adorned by the consistent practice of some of the most difficult and most painful virtues. Trust in Providence, content and resignation in extreme poverty and suffering, the most genuine amiability and the most sincere readiness to assist their brethren, an adherence to their religious opinions which no persecutions and no bribes can shake, a capacity for heroic, transcendent, and prolonged self-sacrifice, may be found in some nations in men who are habitual liars and habitual cheats.

The promotion of industrial veracity is probably the single form in which the growth of manufactures exercises a favourable influence upon morals. It is possible, however, for this virtue to exist in great perfection without any corresponding growth of political veracity, or in other words, of that spirit of impartiality which in matters of controversy desires that all opinions, arguments, and facts should be fully and fairly stated. This habit of what is commonly termed 'fair play' is especially the characteristic of free communities, and it is pre-eminently fostered by political life. The practice of debate creates a sense of the injustice of suppressing one side of a case, which gradually extends through all forms of intellectual life, and becomes an essential element in the national character. But beyond all this there is a still higher form of intellectual virtue. By enlarged intellectual culture, especially by philosophic studies, men come at last to pursue truth for its own sake, to esteem it a duty to emancipate themselves from party spirit, prejudices, and passion, and through love of truth to cultivate a judicial spirit in controversy. They aspire to the intellect not of a sectarian but of a philosopher, to the intellect not of a partisan but of a statesman.

Of these three forms of a truthful spirit the two last may be said to belong exclusively to a highly civilised society. The last especially can hardly be attained by any but a cultivated mind, and is one of the latest flowers of virtue that bloom in the human heart. The growth, however, both of political and philosophical veracity has been unnaturally re-tarded by the opposition of theologians, who made it during many centuries a main object of their policy to suppress all writings that were opposed to their views, and who, when this power had escaped their grasp, proceeded to discourage in every way impartiality of mind and judgment, and to associate it with the notion of sin.

To the observations I have already made concerning the moral effects of industrial life, I shall at present add but two. The first is that an industrial spirit creates two wholly different types of character—a thrifty character and a specu-lating character. Both types grow out of a strong sense of the value and a strong desire for the attainment of material comforts, but they are profoundly different both in their virtues and their vices. The chief characteristic of the one type is caution, that of the other enterprise. Thriftiness is one of the best regulators of life. It produces order, sobriety, moderation, self-restraint, patient industry, and all that cast of virtues which is designated by the term respectability ; but it has also a tendency to form contracted and ungenerous natures, incapable of enthusiasm or lively sympathy. The speculating character, on the other hand, is restless, fiery, and uncertain, very liable to fall into great and conspicuous vices, impatient of routine, but by no means unfavourable to strong feelings, to great generosity or resolution. Which of these two forms the industrial spirit assumes depends upon local circumstances. Thriftiness flourishes chiefly among men placed outside the great stream of commerce, and in positions where wealth is only to be acquired by slow and steady in-dustry, while the speculating character is most common in the great centres of enterprise and of wealth.

In the next place, it may be remarked that industrial habits bring forethought into a new position in the moral type. In early stages of theological belief, men regarding every incident that happens to them as the result of a special divine decree, sometimes esteem it a test of faith and a form of duty to take no precautions for the future, but to leave questions of food and clothing to Providential interposition. On the other hand, in an industrial civilisation, prudent forethought is regarded not simply as lawful, but as a duty, and a duty of the very highest order. A good man of the industrial type deems it a duty not to marry till he has ensured the maintenance of a possible family; if he possesses children, he regulates his expenses not simply by the relation of his income to his immediate wants, but with a constant view to the education of his sons, to the portioning of his daughters, to the future necessities and careers of each member of his family. Constant forethought is the guiding principle of his whole life. No single circumstance is regarded as a better test of the civilisation of a people than the extent to which it is diffused among them. The old doctrine virtually disappears, and is interpreted to mean nothing more than that we should accept with resignation what no efforts and no forethought could avert.

This change is but one of several influences which, as civilisation advances, diminish the spirit of reverence among mankind. Reverence is one of those feelings which, in utilitarian systems, would occupy at best a very ambiguous position; for it is extremely questionable whether the great evils that have grown out of it in the form of religious superstition and political servitude have not made it a source of more unhappiness than happiness. Yet, however doubtful may be its position if estimated by its bearing on happiness and on progress, there are few persons who are not conscious that no character can attain a supreme degree of excellence in which a reverential spirit is wanting. Of all the forms of moral goodness it is that to which the epithet beautiful may be most emphatically applied. Yet the habits of advancing

civilisation are, if I mistake not, on the whole inimical to its
growth. For reverence grows out of a sense of constant
dependence. It is fostered by that condition of religious
thought in which men believe that each incident that befalls
them is directly and specially ordained, and when every
event is therefore fraught with a moral import. It is fostered
by that condition of scientific knowledge in which every portentous natural phenomenon is supposed to be the result of a
direct divine interposition, and awakens in consequence emotions of humility and awe. It is fostered in that stage of
political life when loyalty or reverence for the sovereign is
the dominating passion, when an aristocracy, branching forth
from the throne, spreads habits of deference and subordination through every village, when a revolutionary, a democratic,
and a sceptical spirit are alike unknown. Every great change,
either of belief or of circumstances, brings with it a change
of emotions. The self-assertion of liberty, the levelling of
democracy, the dissecting-knife of criticism, the economical
revolutions that reduce the relations of classes to simple con-
tracts, the agglomeration of population, and the facilities of
locomotion that sever so many ancient ties, are all incompatible with the type of virtue which existed before the power
of tradition was broken, and when the chastity of faith was
yet unstained. Benevolence, uprightness, enterprise, intellectual honesty, a love of freedom, and a hatred of superstition
are growing around us, but we look in vain for that most
beautiful character of the past, so distrustful of self, and so
trustful of others, so simple, so modest, and so devout, which
even when, Ixion-like, it bestowed its affections upon a cloud,
made its very illusions the source of some of the purest
virtues of our nature. In a few minds, the contemplation
of the sublime order of nature produces a reverential feeling,
but to the great majority of mankind it is an incontestable
though mournful fact, that the discovery of controlling and
unchanging law deprives phenomena of their moral signifi

cance, and nearly all the social and political spheres in which reverence was fostered have passed away. Its most beautiful displays are not in nations like the Americans or the modern French, who have thrown themselves most fully into the tendencies of the age, but rather in secluded regions like Styria or the Tyrol. Its artistic expression is found in no work of modern genius, but in the mediæval cathedral, which, mellowed but not impaired by time, still gazes on us in its deathless beauty through the centuries of the past. A superstitious age, like every other phase of human history, has its distinctive virtues, which must necessarily decline before a new stage of progress can be attained.

The virtues and vices growing out of the relation between the sexes are difficult to treat in general terms, both on account of the obvious delicacy of the subject, and also because their natural history is extremely obscured by special causes. In the moral evolutions we have as yet examined, the normal influences are most powerful, and the importance of deranging and modifying circumstances is altogether subsidiary. The expansion of the amiable virtues, the decline of heroism and loyalty, and the growth of industrial habits spring out of changes which necessarily take place under almost all forms of civilisation,[1] and the broad features of the movement are therefore in almost all nations substantially the same. But in the history of sensuality, special causes, such as slavery, religious doctrines, or laws affecting marriage, have been the most powerful agents. The immense changes effected in this field by the Christian religion I shall hereafter examine. In the present chapter I shall content myself with two or three very general remarks relating to the nature of the vice, and to the effect of different stages of civilisation upon its progress.

---

[1] The principal exception being where slavery, coexisting with advanced civilisation, retards or prevents the growth of industrial habits.

There are, I conceive, few greater fallacies than are involved in the method so popular among modern writers of judging the immorality of a nation by its statistics of illegitimate births. Independently of the obvious defect of this method in excluding simple prostitution from our comparison, it altogether neglects the fact that a large number of illegitimate births arise from causes totally different from the great violence of the passions. Such, for example, is the notion prevailing in many country districts of England, that the marriage ceremony has a retrospective virtue, cancelling previous immorality; and such too is the custom so general among some classes on the Continent of forming permanent connections without the sanction either of a legal or a religious ceremony. However deeply such facts may be reprehended and deplored, it would be obviously absurd to infer from them that the nations in which they are most prominent are most conspicuous for the uncontrolled violence of their sensual passions. In Sweden, which long ranked among the lowest in the moral scale, if measured by the number of illegitimate births, the chief cause appears to have been the difficulties with which legislators surrounded marriage.[1] Even in displays of actual and violent passion, there are distinctions to be drawn which statistics are wholly unable to reach. The coarse, cynical, and ostentatious sensuality which forms the most repulsive feature of the French character, the dreamy, languid, and æsthetical sensuality of the Spaniard or the Italian, the furtive and retiring sensuality of some northern nations, though all forms of the same vice, are widely different feelings, and exercise widely different effects upon the prevailing disposition.

In addition to the very important influence upon public morals which climate, I think, undoubtedly exercises in

[1] See Mr. Laing's *Travels in* to have had a similar effect in Sweden. A similar cause is said Bavaria.

stimulating or allaying the passions, it has a powerful indirect action upon the position, character, and tastes of women, by determining the prevalence of indoor or out-of-door life, and also the classes among whom the gift of beauty is diffused. In northern countries the prevailing cast of beauty depends rather on colour than on form. It consists chiefly of a freshness and delicacy of complexion which severe labour and constant exposure necessarily destroy, and which is therefore rarely found in the highest perfection among the very poor. But the southern type is essentially democratic. The fierce rays of the sun only mellow and mature its charms. Its most perfect examples may be found in the hovel as in the palace, and the effects of this diffusion of beauty may be traced both in the manners and the morals of the people.

It is probable that the observance of this form of virtue is naturally most strict in a rude and semi-civilised but not barbarous people, and that a very refined civilisation is not often favourable to its growth. Sensuality is the vice of young men and of old nations. A languid epicureanism is the normal condition of nations which have attained a high intellectual or social civilisation, but which, through political causes, have no adequate sphere for the exertion of their energies. The temptation arising from the great wealth of some, and from the feverish longing for luxury and exciting pleasures in others, which exists in all large towns, has been peculiarly fatal to female virtue, and the whole tendency of the public amusements of civilisation is in the same direction. The rude combats which form the chief enjoyments of barbarians produce cruelty. The dramatic and artistic tastes and the social habits of refined men produce sensuality. Education raises many poor women to a stage of refinement that makes them suitable companions for men of a higher rank, and not suitable for those of their own. Industrial pursuits have, indeed, a favourable influence in promoting habits of self-restraint, and especially in checking the licence of military life; but on the other hand, they greatly increase temptation by encouraging postponement of marriage, and in communities, even more than in individuals, moral inequalities are much more due to differences of temptation than to differences of self-restraint. In large bodies of men a considerable increase of temptation always brings with it an increase, though not necessarily a proportionate increase, of vice. Among the checks on excessive multiplication, the historical influence of voluntary continence has been, it must be feared, very small. Physical and moral evils have alone been decisive, and as these form the two opposite weights, we unhappily very frequently find that the diminution of the one has been followed by the increase of the other. The nearly universal custom of early marriages among the Irish peasantry has alone rendered possible that high standard of female chastity. that intense and jealous sensitiveness respecting female honour, for which, among many failings and some vices, the Irish poor have long been pre-eminent in Europe; but these very marriages are the most conspicuous proofs of the national improvidence, and one of the most fatal obstacles to industrial prosperity. Had the Irish peasants been less chaste, they would have been more prosperous. Had that fearful famine, which in the present century desolated the land, fallen upon a people who thought more of accumulating subsistence than of avoiding sin, multitudes might now be living who perished by literal starvation on the dreary hills of Limerick or Skibbereen.

The example of Ireland furnishes us, however, with a remarkable instance of the manner in which the influence of a moral feeling may act beyond the circumstances that gave it birth. There is no fact in Irish history more singular than the complete, and, I believe, unparalleled absence among the Irish priesthood of those moral scandals which in every continental country occasionally prove the danger of vows of celibacy. The unsuspected purity of the Irish priests in this respect is the more remarkable, because, the government of the country being Protestant, there is no special inquisitorial legislation to ensure it, because of the almost unbounded influence of the clergy over their parishioners, and also because if any just cause of suspicion existed, in the fierce sectarianism of Irish public opinion, it would assuredly be magnified. Considerations of climate are quite inadequate to explain this fact; but the chief cause is, I think, sufficiently obvious. The habit of marrying at the first development of the passions has produced among the Irish peasantry, from whom the priests for the most part spring, an extremely strong feeling of the iniquity of irregular sexual indulgence, which retains its power even over those who are bound to perpetual celibacy.

It will appear evident from the foregoing considerations that, while the essential nature of virtue and vice is unaltered, there is a perpetual, and in some branches an orderly and necessary change, as society advances, both in the proportionate value attached to different virtues in theory, and in the perfection in which they are realised in practice. It will appear too that, while there may be in societies such a thing as moral improvement, there is rarely or never, on a large scale, such a thing as unmixed improvement. We may gain more than we lose, but we always lose something. There are virtues which are continually dying away with advancing civilisation, and even the lowest stage possesses its distinctive excellence. There is no spectacle more piteous or more horrible to a good man than that of an oppressed nationality writhing in anguish beneath a tyrant's yoke; but there is no condition in which passionate, unquestioning self-sacrifice and heroic courage, and the true sentiment of fraternity are more grandly elicited, and it is probable that the triumph of liberty will in these forms not only lessen the moral performances, but even weaken the moral capacities of mankind. War is, no doubt, a fearful evil, but it is the seed-plot of magnanimous virtues, which in a pacific age must

wither and decay.  Even the gambling-table fosters among
its more skilful votaries a kind of moral nerve, a capacity for
bearing losses with calmness, and controlling the force of
the desires, which is scarcely exhibited in equal perfection in
any other sphere.

There is still so great a diversity of civilisation in
existing nations that traversing tracts of space is almost
like traversing tracts of time, for it brings us in contact with
living representatives of nearly every phase of past civilisation.  But these differences are rapidly disappearing before
the unparalleled diffusion and simplification of knowledge,
the still more amazing progress in means of locomotion, and
the political and military causes that are manifestly con-
verting Europe into a federation of vast centralised and
democratic States.  Even to those who believe that the
leading changes are on the whole beneficial, there is much
that is melancholy in this revolution.  Those small States
which will soon have disappeared from the map of Europe,
besides their vast superiority to most great empires in finan-
cial prosperity, in the material well-being of the inhabitants,
and in many cases in political liberty, pacific tastes, and
intellectual progress, form one of the chief refuges of that
spirit of content, repose, and retrospective reverence which
is pre-eminently wanting in modern civilisation, and their
security is in every age one of the least equivocal measures
of international morality.  The monastic system, however
pernicious when enlarged to excess, has undoubtedly contributed to the happiness of the world, by supplying an asylum
especially suited to a certain type of character; and that
vindictive and short-sighted revolution which is extirpating
it from Europe is destroying one of the best correctives of the
excessive industrialism of our age.  It is for the advantage of
a nation that it should attain the most advanced existing
type of progress, but it is extremely questionable whether it
is for the advantage of the community at large that all nations

should attain the same type, even when it is the most advanced. The influence of very various circumstances is absolutely necessary to perfect moral development. Hence, one of the great political advantages of class representation, which brings within the range of politics a far greater variety both of capacities and moral qualities than can be exhibited when one class has an exclusive or overwhelmingly preponderating influence, and also of heterogeneous empires, in which different degrees of civilisation produce different kinds of excellence which react upon and complete one another. In the rude work of India and Australia a type of character is formed which England could ill afford to lose.

The remarks I have now made will be sufficient, I hope, to throw some light upon those great questions concerning the relations of intellectual and moral progress which have of late years attracted so large an amount of attention. It has been contended that the historian of human progress should concentrate his attention exclusively on the intellectual elements; for there is no such thing as moral history, morals being essentially stationary, and the rudest barbarians being in this respect as far advanced as ourselves. In opposition to this view, I have maintained that while what may be termed the primal elements of morals are unaltered, there is a perpetual change in the standard which is exacted, and also in the relative value attached to particular virtues, and that these changes constitute one of the most important branches of general history. It has been contended by other writers that, although such changes do take place, and although they play an extremely great part in the world, they must be looked upon as the result of intellectual causes, changes in knowledge producing changes in morals. In this view, as we have seen, there is some truth, but it can only, I think, be accepted with great qualification. It is one of the plainest of facts that neither the individuals nor the ages most distinguished for intellectual achievements have been most distinguished for moral excellence, and that a high intellectual and material civilisation has often coexisted with much depravity. In some respects the conditions of intellectual growth are not favourable to moral growth. The agglomeration of men in great cities—which are always the centres of progress and enlightenment—is one of the most important causes of material and intellectual advance : but great towns are the peculiar seed-plots of vice, and it is extremely questionable whether they produce any special and equivalent efflorescence of virtue, for even the social virtues are probably more cultivated in small populations, where men live in more intimate relations.    Many of the most splendid outbursts of moral enthusiasm may be traced to an overwhelming force of conviction rarely found in very culti-vated minds, which are keenly sensible to possibilities of error, conflicting arguments, and qualifying circumstances. Civilisation has on the whole been more successful in repress-ing crime than in repressing vice.    It is very favourable to the gentler, charitable, and social virtues, and, where slavery does not exist, to the industrial virtues, and it is the especial nurse of the intellectual virtues ; but it is in general not equally favourable to the production of self-sacrifice, enthu-siasm, reverence, or chastity.

The moral changes, however, which are effected by civili-sation may ultimately be ascribed chiefly to intellectual causes, for these lie at the root of the whole structure of civilised life.    Sometimes, as we have seen, intellectual causes act directly, but more frequently they have only an indirect in-fluence, producing habits of life which in their turn produce new conceptions of duty.    The morals of men are more go-verned by their pursuits than by their opinions.    A type of virtue is first formed by circumstances, and men afterwards make it the model upon which their theories are framed. Thus geographical or other circumstances, that make one nation military and another industrial, will produce in each a realised type of excellence, and corresponding conceptions about the relative importance of different virtues widely different from those which are produced in the other, and this may be the case although the amount of knowledge in the two communities is substantially equal.

Having discussed these questions as fully as the nature of my subject requires, I will conclude this chapter by noticing a few very prevalent errors in the moral judgments of history, and will also endeavour to elucidate some important consequences that may be deduced from the nature of moral types.

It is probable that the moral standard of most men is much lower in political judgments than in private matters in which their own interests are concerned. There is nothing more common than for men who in private life are models of the most scrupulous integrity to justify or excuse the most flagrant acts of political dishonesty and violence; and we should be altogether mistaken if we argued rigidly from such approvals to the general moral sentiments of those who utter them. Not unfrequently too, by a curious moral paradox, political crimes are closely connected with national virtues. A people who are submissive, gentle, and loyal, fall by reason of these very qualities under a despotic government; but this uncontrolled power has never failed to exercise a most pernicious influence on rulers, and their numerous acts of rapacity and aggression being attributed in history to the nation they represent, the national character is wholly misinterpreted.[1] There are also particular kinds both of virtue and of vice which appear prominently before the world, while others of at least equal influence almost escape the notice of history. Thus, for example, the sectarian animosities, the horrible persecutions, the blind hatred of progress, the ungenerous support of every galling disqualification and restraint, the intense class selfishness, the obstinately protracted defence of intellec-

---

[1] This has been, I think, especially the case with the Austrians.

tual and political superstition, the childish but whimsically ferocious quarrels about minute dogmatic distinctions, or dresses,
or candlesticks, which constitute together the main features of
ecclesiastical history, might naturally, though very unjustly,
lead men to place the ecclesiastical type in almost the lowest
rank, both intellectually and morally. These are, in fact, the
displays of ecclesiastical influence which stand in bold relief
in the pages of history. The civilising and moralising influence of the clergyman in his parish, the simple, unostenta-
tious, unselfish zeal with which he educates the ignorant,
guides the erring, comforts the sorrowing, braves the horrors
of pestilence, and sheds a hallowing influence over the dying
hour, the countless ways in which, in his little sphere, he
allays evil passions, and softens manners, and elevates and
purifies those around him—all these things, though very evident to the detailed observer, do not stand out in the same
vivid prominence in historical records, and are continually
forgotten by historians. It is always hazardous to argue
from the character of a corporation to the character of the
members who compose it, but in no other case is this method
of judgment so fallacious as in the history of ecclesiastics, for
there is no other class whose distinctive excellences are less
apparent, and whose mental and moral defects are more
glaringly conspicuous in corporate action. In different nations,
again, the motives of virtue are widely different, and serious
misconceptions arise from the application to one nation of the
measure of another. Thus the chief national virtues of the
French people result from an intense power of sympathy,
which is also the foundation of some of their most beautiful
intellectual qualities, of their social habits, and of their unrivalled influence in Europe. No other nation has so habitual and vivid a sympathy with great struggles for freedom
beyond its border. No other literature exhibits so expansive
and œcumenical a genius, or expounds so skilfully, or appre-
ciates so generously, foreign ideas. In hardly any other land

would a disinterested war for the support of a suffering nationality find so large an amount of support. The national crimes of France are many and grievous, but much will be forgiven her because she loved much. The Anglo-Saxon nations, on the other hand, though sometimes roused to strong but transient enthusiasm, are habitually singularly narrow, unappreciative, and unsympathetic. The great source of their national virtue is the sense of duty, the power of pursuing a course which they believe to be right, independently of all considerations of sympathy or favour, of enthusiasm or success.     Other nations have far surpassed them in many qualities that are beautiful, and in some qualities that are great.    It is the merit of the Anglo-Saxon race that beyond all others it has produced men of the stamp of a Washington or a Hampden ; men careless, indeed, for glory, but very careful of honour ; who made the supreme majesty of moral rectitude the guiding principle of their lives, who proved in the most trying circumstances that no allurements of ambition, and no storms of passion, could cause them to deviate one hair's breadth from the course they believed to be their duty. This was also a Roman characteristic—especially that of Marcus Aurelius.    The unweary, unostentatious, and inglorious crusade of England against slavery may probably be regarded as among the three or four perfectly virtuous pages comprised in the history of nations.

Although it cannot be said that any virtue is the negation of another, it is undoubtedly true that virtues are naturally grouped according to principles of affinity or congruity, which are essential to the unity of the type.    The heroical, the amiable, the industrial, the intellectual virtues form in this manner distinct groups ; and in some cases the development of one group is incompatible, not indeed with the existence, but with the prominence of others.    Content cannot be the leading virtue in a society animated by an intense industrial spirit, nor submission nor tolerance of injuries in a society formed upon a military type, nor intellectual virtues in a society where a believing spirit is made the essential of goodness, yet each of these conditions is the special sphere of some particular class of virtues. The distinctive beauty of a moral type depends not so much on the elements of which it is composed, as on the proportions in which those elements are combined. The characters of Socrates, of Cato, of Bayard, of Fénelon, and of St. Francis are all beautiful, but they differ generically, and not simply in degrees of excellence. To endeavour to impart to Cato the distinctive charm of St. Francis, or to St. Francis that of Cato, would be as absurd as to endeavour to unite in a single statue the beauties of the Apollo and the Laocoon, or in a single landscape the beauties of the twilight and of the meridian sun. Take away pride from the ancient Stoic or the modern Englishman, and you would have destroyed the basis of many of his noblest virtues, but humility was the very principle and root of the moral qualities of the monk. There is no quality virtuous in a woman that is not also virtuous in a man, yet that disposition or hierarchy of virtues which constitutes a perfect woman would be wholly unsuited for a perfect man. The moral is in this respect like the physical type. The beauty of man is not the beauty of woman, nor the beauty of the child as the beauty of the adult, nor the beauty of an Italian as the beauty of an Englishwoman. All types of character are not good, as all types of countenance are not beautiful; but there are many distinct casts of goodness, as there are many distinct casts of beauty.

This most important truth may be stated in a somewhat different form. Whenever a man is eminently deficient in any virtue, it, of course, follows that his character is imperfect, but it does not necessarily follow that he is not in other respects moral and virtuous. There is, however, usually some one virtue, which I may term rudimentary, which is brought forward so prominently before the world, as the first condition of moral excellence, that it may be safely inferred that a man who has absolutely neglected it is entirely indifferent to moral culture. Rudimentary virtues vary in different ages, nations, and classes. Thus, in the great republics of antiquity patriotism was rudimentary, for it was so assiduously cultivated, that it appeared at once the most obvious and the most essential of duties. Among ourselves much private virtue may co-exist with complete indifference to national interests. In the monastic period, and in a somewhat different form in the age of chivalry, a spirit of reverential obedience was rudimentary, and the basis of all moral progress ; but we may now frequently find a good man without it, his moral energies having been cultivated in other directions. Common truthfulness and honesty, as I have already said, are rudimentary virtues in industrial societies, but not in others. Chastity, in England at least, is a rudimentary female virtue, but scarcely a rudimentary virtue among men, and it has not been in all ages, and is not now in all countries, rudimentary among women. There is no more important task devolving upon a moral historian, than to discover in each period the rudimentary virtue, for it regulates in a great degree the position assigned to all others.

From the considerations I have urged, it will appear that there is considerable danger in proposing too absolutely a single character, however admirable, as the model to which all men must necessarily conform. A character may be perfect in its own kind, but no character can possibly embrace all types of perfection ; for, as we have seen, the perfection of a type depends not only upon the virtues that constitute it, but also upon the order and prominence assigned to them. All that can be expected in an ideal is, that it should be perfect of its own kind, and should exhibit the type most needed in its age, and most widely useful to mankind. The Christian type is the glorification of the amiable, as the Stoic type was that of the heroic qualities, and this is one of the reasons why Christianity is so much more fitted than Stoicism to preside over civilisation, for the more society is organised and civilised, the greater is the scope for the amiable, and the less for the heroic qualities.

The history of that moral intolerance which endeavours to reduce all characters to a single type has never, I think, been examined as it deserves, and I shall frequently have occasion to advert to it in the following pages. No one can have failed to observe how common it is for men to make their own tastes or excellences the measure of all goodness, pronouncing all that is broadly different from them to be imperfect or low, or of a secondary value. And this, which is usually attributed to vanity, is probably in most cases much more due to feebleness of imagination, to the difficulty most men have in conceiving in their minds an order of character fundamentally different from their own. A good man can usually sympathise much more with a very imperfect character of his own type than with a far more perfect one of a different type. To this cause, quite as much as to historical causes or occasional divergences of interest, may be traced the extreme difficulty of effecting cordial international friendships, especially in those cases when a difference of race coincides with the difference of nationality. Each nation has a distinct type of excellence, each esteems the virtues in which it excels, and in which its neighbours are often most deficient, incomparably the greatest. Each regards with especial antipathy the vices from which it is most free, and to which its neighbours may be most addicted. Hence arises a mingled feeling of contempt and dislike, from which the more enlightened minds are, indeed, soon emancipated, but which constitutes the popular sentiment.

The type of character of every individual depends partly upon innate temperament and partly upon external circumstances. A warlike, a refined, an industrial society each evokes and requires its specific qualities, and produces its appropriate type. If a man of a different type arise—if, for example, a man formed by nature to exhibit to the highest perfection the virtues of gentleness or meekness, be born in the midst of a fierce military society—he will find no suitable scope for action, he will jar with his age, and his type will be regarded with disfavour. And the effect of this opposition is not simply that he will not be appreciated as he deserves, he will also never succeed in developing his own distinctive virtues as they would have been developed under other circumstances. Everything will be against him — the force of education, the habits of society, the opinions of mankind, even his own sense of duty. All the highest models of excellence about him being formed on a different type, his very efforts to improve his being will dull the qualities in which nature intended him to excel. If, on the other hand, a man with naturally heroic qualities be born in a society which pre-eminently values heroism, he will not only be more appreciated, he will also, under the concurrence of favourable circumstances, carry his heroism to a far higher point than would otherwise have been possible. Hence changing circumstances produce changing types, and hence, too, the possibility of moral history and the necessity of uniting it with general history. Religions, considered as moral teachers, are realised and effective only when their moral teaching is in conformity with the tendency of their age. If any part of it is not so, that part will be either openly abandoned, or refined away, or tacitly neglected. Among the ancients, the co-existence of the Epicurean and Stoical schools, which offered to the world two entirely different archetypes of virtue, secured in a very remarkable manner the recognition of different kinds of excellence; for although each of these schools often attained a pre-eminence, neither ever succeeded in wholly destroying or discrediting the other.

Of the two elements that compose the moral condition of mankind, our generalised knowledge is almost restricted to one. We know much of the ways in which political, social, or intellectual causes act upon character, but scarcely anything of the laws that govern innate disposition, of the reasons and extent of the natural moral diversities of individuals or races. I think, however, that most persons who reflect upon the subject will conclude that the progress of medicine, revealing the physical causes of different moral predispositions, is likely to place a very large measure of knowledge on this point within our reach. Of all the great branches of human knowledge, medicine is that in which the accomplished results are most obviously imperfect and provisional, in which the field of unrealised possibilities is most extensive, and from which, if the human mind were directed to it, as it has been during the past century to locomotive and other industrial inventions, the most splendid results might be expected. Our almost absolute ignorance of the causes of some of the most fatal diseases, and the empirical nature of nearly all our best medical treatment, have been often recognised. The medicine of inhalation is still in its infancy, and yet it is by inhalation that Nature produces most of her diseases, and effects most of her cures. The medical power of electricity, which of all known agencies bears most resemblance to life, is almost unexplored. The discovery of anæsthetics has in our own day opened out a field of inestimable importance, and the proved possibility, under certain physical conditions, of governing by external suggestions the whole current of the feelings and emotions, may possibly contribute yet further to the alleviation of suffering, and perhaps to that euthanasia which Bacon proposed to physicians as an end of their art. But in the eyes both of the philanthropist and of the philosopher, the greatest of all results to be expected in this, or perhaps any other field, are, I conceive, to be looked for in the study of the relations between our physical and our moral natures. He who raises moral pathology to a science, expanding, systema-

tising, and applying many fragmentary observations that
have been already made, will probably take a place among
the master intellects of mankind.   The fastings and bleed-
ings of the mediæval monk, the medicines for allaying or
stimulating the sensual passions, the treatment of nervous
diseases, the moral influences of insanity and of castration, the
researches of phrenology, the moral changes that accompany
the successive stages of physical developments, the instances
of diseases which have altered, sometimes permanently, the
whole complexion of the character, and have acted through
the character upon all the intellectual judgments,[1] are
examples of the kind of facts with which such a science
would deal.   Mind and body are so closely connected that
even those who most earnestly protest against materialism
readily admit that each acts continually upon the other.
The sudden emotion that quickens the pulse, and blanches or
flushes the cheek, and the effect of fear in predisposing to an
epidemic, are familiar instances of the action of the mind
upon the body, and the more powerful and permanent influence of the body upon the disposition is attested by countless observations.   It is probable that this action extends to
all parts of our moral constitution, that every passion or
characteristic tendency has a physical predisposing cause, and
that if we were acquainted with these, we might treat by
medicine the many varieties of moral disease as systematically
as we now treat physical disease.  In addition to its incalculable
practical importance, such knowledge would have a great
philosophical value, throwing a new light upon the filiation
of our moral qualities, enabling us to treat exhaustively the
moral influence of climate, and withdrawing the great question of the influence of race from the impressions of isolated
observers to place it on the firm basis of experiment.   It

[1] See some remarkable instances of this in Cabanis, Rapports du Physique et du Moral de
l'Homme.

would thus form the complement to the labours of the historian.

Such discoveries are, however, perhaps far from attainment, and their discussion does not fall within the compass of this work. My present object is simply to trace the action of external circumstances upon morals, to examine what have been the moral types proposed as ideal in different ages, in what degree they have been realised in practice, and by what causes they have been modified, impaired, or destroyed.

# CHAPTER II.

## THE PAGAN EMPIRE.

ONE of the first facts that must strike a student who examines the ethical teaching of the ancient civilisations is how imperfectly that teaching was represented, and how feebly it was influenced by the popular creed. The moral ideals had at no time been sought in the actions of the gods, and long before the triumph of Christianity, polytheism had ceased to have any great influence upon the more cultivated intellects of mankind.

In Greece we may trace from the earliest time the footsteps of a religion of nature, wholly different from the legends of the mythology. The language in which the first Greek dramatists asserted the supreme authority and universal providence of Zeus was so emphatic, that the Christian Fathers commonly attributed it either to direct inspiration or to a knowledge of the Jewish writings, while later theologians of the school of Cudworth have argued from it in favour of the original monotheism of our race. The philosophers were always either contemptuous or hostile to the prevailing legends. Pythagoras is said to have declared that he had seen Hesiod tied to a brazen pillar in hell, and Homer hung upon a tree surrounded by serpents, on account of the fables they had invented about the gods.[1] Plato, for the same reason, banished the poets from his republic. Stilpo turned to

---

[1] Diog. Laërt. *Pythag.*

ridicule the whole system of sacrifices,[1] and was exiled from
Athens for denying that the Athene of Phidias was a goddess.[2] Xenophanes remarked that each nation attributed to
the gods its distinctive national type, the gods of the
Æthiopians being black, the gods of the Thracians fair and
blue-eyed.[3] Diagoras and Theodorus are said to have denied,
and Protagoras to have questioned the existence of the gods,[4]
while the Epicureans deemed them wholly indifferent to
human affairs, and the Pyrrhonists pronounced our faculties
absolutely incapable of attaining any sure knowledge, either
human or divine. The Cynic Antisthenes said that there were
many popular gods, but there was only one god of nature.[5]
The Stoics, reproducing an opinion which was supported by
Aristotle and attributed to Pythagoras,[6] believed in an all-
pervading soul of nature, but unlike some modern schools
which have adopted this view, they asserted in emphatic
language the doctrine of Providence, and the self-conscious-
ness of the Deity.

In the Roman republic and empire, a general scepticism
had likewise arisen among the philosophers as the first fruit
of intellectual development, and the educated classes were
speedily divided between avowed or virtual atheists, like the
Epicureans,[7] and pure theists, like the Stoics and the Platonists. The first, represented by such writers as Lucretius
and Petronius, regarded the gods simply as the creations of
fear, denied every form of Providence, attributed the world

---

[1] Plutarch, *De Profectibus in Virt.*

[2] Diog. Laërt. *Stilpo.*

[3] Clem. Alexand. *Strom.* vii.

[4] Cicero, *De Nat. Deorum,* i. 1.

[5] Lactant. *Inst. Div.* i. 5.

[6] 'Pythagoras ita definivit quid esset Deus: Animus qui per uni-
versas mundi partes, omnemque na-
turam commeans atque diffusus,
ex quo omnia quæ nascuntur
animalia vitam capiunt.' — Ibid.

Lactantius in this chapter has collected several other philosophic
definitions of the Divinity. See
too Plutarch, *De Placit. Philos.*
Tertullian explains the stoical
theory by an ingenious illustration:
'Stoici enim volunt Deum sic per
materiem decucurrisse quomodo mel
per favos.'—Tert. *De Anima.*

[7] As Cicero says: 'Epicurus re
tollit, oratione relinquit, deos.'—
*De Nat. Deor.* i. 44.

to a concurrence of atoms, and life to spontaneous generation, and regarded it as the chief end of philosophy to banish as illusions of the imagination every form of religious belief. The others formed a more or less pantheistic conception of the Deity, asserted the existence of a Providence,[1] but treated with great contempt the prevailing legends which they endeavoured in various ways to explain. The first systematic theory of explanation appears to have been that of the Sicilian Euhemerus, whose work was translated by Ennius. He pretended that the gods were originally kings, whose history and genealogies he professed to trace, and who after death had been deified by mankind.[2] Another attempt, which in the first period of Roman scepticism was more generally popular, was that of some of the Stoics, who regarded the gods as personifications of the different attributes of the Deity, or of different forces of nature. Thus Neptune was the sea, Pluto was fire, Hercules represented the strength of God, Minerva His wisdom, Ceres His fertilising energy.[3] More than a hundred years before the Empire, Varro had declared that 'the soul of the world is God, and that its parts are true divinities.'[4] Virgil and Manilius described, in lines of singular beauty, that universal spirit, the principle of all life, the efficient cause of all motion, which

---

[1] Sometimes, however, they restricted its operation to the great events of life. As an interlocutor in Cicero says : 'Magna dii curant, parva negligunt.'—Cic. *De Natur. Deor.* ii. 66. Justin Martyr notices (*Trypho,* i.) that some philosophers maintained that God cared for the universal or species, but not for the individual. Seneca maintains that the Divinity has determined all things by an inexorable law of destiny, which He has decreed, but which He Himself obeys. (*De Provident.* v.)

[2] See on this theory Cicero, *De Natur. Deor.* i. 42 ; Lactantius, *Inst. Div.* i. 11.

[3] Diog. Laërt. *Vit. Zeno.* St. Aug. *De Civ. Dei,* iv. 11. Maximus of Tyre, *Dissert.* x. (in some editions xxix.) § 8. Seneca, *De Beneficiis,* iv. 7–8. Cic. *De Natur. Deor.* i. 15. Cicero has devoted the first two books of this work to the stoical theology. A full review of the allegorical and mythical interpretations of paganism is given by Eusebius, *Evang. Præpar.* lib. iii.

[4] St. Aug. *De Civ.* vii. 5.

permeates and animates the globe. Pliny said that 'the world and sky, in whose embrace all things are enclosed, must be deemed a god, eternal, immense, never begotten, and never to perish. To seek things beyond this is of no profit to man, and they transcend the limits of his faculties.'[1] Cicero had adopted the higher Platonic conception of the Deity as mind freed from all taint of matter,[2] while Seneca celebrated in magnificent language ' Jupiter the guardian and ruler of the universe, the soul and spirit, the lord and master of this mundane sphere, . . . the cause of causes, upon whom all things hang. . . . Whose wisdom oversees the world that it may move uncontrolled in its course, . . . from whom all things proceed, by whose spirit we live, . . . who comprises all we see.'[3] Lucan, the great poet of stoicism, rose to a still higher strain, and to one which still more accurately expressed the sentiments of his school, when he described Jupiter as that majestic, all-pervasive spirit, whose throne is virtue and the universe.[4] Quintilian defended the subjugation of the world beneath the sceptre of a single man, on the ground that it was an image of the government of God. Other philosophers contented themselves with asserting the supreme authority of Jupiter Maximus, and reducing the other divinities to mere administrative and angelic functions, or, as the Platonists expressed it, to the position of dæmons. According to some of the Stoics, a final catastrophe would consume the universe, the resuscitated spirits of men and all these minor gods, and the whole creation being absorbed into the great parent spirit, God

---

Plin. *Hist. Nat.* ii. 1.

'Nec vero Deus ipse qui intelligitur a nobis, alio modo intelligi potest nisi mens soluta quædam et libera, segregata ab omni concretione mortali, omnia sentiens et movens, ipsæque prædita motu sempiterno.'—*Tusc. Quæst.* i. 27.

[3] Senec. *Quæst. Nat.* ii. 45.

[4] ' Estne Dei sedes, nisi terra et pontus et aër,

Et cœlum et virtus ? Superos quid quærimus ultra?

Jupiter est quodcumque vides, quodcumque moveris.'

*Pharsal.* ix. 578-80.

would be all in all. The very children and old women ridiculed Cerberus and the Furies[1] or treated them as mere
metaphors of conscience.[2] In the deism of Cicero the popular divinities were discarded, the oracles refuted and ridiculed,
the whole system of divination pronounced a political imposture, and the genesis of the miraculous traced to the exuberance of the imagination, and to certain diseases of the judgment.[3] Before the time of Constantine, numerous books
had been written against the oracles.[4] The greater number
of these had actually ceased, and the ablest writers justly
saw in this cessation an evidence of the declining credulity
of the people, and a proof that the oracles had been a fruit
of that credulity.[5] The Stoics, holding, as was their custom,
aloof from direct religious discussion, dissuaded their disciples from consulting them, on the ground that the gifts of
fortune were of no account, and that a good man should be
content with his conscience, making duty and not success the
object of his life.[6] Cato wondered that two augurs could

[1] 'Quæve anus tam excors in-
veniri potest, quæ illa, quæ quondam credebantur apud inferos por-
tenta, extimescat?'—Cic. De Nat.
Deor. ii. 2.
'Esse aliquos Manes et subterranea
  regna . . .
Nec pueri credunt nisi qui nondum
  ære lavantur.'
       Juv. Sat. ii. 149, 152.
See on this subject a good review
by the Abbé Freppel, Les Pères Apo-
stoliques, leçon viii.
[2] Cicero, De Leg. i. 14 ; Macrobius, In. Som. Scip. i. 10.
[3] See his works De Divinatione
and De Nat. Deorum, which form
a curious contrast to the religious
conservatism of the De Legibus,
which was written chiefly from a
political point of view.
[4] Eusebius, Præp. Evang. lib. iv.
[5] The oracles first gave their

answers in verse, but their bad
poetry was ridiculed, and they
gradually sank to prose, and at
last ceased. Plutarch defended the
inspiration of the bad poetry on the
ground that the inspiring spirit
availed itself of the natural faculties
of the priestess for the expression
of its infallible truths—a theory
which is still much in vogue among
Biblical critics, and is, I believe,
called dynamical inspiration. See
Fontenelle, Hist. des Oracles (1st
ed.), pp. 292–293.
[6] See the famous description of
Cato refusing to consult the oracle
of Jupiter Ammon in Lucan, Phars.
ix. ; and also Arrian, ii. 7. Seneca
beautifully says, ' Vis deos pro-
pitiare ? bonus esto. Satis illos
coluit quisquis imitatus est.'—Ep.
xcv.

meet with gravity.[1]    The Roman general Sertorius made the
forgery of auspicious omens a continual resource in warfare.[2]
The Roman wits made divination the favourite subject of
their ridicule.[3]    The denunciation which the early Greek
moralists launched against the popular ascription of immoral
deeds to the gods was echoed by a long series of later philosophers,[4] while Ovid made these fables the theme of his
mocking *Metamorphoses*, and in his most immoral poem proposed Jupiter as a model of vice.    With an irony not unlike that of Isaiah, Horace described the carpenter deliberat-
ing whether he should convert a shapeless log into a bench
or into a god.[5]    Cicero, Plutarch, Maximus of Tyre, and
Dion Chrysostom either denounced idolatry or defended the
use of images simply on the ground that they were signs
and symbols of the Deity,[6] well suited to aid the devotions

---

[1] Cicero, *De Divin.* ii. 24.

[2] Aulus Gellius, *Noct. Att.* xv. 22.

[3] See a long string of witticisms
collected by Legendre, *Traité de
l'Opinion, ou Mémoires pour servir
a l'Histoire de l'Esprit humain*
(Venise, 1735), tome i. pp. 386–387.

[4] See Cicero, *De Natura Deorum*;
Seneca, *De Brev. Vit.* c. xvi. ; Plin.
*Hist. Nat.* ii. 5 ; Plutarch, *De Su-
perstitione*.

[5] 'Olim truncus eram ficulnus,
inutile lignum,
Cum faber, incertus scamnum
faceretne Priapum,
Maluit esse Deum.'
    *Sat.* I. viii. 1–3.

[6] There is a very curious discussion on this subject, reported to
have taken place between Apollonius of Tyana and an Egyptian
priest. The former defended the
Greek fashion of worshipping the
Divinity under the form of the
human image, sculptured by
Phidias and Praxiteles, this being
the noblest form we can conceive,

and therefore the least inadequate
to the Divine perfections. The
latter defended the Egyptian custom of worshipping animals, because, as he said, it is blasphemous
to attempt to conceive an image of
the Deity, and the Egyptians therefore concentrate the imagination of
the worshipper on objects that are
plainly merely allegorical or symbolical, and do not pretend to offer
any such image (*Philos. Apoll. of
Tyana*, vi. 19). Pliny shortly says,
'Effigiem Dei formamque quærere
imbecillitatis humanæ reor' (*Hist.
Nat.* ii. 5). See too Max. Tyrius,
Diss. xxxviii. There was a legend
that Numa forbade all idols, and
that for 200 years they were unknown in Rome (Plutarch, *Life of
Numa*). Dion Chrysostom said
that the Gods need no statues or
sacrifices, but that by these means
we attest our devotion to them
(*Orat.* xxxi.) On the vanity of rich
idols, see Plutarch, *De Superstitione*; Seneca, *Ep.* xxxi.

of the ignorant. Seneca[1] and the whole school cf Pythagoras objected to the sacrifices.

These examples will be sufficient to show how widely the philosophic classes in Rome were removed from the professed religion of the State, and how necessary it is to seek elsewhere the sources of their moral life. But the opinions of learned men never reflect faithfully those of the vulgar, and the chasm between the two classes was even wider than at present before the dawn of Christianity and the invention of printing. The atheistic enthusiasm of Lucretius and the sceptical enthusiasm of some of the disciples of Carneades were isolated phenomena, and the great majority of the ancient philosophers, while speculating with the utmost freedom in private, or in writings that were read by the few, countenanced, practised, and even defended the religious rites that they despised. It was believed that many different paths adapted to different nations and grades of knowledge converge to the same Divinity, and that the most erroneous religion is good if it forms good dispositions and inspires virtuous actions. The oracle of Delphi had said that the best religion is that of a man's own city. Polybius and Dionysius of Halicarnassus, who regarded all religions simply as political agencies, dilated in rapturous terms upon the devotion of the Romans and the comparative purity of their creed.[2] Varro openly professed the belief that there are religious truths which it is expedient that the people should not know, and falsehoods which they should believe to be true.[3] The Academic Cicero and the Epicurean Cæsar were both high officers of religion. The Stoics taught that every man should duly perform the religious ceremonies of his country.[4]

But the Roman religion, even in its best days, though an

---

[1] Lact. *Inst. Div.* vi. 25.  [3] St. Aug. *De Civ. Dei*, iv. 31.
[2] Dion. Halic. ii.; Polyb. vi. 56.  [4] Epictetus, *Enchir.* xxxix.

admirable system of moral discipline, was never an independent source of moral enthusiasm. It was the creature of the State, and derived its inspiration from political feeling. The Roman gods were not, like those of the Greeks, the creations of an unbridled and irreverent fancy, nor, like those of the Egyptians, representations of the forces of nature; they were for the most part simple allegories, frigid personifications of different virtues, or presiding spirits imagined for the protection of different departments of industry. The religion established the sanctity of an oath, it gave a kind of official consecration to certain virtues, and commemorated special instances in which they had been displayed; its local character strengthened patriotic feeling, its worship of the dead fostered a vague belief in the immortality of the soul,[1] it sustained the supremacy of the father in the family, surrounded marriage with many imposing solemnities, and created simple and reverent characters profoundly submissive to an over-ruling Providence and scrupulously observant of sacred rites. But with all this it was purely selfish. It was simply a method of obtaining prosperity, averting calamity, and reading the future. Ancient Rome produced many heroes, but no saint. Its self-sacrifice was patriotic, not religious. Its religion was neither an independent teacher nor a source of inspiration, although its rites mingled with and strengthened some of the best habits of the people.

But these habits, and the religious reverence with which they were connected, soon disappeared amid the immorality and decomposition that marked the closing years of the Republic and the dawn of the Empire. The stern simplicity of life, which the censors had so zealously and often so tyrannically

---

[1] Cicero, speaking of the worship of deified men, says, 'indicat omnium quidem animos immortales esse, sed fortium bonorumque divinos.' — De Leg. ii. 11. The Roman worship of the dead, which was the centre of the domestic religion, has been recently investigated with much ability by M. Coulanges (La Cité antique)

enforced,[1] was exchanged for a luxury which first appeared after the return of the army of Manlius from Asia,[2] increased to immense proportions after the almost simultaneous conquests of Carthage, Corinth, and Macedonia,[3] received an additional stimulus from the example of Antony,[4] and at last, under the Empire, rose to excesses which the wildest Oriental orgies have never surpassed.[5] The complete subversion of the social and political system of the Republic, the anarchy of civil war, the ever-increasing concourse of strangers, bringing with them new philosophies, customs, and gods, had dissolved or effaced all the old bonds of virtue. The simple juxtaposition of many forms of worship effected what could not have been effected by the most sceptical literature or the most audacious philosophy. The moral influence of religion was almost annihilated. The feeling of reverence was almost extinct. Augustus solemnly degraded the statue of Neptune because his fleet had been wrecked.[6] When Germanicus died, the populace stoned or overthrew the altars of the gods.[7] The idea of sanctity was so far removed from the popular divinities that it became a continual complaint that prayers were offered which the most depraved would blush to pronounce aloud.[8] Amid the corruption of the Empire, we meet with many noble efforts of reform made by philosophers or by emperors, but we find

---

[1] On the minute supervision exercised by the censors on all the details of domestic life, see Aul. Gell. *Noct.* ii. 24 ; iv. 12, 20.

[2] Livy, xxxix. 6.

[3] Vell. Paterculus, i. 11–13 ; Eutropius, iv. 6. Sallust ascribed the decadence of Rome to the destruction of its rival, Carthage.

[4] Plutarch, *De Adulatore et Amico.*

[5] There is much curious information about the growth of Roman luxury in Pliny (*Hist. Nat.* lib.

xxxiv.). The movement of decomposition has been lately fully traced by Mommsen (*Hist. of Rome*); Döllinger (*Jew and Gentile*); Denis (*Hist. des Idées morales dans l'Antiquité*) ; Pressensé (*Hist. des trois premiers Siècles*); in the histories of Champagny, and in the beautiful closing chapters of the *Apôtres* of Renan.

[6] Sueton. *Aug.* xvi.

[7] Ibid. *Calig.* v.

[8] Persius, *Sat.* ii.; Horace, *Ep.* i. 16, vv. 57-60.

scarcely a trace of the moral influence of the old religion. The apotheosis of the emperors consummated its degradation. The foreign gods were identified with those of Rome, and all their immoral legends associated with the national creed.[1] The theatre greatly extended the area of scepticism. Cicero mentions the assenting plaudits with which the people heard the lines of Ennius, declaring that the gods, though real beings, take no care for the things of man.[2] Plutarch tells of a spectator at a theatre rising up with indignation after a recital of the crimes of Diana, and exclaiming to the actor, ' May you have a daughter like her whom you have described!'[3] St. Augustine and other of the Fathers long after ridiculed the pagans who satirised in the theatres the very gods they worshipped in the temples.[4]    Men were still profoundly superstitious, but they resorted to each new religion as to a charm or talisman of especial power, or a system of magic revealing the future.    There existed, too, to a very large extent, a kind of superstitious scepticism which occupies a very prominent place in religious history.    There were multitudes who, declaring that there were no gods, or that the gods never interfered with human affairs, professed with the same breath an absolute faith in all portents, auguries, dreams, and miracles.    Innumerable natural objects, such as comets, meteors, earthquakes, or monstrous births, were supposed to possess a kind of occult or magical virtue, by which they foreshadowed, and in some cases influenced,

---

[1] See, on the identification of the Greek and Egyptian myths, Plutarch's De Iside et Osiride. The Greek and Roman gods were habitually regarded as identical, and Cæsar and Tacitus, in like manner, identified the deities of Gaul and Germany with those of their own country. See Döllinger, Jew and Gentile, vol ii. pp. 160–165.

[2] 'Ego deûm genus esse semper dixi et dicam cœlitum ; Sed eos non curare opinor quid agat hominum genus.' Cicero adds : 'magno plausu loquitur assentiente populo.' — De Divin. ii. 50.

[3] Plutarch, De Superstitione.

[4] St. Aug. De Civ. Dei, vi. 6; Tertul. Apol. 15; Arnobius, Adv. Gentes, iv.

the destinies of men. Astrology, which is the special represe-
sentative of this mode of thought, rose to great prominence.
The elder Pliny notices that in his time a belief was rapidly
gaining ground, both among the learned and among the vulgar, that the whole destiny of man is determined by the star that
presides over his nativity; that God, having ordained this,
never interferes with human affairs, and that the reality
of the portents is due to this pre-ordainment.[1] One of the
later historians of the Empire remarks that numbers who
denied the existence of any divinity believed nevertheless
that they could not safely appear in public, or eat or bathe,
unless they had first carefully consulted the almanac to
ascertain the position of the planet Mercury, or how far the
moon was from the Crab.[2] Except, perhaps, among the peasants in the country districts, the Roman religion, in the
last years of the Republic, and in the first century of the
Empire, scarcely existed, except in the state of a superstition,
and he who would examine the true moral influence of the
time must turn to the great schools of philosophy which had
been imported from Greece.

The vast place which the rival systems of Zeno and Epicurus occupy in the moral history of mankind, and especially in the closing years of the empire of paganism, may

---

[1] 'Pars alia et hanc pellit, as-
troque suo eventus assignat,
nascendi legibus; semelque in
omnes futuros unquam Deo decretum; in reliquum vero otium
datum. Sedere cœpit sententia
hæc pariterque et eruditum vulgus
et rude in eam cursu vadit. Ecce
fulgurum monitus, oraculorum
præscita, aruspicum prædicta,
atque etiam parva dictu, in auguriis
sternumenta et offensiones pedum.'
—Hist. Nat. ii. 5. Pliny himself
expresses great doubt about astrology, giving many examples of men
with different destinies, who had
been born at the same time, and
therefore under the same stars (vii.
50). Tacitus expresses complete
doubt about the existence of Providence. (Ann. vi. 22.) Tiberius is
said to have been very indifferent
to the gods and to the worship of
the temples, being wholly addicted
to astrology and convinced that all
things were pre-ordained. (Suet.
Tib. lxix.)
[2] Ammianus Marcellinus, xxviii.
4.

easily lead us to exaggerate the creative genius of their founders, who, in fact, did little more than give definitions or intellectual expression to types of excellence that had at all times existed in the world. There have ever been stern, upright, self-controlled, and courageous men, actuated by a pure sense of duty, capable of high efforts of self-sacrifice, somewhat intolerant of the frailties of others, somewhat hard and unsympathising in the ordinary intercourse of society, but rising to heroic grandeur as the storm lowered upon their path, and more ready to relinquish life than the cause they believed to be true. There have also always been men of easy tempers and of amiable disposition, gentle, benevolent, and pliant, cordial friends and forgiving enemies, selfish at heart, yet ever ready, when it is possible, to unite their gratifications with those of others, averse to all enthusiasm, mysticism, utopias, and superstition, with little depth of character or capacity for self-sacrifice, but admirably fitted to impart and to receive enjoyment, and to render the course of life easy and harmonious. The first are by nature Stoics, and the second Epicureans, and if they proceed to reason about the *summum bonum* or the affections, it is more than probable that in each case their characters will determine their theories. The first will estimate self-control above all other qualities, will disparage the affections, and will endeavour to separate widely the ideas of duty and of interest, while the second will systematically prefer the amiable to the heroic, and the utilitarian to the mystical.

But while it is undoubtedly true that in these matters character usually determines opinion, it is not less true that character is itself in a great measure governed by national circumstances. The refined, artistic, sensual civilisations of Greece and Asia Minor might easily produce fine examples of the Epicurean type, but Rome was from the earliest times pre-eminently the home of stoicism. Long before the Romans had begun to reason about philosophy, they had exhibited it in action, and in their speculative days it was to this doctrine that the noblest minds naturally tended. A great nation engaged in perpetual wars in an age when success in warfare depended neither upon wealth nor upon mechanical genius, but upon the constant energy of patriotic enthusiasm, and upon the unflinching maintenance of military discipline, the whole force of the national character tended to the production of a single definite type. In the absolute authority accorded to the father over the children, to the husband over the wife, to the master over the slave, we may trace the same habits of discipline that proved so formidable in the field. Patriotism and military honour were indissolubly connected in the Roman mind. They were the two sources of national enthusiasm, the chief ingredients of the national conception of greatness. They determined irresistibly the moral theory which was to prove supreme.

Now war, which brings with it so many demoralising influences, has, at least, always been the great school of heroism. It teaches men how to die. It familiarises the mind with the idea of noble actions performed under the influence, not of personal interest, but of honour and of enthusiasm. It elicits in the highest degree strength of character, accustoms men to the abnegation needed for simultaneous action, compels them to repress their fears, and establish a firm control over their affections. Patriotism, too, leads them to subordinate their personal wishes to the interests of the society in which they live. It extends the horizon of life, teaching men to dwell among the great men of the past, to derive their moral strength from the study of heroic lives, to look forward continually, through the vistas of a distant future, to the welfare of an organisation which will continue when they have passed away. All these influences were developed in Roman life to a degree which can now never be reproduced. War, for the reasons I have stated, was far more than at present the school of heroic virtues. Patriotism, in the absence of any strong theological passion, had assumed a transcendent power. The citizen, passing continually from political to military life, exhibited to perfection the moral effects of both. The habits of command formed by a long period of almost universal empire, and by the aristocratic organisation of the city, contributed to the elevation, and also to the pride, of the national character.

It will appear, I think, sufficiently evident, from these considerations, that the circumstances of the Roman people tended inevitably to the production of a certain type of character, which, in its essential characteristics, was the type of stoicism. In addition to the predisposition which leads men in their estimate of the comparative excellence of different qualities to select for the highest eulogy those which are most congruous to their own characters, this fact derives a great importance from the large place which the biographical element occupied in ancient ethical teaching. Among Christians the ideals have commonly been either supernatural beings or men who were in constant connection with supernatural beings, and these men have usually been either Jews or saints, whose lives were of such a nature as to isolate them from most human sympathies, and to efface as far as possible the national type. Among the Greeks and Romans the examples of virtue were usually their own fellow-countrymen; men who had lived in the same moral atmosphere, struggled for the same ends, acquired their reputation in the same spheres, exhibited in all their intensity the same national characteristics as their admirers. History had assumed a didactic character it has now almost wholly lost. One of the first tasks of every moralist was to collect traits of character illustrating the precepts he enforced. Valerius Maximus represented faithfully the method of the teachers of antiquity when he wrote his book giving a catalogue of different moral qualities, and illustrating each by a profusion of examples derived from the history of his own or of foreign nations.

'Whenever,' said Plutarch, 'we begin an enterprise, or take possession of a charge, or experience a calamity, we place before our eyes the example of the greatest men of our own or of bygone ages, and we ask ourselves how Plato or Epaminondas, Lycurgus or Agesilaus, would have acted. Looking into these personages as into a faithful mirror, we can remedy our defects in word or deed. . . . Whenever any perplexity arrives, or any passion disturbs the mind, the student of philosophy pictures to himself some of those who have been celebrated for their virtue, and the recollection sustains his tottering steps and prevents his fall.'[1]

Passages of this kind continually occur in the ancient moralists,[2] and they show how naturally the highest type of national excellence determined the prevailing school of moral philosophy, and also how the influence of the heroic period of national history would act upon the best minds in the subsequent and wholly different phases of development. It was therefore not surprising that during the Empire, though the conditions of national life were profoundly altered, Stoicism should still be the philosophical religion, the great source and regulator of moral enthusiasm. Epicureanism had, indeed, spread widely in the Empire,[3] but it proved little more than a principle of disintegration or an apology for vice, or at best the religion of tranquil and indifferent natures animated by no strong moral enthusiasm. It is indeed true that Epicurus had himself been a man of the most blameless character, that his doctrines were at first carefully distinguished from the coarse sensuality of the Cyrenaic school which had preceded them, that they admitted in theory almost every form of virtue, and that the school had produced

---

[1] *De Profectibus in Virt.* It was originally the custom at Roman feasts to sing to a pipe the actions and the virtues of the greatest men. (Cic. *Tusc. Quæst.* iv.)
[2] E.g. Epictetus, *Ench.* lii.

Seneca is full of similar exhortations.
[3] According to Cicero, the first Latin work on philosophy was by the Epicurean Amafanius. (*Tusc. Quæst.* iv.)

many disciples who, if they had not attained the highest
grades of excellence, had at least been men of harmless lives,
intensely devoted to their master, and especially noted for
the warmth and constancy of their friendships.[1] But a
school which placed so high a value on ease and pleasure was
eminently unfit to struggle against the fearful difficulties that
beset the teachers of virtue amid the anarchy of a military
despotism, and the virtues and the vices of the Romans were
alike fatal to its success. All the great ideals of Roman excellence belonged to a different type. Such men as a Decius
or a Regulus would have been impossible in an Epicurean
society, for even if their actuating emotion were no nobler than
a desire for posthumous fame, such a desire could never grow
powerful in a moral atmosphere charged with the shrewd,
placid, unsentimental utilitarianism of Epicurus. On the
other hand, the distinctions the Epicureans had drawn between more or less refined pleasures and their elevated
conceptions of what constitutes the true happiness of men,
were unintelligible to the Romans, who knew how to sacri-

---

[1] See on the great perfection of
the character of Epicurus his life
by Diogenes Laërtius, and on the
purity of the philosophy he taught
and the degree in which it was distorted and misrepresented by his
Roman followers, Seneca *De Vita
Beata*, c. xii. xiii. and *Ep.* xxi.
Gassendi, in a very interesting little
work entitled *Philosophiæ Epicuri
Syntagma*, has abundantly proved
the possibility of uniting Epicurean
principles with a high code of
morals. But probably the most
beautiful picture of the Epicurean
system is the first book of the *De
Finibus*, in which Cicero endeavours
to paint it as it would have been
painted by its adherents. When
we remember that the writer of
this book was one of the most
formidable and unflinching opponents of Epicureanism in all the
ancient world, it must be owned
that it would be impossible to find
a grander example of that noble
love of truth, that sublime and
scrupulous justice to opponents,
which was the pre-eminent glory of
ancient philosophers, and which,
after the destruction of philosophy,
was for many centuries almost unknown in the world. It is impossible to doubt that Epicureanism
was logically compatible with a very
high degree of virtue. It is, I
think, equally impossible to doubt
that its practical tendency was towards vice.

fice enjoyment, but who, when pursuing it, gravitated naturally to the coarsest forms. The mission of Epicureanism was therefore chiefly negative. The anti-patriotic tendency of its teaching contributed to that destruction of national feeling which was necessary to the rise of cosmopolitanism, while its strong opposition to theological beliefs, supported by the genius and enthusiasm of Lucretius, told powerfully upon the decaying faith.

Such being the functions of Epicureanism, the constructive or positive side of ethical teaching devolved almost exclusively upon Stoicism; for although there were a few philosophers who expressed themselves in strong opposition to some portions of the Stoical system, their efforts usually tended to no more than a modification of its extreme and harshest features. The Stoics asserted two cardinal principles —that virtue was the sole legitimate object to be aspired to, and that it involved so complete an ascendancy of the reason as altogether to extinguish the affections. The Peripatetics and many other philosophers, who derived their opinions chiefly from Plato, endeavoured to soften down the exaggeration of these principles. They admitted that virtue was an object wholly distinct from interest, and that it should be the leading motive of life; but they maintained that happiness was also a good, and a certain regard for it legitimate. They admitted that virtue consisted in the supremacy of the reason over the affections, but they allowed the exercise of the latter within restricted limits. The main distinguishing features, however, of Stoicism, the unselfish ideal and the controlling reason, were acquiesced in, and each represents an important side of the ancient conception of excellence which we must now proceed to examine.

In the first we may easily trace the intellectual expression of the high spirit of self-sacrifice which the patriotic enthusiasm had elicited. The spirit of patriotism has this peculiar characteristic, that, while it has evoked acts of heroism which are both very numerous and very sublime, it has done so without presenting any prospect of personal immortality as a reward. Of all the forms of human heroism, it is probably the most unselfish. The Spartan and the Roman died for his country because he loved it. The martyr's ecstasy of hope had no place in his dying hour. He gave up all he had, he closed his eyes, as he believed, for ever, and he asked for no reward in this world or in the next. Even the hope of posthumous fame—the most refined and supersensual of all that can be called reward—could exist only for the most conspicuous leaders. It was examples of this nature that formed the culminations or ideals of ancient systems of virtue, and they naturally led men to draw a very clear and deep distinction between the notions of interest and of duty. It may, indeed, be truly said, that while the conception of what constituted duty was often very imperfect in antiquity, the conviction that duty, as distinguished from every modification of selfishness, should be the supreme motive of life was more clearly enforced among the Stoics than in any later society.

The reader will probably have gathered from the last chapter that there are four distinct motives which moral teachers may propose for the purpose of leading men to virtue. They may argue that the disposition of events is such that prosperity will attend a virtuous life, and adversity a vicious one—a proposition they may prove by pointing to the normal course of affairs, and by asserting the existence of a special Providence in behalf of the good in the present world, and of rewards and punishments in the future. As far as these latter arguments are concerned, the efficacy of such teaching rests upon the firmness with which certain theological tenets are held, while the force of the first considerations will depend upon the degree and manner in which society is organised, for there are undoubtedly some conditions of society in which a perfectly upright life has not even a general tendency to prosperity. The peculiar circumstances and dispositions of individuals will also influence largely the way in which they receive such teaching, and, as Cicero observed, 'what one utility has created, another will often destroy.'

They may argue, again, that vice is to the mind what disease is to the body, and that a state of virtue is in consequence a state of health. Just as bodily health is desired for its own sake, as being the absence of a painful, or at least displeasing state, so a well-ordered and virtuous mind may be valued for its own sake, and independently of all the external good to which it may lead, as being a condition of happiness; and a mind distracted by passion and vice may be avoided, not so much because it is an obstacle in the pursuit of prosperity, as because it is in itself essentially painful and disturbing. This conception of virtue and vice as states of health or sickness, the one being in itself a good and the other in itself an evil, was a fundamental proposition in the ethics of Plato.[1] It was admitted, but only to a subsidiary place, by the Stoics,[2] and has passed more or less

---

[1] Mr. Grote gives the following very clear summary of Plato's ethical theory, which he believes to be original:—'Justice is in the mind a condition analogous to good health and strength in the body. Injustice is a condition analogous to sickness, corruption, impotence in the body. . . . To possess a healthy body is desirable for its consequences as a means towards other constituents of happiness, but it is still more desirable in itself as an essential element of happiness *per se*, i.e., the negation of sickness, which would of itself make us miserable. . . . In like manner, the just mind blesses the possessor twice: first and chiefly by bringing to him happiness in itself; next, also, as it leads to ulterior happy results. The unjust mind is a curse to its possessor in itself and apart from results, though it also leads to ulterior results which render it still more a curse to him.'—Grote's *Plato*, vol. iii. p. 131. According to Plutarch, Aristo of Chio defined virtue as 'the health of the soul.' (*De Virtute Morali*.)

[2] 'Beata est ergo vita conveniens naturæ suæ; quæ non aliter contingere potest quam si primum sana mens est et in perpetuâ possessione sanitatis suæ.'—Seneca, *De Vita Beata*, c. iii.

into all the succeeding systems. It is especially favourable to large and elevating conceptions of self-culture, for it leads men to dwell much less upon isolated acts of virtue or vice than upon the habitual condition of mind from which they spring.

It is possible, in the third place, to argue in favour of virtue by offering as a motive that sense of pleasure which follows the deliberate performance of a virtuous act. This emotion is a distinct and isolated gratification following a distinct action, and may therefore be easily separated from that habitual placidity of temper which results from the extinction of vicious and perturbing impulses. It is this theory which is implied in the common exhortations to enjoy ' the luxury of doing good,' and though especially strong in acts of benevolence, in which case sympathy with the happiness created intensifies the feeling, this pleasure attends every kind of virtue.

These three motives of action have all this common characteristic, that they point as their ultimate end to the happiness of the agent. The first seeks that happiness in external circumstances; the second and third in psychological conditions. There is, however, a fourth kind of motive which may be urged, and which is the peculiar characteristic of the intuitive school of moralists and the stumbling-block of its opponents. It is asserted that we are so constituted that the notion of duty furnishes in itself a natural motive of action of the highest order, wholly distinct from all the refinements and modifications of self-interest. The coactive force of this motive is altogether independent of surrounding circumstances, and of all forms of belief. It is equally true for the man who believes and for the man who rejects the Christian faith, for the believer in a future world and for the believer in the mortality of the soul. It is not a question of happiness or unhappiness, of reward or punishment, but of a generically different nature. Men feel that a certain course of life is the natural end of their being, and they feel bound, even at the expense of happiness, to pursue it. They feel that certain acts are essentially good and noble, and others essentially base and vile, and this perception leads them to pursue the one and to avoid the other, irrespective of all considerations of enjoyment.

I have recurred to these distinctions, which were more fully discussed in the last chapter, because the school of philosophy we are reviewing furnishes the most perfect of all historical examples of the power which the higher of these motives can exercise over the mind. The coarser forms of self-interest were in stoicism absolutely condemned. It was one of the first principles of these philosophers that all things that are not in our power should be esteemed indifferent ; that the object of all mental discipline should be to withdraw the mind from all the gifts of fortune, and that prudence must in consequence be altogether excluded from the motives of virtue. To enforce these principles they continually dilated upon the vanity of human things, and upon the majesty of the independent mind, and they indulged, though scarcely more than other sects, in many exaggerations about the impassive tranquillity of the sage.[1] In the Roman empire stoicism flourished at a period .which, beyond almost any other, seemed unfavourable to such teaching. There were reigns when, in the emphatic words of Tacitus, ' virtue was a sentence of death.' In no period had brute force more completely triumphed, in none was the thirst for material advantages more intense, in very few was vice more ostentatiously glorified. Yet in the midst of all these circumstances the Stoics taught a philosophy which was not a compromise, or an attempt to moderate the popular excesses, but which

---

[1] The famous paradox that 'the sage could be happy even in the bull of Phalaris,' comes from the writings not of Zeno but of Epicurus —though the Stoics adopted and greatly admired it. (Cic. *Tusc.* ii. See Gassendi, *Philos. Epicuri Syntagma*, pars iii. c. 1.)

was rather in its austere sanctity the extreme antithesis of
all that the prevailing examples and their own interests could
dictate. And these men were no impassioned fanatics, fired
with the prospect of coming glory. They were men from
whose motives of action the belief in the immortality of the
soul was resolutely excluded. In the scepticism that accompanied the first introduction of philosophy into Rome, in the
dissolution of the old fables about Tartarus and the Styx,
and the dissemination of Epicureanism among the people,
this doctrine had sunk very low, notwithstanding the beautiful
reasonings of Cicero and the religious faith of a few who
clung like Plutarch to the mysteries in which it was
perpetuated. An interlocutor in Cicero expressed what
was probably a common feeling when he acknowledged that,
with the writings of Plato before him, he could believe and
realise it; but when he closed the book, the reasonings
seemed to lose their power, and the world of spirits grew
pale and unreal.[1] If Ennius could elicit the plaudits of a
theatre when he proclaimed that the gods took no part in
human affairs, Cæsar could assert in the senate, without
scandal and almost without dissent, that death was the
end of all things.[2] Pliny, perhaps the greatest of Roman
scholars, adopting the sentiment of all the school of Epicurus, describes the belief in a future life as a form of madness,
a puerile and a pernicious illusion.[3] The opinions of the
Stoics were wavering and uncertain. Their first doctrine was
that the soul of man has a future and independent, but not

---

[1] 'Sed nescio quomodo dum lego
assentior; cum posui librum et
mecum ipse de immortalitate
animorum cœpi cogitare, as-
sensio omnis illa elabitur.'—Cic.
Tusc. i.

[2] Sallust, Catilina, cap. li.

[3] See that most impressive passage (Hist. Nat. vii. 56). That
the sleep of annihilation is the

happiest end of man is a favourite
thought of Lucretius. Thus:
'Nil igitur mors est, ad nos neque
pertinet hilum,
Quandoquidem natura animi mor-
talis habetur.'—iii. 842.
This mode of thought has been recently expressed in Mr. Swinburne's
very beautiful poem on The Garden
of Proserpine.

an eternal existence, that it survives until the last conflagration which was to destroy the world, and absorb all finite things into the all-pervading soul of nature. Chrysippus, however, restricted to the best and noblest souls this future existence, which Cleanthes had awarded to all,[1] and among the Roman Stoics even this was greatly doubted. The belief that the human soul is a detached fragment of the Deity naturally led to the belief that after death it would be reabsorbed into the parent Spirit. The doctrine that there is no real good but virtue deprived the Stoics of the argument for a future world derived from unrequited merit and unpunished crime, and the earnestness with which they contended that a good man should act irrespectively of reward inclined them, as it is said to have inclined some Jewish thinkers,[2] to the denial of the existence of the reward.[3] Panætius, the founder of Roman stoicism, maintained that the soul perished with the body,[4] and his opinion was followed by Epictetus,[5] and Cornutus.[6] Seneca contradicted himself on the subject.[7]

---

[1] Diog. Laërtius. The opinion of Chrysippus seems to have prevailed, and Plutarch (*De Placit. Philos.*) speaks of it as that of the school. Cicero sarcastically says, 'Stoici autem usuram nobis largiuntur, tanquam cornicibus: diu mansuros aiunt animos; semper, negant.'—*Tusc. Disp.* i. 31.

[2] It has been very frequently asserted that Antigonus of Socho having taught that virtue should be practised for its own sake, his disciple, Zadok, the founder of the Sadducees, inferred the non-existence of a future world; but the evidence for this whole story is exceedingly unsatisfactory. The reader may find its history in a very remarkable article by Mr. Twisleton on *Sadducees*, in Smith's *Biblical Dictionary*.

[3] On the Stoical opinions about a future life see Martin, *La Vie future* (Paris, 1858); Courdaveaux *De l'immortalité de l'âme dans le Stoïcisme* (Paris, 1857); and Alger's *Critical Hist. of the Doctrine of a Future Life* (New York, 1866).

[4] His arguments are met by Cicero in the *Tusculans.*

[5] See a collection of passages from his discourses collected by M. Courdaveaux, in the introduction to his French translation of that book.

[6] Stobæus, *Eclog. Physic.* lib. i. cap. 52.

[7] In his consolations to Marcia, he seems to incline to a belief in the immortality, or at least the future existence, of the soul. In many other passages, however, he speaks of it as annihilated at death.

Marcus Aurelius never rose beyond a vague and mournful aspiration. Those who believed in a future world believed in it faintly and uncertainly, and even when they accepted it as a fact, they shrank from proposing it as a motive. The whole system of Stoical ethics, which carried self-sacrifice to a point that has scarcely been equalled, and exercised an influence which has rarely been surpassed, was evolved without any assistance from the doctrine of a future life.[1] Pagan antiquity has bequeathed us few nobler treatises of morals than the 'De Officiis' of Cicero, which was avowedly an expansion of a work of Panætius.[2] It has left us no grander example than that of Epictetus, the sickly, deformed slave of a master who was notorious for his barbarity, enfranchised late in life, but soon driven into exile by Domitian ; who, while sounding the very abyss of human misery, and looking forward to death as to simple decomposition, was yet so filled with the sense of the Divine presence that his life was one continued hymn to Providence, and his writings and his example, which appeared to his contemporaries almost the ideal of human goodness, have not lost their consoling power through all the ages and the vicissitudes they have survived.[3]

---

[1] 'Les Stoïciens ne faisaient aucunement dépendre la morale de la perspective des peines ou de la rémunération dans une vie future. . . . La croyance à l'immortalité de l'âme n'appartenait donc, selon leur manière de voir, qu'à la physique, c'est-à-dire à la psychologie.' —Degerando, *Hist. de la Philos.* tome iii. p. 56.

[2] 'Panætius igitur, qui sine controversia de officiis accuratissime disputavit, quemque nos, correctione quadam adhibita, potissimum secuti sumus.'—*De Offic.* iii. 2.

[3] Marcus Aurelius thanks Providence, as for one of the great blessings of his life, that he had been made acquainted with the writings of Epictetus. The story is well known how the old philosopher warned his master, who was beating him, that he would soon break his leg, and when the leg was broken, calmly remarked, 'I told you you would do so.' Celsus quoted this in opposition to the Christians, asking, 'Did your leader under suffering ever say anything so noble?' Origen finely replied, 'He did what was still nobler—He kept silence.' A Christian anchorite (some say St. Nilus, who lived in the beginning of the fifth century)

There was, however, another form of immortality which
exercised a much greater influence among the Roman moralists. The desire for reputation, and especially for posthumous reputation—that 'last infirmity of noble minds'[1]—
assumed an extraordinary prominence among the springs of
Roman heroism, and was also the origin of that theatrical
and overstrained phraseology which the greatest of ancient
moralists rarely escaped.[2] But we should be altogether in
error if we inferred, as some have done, that paganism never
rose to the conception of virtue concealing itself from the
world, and consenting voluntarily to degradation. No
characters were more highly appreciated in antiquity than
those of men who, through a sense of duty, opposed the
strong current of popular favour; of men like Fabius, who
consented for the sake of their country to incur the reputation that is most fatal to a soldier;[3] of men like Cato, who
remained unmoved among the scoffs, the insults, and the
ridicule of an angry crowd.[4] Cicero, expounding the principles of Stoicism, declared that no one has attained to true
philosophy who has not learnt that all vice should be
avoided, 'though it were concealed from the eyes of gods and
men,'[5] and that no deeds are more laudable than those which
are done without ostentation, and far from the sight of men.[6]

---

was so struck with the *Enchiridion*
of Epictetus, that he adapted it to
Christian use. The conversations
of Epictetus, as reported by Arrian,
are said to have been the favourite
reading of Toussaint l'Ouverture.

[1] Tacitus had used this expression
before Milton : 'Quando etiam sa-
pientibus cupido gloriæ novissima
exuitur.'—*Hist.* iv. 6.

[2] Two remarkable instances have
come down to us of eminent writers
begging historians to adorn and
even exaggerate their acts. See
the very curious letters of Cicero

to the historian Lucceius (*Ep. ad
Divers.* v. 12); and of the younger
Pliny to Tacitus (*Ep.* vii. 33).
Cicero has himself confessed that
he was too fond of glory.

[3] 'Unus homo nobis cunctando
restituit rem;
Non ponebat enim rumores ante
salutem.'—Ennius.

[4] See the beautiful description of
Cato's tranquillity under insults.
Seneca, *De Ira*, ii. 33; *De Const.
Sap.* 1, 2.

[5] *De Officiis*, iii. 9.

[6] *Tusc.* ii. 26.

14

The writings of the Stoics are crowded with sentences to the same effect. 'Nothing for opinion, all for conscience.'[1] 'He who wishes his virtue to be blazed abroad is not labouring for virtue but for fame.'[2] 'No one is more virtuous than the man who sacrifices the reputation of a good man rather than sacrifice his conscience.'[3] 'I do not shrink from praise, but I refuse to make it the end and term of right.'[4] 'If you do anything to please men, you have fallen from your estate.'[5] 'Even a bad reputation nobly earned is pleasing.'[6] 'A great man is not the less great when he lies vanquished and prostrate in the dust.'[7] 'Never forget that it is possible to be at once a divine man, yet a man unknown to all the world.'[8] 'That which is beautiful is beautiful in itself; the praise of man adds nothing to its quality.'[9] Marcus Aurelius, following an example that is ascribed to Pythagoras, made it a special object of mental discipline, by continually meditating on death, and evoking, by an effort of the imagination, whole societies that had passed away, to acquire a realised sense of the vanity of posthumous fame. The younger Pliny painted faithfully the ideal of Stoicism when he described one of his friends as a man 'who did nothing for ostentation, but all for conscience; who sought the reward of virtue in itself, and not in the praise of man.'[10] Nor were the Stoics less emphatic in distinguishing the obligation from the attraction of virtue. It was on this point that they separated from the more refined Epicureans, who were often willing to sublimate to the highest degree the kind of pleasure they proposed as an object, provided only it were admitted that pleasure is necessarily the ultimate end of our actions. But this the Stoics firmly denied. 'Pleasure,' they

---

[1] Seneca, *De Vit. Beat.* c. xx.
[2] Seneca. *Ep.* cxiii.
[3] Seneca, *Ep.* lxxxi.
[4] Persius, *Sat.* i. 45-47.
[5] Epictetus, *Ench.* xxiii.
[6] Seneca, *De Ira*, iii. 41.
[7] Seneca, *Cons. ad Helv.* xiii.
[8] Marc. Aur. vii. 67
[9] Marc. Aur. iv. 20.
[10] Pliny, *Ep.* i. 22.

argued, 'is the companion, not the guide, of our course.'[1] 'We do not love virtue because it gives us pleasure, but it gives us pleasure because we love it.'[2] 'The wise man will not sin, though both gods and men should overlook the deed, for it is not through the fear of punishment or of shame that he abstains from sin. It is from the desire and obligation of what is just and good.'[3] 'To ask to be paid for virtue is as if the eye demanded a recompense for seeing, or the feet for walking.'[4] In doing good, man 'should be like the vine which has produced grapes, and asks for nothing more after it has produced its proper fruit.'[5] His end, according to these teachers, is not to find peace either in life or in death. It is to do his duty, and to tell the truth.

The second distinguishing feature of Stoicism I have noticed was the complete suppression of the affections to make way for the absolute ascendancy of reason. There are two great divisions of character corresponding very nearly to the Stoical and Epicurean temperaments I have described— that in which the will predominates, and that in which the desires are supreme. A good man of the first class is one whose will, directed by a sense of duty, pursues the course he believes to be right, in spite of strong temptations to pursue an opposite course, arising either from his own passions and tendencies, or from the circumstances that surround him. A good man of the second class is one who is so happily consti-tuted that his sympathies and desires instinctively tend to virtuous ends. The first character is the only one to which we can, strictly speaking, attach the idea of merit, and it is also the only one which is capable of rising to high efforts of

---

[1] 'Non dux, sed comes voluptas.' — De Vit. Beat. c. viii.

[2] 'Voluptas non est merces nec causa virtutis sed accessio; nec quia delectat placet sed quia placet de-lectat.'—Ibid., c. ix.

[3] Peregrinus apud Aul. Gellius, xii. 11. Peregrinus was a Cynic, but his doctrine on this point was identical with that of the Stoics.

[4] Marc. Aurel. ix. 42.

[5] Marc. Aurel. v. 6.

continuous and heroic self-sacrifice; but on the other hand there is a charm in the spontaneous action of the unforced desires which disciplined virtue can perhaps never attain. The man who is consistently generous through a sense of duty, when his natural temperament impels him to avarice, and when every exercise of benevolence causes him a pang, deserves in the very highest degree our admiration; but he whose generosity costs him no effort, but is the natural gratification of his affections, attracts a far larger measure of our love. Corresponding to these two casts of character, we find two distinct theories of education, the aim of the one being chiefly to strengthen the will, and that of the other to guide the desires. The principal examples of the first are the Spartan and Stoical systems of antiquity, and, with some modifications, the asceticism of the Middle Ages. The object of these systems was to enable men to endure pain, to repress manifest and acknowledged desires, to relinquish enjoyments, to establish an absolute empire over their emotions. On the other hand, there is a method of education which was never more prevalent than in the present day, which exhausts its efforts in making virtue attractive, in associating it with all the charms of imagination and of prosperity, and in thus insensibly drawing the desires in the wished-for direction. As the first system is especially suited to a disturbed and military society, which requires and elicits strong efforts of the will, and is therefore the special sphere of heroic virtues, so the latter belongs naturally to a tranquil and highly organised civilisation, which is therefore very favourable to the amiable qualities, and it is probable that as civilisation advances, the heroic type will, in consequence, become more and more rare, and a kind of self-indulgent goodness more common. The circumstances of the ancient societies led them to the former type, of which the Stoics furnished the extreme expression in their doctrine that the affections are of the nature of a disease[1]—a doctrine which they justified by the same kind of arguments as those which are now often employed by metaphysicians to prove that love, anger, and the like can only be ascribed by a figure of speech to the Deity. Perturbation, they contended, is necessarily imperfection, and none of its forms can in consequence be ascribed to a perfect being. We have a clear intuitive perception that reason is the highest, and should be the directing power of an intelligent being; but every act which is performed at the instigation of the emotions is withdrawn from the empire of reason. Hence it was inferred that while the will should be educated to act habitually in the direction of virtue, even the emotions that seem most fitted to second it should be absolutely proscribed. Thus Seneca has elaborated at length the distinction between clemency and pity, the first being one of the highest virtues, and the latter a positive vice. Clemency, he says, is an habitual disposition to gentleness in the application of punishments. It is that moderation which remits something of an incurred penalty, it is the opposite of cruelty, which is an habitual disposition to rigour. Pity, on the other hand, bears to clemency the same kind of relation as superstition to religion. It is the weakness of a feeble mind that flinches at the sight of suffering. Clemency is an act of judgment, but pity disturbs the judgment. Clemency adjudicates upon the proportion between suffering and guilt. Pity contemplates only suffering, and gives no

---

[1] Seneca, however, in one of his letters (*Ep.* lxxv.), subtilises a good deal on this point. He draws a distinction between affections and maladies. The first, he says, are irrational, and therefore reprehensible movements of the soul, which, if repeated and unrepressed, tend to form an irrational and evil habit, and to the last he in this letter restricts the term disease. He illustrates this distinction by observing that colds and any other slight ailments, if unchecked and neglected, may produce an organic disease. The wise man, he says, is wholly free from moral disease, but no man can completely emancipate himself from affections, though he should make this his constant object.

thought to its cause. Clemency, in the midst of its noblest efforts, is perfectly passionless; pity is unreasoning emotion. Clemency is an essential characteristic of the sage; pity is only suited for weak women and for diseased minds. 'The sage will console those who weep, but without weeping with them; he will succour the shipwrecked, give hospitality to the proscribed, and alms to the poor, . . . restore the son to the mother's tears, save the captive from the arena, and even bury the criminal; but in all this his mind and his counten- ance will be alike untroubled. He will feel no pity. He will succour, he will do good, for he is born to assist his fellows, to labour for the welfare of mankind, and to offer to each one his part. . . . His countenance and his soul will betray no emotion as he looks upon the withered legs, the tattered rags, the bent and emaciated frame of the beggar. But he will help those who are worthy, and, like the gods, his leaning will be towards the wretched. . . . It is only diseased eyes that grow moist in beholding tears in other eyes, as it is no true sympathy, but only weakness of nerves, that leads some to laugh always when others laugh, or to yawn when others yawn.'[1]

Cicero, in a sentence which might be adopted as the motto of Stoicism, said that Homer 'attributed human qualities to the gods; it would have been better to have imparted divine qualities to men.' The remarkable passage I have just cited serves to show the extremes to which the Stoics pushed this imitation. And indeed, if we compare the different virtues that have flourished among Pagans and Christians, we invariably find that the prevailing type of excellence among the former is that in which the will and judgment, and among the latter that in which the emotions, are most prominent. Friendship rather than love, hospitality rather than charity, magnanimity rather than tenderness,

---

[1] *De Clem.* ii. 6, 7.

clemency rather than sympathy, are the characteristics of ancient goodness. The Stoics, who carried the suppression of the emotions farther than any other school, laboured with great zeal to compensate the injury thus done to the benevolent side of our nature, by greatly enlarging the sphere of reasoned and passionless philanthropy. They taught, in the most emphatic language, the fraternity of all men, and the consequent duty of each man consecrating his life to the welfare of others. They developed this general doctrine in a series of detailed precepts, which, for the range, depth, and beauty of their charity, have never been surpassed. They even extended their compassion to crime, and adopting the paradox of Plato, that all guilt is ignorance,[1] treated it as an involuntary disease, and declared that the only legitimate ground of punishment is prevention.[2] But, however fully they might reconcile in theory their principles with the widest and most active benevolence, they could not wholly counteract the practical evil of a system which declared war against the whole emotional side of our being, and reduced human virtue to a kind of majestic egotism ; proposing as examples Anaxagoras, who, when told that his son had died, simply observed, 'I never supposed that I had begotten an immortal;' or Stilpo, who, when his country had been ruined, his native city captured, and his daughters carried away as slaves or as concubines, boasted that he had lost nothing, for the sage is independent of circumstances.[3] The framework or theory of

---

[1] 'Peccantes vero quid habet cur oderit, cum error illos in hujusmodi delicta compellat?'—Sen. De Ira, i. 14. This is a favourite thought of Marcus Aurelius, to which he reverts again and again. See, too, Arrian, i. 18.

[2] 'Ergo ne homini quidem nocebimus quia peccavit sed ne peccet, nec unquam ad præteritum sed ad futurum pœna referetur.'—Ibid. ii. 31. In the philosophy of Plato, on the other hand, punishment was chiefly expiatory and purificatory. (Lerminier, Introd. à l'Histoire du Droit, p. 123.)

[3] Seneca, De Constant. Sap. v. Compare and contrast this famous sentence of Anaxagoras with that of one of the early Christian hermits. Someone told the hermit that his father was dead. 'Cease your blasphemy,' he answered, 'my father is immortal.' — Socrates, Eccl. Hist. iv. 23.

HISTORY OF EUROPEAN MORALS.

benevolence might be there, but the animating spirit was
absent. Men who taught that the husband or the father
should look with perfect indifference on the death of his wife
or his child, and that the philosopher, though he may shed
tears of pretended sympathy in order to console his suffering
friend, must suffer no real emotion to penetrate his breast,[1]
could never found a true or lasting religion of benevolence.
Men who refused to recognise pain and sickness as evils were
scarcely likely to be very eager to relieve them in others.

In truth, the Stoics, who taught that all virtue was conformity to nature, were, in this respect, eminently false to
their own principle. Human nature, as revealed to us by
reason, is a composite thing, a constitution of many parts
differing in kind and dignity, a hierarchy in which many
powers are intended to co-exist, but in different positions of
ascendancy or subordination. To make the higher part of
our nature our whole nature, is not to restore but to muti-
late humanity, and this mutilation has never been attempted
without producing grave evils. As philanthropists, the
Stoics, through their passion for unity, were led to the extirpation of those emotions which nature intended as the chief
springs of benevolence. As speculative philosophers, they
were entangled by the same desire in a long train of pitiable
paradoxes. Their famous doctrines that all virtues are equal,
or, more correctly, are the same, that all vices are equal, that
nothing is an evil which does not affect our will, and that
pain and bereavement are, in consequence, no ills,[2] though

---

[1] Epictetus, *Ench.* 16, 18.
[2] The dispute about whether
anything but virtue is a good, was,
in reality, a somewhat childish
quarrel about words; for the Stoics,
who indignantly denounced the
Peripatetics for maintaining the
affirmative, admitted that health,
friends, &c., should be sought not
as 'goods' but as 'preferables.'

See a long discussion on this matter
in Cicero (*De Finib.* lib. iii. iv.).
The Stoical doctrine of the equality
of all vices was formally repudiated
by Marcus Aurelius, who maintained (ii. 10), with Theophrastus,
that faults of desire were worse
than faults of anger. The other
Stoics, while dogmatically asserting
the equality of all virtues as well

partially explained away and frequently disregarded by the
Roman Stoics, were yet sufficiently prominent to give their
teaching something of an unnatural and affected appearance.
Prizing only a single object, and developing only a single side
of their nature, their minds became narrow and their views
contracted. Thus, while the Epicureans, urging men to
study nature in order to banish superstition, endeavoured to
correct that ignorance of physical science which was one of
the chief impediments to the progress of the ancient mind,
the Stoics for the most part disdained a study which was
other than the pursuit of virtue.[1] While the Epicurean poet
painted in magnificent language the perpetual progress of
mankind, the Stoic was essentially retrospective, and exhausted his strength in vain efforts to restore the simplicity
of a by-gone age. While, too, the school of Zeno produced
many of the best and greatest men who have ever lived, it
must be acknowledged that its records exhibit a rather unusual number of examples of high professions falsified in
action, and of men who, displaying in some forms the most
undoubted and transcendent virtue, fell in others far below
the average of mankind. The elder Cato, who, though not
a philosopher, was a model of philosophers, was conspicuous
for his inhumanity to his slaves.[2] Brutus was one of the
most extortionate usurers of his time, and several citizens

as the equality of all vices, in their
particular judgments graduated
their praise or blame much in the
same way as the rest of the world.
[1] See Seneca (*Ep.* lxxxix.). Seneca himself, however, has devoted
a work to natural history, but the
general tendency of the school was
certainly to concentrate all attention upon morals, and all, or nearly
all the great naturalists were Epicureans. Cicero puts into the
mouth of the Epicurean the sentence, 'Omnium autem rerum na-

tura cognita levamur superstitione,
liberamur mortis metu, non con-
turbamur ignoratione rerum' (*De
Fin.* i.); and Virgil expressed an
eminently Epicurean sentiment in
his famous lines :—
'Felix, qui potuit rerum cognoscere
    causas,
Quique metus omnes et inexorabile
    fatum
Subjecit pedibus, strepitumque
    Acherontis avari.'
            *Georg.* 490–492.
[2] Plutarch, *Cato Major.*

of Salamis died of starvation, imprisoned because they could not pay the sum he demanded.[1] No one eulogised more eloquently the austere simplicity of life which Stoicism advocated than Sallust, who in a corrupt age was notorious for his rapacity. Seneca himself was constitutionally a nervous and timid man, endeavouring, not always with success, to support himself by a sublime philosophy. He guided, under circumstances of extreme difficulty, the cause of virtue, and his death is one of the noblest antiquity records; but his life was deeply marked by the taint of flattery, and not free from the taint of avarice, and it is unhappily certain that he lent his pen to conceal or varnish one of the worst crimes of Nero. The courage of Lucan failed signally under torture, and the flattery which he bestowed upon Nero, in his 'Pharsalia,' ranks with the Epigrams of Martial as probably the extreme limit of sycophancy to which Roman literature descended.

While, too, the main object of the Stoics was to popularise philosophy, the high standard of self-control they exacted rendered their system exceedingly unfit for the great majority of mankind, and for the ordinary condition of affairs. Life is history, not poetry. It consists mainly of little things, rarely illumined by flashes of great heroism, rarely broken by great dangers, or demanding great exertions. A moral system, to govern society, must accommodate itself to common characters and mingled motives. It must be capable of influencing natures that can never rise to an heroic level. It must tincture, modify, and mitigate where it cannot eradicate or transform. In Christianity there are always a few persons seeking by continual and painful efforts to reverse or extinguish the ordinary feelings of humanity, but in the great majority of cases the influence of the religious principle upon the mind, though very real, is not of a nature

---

[1] Cicero, *Ad Attic.* vi. 2.

to cause any serious strain or struggle. It is displayed in a certain acquired spontaneity of impulse. It softens the character, purifies and directs the imagination, blends insensibly with the habitual modes of thought, and, without revolutionising, gives a tone and bias to all the forms of action. But Stoicism was simply a school of heroes. It recognised no gradations of virtue or vice. It condemned all emotions, all spontaneity, all mingled motives, all the principles, feelings, and impulses upon which the virtue of common men mainly depends. It was capable of acting only on moral natures that were strung to the highest tension, and it was therefore naturally rejected by the multitude.

The central conception of this philosophy of self-control was the dignity of man. Pride, which looks within, making man seek his own approbation, as distinguished from vanity, which looks without, and shapes its conduct according to the opinions of others, was not cnly permitted in Stoicism, it was even its leading moral agent. The sense of virtue, as I have elsewhere observed, occupies in this system much the same place as the sense of sin in Christianity. Sin, in the conception of the ancients, was simply disease, and they deemed it the part of a wise man to correct it, but not to dwell upon its circumstances. In the many disquisitions which Epictetus and others have left us concerning the proper frame of mind in which man should approach death, repentance for past sin has absolutely no place, nor do the ancients appear to have ever realised the purifying and spiritualising influence it exercises upon character. And while the reality of moral disease was fully recognised, while a lofty and indeed unattainable ideal was continually proposed, no one doubted the essential excellence of human nature, and very few doubted the possibility of man acquiring by his own will a high degree of virtue. In this last respect there was a wide difference between the teaching of the Roman moralists and of the Greek poets.[1] Homer continually represents courage, anger, and the like, as the direct inspiration of Heaven. Æschylus, the great poet of fatalism, regards every human passion as but a single link in the great chain of causes forged by the inexorable will of Zeus. There are, indeed, few grander things in poetry than his picture of the many and various motives that urged Clytemnestra to the slaughter of Agamemnon—revenge for her murdered daughter, love for Ægisthus, resentment at past breaches of conjugal duty, jealousy of Cassandra, all blending in that fierce hatred that nerved her arm against her husband's life; while above all this tumult of passion the solemn song of Cassandra proclaimed that the deed was but the decree of Heaven, the harvest of blood springing from the seed of crime, the accomplishment of the ancient curse that was destined to cling for ever to the hapless race of Atreus. Before the body of the murdered king, and in presence of the wildest paroxysms of human passion, the bystanders bowed their heads, exclaiming, ' Zeus has willed it—Zeus the supreme Ruler, the God who does all; for what can happen in the world without the will of Zeus?'

But conceptions of this kind had little or no place in the philosophy of Rome. The issue of human enterprises and the disposition of the gifts of fortune were recognised as under the control of Providence; but man was master of his own feelings, and was capable of attaining such excellence that he might even challenge comparison with the gods. Audacious as such sentiments may now appear, they were common to most schools of Roman moralists. ' We boast justly of our own virtue,' said the eclectic Cicero, ' which we could not do if we derived it from the Deity and not from ourselves.'

---

[1] This contrast is noticed and largely illustrated by M. Montée in his interesting little work Le Stoïcisme à Rome, and also by Legendre in his Traité de l'Opinion, ou Mémoires pour servir à l'histoire de l'esprit humain (Venise, 1735).

'All mortals judge that fortune is to be received from the gods and wisdom from ourselves.'[1] The Epicurean Horace, in his noblest ode, described the just man, confident in his virtue, undaunted amid the crash of worlds, and he tells us to pray only for those things which Jupiter gives and takes away. 'He gives life, he gives wealth; an untroubled mind I secure for myself.'[2] 'The calm of a mind blest in the consciousness of its virtue,' was the expression of supreme felicity the Epicureans had derived from their master.[3] Lucretius, in a magnificent passage, designates Epicurus as a god, and boasts that the popular divinities dwindle into insignificance before him. Ceres, he says, gave men corn, and Bacchus wine, but Epicurus the principles of virtue. Hercules conquered monsters, Epicurus conquered vice.[4] 'Pray,' said Juvenal, 'for a healthy mind in a healthy body. Ask for a brave soul unscared by death. . . . But there are things you can give yourself.'[5] 'Misfortune, and losses, and calumny,' said Seneca, 'disappear before virtue as the taper before the sun.'[6] 'In one point the sage is superior to God. God owes it to His nature not to fear, but the sage owes it to himself. Sublime condition! he joins the frailty of a man to the security of a god.'[7] 'Except for immortality,' he elsewhere writes, 'the sage is like to God.'[8] 'It is the characteristic of a wise man,'

---

[1] 'Atque hoc quidem omnes mortales sic habent . . . commoditatem prosperitatemque vitæ a diis se habere, virtutem autem nemo unquam acceptam deo retulit. Nimirum recte. Propter virtutem enim jure laudamur et in virtute recte gloriamur. Quod non contingeret si id donum a deo, non a nobis haberemus.'—Cicero, De Nat. Deor. iii. 36.
[2] Ep. i. 18.
[3] Seneca. Ep. lxvi.
[4] Lucretius, v. It was a Greek proverb, that Apollo begat Æscu-

lapius to heal the body, and Plato to heal the soul. (Legendre, Traité de l'Opinion, tome i. p. 197.)
[5] 'Orandum est ut sit mens sana in corpore sano:
Fortem posce animum, mortis terrore carentem. . . .
Monstro, quod ipse tibi possis dare.'
Juvenal, Sat. x. 356.
Marcus Aurelius recommends prayer, but only that we may be freed from evil desires. (ix. 11.)
[6] Seneca. Ep. lxvi.
[7] Ibid. Ep. liii.
[8] De Const. Sap. viii.

added Epictetus, 'that he looks for all his good and evil from himself.' · 'As far as his rational nature is concerned, he is in no degree inferior to the gods.'[2]

There were, however, other veins of thought exhibited in stoicism which greatly modified and sometimes positively contradicted this view of the relations of man to the Deity. The theology of the Stoics was an ill-defined, uncertain, and somewhat inconsistent Pantheism; the Divinity was especially worshipped under the two aspects of Providence and moral goodness, and the soul of man was regarded as 'a detached fragment of the Deity,'[3] or as at least pervaded and accompanied by a divine energy. 'There never,' said Cicero, 'was a great man, without an inspiration from on high.'[4] 'Nothing,' said Seneca, 'is closed to God. He is present in our conscience. He intervenes in our thoughts.'[5] 'I tell thee, Lucilius,' he elsewhere writes, 'a sacred spirit dwells within us, the observer and the guardian of our good and evil deeds. . . . No man is good without God. Who, save by His assistance, can rise above fortune? He gives noble and lofty counsels. A God (what God I know not) dwells in every good man.'[6] 'Offer to the God that is in thee,' said Marcus Aurelius, 'a manly being, a citizen, a soldier at his post ready to depart from life as soon as the trumpet sounds.'[7] 'It is sufficient to believe in the Genius who is within us, and to honour him by a pure worship.'[8]

Passages of this kind are not unfrequent in Stoical writings. More commonly, however, virtue is represented as a human act imitating God. This was the meaning of

---

[1] *Ench.* xlviii.
[2] Arrian, i. 12.
[3] Arrian, ii. 8. The same doctrine is strongly stated in Seneca, *Ep.* xcii.
[4] Cicero, *De Nat. Deor.* ii. 66.
[5] *Ep.* lxxxiii. Somewhat similar sentiments are attributed to Thales and Bion (Diog. Laërt.).

[6] *Ep.* xli. There are some beautiful sentiments of this kind in Plutarch's treatise, *De Sera Numinis Vindicta.* It was a saying of Pythagoras, that 'we become better as we approach the gods.'
[7] Marc. Aur. iii. 5.
[8] Marcus Aurelius.

the Platonic maxim, 'follow God,' which the Stoics continually repeated, which they developed in many passages of the most touching and beautiful piety, and to which they added the duty of the most absolute and unquestioning submission to the decrees of Providence. Their doctrine on this latter point harmonised well with their antipathy to the emotional side of our being. 'To weep, to complain, to groan, is to rebel;'[1] 'to fear, to grieve, to be angry, is to be a deserter.'[2] 'Remember that you are but an actor, acting whatever part the Master has ordained. It may be short, or it may be long. If He wishes you to represent a poor man, do so heartily; if a cripple, or a magistrate, or a private man, in each case act your part with honour.'[3] 'Never say of anything that you have lost it, but that you have restored it; your wife and child die—you have restored them; your farm is taken from you—that also is restored. It is seized by an impious man. What is it to you by whose instrumentality He who gave it reclaims it?'[4] 'God does not keep a good man in prosperity; He tries, He strengthens him, He prepares him for Himself.'[5] 'Those whom God approves, whom He loves, He hardens, He proves, He exercises; but those whom He seems to indulge and spare, He preserves for future ills.'[6] With a beautiful outburst of submissive gratitude, Marcus Aurelius exclaims, 'Some have said, Oh, dear city of Cecrops!—but thou, canst thou say, Oh, dear city of Jupiter? . . . All that is suitable to thee, oh world, is suitable to me.'[7]

These passages, which might be indefinitely multiplied, serve to show how successfully the Stoics laboured, by dilating upon the conception of Providence, to mitigate the arrogance which one aspect of their teaching unquestionably displayed. But in this very attempt another danger was incurred, upon

---

[1] Seneca, *Præf. Nat. Quæst.* iii.
[2] Marc. Aur. x. 25.
[3] Epict. *Ench.* xvii.
[4] Epict. *Ench.* xi.
[5] Seneca, *De Prov.* i.
[6] Ibid. iv.
[7] Marc. Aurel. ii. **2, 3.**

which a very large proportion of the moral systems of all ages have been wrecked. A doctrine which thus enjoins absolute submission to the decrees of Providence,[1] which proscribes the affections, and which represents its disciples as altogether independent of surrounding circumstances, would in most conditions of society have led necessarily to quietism, and proved absolutely incompatible with active virtue. Fortunately, however, in the ancient civilisations the idea of virtue had from the earliest times been so indissolubly connected with that of political activity that the danger was for a long period altogether avoided. The State occupied in antiquity a prominence in the thoughts of men which it never has attained in modern times. The influence of patriotism thrilled through every fibre of moral and intellectual life. The most profound philosophers, the purest moralists, the most sublime poets, had been soldiers or statesmen. Hence arose the excessive predominance occasionally accorded to civic virtues in ancient systems of ethics, and also not a few of their most revolting paradoxes. Plato advocated community of wives mainly on the ground that the children produced would be attached more exclusively to their country.[2] Aristotle may be almost said to have made the difference between Greek and barbarian the basis of his moral code.

---

[1] The language in which the Stoics sometimes spoke of the inexorable determination of all things by Providence would appear logically inconsistent with free will. In fact, however, the Stoics asserted the latter doctrine in unequivocal language, and in their practical ethics even exaggerated its power. Aulus Gellius (*Noct. Att.* vi. 2) has preserved a passage in which Chrysippus exerted his subtlety in reconciling the two things. See, too, Arrian, i. 17.

[2] We have an extremely curious illustration of this mode of thought in a speech of Archytas of Tarentum on the evils of sensuality, which Cicero has preserved. He considers the greatest of these evils to be that the vice predisposes men to unpatriotic acts. ' Nullam capitaliorem pestem quam corporis voluptatem, hominibus a natura datam. . . . . Hinc patriæ proditiones, hinc rerumpublicarum eversiones, hinc cum hostibus clandestina colloquia nasci,' etc.—Cicero, *De Senect.* xii.

The Spartan legislation was continually extolled as an ideal, as the Venetian constitution by the writers of the seventeenth century. On the other hand, the contact of the spheres of speculation and of political activity exercised in one respect a very beneficial influence upon ancient philosophies. Patriotism almost always occupied a prominence in the scale of duties, which forms a striking contrast to the neglect or discredit into which it has fallen among modern teachers. We do, indeed, read of an Anaxagoras pointing to heaven as to his true country, and pronouncing exile to be no evil, as the descent to the infernal regions is the same from every land;[1] but such sentiments, though not unknown among the Epicureans and the Cynics, were diametrically opposed to the prevailing tone. Patriotism was represented as a moral duty, and a duty of the highest order. Cicero only echoed the common opinion of antiquity in that noble passage, in which he asserts that the love we owe our country is even holier and more profound than that we owe our nearest kinsman, and that he can have no claim to the title of a good man who even hesitates to die in its behalf.[2]

A necessary consequence of this prominence of patriotism was the practical character of most ancient ethics. We find, indeed, moralists often exhorting men to moderate their ambition, consoling them under political adversity, and urging that there are some circumstances under which an upright man should for a time withdraw from public affairs;[3] but the general duty of taking part in political life was emphatically asserted, and the vanity of the quietist theory of life not only maintained, but even somewhat exaggerated. Thus

---

Diog. Laërt. *Anax.*

[2] 'Cari sunt parentes, cari liberi, propinqui, familiares; sed omnes omnium caritates patria una complexa est; pro qua quis bonus dubitet mortem oppetere si ei sit profuturus?'—*De Offic.* i. 17.

[3] See Seneca, *Consol. ad Helviam* and *De Otio Sapien.*; and Plutarch, *De Exilio.* The first of these works is the basis of one of the most beautiful compositions in the English language, Bolingbroke's *Reflections on Exile.*

15

Cicero declared that 'all virtue is in action.'[1] The younger Pliny mentions that he once lamented to the Stoic Euphrates the small place which his official duties left for philosophical pursuits; but Euphrates answered that the discharge of public affairs and the administration of justice formed a part, and the most important part, of philosophy, for he who is so engaged is but practising the precepts of the schools.[2] It was a fundamental maxim of the Stoics that humanity is a body in which each limb should act solely and continually with a view to the interests of the whole. Marcus Aurelius, the purest mind of the sect, was for nineteen years the active ruler of the civilised globe. Thrasea, Helvidius, Cornutus, and a crowd of others who had adopted Stoicism as a religion, lived, and in many cases died, in obedience to its precepts, struggling for the liberties of their country in the darkest hours of tyranny.

Men who had formed such high conceptions of duty, who had bridled so completely the tumult of passion, and whose lives were spent in a calm sense of virtue and of dignity, were little likely to be assailed by the superstitious fears that are the nightmare of weaker men. The preparation for death was deemed one of the chief ends of philosophy.[3] The thought of a coming change assisted the mind in detaching itself from the gifts of fortune, and the extinction of all superstitious terrors completed the type of self-reliant majesty which Stoicism had chosen for its ideal. But while it is certain that no philosophers expatiated upon death with a grander eloquence, or met it with a more placid courage, it can hardly be denied that their constant disquisitions forced it into an unhealthy prominence, and somewhat discoloured their whole view of life. 'The Stoics,' as Bacon has said, bestowed too much cost on death, and by their preparations

[1] De Officiis.
[2] Epist. i. 10.
[3] 'Tota enim philosophorum vita, ut ait idem, commentatio mortis est.'—Cicero, Tusc. i. 30, ad fin.

made it more fearful.'[1] There is a profound wisdom in the maxims of Spinoza, that 'the proper study of a wise man is not how to die, but how to live,' and that 'there is no subject on which the sage will think less than death.'[2] A life of active duty is the best preparation for the end, and so large a part of the evil of death lies in its anticipation, that an attempt to deprive it of its terrors by constant meditation almost necessarily defeats its object, while at the same time it forms an unnaturally tense, feverish, and tragical character, annihilates the ambition and enthusiasm that are essential to human progress, and not unfrequently casts a chill and a deadness over the affections.

Among the many half-pagan legends that were connected with Ireland during the middle ages, one of the most beautiful is that of the islands of life and of death. In a certain lake in Munster it is said there were two islands; into the first death could never enter, but age and sickness, and the weariness of life, and the paroxysms of fearful suffering were all known there, and they did their work till the inhabitants, tired of their immortality, learned to look upon the opposite island as upon a haven of repose : they launched their barks upon the gloomy waters; they touched its shore and they were at rest.[3]

This legend, which is far more akin to the spirit of paganism than to that of Christianity, and is in fact only another form of the myth of Tithonus, represents with great fidelity the aspect in which death was regarded by the exponents of Stoicism. There was much difference of opinion and of certitude in the judgments of the ancient philosophers

---

[1] *Essay on Death.*
[2] Spinoza, *Ethics,* iv. 67.
[3] Camden. Montalembert notices a similar legend as existing in Brittany (*Les Moines d'Occident,* tome ii. p. 287). Procopius (*De Bello Goth.* iv. 20) says that it is impossible for men to live in the west of Britain, and that the district is believed to be inhabited by the souls of the dead.

concerning the future destinies of the soul, but they were unanimous in regarding death simply as a natural rest, and in attributing the terrors that were connected with it to a diseased imagination. Death, they said, is the only evil that does not afflict us when present. While we are, death is not, when death has come we are not. It is a false belief that it only follows, it also precedes, life. It is to be as we were before we were born. The candle which has been extinguished is in the same condition as before it was lit, and the dead man as the man unborn. Death is the end of all sorrow. It either secures happiness or ends suffering. It frees the slave from his cruel master, opens the prison door, calms the qualms of pain, closes the struggles of poverty. It is the last and best boon of nature, for it frees man from all his cares. It is at worst but the close of a banquet we have enjoyed. Whether it be desired or whether it be shunned, it is no curse and no evil, but simply the resolution of our being into its primitive elements, the law of our nature to which it is our duty cheerfully to conform.

Such were the leading topics that were employed in that beautiful literature of ' Consolations,' which the academic Crantor is said to have originated, and which occupies so large a place in the writings of Cicero, Plutarch, and the Stoics. Cicero, like all the school of Plato, added to these motives a very firm and constant reference to the immortality of the soul. Plutarch held the same doctrine with equal assurance, but he gave it a much less conspicuous position in his ' Consolations,' and he based it not upon philosophical grounds, but upon the testimonies of the oracles, and upon the mysteries of Bacchus.[1] Among the Stoics the doctrine shone with a faint and uncertain light, and was seldom or never adopted as a motive. But that which is most impressive to a student who turns from the religious literature of

---

[1] In his *De Sera Numinis Vindicta* and his *Consolatio ad Uxorem*.

Christianity to the pagan philosophies, is the complete
absence in the latter of all notion concerning the penal character of death.    Death, according to Socrates,[1] either
extinguishes life or emancipates it from the thraldom of the
body.    Even in the first case it is a blessing, in the last it is
the greatest of boons.    'Accustom yourself,' said Epicurus,
'to the thought that death is indifferent; for all good and all
evil consist in feeling, and what is death but the privation of
feeling?'[2]    'Souls either remain after death,' said Cicero, 'or
they perish in death.    If they remain they are happy; if they
perish they are not wretched.'[3]    Seneca, consoling Polybius
concerning the death of his brother, exhorts his friend to
think, 'if the dead have any sensations, then my brother, let
loose as it were from a lifelong prison, and at last enjoying
his liberty, looks down from a loftier height on the wonders
of nature and on all the deeds of men, and sees more clearly
those divine things which he had so long sought in vain to
understand.    But why should I be afflicted for one who is
either happy or is nothing?    To lament the fate of one who
is happy is envy; to lament the fate of a nonentity is
madness.'[4]

But while the Greek and Roman philosophers were on
this point unanimous, there was a strong opposing current in
the popular mind.    The Greek word for superstition signifies
literally, fear of gods or dæmons, and the philosophers
sometimes represent the vulgar as shuddering at the thought
of death, through dread of certain endless sufferings to which
it would lead them.    The Greek mythology contains many
fables on the subject.    The early Greek vases occasionally

---

[1] In the *Phædo, passim.* See,
too, Marc. Aurelius, ii. 12.
[2] See a very striking letter of
Epicurus quoted by Diogenes Laërt.
in his life of that philosopher.
Except a few sentences, quoted by
other writers, these letters were all
that remained of the works of
Epicurus, till the recent discovery
of one of his treatises at Hercula-
neum.
[3] *Tusc. Quæst.* i.
[4] *Consol. ad Polyb.* xxvii.

represent scenes of infernal torments, not unlike those of the mediæval frescoes.[1] The rapture with which Epicureanism was received, as liberating the human mind from the thraldom of superstitious terrors, shows how galling must have been the yoke. In the poem of Lucretius, in occasional passages of Cicero and other Latin moralists, above all, in the treatise of Plutarch ' On Superstition,' we may trace the deep impression these terrors had made upon the populace, even during the later period of the Republic, and during the Empire. To destroy them was represented as the highest function of philosophy. Plutarch denounced them as the worst calumny against the Deity, as more pernicious than atheism, as the evil consequences of immoral fables, and he gladly turned to other legends which taught a different lesson. Thus it was related that when, during a certain festival at Argos, the horses that were to draw the statue of Juno to the temple were detained, the sons of the priestess yoked themselves to the car, and their mother, admiring their piety, prayed the goddess to reward them with whatever boon was the best for man. Her prayer was answered —they sank asleep and died.[2] In like manner the architects of the great temple of Apollo at Delphi, prayed the god to select that reward which was best. The oracle told them in reply to spend seven days in rejoicing, and on the following night their reward would come. They too died in sleep.[3] The swan was consecrated to Apollo because its dying song was believed to spring from a prophetic impulse.[4] The Spanish Celts raised temples, and sang hymns of praise to death.[5] No

---

[1] Maury, *Hist. des Religions de la Grèce antique*, tom. i. pp. 582–588. M. Ravaisson, in his Memoir on Stoicism (*Acad. des Inscriptions et Belles-lettres*, tom. xxi.) has enlarged on the terrorism of paganism, but has, I think, exaggerated it. Religions which selected games as

the natural form of devotion can never have had any very alarming character.

[2] Plutarch, *Ad Apollonium.*
[3] Ibid.
[4] Cic. *Tusc. Quæst.* i.
[5] Philost. Apoll. of Tyan. v. 4. Hence their passion for suicide,

philosopher of antiquity ever questioned that a good man, reviewing his life, might look upon it without shame and even with positive complacency, or that the reverence with which men regard heroic deaths is a foretaste of the sentence of the Creator. To this confidence may be traced the tranquil courage, the complete absence of all remorse, so conspicuous in the closing hours of Socrates, and of many other of the sages of antiquity. There is no fact in religious history more startling than the radical change that has in this respect passed over the character of devotion. It is said of Chilon, one of the seven sages of Greece, that at the close of his career he gathered his disciples around him, and congratulated himself that in a long life he could recall but a single act that saddened his dying hour. It was that, in a perplexing dilemma, he had allowed his love of a friend in some slight degree to obscure his sense of justice.[1] The writings of Cicero in his old age are full of passionate aspirations to a future world, unclouded by one regret or by one fear. Seneca died tranquilly, bequeathing to his friends 'the most precious of his possessions, the image of his life.'[2] Titus on his deathbed declared that he could remember only a single act with which to reproach himself.[3] On the last night in which Antoninus Pius lived, the tribune came to ask for the pass-word of the night. The dying emperor gave him ' æquanimitas.'[4] Julian, the last great representative of his expiring creed, caught up the same majestic strain. Amid

---

which Silius Italicus commemorates in lines which I think very beautiful:—

' Prodiga gens animæ et properare facillima mortem ;
Namque ubi transcendit florentes viribus annos
Impatiens ævi, spernit novisse senectam
Et fati modus in dextra est.'—i. 225-228.

Valerius Maximus (ii. vi. § 12) speaks of Celts who celebrated the birth of men with lamentation, and their deaths with joy.
[1] Aulus Gellius, Noctes, i. 3.
[2] Tacitus, Annales, xv. 62.
[3] Sueton. Titus, 10.
[4] Capitolinus, Antoninus.

the curses of angry priests, and the impending ruin of the cause he loved, he calmly died in the consciousness of his virtue; and his death, which is among the most fearless that antiquity records, was the last protest of philosophic paganism against the new doctrine that had arisen.[1]

It is customary with some writers, when exhibiting the many points in which the ancient philosophers anticipated Christian ethics, to represent Christianity as if it were merely a development or authoritative confirmation of the highest teaching of paganism, or as if the additions were at least of such a nature that there is but little doubt that the best and purest spirits of the pagan world, had they known them, would have gladly welcomed them. But this conception, which contains a large amount of truth if applied to the teaching of many Protestants, is either grossly exaggerated or absolutely false if applied to that of the patristic period or of mediæval Catholicism. On the very subject which the philosophers deemed the most important their unanimous conclusion was the extreme antithesis of the teaching of Catholicism. The philosophers taught that death is 'a law and not a punishment;'[2] the fathers taught that it is a penal infliction introduced into the world on account of the sin of Adam, which was also the cause of the appearance of all noxious plants, of all convulsions in the material globe, and, as was sometimes asserted, even of a diminution of the light of the sun. The first taught that death was the end of suffering; they ridiculed as the extreme of folly the notion that

---

[1] See the beautiful account of his last hours given by Ammianus Marcellinus and reproduced by Gibbon. There are some remarks well worth reading about the death of Julian, and the state of thought that rendered such a death possible, in Dr. Newman's *Discourses on University Education*, lect. ix.

[2] 'Lex non pœna mors' was a favourite saying among the ancients. On the other hand, Tertullian very distinctly enunciated the patristic view, 'Qui autem primordia hominis novimus, audenter determinamus mortem non ex natura secutam hominem sed ex culpa.'—*De Anima*, 52.

physical evils could await those whose bodies had been reduced to ashes, and they dwelt with emphatic eloquence upon the approaching, and, as they believed, final extinction of superstitious terrors. The second taught that death to the vast majority of the human race is but the beginning of endless and excruciating tortures—tortures before which the most ghastly of terrestrial sufferings dwindle into insignificance—tortures which no courage could defy—which none but an immortal being could endure. The first represented man as pure and innocent until his will had sinned; the second represented him as under a sentence of condemnation at the very moment of his birth. 'No funeral sacrifices,' said a great writer of the first school, 'are offered for children who die at an early age, and none of the ceremonies practised at the funerals of adults are performed at their tombs, for it is believed that infants have no hold upon earth or upon terrestrial affections. . . . The law forbids us to honour them because it is irreligious to lament for those pure souls who have passed into a better life and a happier dwelling-place.'[1] 'Whosoever shall tell us,' said a distinguished exponent of the patristic theology, 'that infants shall be quickened in Christ who die without partaking in His Sacrament, does both contradict the Apostle's teaching and condemn the whole Church. . . . And he that is not quickened in Christ must remain in that condemnation of which the Apostle speaks, "by one man's offence condemnation came upon all men to condemnation." To which condemnation infants are born liable as all the Church believes.'[2] The one school endeavoured to plant its foundations in the moral nature of mankind, by proclaiming that man can become acceptable to the Deity by his own virtue, and by this alone, that all sacrifices, rites, and forms are indifferent, and that the true worship of God is the recognition and imitation of His

---

[1] Plutarch, *Ad Uxorem*.    [2] St. Augustine, *Epist.* 166

goodness. According to the other school, the most heroic efforts
of human virtue are insufficient to avert a sentence of eternal
condemnation, unless united with an implicit belief in the
teachings of the Church, and a due observance of the rites it
enjoins. By the philosophers the ascription of anger and
vengeance to the Deity, and the apprehension of future
torture at His hands, were unanimously repudiated;[1] by
the priests the opposite opinion was deemed equally cen-
surable.[2]

These are fundamental points of difference, for they relate
to the fundamental principles of the ancient philosophy. The
main object of the pagan philosophers was to dispel the terrors
the imagination had cast around death, and by destroying
this last cause of fear to secure the liberty of man. The
main object of the Catholic priests has been to make death in
itself as revolting and appalling as possible, and by representing escape from its terrors as hopeless, except by complete
subjection to their rule, to convert it into an instrument of
government. By multiplying the dancing or warning skeletons, and other sepulchral images representing the loathsome-
ness of death without its repose; by substituting inhumation
for incremation, and concentrating the imagination on the
ghastliness of decay; above all, by peopling the unseen world
with demon phantoms and with excruciating tortures, the
Catholic Church succeeded in making death in itself unspeakably terrible, and in thus preparing men for the consolations
it could offer. Its legends, its ceremonies, its art,[3] its dog-

---

[1] 'At hoc quidem commune est
omnium philosophorum, non eorum
modo qui deum nihil habere ipsum
negotii dicunt, et nihil exhibere
alteri; sed eorum etiam, qui deum
semper agere aliquid et moliri
volunt, numquam nec irasci deum
nec nocere.'—Cic. De Offic. iii. 28.

[2] See the refutation of the

philosophic notion in Lactantius,
De Ira Dei.

[3] 'Revelation,' as Lessing observes in his essay on this subject,
'has made Death the "king of terrors." the awful offspring of sin
and the dread way to its punishment; though to the imagination
of the ancient heathen world,

matic teaching, all conspired to this end, and the history of
its miracles is a striking evidence of its success. The great
majority of superstitions have ever clustered around two
centres—the fear of death and the belief that every phenomenon of life is the result of a special spiritual interposition.
Among the ancients they were usually of the latter kind.
Auguries, prophecies, interventions in war, prodigies avenging
the neglect of some rite or marking some epoch in the fortunes of a nation or of a ruler, are the forms they usually
assumed. In the middle ages, although these were very
common, the most conspicuous superstitions took the form of
visions of purgatory or hell, conflicts with visible demons,
or Satanic miracles. Like those mothers who govern their
children by persuading them that the dark is crowded with
spectres that will seize the disobedient, and who often succeed
in creating an association of ideas which the adult man is
unable altogether to dissolve, the Catholic priests resolved to
base their power upon the nerves ; and as they long exercised
an absolute control over education, literature, and art, they
succeeded in completely reversing the teaching of ancient
philosophy, and in making the terrors of death for centuries
the nightmare of the imagination.

There is, indeed, another side to the picture. The vague
uncertainty with which the best pagans regarded death passed
away before the teaching of the Church, and it was often
replaced by a rapture of hope, which, however, the doctrine
of purgatory contributed at a later period largely to quell.
But, whatever may be thought of the justice of the Catholic
conception of death or of its influence upon human happiness,
it is plain that it is radically different from that of the pagan
philosophers. That man is not only an imperfect but a fallen
being, and that death is the penal consequence of his sin,

---

Greek or Etrurian, he was a
youthful genius—the twin brother
of Sleep, or a lusty boy with a
torch held downwards.'—Coleridge's *Biographia Litteraria*, cap.
xxii., note by Sara Coleridge.

was a doctrine profoundly new to mankind, and it has exercised an influence of the most serious character upon the moral history of the world.

The wide divergence of the classical from the Catholic conception of death appears very plainly in the attitude which each system adopted towards suicide. This is, perhaps, the most striking of all the points of contrast between the teaching of antiquity, and especially of the Roman Stoics, on the one hand, and that of almost all modern moralists on the other. It is indeed true that the ancients were by no means unanimous in their approval of the act. Pythagoras, to whom so many of the wisest sayings of antiquity are ascribed, is said to have forbidden men ' to depart from their guard or station in life without the order of their commander, that is, of God.'[1] Plato adopted similar language, though he permitted suicide when the law required it, and also when men had been struck down by intolerable calamity, or had sunk to the lowest depths of poverty.[2] Aristotle condemned it on civic grounds, as being an injury to the State.[3] The roll of Greek suicides is not long, though it contains some illustrious names, among others those of Zeno and Cleanthes.[4] In Rome, too, where suicide acquired a greater prominence, its lawfulness was by no means accepted as an axiom, and the story of Regulus,

---

[1] 'Vetat Pythagoras injussu imperatoris, id est Dei, de præsidio et statione vitæ decedere.'—Cic. *De Senec.* xx. If we believe the very untrustworthy evidence of Diog. Laërtius (*Pythagoras*) the philosopher himself committed suicide by starvation.

[2] See his *Laws*, lib. ix. In his *Phædon*, however, Plato went further, and condemned all suicide. Libanius says (*De Vita Sua*) that the arguments of the *Phædon* prevented him from committing suicide after the death of Julian. On the

other hand, Cicero mentions a certain Cleombrotus, who was so fascinated by the proof of the immortality of the soul in the *Phædon* that he forthwith cast himself into the sea. Cato, as is well known, chose this work to study, the night he committed suicide.

[3] Arist. *Ethic.* v.

[4] See a list of these in Lactantius' *Inst. Div.* iii. 18. Many of these instances rest on very doubtful evidence.

whether it be a history or a legend, shows that the patient
endurance of suffering was once the supreme ideal.[1] Virgil
painted in gloomy colours the condition of suicides in the
future world.[2] Cicero strongly asserted the doctrine of
Pythagoras, though he praised the suicide of Cato.[3] Apuleius,
expounding the philosophy of Plato, taught that ' the wise man
never throws off his body except by the will of God.'[4] Cæsar,
Ovid, and others urged that in extreme distress it is easy to
despise life, and that true courage is shown in enduring it.[5]
Among the Stoics themselves, the belief that no man may
shrink from a duty co-existed with the belief that every man
has a right to dispose of his own life. Seneca, who emphatically advocated suicide, admits that there were some who
deemed it wrong, and he himself attempted to moderate what
he termed ' the passion for suicide', that had arisen among his
disciples.[6] Marcus Aurelius wavers a little on the subject,
sometimes asserting the right of every man to leave life when

---

[1] Adam Smith's *Moral Sentiments*, part vii. § 2.

[2] ' Proxima deinde tenent mœsti
loca qui sibi lethum
Insontes peperere manu, lucemque
perosi
Projecere animas. Quam vellent
æthere in alto
Nunc et pauperiem et duros per-
ferre labores.'—*Æneid*, vi. 434-
437.

[3] Cicero has censured suicide in
his *De Senectute*, in the *Somn.
Scipionis*, and in the *Tusculans*.
Concerning the death of Cato, he
says, that the occasion was such as
to constitute a divine call to leave
life.—*Tusc.* i.

[4] Apuleius, *De Philos Plat.*
lib. i.

[5] Thus Ovid :—

' Rebus in adversis facile est con-
temnere vitam,
Fortiter ille facit qui miser
esse potest.'

See, too, Martial, xi. 56.

[6] Especially *Ep.* xxiv. Seneca
desires that men should not commit
suicide with panic or trepidation.
He says that those condemned to
death should await their execution,
for ' it is a folly to die through fear
of death ;' and he recommends
men to support old age as long as
their faculties remain unimpaired.
On this last point, however, his
language is somewhat contradictory. There is a good review of
the opinions of the ancients in
general, and of Seneca in particular, on this subject in Justus Lipsius' *Manuductio ad Stoicam Philo-
sophiam*, lib. iii. dissert. 22, 23,
from which I have borrowed much.

he pleases, sometimes inclining to the Platonic doctrine that man is a soldier of God, occupying a post which it is criminal to abandon.[1] Plotinus and Porphyry argued strongly against all suicide.[2]

But, notwithstanding these passages, there can be no question that the ancient view of suicide was broadly and strongly opposed to our own. A general approval of it floated down through most of the schools of philosophy, and even to those who condemned it, it never seems to have assumed its present aspect of extreme enormity. This was in the first instance due to the ancient notion of death; and we have also to remember that when a society once learns to tolerate suicide, the deed, in ceasing to be disgraceful, loses much of its actual criminality, for those who are most firmly convinced that the stigma and suffering it now brings upon the family of the deceased do not constitute its entire guilt, will readily acknowledge that they greatly aggravate it. In the conditions of ancient thought, this aggravation did not exist. Epicurus exhorted men ' to weigh carefully, whether they would prefer death to come to them, or would themselves

------

[1] In his *Meditations*, ix. 3, he speaks of the duty of patiently awaiting death. But in iii. 1, x. 8, 22–32, he clearly recognises the right of suicide in some cases, especially to prevent moral degeneracy. It must be remembered that the *Meditations* of Marcus Aurelius were private notes for his personal guidance, that all the Stoics admitted it to be wrong to commit suicide in cases where the act would be an injury to society, and that this consideration in itself would be sufficient to divert an emperor from the deed. Antoninus, the uncle, predecessor, and model of M. Aurelius, had considered it his duty several times to prevent Hadrian from committing suicide (Spartianus, *Hadrianus*). According to Capitolinus, Marcus Aurelius in his last illness purposely accelerated his death by abstinence. The duty of not hastily, or through cowardice, abandoning a path of duty, and the right of man to quit life when it appears intolerable, are combined very clearly by Epictetus, *Arrian*, i. 9; and the latter is asserted in the strongest manner, i. 24–25.

[2] Porphyry, *De Abst. Carnis*, ii. 47; Plotinus, 1st Enn. ix. Porphyry says (*Life of Plotinus*) that Plotinus dissuaded him from suicide. There is a good epitome of the arguments of this school against suicide in Macrobius, *In Som. Scip.* 1.

go to death;[1] and among his disciples, Lucretius, the illustrious poet of the sect, died by his own hand,[2] as did also Cassius the tyrannicide, Atticus the friend of Cicero,[3] the voluptuary Petronius,[4] and the philosopher Diodorus.[5] Pliny described the lot of man as in this respect at least superior to that of God, that man has the power of flying to the tomb,[6] and he represented it as one of the greatest proofs of the bounty of Providence, that it has filled the world with herbs, by which the weary may find a rapid and a painless death.[7] One of the most striking figures that a passing notice of Cicero brings before us, is that of Hegesias, who

---

[1] Quoted by Seneca, *Ep.* xxvi. Cicero states the Epicurean doctrine to be, 'Ut si tolerabiles sint dolores, feramus, sin minus æquo animo e vita, cum ea non placet, tanquam e theatro, exeamus' (*De Finib.* i. 15); and again, 'De Diis immortalibus sine ullo metu vera sentit. Non dubitat, si ita melius sit, de vita migrare.'— Id. i. 19.

[2] This is noticed by St. Jerome.

[3] Corn. Nepos, *Atticus.* He killed himself when an old man, to shorten a hopeless disease.

[4] Petronius, who was called the arbitrator of tastes ('elegantiæ arbiter'), was one of the most famous voluptuaries of the reign of Nero. Unlike most of his contemporaries, however, he was endowed with the most exquisite and refined taste; his graceful manners fascinated all about him, and made him in matters of pleasure the ruler of the Court. Appointed Proconsul of Bithynia, and afterwards Consul, he displayed the energies and the abilities of a statesman. A Court intrigue threw him out of favour; and believing that his death was resolved on, he determined to anticipate it by suicide. Calling his friends about him, he opened his veins, shut them, and opened them again; prolonged his lingering death till he had arranged his affairs; discoursed in his last moments, not about the immortality of the soul or the dogmas of philosophers, but about the gay songs and epigrams of the hour; and partaking of a cheerful banquet, died as recklessly as he had lived. (Tacit. *Annal.* xvi 18–19.) It has been a matter of much dispute whether or not this Petronius was the author of the *Satyricon,* one of the most licentious and repulsive works in Latin literature.

[5] Seneca, *De Vita Beata,* xix.

[6] 'Imperfectæ vero in homine naturæ præcipua solatia, ne Deum quidem posse omnia; namque nec sibi potest mortem consciscere si velit, quod homini dedit optimum in tantis vitæ pœnis.'—*Hist. Nat.* ii. 5.

[7] *Hist. Nat.* ii. 63. We need not be surprised at this writer thus speaking of sudden death, 'Mortes repentinæ (hoc est summa vitæ felicitas),' vii. 54.

was surnamed by the ancients 'the orator of death.' A conspicuous member of that Cyrenaic school which esteemed the pursuit of pleasure the sole end of a rational being, he taught that life was so full of cares, and its pleasure so fleeting and so alloyed, that the happiest lot for man was death; and such was the power of his eloquence, so intense was the fascination he cast around the tomb, that his disciples embraced with rapture the consequence of his doctrine, multitudes freed themselves by suicide from the troubles of the world, and the contagion was so great, that Ptolemy, it is said, was compelled to banish the philosopher from Alexandria.[1]

But it was in the Roman Empire and among the Roman Stoics that suicide assumed its greatest prominence, and its philosophy was most fully elaborated. From an early period self-immolation, like that of Curtius or Decius, had been esteemed in some circumstances a religious rite, being, as has been well suggested, probably a lingering remnant of the custom of human sacrifices,[2] and towards the closing days of paganism many influences conspired in the same direction. The example of Cato, who had become the ideal of the Stoics, and whose dramatic suicide was the favourite subject of their eloquence,[3] the indifference to death produced by the great multiplication of gladiatorial shows, the many instances of barbarian captives, who, sooner than slay their fellow-countrymen, or minister to the pleasures of their conquerors, plunged their lances into their own necks, or found

---

[1] *Tusc. Quæst.* lib. 1. Another remarkable example of an epidemic of suicide occurred among the young girls of Miletus. (*Aul. Gell.* xv. 10.)

[2] Sir Cornewall Lewis, *On the Credibility of Early Roman History,* vol. ii. p. 430. See, too, on this class of suicides, Cromaziano, *Istorica Critica del Suicidio* (Venezia,

1788), pp. 81–82. The real name of the author of this book (which is, I think, the best history of suicide) was Buonafede. He was a Celestine monk. The book was first published at Lucca in 1761. It was translated into French in 1841.

[3] Senec. *De Provid.* ii.; *Ep.* xxiv.

otner and still more horrible roads to freedom,[1] the custom
of compelling political prisoners to execute their own sentence,
and, more than all, the capricious and atrocious tyranny
of the Cæsars,[2] had raised suicide into an extraordinary
prominence. Few things are more touching than the passionate joy with which, in the reign of Nero, Seneca clung
to it as the one refuge for the oppressed, the last bulwark
of the tottering mind. 'To death alone it is due that life
is not a punishment, that, erect beneath the frowns of
fortune, I can preserve my mind unshaken and master of
itself. I have one to whom I can appeal. I see before me
the crosses of many forms. . . . I see the rack and the scourge,
and the instruments of torture adapted to every limb and to
every nerve; but I also see Death. She stands beyond my
savage enemies, beyond my haughty fellow-countrymen.
Slavery loses its bitterness when by a step I can pass to
liberty. Against all the injuries of life, I have the refuge of
death.'[3] 'Wherever you look, there is the end of evils. You
see that yawning precipice—there you may descend to
liberty. You see that sea, that river, that well—liberty sits
at the bottom. . . . Do you seek the way to freedom?—you
may find it in every vein of your body.'[4] 'If I can choose
between a death of torture and one that is simple and easy,
why should I not select the latter? As I choose the ship
in which I will sail, and the house I will inhabit, so I will
choose the death by which I will leave life. . . . In no matter more than in death should we act according to our desire.
Depart from life as your impulse leads you, whether it be by
the sword, or the rope, or the poison creeping through the
veins; go your way, and break the chains of slavery. Man
should seek the approbation of others in his life; his death

---

[1] See some examples of this in
Seneca, *Ep.* lxx.
[2] See a long catalogue of suicides arising from this cause, in
Cromaziano, *Ist. del Suicidio*, pp.
112-.14.
[3] *Consol. ad Marc.* c. xx.
[4] *De Ira*, iii. 15

16

concerns himself alone. That is the best which pleases him most. . . . The eternal law has decreed nothing better than this, that life should have but one entrance and many exits. Why should I endure the agonies of disease, and the cruelties of human tyranny, when I can emancipate myself from all my torments, and shake off every bond? For this reason, but for this alone, life is not an evil—that no one is obliged to live. The lot of man is happy, because no one continues wretched but by his fault. If life pleases you, live. If not, you have a right to return whence you came.'[1]

These passages, which are but a few selected out of very many, will sufficiently show the passion with which the most influential teacher of Roman Stoicism advocated suicide. As a general proposition, the law recognised it as a right, but two slight restrictions were after a time imposed.[2] It had

[1] *Ep.* lxx.

[2] See Donne's *Biathanatos* (London, 1700), pp. 56–57. Gibbon's *Decline and Fall*, ch. xliv. Blackstone, in his chapter on suicide, quotes the sentence of the Roman lawyers on the subject: 'Si quis impatientia doloris aut tædio vitæ aut morbo aut furore aut pudore mori maluit non animadvertatur in eum.' Ulpian expressly asserts that the wills of suicides were recognised by law, and numerous examples of the act, notoriously prepared and publicly and gradually accomplished, prove its legality in Rome. Suetonius, it is true, speaks of Claudius accusing a man for having tried to kill himself (Claud. xvi.), and Xiphilin says (lxix. 8) that Hadrian gave special permission to the philosopher Euphrates to commit suicide, 'on account of old age and disease;' but in the first case it appears from the context that a reproach

and not a legal action was meant, while Euphrates, I suppose, asked permission to show his loyalty to the emperor, and not as a matter of strict necessity. There were, however, some Greek laws condemning suicide, probably on civic grounds. Josephus mentions (*De Bell. Jud.* iii. 8) that in some nations 'the right hand of the suicide was amputated, and that in Judea the suicide was only buried after sunset.' A very strange law, said to have been derived from Greece, is reported to have existed at Marseilles. Poison was kept by the senate of the city, and given to those who could prove that they had sufficient reason to justify their desire for death, and all other suicide was forbidden. The law was intended, it was said, to prevent hasty suicide, and to make deliberate suicide as rapid and painless as possible. (Valer. Maximus, ii. 6, § 7.) In the Reign

become customary with many men who were accused of political offences to commit suicide before trial, in order to prevent the ignominious exposure of their bodies and the confiscation of their goods; but Domitian closed this resource by ordaining that the suicide of an accused person should entail the same consequences as his condemnation. Hadrian afterwards assimilated the suicide of a Roman soldier to desertion.[1] With these exceptions, the liberty appears to have been absolute, and the act was committed under the most various motives. The suicide of Otho, who is said to have killed himself to avoid being a second time a cause of civil war, was extolled as equal in grandeur to that of Cato.[2] In the Dacian war, the enemy, having captured a distinguished Roman general named Longinus, endeavoured to extort terms from Trajan as a condition of his surrender, but Longinus, by taking poison, freed the emperor from his embarrassment.[3] On the death of Otho, some of his soldiers, filled with grief and admiration, killed themselves before his corpse,[4] as did also a freedman of Agrippina, at the funeral of the empress.[5] Before the close of the Republic, an enthusiastic partisan of one of the factions in the chariot races flung himself upon the pile on which the body of a favourite coachman was consumed, and perished in the flames.[6] A Roman, unmenaced in his

---

of Terror in France, a law was made similar to that of Domitian. (Carlyle's *Hist. of the French Revolution*, book v. c. ii.)

[1] Compare with this a curious 'order of the day,' issued by Napoleon in 1802, with the view of checking the prevalence of suicide among his soldiers. (Lisle, *Du Suicide*, pp. 462-463.)

[2] See Suetonius, *Otho*, c. x.-xi., and the very fine description in Tacitus, *Hist.* lib. ii. c. 47-49. Martial compares the death of Otho to that of Cato:

'Sit Cato, dum vivit, sane vel Cæsare major;
Dum moritur, numquid major
Othone fuit?'—*Ep.* vi. 32.

[3] Xiphilin, lxviii. 12.

[4] Tacit. *Hist.* ii. 49. Suet. *Otho*, 12. Suetonius says that, in addition to these, many soldiers who were not present killed themselves on hearing the news.

[5] Ibid. *Annal.* xiv. 9.

[6] Plin. *Hist. Nat.* vii. 54. The opposite faction attributed this suicide to the maddening effects of the perfumes burnt on the pile.

fortune, and standing high in the favour of his sovereign, killed himself under Tiberius, because he could not endure to witness the crimes of the empire.[1] Another, being afflicted by an incurable malady, postponed his suicide till the death of Domitian, that at least he might die free, and on the assassination of the tyrant, hastened cheerfully to the tomb.[2] The Cynic Peregrinus announced that, being weary of life, he would on a certain day depart, and, in presence of a large concourse, he mounted the funeral pile.[3] Most frequently, however, death was regarded as 'the last physician of disease,'[4] and suicide as the legitimate relief from intolerable suffering. 'Above all things,' said Epictetus, 'remember that the door is open. Be not more timid than boys at play. As they, when they cease to take pleasure in their games, declare they will no longer play, so do you, when all things begin to pall upon you, retire ; but if you stay, do not complain.'[5] Seneca declared that he who waits the extremity of old age is not 'far removed from a coward,' 'as he is justly regarded as too much addicted to wine who drains the flask to the very dregs.' ' I will not relinquish old age,' he added, 'if it leaves my better part intact. But if it begins to shake my mind, if it destroys its faculties one by one, if it leaves me not life but breath, I will depart from the putrid or tottering edifice. I will not escape by death from disease so long as it may be healed, and leaves my mind unimpaired. I will not raise my hand against myself on account of pain, for so to die is to be conquered. But if I know that I must suffer without hope of relief, I will depart, not through fear of the pain itself, but because it prevents all for which I would live.'[6] 'Just as a landlord,' said Musonius, 'who has not received his rent, pulls

---

[1] Tacit. *Annal.* vi. 26.
[2] Plin. *Ep.* i. 12.
[3] This history is satirically and unfeelingly told by Lucian. See,

too, Ammianus Marcellinus, **xxix.** 1.
[4] Sophocles.
[5] Arrian, i. 24.
[6] Seneca, *Ep.* lviii.

down the doors, removes the rafters, and fills up the well, so I seem to be driven out of this little body, when nature, which has let it to me, takes away, one by one, eyes and ears, hands and feet. I will not, therefore, delay longer, but will cheerfully depart as from a banquet.'[1]

This conception of suicide as an euthanasia, an abridgment of the pangs of disease, and a guarantee against the dotage of age, was not confined to philosophical treatises. We have considerable evidence of its being frequently put in practice. Among those who thus abridged their lives was Silius Italicus, one of the last of the Latin poets.[2] The younger Pliny describes in terms of the most glowing admiration the conduct of one of his friends, who, struck down by disease, resolved calmly and deliberately upon the path he should pursue. He determined, if the disease was only dangerous and long, to yield to the wishes of his friends and await the struggle ; but if the issue was hopeless, to die by his own hand. Having reasoned on the propriety of this course with all the tranquil courage of a Roman, he summoned a council of physicians, and, with a mind indifferent to either fate, he calmly awaited their sentence.[3] The same writer mentions the case of a man who was afflicted with a horrible disease, which reduced his body to a mass of sores. His wife, being convinced that it was incurable, exhorted her husband to shorten his sufferings ; she nerved and encouraged him to the effort, and she claimed it as her privilege to accompany him to the grave. Husband and wife, bound

---

[1] Stobæus. One of the most deliberate suicides recorded was that of a Greek woman of ninety years old.—Val. Maxim. ii. 6, § 8.
[2] Plin. *Ep.* iii. 7. He starved himself to death.
[3] *Ep.* i. 22. Some of Pliny's expressions are remarkable :—'Id ego arduum in primis et præcipua laude dignum put ). Nam impetu quodam et instinctu procurrere ad mortem, commune cum multis deliberare vero et causas ejus ex pendere, utque suaserit ratio, vitæ mortisque consilium suscipere vel ponere, ingentis est animi.' In this case the doctors pronounced that recovery was possible, and the suicide was in consequence averted.

together, plunged into a lake.[1]  Seneca, in one of his letters, has left us a detailed description of the death-bed of one of the Roman suicides.  Tullius Marcellinus, a young man of remarkable abilities and very earnest character, who had long ridiculed the teachings of philosophy, but had ended by embracing it with all the passion of a convert, being afflicted with a grave and lingering though not incurable disease, resolved at length upon suicide.  He gathered his friends around him, and many of them entreated him to continue in life.  Among them, however, was one Stoical philosopher, who addressed him in what Seneca terms the very noblest of discourses. He exhorted him not to lay too much stress upon the question he was deciding, as if existence was a matter of great importance.  He urged that life is a thing we possess in common with slaves and animals, but that a noble death should indeed be prized, and he concluded by recommending suicide. Marcellinus gladly embraced the counsel which his own wishes had anticipated.  According to the advice of his friend, he distributed gifts among his faithful slaves, consoled them on their approaching bereavement, abstained during three days from all food, and at last, when his strength had been wholly exhausted, passed into a warm bath and calmly died, describing with his last breath the pleasing sensations that accompanied receding life.[2]

The doctrine of suicide was indeed the culminating point of Roman Stoicism.  The proud, self-reliant, unbending character of the philosopher could only be sustained when he felt that he had a sure refuge against the extreme forms of suffering or of despair.  Although virtue is not a mere creature of interest, no great system has ever yet flourished which did not present an ideal of happiness as well as an ideal of duty.  Stoicism taught men to hope little, but to fear nothing.

---

[1] Lib. vi. *Ep.* xxiv.
[2] *Ep.* lxxvii.  On the former career of Marcellinus, see *Ep.* xxix.

It did not array death in brilliant colours, as the path to
positive felicity, but it endeavoured to divest it, as the end
of suffering, of every terror. Life lost much of its bitterness
when men had found a refuge from the storms of fate, a
speedy deliverance from dotage and pain. Death ceased to
be terrible when it was regarded rather as a remedy than as
a sentence. Life and death in the Stoical system were attuned
to the same key. The deification of human virtue, the total
absence of all sense of sin, the proud stubborn will that deemed
humiliation the worst of stains, appeared alike in each. The
type of its own kind was perfect. All the virtues and all the
majesty that accompany human pride, when developed to the
highest point, and directed to the noblest ends, were here displayed. All those which accompany humility and self-abase-
ment were absent.

I desire at this stage of our enquiry to pause for a moment,
in order to retrace briefly the leading steps of the foregoing
argument, and thus to bring into the clearest light the connection which many details and quotations may have occasionally obscured. Such a review will show at a single glance
in what respects Stoicism was a result of the pre-existent state
of society, and in what respects it was an active agent, how
far its influence was preparing the way for Christian ethics,
and how far it was opposed to them.

We have seen, then, that among the Romans, as among
other people, a very clear and definite type of moral excellence
was created before men had formed any clear intellectual
notions of the nature and sanctions of virtue. The characters
of men are chiefly governed by their occupations, and the republic being organised altogether with a view to military
success, it had attained all the virtues and vices of a military
society. We have seen, too, that at all times, but most
especially under the conditions of ancient warfare, military life
is very unfavourable to the amiable, and very favourable to
the heroic virtues. The Roman had learnt to value force

very highly.  Being continually engaged in inflicting pain, his natural or instinctive humanity was very low.  His moral feelings were almost bounded by political limits, acting only, and with different degrees of intensity, towards his class, his country, and its allies.  Indomitable pride was the most prominent element of his character.  A victorious army which is humble or diffident, or tolerant of insult, or anxious to take the second place, is, indeed, almost a contradiction of terms.  The spirit of patriotism, in its relation to foreigners, like that of political liberty in its relation to governors, is a spirit of constant and jealous self-assertion ; and although both are very consonant with high morality and great self-devotion, we rarely find that the grace of genuine humility can flourish in a society that is intensely pervaded by their influence.  The kind of excellence that found most favour in Roman eyes was simple, forcible, massive, but coarse-grained.  Subtilty of motives, refinements of feelings, delicacies of susceptibility, were rarely appreciated.

This was the darker side of the picture.  On the other hand, the national character, being formed by a profession in which mercenary considerations are less powerful, and splendid examples of self-devotion more frequent, than in any other, had early risen to a heroic level.  Death being continually confronted, to meet it with courage was the chief test of virtue.  The habits of men were unaffected, frugal, honourable, and laborious.  A stern discipline pervading all ages and classes of society, the will was trained, to an almost unexampled degree, to repress the passions, to endure suffering and opposition, to tend steadily and fearlessly towards an unpopular end.  A sense of duty was very widely diffused, and a deep attachment to the interests of the city became the parent of many virtues.

Such was the type of excellence the Roman people had attained at a time when its intellectual cultivation produced philosophical discussions, and when numerous Greek professors, attracted partly by political events, and partly by the patronage of Scipio Æmilianus, arrived at Rome, bringing with them the tenets of the great schools of Zeno and Epicurus, and of the many minor sects that clustered around them. Epicureanism being essentially opposed to the pre-existing type of virtue, though it spread greatly, never attained the position of a school of virtue. Stoicism, taught by Panætius of Rhodes, and soon after by the Syrian Posidonius, became the true religion of the educated classes. It furnished the principles of virtue, coloured the noblest literature of the time, and guided all the developments of moral enthusiasm.

The Stoical system of ethics was in the highest sense a system of independent morals. It taught that our reason reveals to us a certain law of nature, and that a desire to conform to this law, irrespectively of all considerations of reward or punishment, of happiness or the reverse, is a possible and a sufficient motive of virtue. It was also in the highest sense a system of discipline. It taught that the will, acting under the complete control of the reason, is the sole principle of virtue, and that all the emotional part of our being is of the nature of a disease. Its whole tendency was therefore to dignify and strengthen the will, and to degrade and suppress the desires. It taught, moreover, that man is capable of attaining an extremely high degree of moral excellence, that he has nothing to fear beyond the present life, that it is essential to the dignity and consistence of his character that he should regard death without dismay, and that he has a right to hasten it if he desires.

It is easy to see that this system of ethics was strictly consonant with the type of character the circumstances of the Roman people had formed. It is also manifest that while the force of circumstances had in the first instance secured its ascendancy, the energy of will which it produced would enable it to offer a powerful resistance to the tendencies of an altered condition of society. This was pre-eminently

shown in the history of Roman Stoicism. The austere
purity of the writings of Seneca and his school is a fact
probably unique in history, when we consider, on the one
hand, the intense and undisguised depravity of the Empire,
and on the other, the prominent position of most of the
leading Stoics in the very centre of the stream. More than
once in later periods did great intellectual brilliancy coincide
with general depravity, but on none of these occasions was
this moral phenomenon reproduced. In the age of Leo X.,
in the age of the French Regency, or of Lewis XV., we look
in vain for high moral teaching in the centre of Italian or of
Parisian civilisation. The true teachers of those ages were
the reformers, who arose in obscure towns of Germany or
Switzerland, or that diseased recluse who, from his solitude
near Geneva, fascinated Europe by the gleams of a dazzling
and almost peerless eloquence, and by a moral teaching
which, though often feverish, paradoxical, and unpractical,
abounded in passages of transcendent majesty and of the
most entrancing purity and beauty. But even the best
moral teachers who rose in the centres of the depraved
society felt the contagion of the surrounding vice. Their
ideal was depressed, their austerity was relaxed, they appealed
to sordid and worldly motives, their judgments of character
were wavering and uncertain, their whole teaching was of
the nature of a compromise. But in ancient Rome, if the
teachers of virtue acted but feebly upon the surrounding
corruption, their own tenets were at least unstained. The
splendour of the genius of Cæsar never eclipsed the moral
grandeur of the vanquished Cato, and amid all the dramatic
vicissitudes of civil war and of political convulsion, the
supreme authority of moral distinctions was never forgotten.
The eloquence of Livy was chiefly employed in painting
virtue, the eloquence of Tacitus in branding vice. The
Stoics never lowered their standard because of the depravity
around them, and if we trace in their teaching any reflection

of the prevailing worship of enjoyment, it is only in the passionate intensity with which they dwelt upon the tranquillity of the tomb.

But it is not sufficient for a moral system to form a bulwark against vice, it must also be capable of admitting those extensions and refinements of moral sympathies which advancing civilisation produces, and the inflexibility of its antagonism to evil by no means implies its capacity of enlarging its conceptions of good. During the period which elapsed between the importation of Stoical tenets into Rome and the ascendancy of Christianity, an extremely important transformation of moral ideas had been effected by political changes, and it became a question how far the new elements could coalesce with the Stoical ideal, and how far they tended to replace it by an essentially different type. These changes were twofold, but were very closely connected. They consisted of the increasing prominence of the benevolent or amiable, as distinguished from the heroic qualities, and of the enlargement of moral sympathies, which having at first comprised only a class or a nation, came at last, by the destruction of many artificial barriers, to include all classes and all nations. The causes of these changes—which were the most important antecedents of the triumph of Christianity—are very complicated and numerous, but it will, I think, be possible to give in a few pages a sufficiently clear outline of the movement.

It originated in the Roman Empire at the time when the union of the Greek and Latin civilisations was effected by the conquest of Greece. The general humanity of the Greeks had always been incomparably greater than that of the Romans. The refining influence of their art and literature, their ignorance of gladiatorial games, and their comparative freedom from the spirit of conquest, had separated them widely from their semi-barbarous conquerors, and had given a peculiar softness and tenderness to their ideal

characters.   Pericles, who, when the friends who had
gathered round his death-bed, imagining him to be insensible,
were recounting his splendid deeds, told them that they had
forgotten his best title to fame—that 'no Athenian had ever
worn mourning on his account;' Aristides, praying the gods
that those who had banished him might never be compelled
by danger or suffering to recall him; Phocion, when unjustly
condemned, exhorting his son never to avenge his death, all
represent a type of character of a milder kind than that
which Roman influences produced.   The plays of Euripides
had been to the ancient world the first great revelation of
the supreme beauty of the gentler virtues.   Among the many
forms of worship that flourished at Athens, there was an
altar which stood alone, conspicuous and honoured beyond
all others.   The suppliants thronged around it, but no image
of a god, no symbol of dogma was there.   It was dedicated
to Pity, and was venerated through all the ancient world as
the first great assertion among mankind of the supreme
sanctity of Mercy.[1]

But while the Greek spirit was from a very early period

---

[1] See the very beautiful lines of
Statius:—

'Urbe fuit media nulli concessa
        potentum
Ara Deum, mitis posuit Clementia
    sedem:
Et miseri fecere sacram, sine sup-
    plice numquam
Illa novo; nulla damnavit vota
    repulsa.
Auditi quicunque rogant, noc-
    tesque diesque
Ire datum, et solis numen placare
    querelis.
Parca superstitio; non thurea
    flamma, nec altus
Accipitur sanguis, lachrymis al-
    taria sudant. . .

Nulla autem effigies, nulli com
    missa metallo
Forma Deæ, mentes habitare et
    pectora gaudet.
Semper habet trepidos, semper
    locus horret egenis
Cœtibus, ignotæ tantum felicibus
    aræ.'—Thebaid, xii. 481-496.

This altar was very old, and was
said to have been founded by the
descendants of Hercules. Diodorus
of Sicily, however, makes a Syra-
cusan say that it was brought from
Syracuse (lib. xiii. 22).   Marcus
Aurelius erected a temple to 'Bene-
ficentia' on the Capitol. (Xiphilin,
lib. lxxi. 34.)

distinguished for its humanity, it was at first as far removed from cosmopolitanism as that of Rome. It is well known that Phrynichus was fined because in his 'Conquest of Miletus' he had represented the triumph of barbarians over Greeks.[1] His successor, Æschylus, deemed it necessary to violate all dramatic probabilities by making the Persian king and courtiers continually speak of themselves as barbarians. Socrates, indeed, had proclaimed himself a citizen of the world,[2] but Aristotle taught that Greeks had no more duties to barbarians than to wild beasts, and another philosopher was believed to have evinced an almost excessive range of sympathy when he declared that his affections extended beyond his own State, and included the whole people of Greece. But the dissolving and disintegrating philosophical discussions that soon followed the death of Socrates, strengthened by political events, tended powerfully to destroy this feeling. The traditions that attached Greek philosophy to Egypt, the subsequent admiration for the schools of India to which Pyrrho and Anaxarchus are said to have resorted,[3] the prevalence of Cynicism and Epicureanism, which agreed in inculcating indifference to political life, the complete decomposition of the popular national religions, and the incompatibility of a narrow local feeling with great knowledge and matured civilisation, were the intellectual causes of the change, and the movement of expansion received a great political stimulus when Alexander eclipsed the glories of Spartan and Athenian history by the vision of universal empire, accorded to the conquered nations the privileges of the conquerors, and

---

[1] Herodotus, vi. 21.
[2] See Arrian's *Epictetus*, i. 9. The very existence of the word φιλανθρωπία shows that the idea was not altogether unknown.
[3] Diog. Laërt. *Pyrrho*. There was a tradition that Pythagoras had himself penetrated to India, and learnt philosophy from the gymnosophists. (Apuleius, *Florid* lib. ii. c. 15.)

created in Alexandria a great centre both of commercial inter-course and of philosophical eclecticism.[1]

It is evident, therefore, that the prevalence of Greek ideas in Rome would be in a two-fold way destructive of narrow national feelings. It was the ascendancy of a people who were not Romans, and of a people who had already become in a great degree emancipated from local sentiments. It is also evident that the Greeks having had for several centuries a splendid literature, at a time when the Romans had none, and when the Latin language was still too rude for literary purposes, the period in which the Romans first emerged from a purely military condition into an intelligent civilisation would bring with it an ascendancy of Greek ideas. Fabius Pictor and Cincius Alimentus, the earliest native Roman his-torians, both wrote in Greek,[2] and although the poems of Ennius, and the 'Origines' of Marcus Cato, contributed largely to improve and fix the Latin language, the precedent was not at once discontinued.[3]    After the conquest of Greece, the political ascendancy of the Romans and the intellectual ascendancy of Greece were alike universal.[4]    The conquered

---

[1] This aspect of the career of Alexander was noticed in a re-markable passage of a treatise ascribed to Plutarch (*De Fort. Alex.*). 'Conceiving he was sent by God to be an umpire between all, and to unite all together, he reduced by arms those whom he could not conquer by persuasion, and formed of a hundred diverse nations one single universal body, mingling, as it were, in one cup of friendship the customs, marriages, and laws of all. He desired that all should regard the whole world as their common country, . . . that every good man should be esteemed a Hellene, every evil man a bar-barian.' See on this subject the third lecture of Mr. Merivale (whose

translation of Plutarch I have bor-rowed) *On the Conversion of the Roman Empire.*

[2] They were both born about B.C. 250. See Sir C. Lewis, *Credi-bility of Early Roman History*, vol. i. p. 82.

[3] Aulus Gellius mentions the indignation of Marcus Cato against a consul named Albinus, who had written in Greek a Roman history, and prefaced it by an apology for his faults of style, on the ground that he was writing in a foreign language. (*Noct Att.* xi. 8.)

[4] See a vivid picture of the Greek influence upon Rome, in Mommsen's *Hist. of Rome* (Eng. trans.), vol. iii. pp. 423–426.

people, whose patriotic feelings had been greatly enfeebled by the influences I have noticed, acquiesced readily in their new condition, and notwithstanding the vehement exertions of the conservative party, Greek manners, sentiments, and ideas soon penetrated into all classes, and moulded all the forms of Roman life. The elder Cato, as an acute observer has noticed, desired all Greek philosophers to be expelled from Rome. The younger Cato made Greek philosophers his most intimate friends.[1] Roman virtue found its highest expression in Stoicism. Roman vice sheltered itself under the name of Epicurus. Diodorus of Sicily and Polybius first sketched in Greek the outlines of universal history. Dionysius of Halicarnassus explored Roman antiquities. Greek artists and Greek architects thronged the city; but the first, under Roman influence, abandoned the ideal for the portrait, and the second degraded the noble Corinthian pillar into the bastard composite.[2] The theatre, which now started into sudden life, was borrowed altogether from the Greeks. Ennius and Pacuvius imitated Euripides; Cæcilius, Plautus, Terence, and Nævius devoted themselves chiefly to Menander. Even the lover in the days of Lucretius painted his lady's charms in Greek.[3] Immense sums were given for Greek literary slaves, and the attractions of the capital drew to Rome nearly all that was brilliant in Athenian society.

While the complete ascendancy of the intellect and manners of Greece was destroying the simplicity of the old Roman type, and at the same time enlarging the range of

---

[1] Plin. Hist. Nat. vii. 31.
[2] See Friedlænder, Mœurs romaines du règne d'Auguste à la fin des Antonins (French trans., 1865), tome i. pp. 6–7.
[3] See the curious catalogue of Greek love terms in vogue (Lucretius, lib. iv. line 1160, &c.). Juvenal, more than a hundred years later, was extremely angry with the Roman ladies for making love in Greek (Sat. vi. lines 190–195). Friedlænder remarks that there is no special term in Latin for to ask in marriage (tome i. p. 354).

Roman sympathies, an equally powerful influence was break-ing down the aristocratic and class feeling which had so long raised an insurmountable barrier between the nobles and the plebeians. Their long contentions had issued in the civil wars, the dictatorship of Julius Cæsar, and the Empire, and these changes in a great measure obliterated the old lines of demarcation. Foreign wars, which develop with great inten-sity distinctive national types, and divert the public mind from internal changes, are usually favourable to the conser-vative spirit; but civil wars are essentially revolutionary, for they overwhelm all class barriers and throw open the highest prizes to energy and genius. Two very remarkable and alto-gether unprecedented illustrations of this truth occurred at Rome. Ventidius Bassus, by his military skill, and by the friendship of Julius Cæsar, and afterwards of Antony, rose from the position of mule-driver to the command of a Roman army, and at last to the consulate,[1] which was also attained, about 40 B.C., by the Spaniard Cornelius Balbus.[2] Augustus, though the most aristocratic of emperors, in order to dis-courage celibacy, permitted all citizens who were not senators to intermarry with freedwomen. The empire was in several distinct ways unfavourable to class distinctions. It was for the most part essentially democratic, winning its popularity from the masses of the people, and crushing the senate, which had been the common centre of aristocracy and of freedom. A new despotic power, bearing alike on all classes, reduced them to an equality of servitude. The emperors were them-selves in many cases the mere creatures of revolt, and their policy was governed by their origin. Their jealousy struck

---

[1] Aul. Gell. *Noct.* xv. 4; Vell. Paterculus, ii. 65. The people were much scandalised at this elevation, and made epigrams about it. There is a curious catalogue of men who at different times rose in Rome from low positions to power and dignity. in Legendre, *Traité de l'Opinion*, tome ii. pp. 254–255.

[2] Dion Cassius, xlviii. 32. Plin *Hist. Nat.* v. 5; vii. 44.

down many of the nobles, while others were ruined by the
public games, which it became customary to give, or by the
luxury to which, in the absence of political occupations, they
were impelled, and the relative importance of all was diminished by the new creations. The ascendancy of wealth
began to pass into new quarters. Delators, or political in-
formers, encouraged by the emperors, and enriched by the
confiscated properties of those whose condemnation they had
procured, rose to great influence. From the time of Caligula,
for several reigns, the most influential citizens were freedmen,
who occupied the principal offices in the palace, and usually
obtained complete ascendancy over the emperors. Through
them alone petitions were presented. By their instrumentality the Imperial favours were distributed. They sometimes
dethroned the emperors. They retained their power unshaken through a succession of revolutions. In wealth, in
power, in the crowd of their courtiers, in the splendour of
their palaces in life, and of their tombs in death, they eclipsed
all others, and men whom the early Roman patricians would
have almost disdained to notice, saw the proudest struggling
for their favour.[1]

Together with these influences many others of a kindred
nature may be detected. The colonial policy which the
Gracchi had advocated was carried out at Narbonne, and
during the latter days of Julius Cæsar, to the amazement and
scandal of the Romans, Gauls of this province obtained seats
in the senate.[2] The immense extent of the empire made it
necessary for numerous troops to remain during long periods
of time in distant provinces, and the foreign habits that were
thus acquired began the destruction of the exclusive feelings
of the Roman army, which the subsequent enrolment of

[1] The history of the influence
of freedmen is minutely traced by
Friedlænder, *Mœurs romaines du
règne d'Auguste à la fin des Antonins*,
tome i. pp. 58–93.  Statius and
Martial sang their praises.
[2] See Tacit. *Ann.* vi. 23–26.

17

barbarians completed. The public games, the immense luxury, the concentration of power, wealth, and genius, made Rome the centre of a vast and ceaseless concourse of strangers, the focus of all the various philosophies and religions of the empire, and its population soon became an amorphous, heterogeneous mass, in which all nations, customs, languages, and creeds, all degrees of virtue and vice, of refinement and barbarism, of scepticism and credulity, intermingled and interacted. Travelling had become more easy and perhaps more frequent than it has been at any other period before the nineteenth century. The subjection of the whole civilised world to a single rule removed the chief obstacles to locomotion. Magnificent roads, which modern nations have rarely rivalled and never surpassed, intersected the entire empire, and relays of post-horses enabled the voyager to proceed with an astonishing rapidity. The sea, which, after the destruction of the fleets of Carthage, had fallen almost completely under the dominion of pirates, had been cleared by Pompey. The European shores of the Mediterranean and the port of Alexandria were thronged with vessels. Romans traversed the whole extent of the empire on political, military, or commercial errands, or in search of health, or knowledge, or pleasure.[1] The entrancing beauties of Como and of Tempe, the luxurious manners of Baiæ and Corinth, the schools, commerce, climate, and temples of Alexandria, the soft winters of Sicily, the artistic wonders and historic recollections of Athens and the Nile, the great colonial interests of Gaul, attracted their thousands, while Roman luxury needed the products of the remotest lands, and the demand for animals for the amphitheatre spread Roman enterprise into the wildest deserts. In the capital, the toleration accorded to different creeds was such that the city soon became a miniature of the

---

[1] On the Roman journeys, see the almost exhaustive dissertation of Friedlænder, tome ii.

world. Almost every variety of charlatanism and of belief displayed itself unchecked, and boasted its train of proselytes. Foreign ideas were in every form in the ascendant. Greece, which had presided over the intellectual development of Rome, acquired a new influence under the favouring policy of Hadrian, and Greek became the language of some of the later as it had been of the earliest writers. Egyptian religions and philosophies excited the wildest enthusiasm. As early as the reign of Augustus there were many thousands of Jewish residents at Rome,[1] and their manners and creed spread widely among the people.[2] The Carthaginian Apuleius,[3] the Gauls Florus and Favorinus, the Spaniards Lucan, Columella, Martial, Seneca, and Quintilian, had all in their different departments a high place in Roman literature or philosophy.

In the slave world a corresponding revolution was taking place. The large proportion of physicians and sculptors who were slaves, the appearance of three or four distinguished authors in the slave class, the numerous literary slaves imported from Greece, and the splendid examples of courage, endurance, and devotion to their masters furnished by slaves during the civil wars, and during some of the worst periods of the Empire, were bridging the chasm between the servile and the free classes, and the same tendency was more powerfully stimulated by the vast numbers and overwhelming influence of the freedmen. The enormous scale and frequent

---

Joseph. (*Antiq.* xvii. 11, § 1) says above 8,000 Jews resident in Rome took part in a petition to Cæsar. If these were all adult males, the total number of Jewish residents must have been extremely large.

[2] See the famous fragment of Seneca cited by St. Augustin (*De Civ. Dei*, vi. 11): 'Usque eo sceleratissimæ gentis consuetudo convaluit, ut per omnes jam terras recepta sit: victi victoribus leges dederunt.' There are numerous scattered allusions to the Jews in Horace, Juvenal, and Martial.

[3] The Carthaginian influence was specially conspicuous in early Christian history. Tertullian and Cyprian (both Africans) are justly regarded as the founders of Latin theology. (See Milman's *Latin Christianity* (ed. 1867), vol. i. pp. 35-36.)

fluctuations of the great Roman establishments, and the innumerable captives reduced to slavery after every war, rendered manumission both frequent and easy, and it was soon regarded as a normal result of faithful service. Many slaves bought their freedom out of the savings which their masters always permitted them to make. Others paid for it by their labour after their emancipation. Some masters emancipated their slaves in order to obtain their part in the distribution of corn, others to prevent the discovery of their own crimes by the torture of their slaves, others through vanity, being desirous of having their funerals attended by a long train of freedmen, very many simply as a reward for long service.[1] The freedman was still under what was termed the patronage of his former master; he was bound to him by what in a later age would have been called a feudal tie, and the political and social importance of a noble depended in a very great degree upon the multitude of his clients. The children of the emancipated slave were in the same relation to the patron, and it was only in the third generation that all disqualifications and restraints were abrogated. In consequence of this system, manumission was often the interest of the master. In the course of his life he enfranchised individual slaves. On his death-bed or by his will he constantly emancipated multitudes. Emancipation by testament acquired such dimensions, that Augustus found it necessary to restrict the power; and he made several limitations, of which the most important was that no one should emancipate by his will more than one hundred of his slaves.[2] It was once proposed that the slaves should be distinguished by a special dress, but the proposition was abandoned because their number was so great that to

---

[1] Milc had emancipated some slaves to prevent them from being tortured as witnesses. (Cic. *Pro Milo.*) This was made illegal. The other reasons for enfranchisement are given by Dion. Halicarn. *Antiq.* lib. iv.

[2] This subject is fully treated by Wallon, *Hist. de l'Esclavage dans l'Antiquité.*

reveal to them their strength would be to place the city at their mercy.[1] Even among those who were not slaves, the element that was derived from slavery soon preponderated. The majority of the free population had probably either themselves been slaves, or were descended from slaves, and men with this tainted lineage penetrated to all the offices of the State.[2] 'There was,' as has been well said, 'a circulation of men from all the universe. Rome received them slaves, and sent them back Romans.'[3]

It is manifest how profound a change had taken place since the Republican days, when the highest dignities were long monopolised by a single class, when the censors repressed with a stringent severity every form or exhibition of luxury, when the rhetoricians were banished from the city, lest the faintest tinge of foreign manners should impair the stern simplicity of the people, and when the proposal to transfer the capital to Veii, after a great disaster, was rejected on the ground that it would be impious to worship the Roman deities anywhere but on the Capitol, or for the Flamens and the Vestals to emigrate beyond the walls.[4]

The greater number of these tendencies to universal fusion or equality were blind forces resulting from the stress of circumstances, and not from any human forethought, or were agencies that were put in motion for a different object. It must, however, be acknowledged that a definite theory of policy had a considerable part in accelerating the movement. The policy of the Republic may be broadly described as a policy of conquest, and that of the Empire as a policy of preservation. The Romans having acquired a vast dominion, were met by the great problem which every first-class power is called upon to solve—by what means many communities,

---

[1] Senec. *De Clemen.* i. 24.
See, on the prominence and the insolence of the freedmen, Tacit. *Annal.* iii. 26–27.

[3] Montesquieu, *Décadence des Romains*, ch. xiii.
[4] See the very curious speech attributed to Camillus (Livy, v. 52).

with different languages, customs, characters, and traditions, can be retained peaceably under a single ruler. In modern times, this difficulty has been most successfully met by local legislatures, which, if they supply a 'line of cleavage,' a nucleus around which the spirit of opposition may form, have on the other hand the priceless advantage of giving the annexed people a large measure of self-government, a centre and safety-valve of local public opinion, a sphere for local ambitions, and a hierarchy of institutions adapted to the distinctive national type. Under no other conditions can a complex empire be carried on with so little strain, or effort, or humiliation, or its inevitable final dissolution be effected with so little danger or convulsion. But local legislatures, which are the especial glory of English statesmanship, belong exclusively to modern civilisation. The Roman method of conciliation was, first of all, the most ample toleration of the customs, religion, and municipal freedom of the conquered, and then their gradual admission to the privileges of the conqueror. By confiding to them in a great measure the defence of the empire, by throwing open to them the offices of State, and especially by according to them the right of Roman citizenship, which had been for centuries jealously restricted to the inhabitants of Rome, and was afterwards only conceded to Italy and Cisalpine Gaul, the emperors sought to attach them to their throne. The process was very gradual, but the whole movement of political emancipation attained its completion when the Imperial throne was occupied by the Spaniard Trajan, and by Pertinax, the son of a freedman, and when an edict of Caracalla extended the rights of Roman citizenship to all the provinces of the empire.

It will appear evident, from the foregoing sketch, that the period which elapsed between Panætius and Constantine exhibited an irresistible tendency to cosmopolitanism. The convergence, when we consider the number, force, and harmony of the influences that composed it, is indeed unexampled

in history. The movement extended through all the fields of
religious, philosophical, political, industrial, military, and domestic life. The character of the people was completely transformed, the landmarks of all its institutions were removed,
the whole principle of its organisation was reversed. It would
be impossible to find a more striking example of the manner
in which events govern character, destroying old habits and
associations, and thus altering that national type of excellence
which is, for the most part, the expression or net moral result
of the national institutions and circumstances. The effect of
the movement was, no doubt, in many respects evil, and some
of the best men, such as the elder Cato and Tacitus, opposed
it, as leading to the demoralisation of the empire; but if it
increased vice, it also gave a peculiar character to virtue. It
was impossible that the conception of excellence, formed in a
society where everything conspired to deepen class divisions
and national jealousies and antipathies, should be retained
unaltered in a period of universal intercourse and amalgamation. The moral expression of the first period is obviously
to be found in the narrower military and patriotic virtues;
that of the second period in enlarged philanthropy and
sympathy.

The Stoical philosophy was admirably fitted to preside over
this extension of sympathies. Although it proved itself in
every age the chief school of patriots, it recognised also, from
the very first, and in the most unequivocal manner, the fraternity of mankind. The Stoic taught that virtue alone is a
good, and that all other things are indifferent; and from this
position he inferred that birth, rank, country, or wealth are
the mere accidents of life, and that virtue alone makes one
man superior to another. He taught also that the Deity is
an all-pervading Spirit, animating the universe, and revealed
with especial clearness in the soul of man; and he concluded
that all men are fellow-members of a single body, united by
participation in the same Divine Spirit. These two doctrines

formed part of the very first teaching of the Stoics, but it was
the special glory of the Roman teachers, and an obvious result
of the condition of affairs I have described, to have brought
them into full relief. One of the most emphatic as well as
one of the earliest extant assertions of the duty of 'charity to
the human race,'[1] occurs in the treatise of Cicero upon duties,
which was avowedly based upon Stoicism. Writing at a
period when the movement of amalgamation had for a generation been rapidly proceeding,[2] and adopting almost without
restriction the ethics of the Stoics, Cicero maintained the
doctrine of universal brotherhood as distinctly as it was afterwards maintained by the Christian Church. 'This whole
world,' he tells us, 'is to be regarded as the common city of
gods and men.'[3] 'Men were born for the sake of men, that
each should assist the others.'[4] 'Nature ordains that a man
should wish the good of every man, whoever he may be, for
this very reason, that he is a man.'[5] 'To reduce man to the
duties of his own city and to disengage him from duties to
the members of other cities, is to break the universal society
of the human race.'[6] 'Nature has inclined us to love men,
and this is the foundation of the law.'[7] The same principles
were reiterated with increasing emphasis by the later Stoics.
Adopting the well-known line which Terence had translated
from Menander, they maintained that man should deem
nothing human foreign to his interest. Lucan expatiated
with all the fervour of a Christian poet upon the time when
'the human race will cast aside its weapons, and when all
nations will learn to love.'[8] 'The whole universe,' said

---

[1] 'Caritas generis humani.'—*De Finib.* So, too, he speaks (*De Leg.* i. 23) of every good man as 'civis totius mundi.'

[2] He speaks of Rome as 'civitas ex nationum conventu constituta.'

[3] *De Legib.* i. 7.    [4] *De Offic.*

[5] Ibid. iii. 6.

[6] *De Offic.* iii. 6.

[7] *De Legib.* i. 15.

[8] 'Tunc genus humanum positis
    sibi consulat armis,
Inque vicem gens omnis amet.'
    —*Pharsalia*, vi.

Seneca, 'which you see around you, comprising all things, both divine and human, is one. We are members of one great body. Nature has made us relatives when it begat us from the same materials and for the same destinies. She planted in us a mutual love, and fitted us for a social life.'[1] 'What is a Roman knight, or freedman, or slave? These are but names springing from ambition or from injury.'[2] 'I know that my country is the world, and my guardians are the gods.'[3] 'You are a citizen,' said Epictetus, 'and a part of the world. . . . The duty of a citizen is in nothing to consider his own interest distinct from that of others, as the hand or foot, if they possessed reason and understood the law of nature, would do and wish nothing that had not some relation to the rest of the body.'[4] 'An Antonine,' said Marcus Aurelius, 'my country is Rome ; as a man, it is the world.'[5]

So far Stoicism appears fully equal to the moral requirements of the age. It would be impossible to recognise more cordially or to enforce more beautifully that doctrine of universal brotherhood for which the circumstances of the Roman Empire had made men ripe. Plato had said that no one is born for himself alone, but that he owes himself in part to his country, in part to his parents, and in part to his friends. The Roman Stoics, taking a wider survey, declared that man is born not for himself but for the whole world.[6] And their doctrine was perfectly consistent with the original principles of their school.

But while Stoicism was quite capable of representing the widening movement, it was not equally capable of representing the softening movement of civilisation. Its condemnation

---

[1] *Ep.* xcv.
[2] *Ep.* xxxi.
[3] *De Vita Beata*, xx.
[4] Arrian, ii. 10.
[5] vi. 44.

[6] ' Hæc duri immota Catonis

Secta fuit, servare modum,
finemque tenere,
Naturamque sequi, patriæque
impendere vitam,
Nec sibi sed toti genitum se
credere mundo.'
Lucan, *Phars.* ii. 380–383.

of the affections, and its stern, tense ideal, admirably fitted
for the struggles of a simple military age, were unsuited for
the mild manners and luxurious tastes of the age of the
Antonines. A class of writers began to arise who, like the
Stoics, believed virtue, rather than enjoyment, to be the
supreme good, and who acknowledged that virtue consisted
solely of the control which the enlightened will exercises
over the desires, but who at the same time gave free scope to
the benevolent affections and a more religious and mystical
tone to the whole scheme of morals. Professing various
speculative doctrines, and calling themselves by many names
—eclectics, peripatetics, or Platonists—they agreed in forming or representing a moral character, less strong, less sublime,
less capable of endurance and heroism, less conspicuous for
energy of will, than that of the Stoics, but far more tender
and attractive. The virtues of force began to recede, and the
gentler virtues to advance, in the moral type. Insensibility
to suffering was no longer professed; indomitable strength
was no longer idolised, and it was felt that weakness and
sorrow have their own appropriate virtues.[1] The works of
these writers are full of delicate touches which nothing but
strong and lively feelings could have suggested. We find this
in the well-known letter of Pliny on the death of his slaves,[2]
in the frequent protests against the ostentation of indifference
with which the Stoics regarded the loss of their friends, in
many instances of simple, artless pathos, which strike the
finest chords of our nature. When Plutarch, after the death
of his daughter, was writing a letter of consolation to his wife,

There is a passage on this
subject in one of the letters of
Pliny, which I think extremely remarkable, and to which I can recall
no pagan parallel :—' Nuper me
cujusdam amici languor admonuit,
optimos esse nos dum infirmi sumus.
Quem enim infirmum aut avaritia
aut libido solicitat? Non amoribus
servit, non appetit honores . . .
tunc deos, tunc hominem esse se
meminit.'—Plin. *Ep.* vii. 26.
[2] *Ep.* viii. 16. He says : 'Hominis est enim affici dolore, sentire
resistere tamen, et solatia admittere,
non solatiis non egere.'

we find him turning away from all the commonplaces of the Stoics as the recollection of one simple trait of his little child rushed upon his mind :—'She desired her nurse to press even her dolls to the breast. She was so loving that she wished everything that gave her pleasure to share in the best of what she had.'

Plutarch, whose fame as a biographer has, I think, unduly eclipsed his reputation as a moralist, may be justly regarded as the leader of this movement, and his moral writings may be profitably compared with those of Seneca, the most ample exponent of the sterner school. Seneca is not unfrequently self-conscious, theatrical, and overstrained. His precepts have something of the affected ring of a popular preacher. The imperfect fusion of his short sentences gives his style a disjointed and, so to speak, granulated character, which the Emperor Caligula happily expressed when he compared it to sand without cement; yet he often rises to a majesty of eloquence, a grandeur both of thought and of expression, that few moralists have ever rivalled. Plutarch, though far less sublime, is more sustained, equable, and uniformly pleasing. The Montaigne of antiquity, his genius coruscates playfully and gracefully around his subject; he delights in illustrations which are often singularly vivid and original, but which, by their excessive multiplication, appear sometimes rather the texture than the ornament of his discourse. A gentle, tender spirit, and a judgment equally free from paradox, exaggeration, and excessive subtilty, are the characteristics of all he wrote. Plutarch excels most in collecting motives of consolation ; Seneca in forming characters that need no consolation. There is something of the woman in Plutarch ; Seneca is all a man. The writings of the first resemble the strains of the flute, to which the ancients attributed the power of calming the passions and charming away the clouds of sorrow, and drawing men by a gentle suasion into the paths of virtue ; the writings of the other are like the trumpet-blast, which kindles the soul with an heroic courage. The first is most fitted to console a mother sorrowing over her dead child, the second to nerve a brave man, without flinching and without illusion, to grapple with an inevitable fate.

The elaborate letters which Seneca has left us on distinctive tenets of the Stoical school, such as the equality of vices or the evil of the affections, have now little more than an historic interest; but the general tone of his writings gives them a permanent importance, for they reflect and foster a certain type of excellence which, since the extinction of Stoicism, has had no adequate expression in literature. The prevailing moral tone of Plutarch, on the other hand, being formed mainly on the prominence of the amiable virtues, has been eclipsed or transcended by the Christian writers, but his definite contributions to philosophy and morals are more important than those of Seneca. He has left us one of the best works on superstition, and one of the most ingenious works on Providence, we possess. He was probably the first writer who advocated very strongly humanity to animals on the broad ground of universal benevolence, as distinguished from the Pythagorean doctrine of transmigration, and he was also remarkable, beyond all his contemporaries, for his high sense of female excellence and of the sanctity of female love.

The Romans had at all times cared more for the practical tendency of a system of philosophy than for its logical or speculative consistency. One of the chief attractions of Stoicism, in their eyes, had been that its main object was not to build a system of opinion, but to propose a pattern of life,[1] and Stoicism itself was only adapted to the Roman character after it had been simplified by Panætius.[2] Although the system could never free itself altogether from that hardness which rendered it so unsuited for an advanced civilisation, it

---

[1] This characteristic of Stoicism is well noticed in Grant's *Aristotle*, vol. i. p. 254. The first volume of this work contains an extremely good review of the principles of the Stoics.

[2] Cic. *De Finib*. lib. iv.

was profoundly modified by the later Stoics, who rarely scrupled to temper it by the admixture of new doctrines. Seneca himself was by no means an unmixed Stoic. If Epictetus was more nearly so, this was probably because the extreme hardship he underwent made him dwell more than his contemporaries upon the importance of fortitude and endurance. Marcus Aurelius was surrounded by the disciples of the most various schools, and his Stoicism was much tinctured by the milder and more religious spirit of Platonism. The Stoics, like all other men, felt the moral current of the time, though they yielded to it less readily than some others. In Thrasea, who occupied in his age a position analogous to that of Cato in an earlier period, we find little or nothing of the asperity and hardness of his great prototype. In the writings of the later Stoics, if we find the same elements as in those of their predecessors, these elements are at least combined in different proportions.

In the first place, Stoicism became more essentially religious. The Stoical character, like all others of a high order, had always been reverential; but its reverence differed widely from that of Christians. It was concentrated much less upon the Deity than upon virtue, and especially upon virtue as exhibited in great men. When Lucan, extolling his hero, boasted that 'the gods favoured the conquering cause, but Cato the conquered,' or when Seneca described ' the fortune of Sulla' as ' the crime of the gods,' these sentences, which sound to modern ears grossly blasphemous, appear to have excited no murmur. We have already seen the audacious language with which the sage claimed an equality with the Divinity. On the other hand, the reverence for virtue apart from all conditions of success, and especially for men of the stamp of Cato, who through a strong moral conviction struggled bravely, though unsuccessfully, against force, genius, or circumstances, was perhaps more steady and more passionate than in any later age. The duty of absolute

submission to Providence, as I have already shown, was continually inculcated, and the pantheistic notion of all virtue
being a part or emanation of the Deity was often asserted,
but man was still the centre of the Stoic's scheme, the ideal
to which his reverence and devotion aspired.    In later
Stoicism this point of view was gradually changed.  Without
any formal abandonment of their pantheistic conceptions, the
language of philosophers recognised with much greater clearness a distinct and personal Divinity.    Every page of Epictetus and Marcus Aurelius is impregnated with the deepest
religious feeling.  ' The first thing to learn,' said the former,
' is that there is a God, that His knowledge pervades the
whole universe, and that it extends not only to our acts but
to our thoughts and feelings. . . .  He who seeks to please
the gods must labour as far as lies in him to resemble them.
He must be faithful as God is faithful, free as He is free,
beneficent as He is beneficent, magnanimous as He is magnanimous.'[1]  'To have God for our maker and father and
guardian, should not that emancipate us from all sadness and
from all fear?'[2]  'When you have shut your door and
darkened your room, say not to yourself you are alone.  God
is in your room, and your attendant genius likewise.  Think
not that they need the light to see what you do.[3]  What can
I, an old man and a cripple, do but praise God?   If I were
a nightingale, I would discharge the office of a nightingale;
if a swan, that of a swan.  But I am a reasonable being;
my mission is to praise God, and I fulfil it; nor shall I ever,
as far as lies in me, shrink from my task, and I exhort you
to join in the same song of praise.'[4]

The same religious character is exhibited, if possible,
in a still greater degree in the 'Meditations of Marcus
Aurelius; but in one respect the ethics of the emperor differ

[1] Arrian, *Epict.* ii. 14.          [3] Ibid. i. 14.
[2] Ibid. i. 9.                      [4] Ibid. i. 16.

widely from those of the slave. In Epictetus we invariably find the strongest sense of the majesty of man. As the child of the Deity, as a being capable of attaining the most exalted virtue, he magnified him to the highest point, and never more so than in the very passage in which he exhorted his disciples to beware of haughtiness. The Jupiter Olympus of Phidias, he reminds them, exhibits no arrogance, but the unclouded serenity of perfect confidence and strength.[1] Marcus Aurelius, on the other hand, dwelt rather on the weakness than on the force of man, and his meditations breathe a spirit, if not of Christian humility, at least of the gentlest and most touching modesty. He was not, it is true, like some later saints, who habitually apply to themselves language of reprobation which would be exaggerated if applied to the murderer or the adulterer. He did not shrink from recognising human virtue as a reality, and thanking Providence for the degree in which he had attained it, but he continually reviewed with an unsparing severity the weaknesses of his character, he accepted and even solicited reproofs from every teacher of virtue, he made it his aim, in a position of supreme power, to check every emotion of arrogance and pride, and he set before him an ideal of excellence which awed and subdued his mind.

Another very remarkable feature of later Stoicism was its increasingly introspective character. In the philosophy of Cato and Cicero, virtue was displayed almost exclusively in action. In the later Stoics, self-examination and purity of thought were continually inculcated. There are some writers who, with an obstinacy which it is more easy to explain than to excuse, persist, in defiance of the very clearest evidence to the contrary, in representing these virtues as exclusively Christian, and in maintaining, without a shadow of proof, that the place they undeniably occupy in the later

---

[1] Arrian, ii. 8.

Roman moralists was due to the direct or indirect influence of the new faith. The plain fact is that they were fully known to the Greeks, and both Plato and Zeno even exhorted men to study their dreams, on the ground that these often reveal the latent tendencies of the disposition.[1] Pythagoras urged his disciples daily to examine themselves when they retired to rest,[2] and this practice soon became a recognised part of the Pythagorean discipline.[3] It was introduced into Rome with the school before the close of the Republic. It was known in the time of Cicero[4] and Horace.[5] Sextius, one of the masters of Seneca, a philosopher of the school of Pythagoras, who flourished chiefly before the Christian era, was accustomed daily to devote a portion of time to self-examination; and Seneca, who at first inclined much to the tenets of Pythagoras,[6] expressly tells us that it was from Sextius he learnt the practice.[7] The increasing prominence of the Pythagorean philosophy which accompanied the invasion of Oriental creeds, the natural tendency of the empire, by closing the avenues of political life, to divert the attention from action to emotion, and also the increased latitude allowed to the play of the sympathies or affections by the later Stoics, brought this emotional part of virtue into great prominence. The letters of Seneca are a kind of moral medicine applied for the most part to the cure of different

---

[1] Plutarch, De Profect. in Virt. This precept was enforced by Bishop Sanderson in one of his sermons. (Southey's Commonplace Book, vol. i. p. 92.)

[2] Diog. Laërt. Pythagoras.

[3] Thus Cicero makes Cato say: 'Pythagoreorumque more, exercendæ memoriæ gratia, quid quoque die dixerim, audiverim, egerim, commemoro vesperi.'—De Senect. xi.

[4] Ibid.

[5] Sermon, i. 4.

[6] He even gave up, for a time, eating meat, in obedience to the Pythagorean principles. (Ep. cviii.) Seneca had two masters of this school, Sextius and Sotion. He was at this time not more than seventeen years old. (See Aubertin, Étude critique sur les Rapports supposés entre Sénèque et St. Paul, p. 156.)

[7] See his very beautiful description of the self-examination of Sextius and of himself. (De Ira, iii. 36.)

infirmities of character. Plutarch, in a beautiful treatise on
'The Signs of Moral Progress,' treated the culture of the
feelings with delicate skill. The duty of serving the Divinity
with a pure mind rather than by formal rites became a
commonplace of literature, and self-examination one of the
most recognised of duties. Epictetus urged men so to purify
their imaginations, that at the sight of a beautiful woman
they should not even mentally exclaim, ' Happy her husband!'[1] The meditations of Marcus Aurelius, above all,
are throughout an exercise of self-examination, and the duty
of watching over the thoughts is continually inculcated.

It was a saying of Plutarch that Stoicism, which sometimes exercised a prejudicial and hardening influence upon
characters that were by nature stern and unbending, proved
peculiarly useful as a cordial to those which were naturally
gentle and yielding. Of this truth we can have no better
illustration than is furnished by the life and writings of
Marcus Aurelius, the last and most perfect representative
of Roman Stoicism. A simple, childlike, and eminently
affectionate disposition, with little strength of intellect or
perhaps originally of will, much more inclined to meditation,
speculation, solitude, or friendship, than to active and public
life, with a profound aversion to the pomp of royalty and
with a rather strong natural leaning to pedantry, he had
embraced the fortifying philosophy of Zeno in its best form,
and that philosophy made him perhaps as nearly a perfectly
virtuous man as has ever appeared upon our world. Tried
by the chequered events of a reign of nineteen years, presiding over a society that was profoundly corrupt, and over a
city that was notorious for its license, the perfection of his
character awed even calumny to silence, and the spontaneous
sentiment of his people proclaimed him rather a god than a
man.[2] Very few men have ever lived concerning whose

---

[1] Arrian, ii. 18. Compare the
*Manual* of Epictetus, xxxiv.

[2] 'Quod de Romulo ægre credi
tum est, omnes pari consensu

inner life we can speak so confidently. His 'Meditations,' which form one of the most impressive, form also one of the truest books in the whole range of religious literature. They consist of rude fragmentary notes without literary skill or arrangement, written for the most part in hasty, broken, and sometimes almost unintelligible sentences amid the turmoil of a camp,[1] and recording, in accents of the most penetrating sincerity, the struggles, doubts, and aims of a soul of which, to employ one of his own images, it may be truly said that it possessed the purity of a star, which needs no veil to hide its nakedness. The undisputed master of the whole civilised world, he set before him as models such men as Thrasea and Helvidius, as Cato and Brutus, and he made it his aim to realise the conception of a free State in which all citizens are equal, and of a royalty which makes it its first duty to respect the liberty of the citizens.[2] His life was passed in unremitting activity. For nearly twelve years he was absent with armies in the distant provinces of the empire ; and although his political capacity has been much and perhaps justly questioned, it is impossible to deny the unwearied zeal with which he discharged the duties of his great position. Yet few men have ever carried farther the virtue of little things, the delicate moral tact and the minute scruples which, though often exhibited by women and by secluded religionists, very rarely survive much contact with active life. The solicitude with which he endeavoured to persuade two jealous rhetoricians to abstain during their debates from retorts that might destroy their friendship,[3] the careful gratitude with which, in a camp in Hungary, he recalled every moral obligation he

---

præsumserunt, Marcum cœlo receptum esse.'—Aur. Vict. Epit. xvi. 'Deusque etiam nunc habetur.'—Capitolinus.

[1] The first book of his Meditations was written on the borders of

the Granua, in Hungary.

[2] i. 14.

[3] See his touching letter to Fronto, who was about to engage in a debate with Herod Atticus.

could trace, even to the most obscure of his tutors,[1] his anxiety to avoid all pedantry and mannerism in his conduct,[2] and to repel every voluptuous imagination from his mind,[3] his deep sense of the obligation of purity,[4] his laborious efforts to correct a habit of drowsiness into which he had fallen, and his self-reproval when he had yielded to it,[5] become all, I think, inexpressibly touching when we remember that they were exhibited by one who was the supreme ruler of the civilised globe, and who was continually engaged in the direction of the most gigantic interests. But that which is especially remarkable in Marcus Aurelius is the complete absence of fanaticism in his philanthropy. Despotic monarchs sincerely anxious to improve mankind are naturally led to endeavour, by acts of legislation, to force society into the paths which they believe to be good, and such men, acting under such motives, have sometimes been the scourges of mankind. Philip II. and Isabella the Catholic inflicted more suffering in obedience to their consciences than Nero and Domitian in obedience to their lusts. But Marcus Aurelius steadily resisted the temptation. 'Never hope,' he once wrote, 'to realise Plato's Republic. Let it be sufficient that you have in some slight degree ameliorated mankind, and do not think that amelioration a matter of small importance. Who can change the opinions of men? and without a change of sentiments what can you make but reluctant slaves and hypocrites?'[6] He promulgated many laws inspired by a spirit of the purest benevolence. He

---

[1] i 6–15. The eulogy he passed on his Stoic master Apollonius is worthy of notice. Apollonius furnished him with an example of the combination of extreme firmness and gentleness.

[2] E.g. 'Beware of Cæsarising.' (vi. 30.) 'Be neither a tragedian nor a courtesan.' (v. 28.) 'Be

just and temperate and a follower of the gods; but be so with simplicity, for the pride of modesty is the worst of all.' (xii. 27.)

[3] iii. 4.

[4] i. 17.

[5] v. 1.

[6] ix. 29.

mitigated the gladiatorial shows.   He treated with invariable
deference the senate, which was the last bulwark of political
freedom.   He endowed many chairs of philosophy which
were intended to diffuse knowledge and moral teaching
through the people.   He endeavoured by the example of his
Court to correct the extravagances of luxury that were prevalent, and he exhibited in his own career a perfect model of
an active and conscientious administrator ; but he made no
rash efforts to force the people by stringent laws out of the
natural channel of their lives.   Of the corruption of his subjects he was keenly sensible, and he bore it with a mournful
but gentle patience.   We may trace in this respect the milder
spirit of those Greek teachers who had diverged from Stoicism, but it was especially from the Stoical doctrine that all
vice springs from ignorance that he derived his rule of life,
and this doctrine, to which he repeatedly recurred, imparted
to all his judgments a sad but tender charity.   'Men were
made for men ; correct them, then, or support them.'[1]   'If
they do ill, it is evidently in spite of themselves and through
ignorance.'[2]   'Correct them if you can; if not, remember
that patience was given you to exercise it in their behalf.'[3]
'It would be shameful for a physician to deem it strange that
a man was suffering from fever.'[4]   'The immortal gods consent for countless ages to endure without anger, and even to
surround with blessings, so many and such wicked men ; but
thou who hast so short a time to live, art thou already weary,
and that when thou art thyself wicked?'[5]   'It is involuntarily that the soul is deprived of justice, and temperance,
and goodness, and all other virtues.   Continually remember
this ; the thought will make you more gentle to all mankind.'[6]
'It is right that man should love those who have offended
him.   He will do so when he remembers that all men are his

[1] viii. 59.                    [4] viii. 15.
[2] xi. 18.                      [5] vii. 70.
[3] ix. 11.                      [6] vii. 63.

relations, and that it is through ignorance and involuntarily that they sin—and then we all die so soon.'[1]

The character of the virtue of Marcus Aurelius, though exhibiting the softening influence of the Greek spirit which in his time pervaded the empire, was in its essentials strictly Roman.[2] Though full of reverential gratitude to Providence, we do not find in him that intense humility and that deep and subtle religious feeling which were the principles of Hebrew virtue, and which have given the Jewish writers so great an ascendancy over the hearts of men. Though borne naturally and instinctively to goodness, his 'Meditations' do not display the keen æsthetical sense of the beauty of virtue which was the leading motive of Greek morals, and which the writing of Plotinus afterwards made very familiar to the Roman world. Like most of the best Romans, the principle of his virtue was the sense of duty, the conviction of the existence of a law of nature to which it is the aim and purpose of our being to conform. Of secondary motives he appears to have been little sensible. The belief in a superintending Providence was the strongest of his religious convictions, but even that was occasionally overcast. On the subject of a future world his mind floated in a desponding doubt. The desire for posthumous fame he deemed it his duty systematically to mortify. While most writers of his school regarded death chiefly as the end of sorrows, and dwelt upon it in order to dispel its terrors, in Marcus Aurelius it is chiefly represented as the last great demonstration of the vanity of earthly things. Seldom, indeed, has such active and unrelaxing virtue been united with so little enthusiasm,

[1] vii. 22.
[2] Mr. Maurice, in this respect, compares and contrasts him very happily with Plutarch. 'Like Plutarch, the Greek and Roman characters were in Marcus Aurelius remarkably blended; but, unlike Plutarch, the foundation of his mind was Roman. He was a student that he might more effectually carry on the business of an emperor.'—*Philosophy of the First Six Centuries*, p. 32.

and been cheered by so little illusion of success. 'There is
but one thing,' he wrote, 'of real value—to cultivate truth
and justice, and to live without anger in the midst of lying
and unjust men.'[1]

The command he had acquired over his feelings was so
great that it was said of him that his countenance was never
known to betray either elation or despondency.[2] We, however,
who have before us the records of his inner life, can have no
difficulty in detecting the deep melancholy that overshadowed
his mind, and his closing years were darkened by many and
various sorrows. His wife, whom he dearly loved and
deeply honoured, and who, if we may believe the Court
scandals that are reported by historians, was not worthy of
his affection,[3] had preceded him to the tomb. His only sur-
viving son had already displayed the vicious tendencies that
afterwards made him one of the worst of rulers. The philosophers, who had instructed him in his youth, and to whom
he had clung with an affectionate friendship, had one by one
disappeared, and no new race had arisen to supply their
place. After a long reign of self-denying virtue, he saw the
decadence of the empire continually more apparent. The
Stoical school was rapidly fading before the passion for
Oriental superstitions. The barbarians, repelled for a time,
were again menacing the frontiers, and it was not difficult to
foresee their future triumph. The mass of the people had

---

[1] vi. 47.
[2] Capitolinus, Aurelius Victor.
[3] M. Suckau, in his admirable
*Étude sur Marc-Aurèle*, and M.
Renan, in a very acute and learned
*Examen de quelques faits relatifs à
l'impératrice Faustine* (read before
the Institut, August 14, 1867),
have shown the extreme uncertainty of the stories about the
debaucheries of Faustina, which
the biographers of Marcus Aurelius

have collected. It will be observed
that the emperor himself has left
an emphatic testimony to her
virtue, and to the happiness he
derived from her (i. 17); that the
earliest extant biographer of Marcus Aurelius was a generation
later; and that the infamous
character of Commodus naturally
predisposed men to imagine that
he was not the son of so perfect an
emperor.

become too inert and too corrupt for any efforts to regenerate
them. A fearful pestilence, followed by many minor calamities,
had fallen upon the land and spread misery and panic through
many provinces. In the midst of these calamities, the emperor was struck down with a mortal illness, which he bore
with the placid courage he had always displayed, exhibiting
in almost the last words he uttered his forgetfulness of self
and his constant anxiety for the condition of his people.[1]
Shortly before his death he dismissed his attendants, and,
after one last interview, his son, and he died as he long had
lived, alone.[2]

Thus sank to rest in clouds and darkness the purest and
gentlest spirit of all the pagan world, the most perfect model
of the later Stoics. In him the hardness, asperity, and arrogance of the sect had altogether disappeared, while the
affectation its paradoxes tended to produce was greatly
mitigated. Without fanaticism, superstition, or illusion, his
whole life was regulated by a simple and unwavering sense
of duty. The contemplative and emotional virtues which
Stoicism had long depressed, had regained their place, but the
active virtues had not yet declined. The virtues of the hero
were still deeply honoured, but gentleness and tenderness had
acquired a new prominence in the ideal type.

But while the force of circumstances was thus developing
the ethical conceptions of antiquity in new directions, the
mass of the Roman people were plunged in a condition of
depravity which no mere ethical teaching could adequately
correct. The moral condition of the empire is, indeed, in some
respects one of the most appalling pictures on record, and
writers have much more frequently undertaken to paint or
even to exaggerate its enormity than to investigate the circumstances by which it may be explained. Such circumstances,

---

' Quid me fletis, et non magis   cogitatis ?'   Capitolinus, *M. Aure-*
de pestilentia et communi morte   *lius.*        [2] Ibid.

however, must unquestionably exist. There is no reason to
believe that the innate propensities of the people were worse
during the Empire than during the best days of the Republic.
The depravity of a nation is a phenomenon which, like all
others, may be traced to definite causes, and in the instance
before us they are not difficult to discover.

I have already said that the virtue of the Romans was a
military and patriotic virtue, formed by the national institutions, and to which religious teaching was merely accessory.
The domestic, military, and censorial discipline, concurring
with the general poverty and also with the agricultural pursuits of the people, had created the simplest and most austere
habits, while the institutions of civic liberty provided ample
spheres for honourable ambition. The nobles, being the
highest body in a free State, and being at the same time continually confronted by a formidable opposition under the
guidance of the tribunes, were ardently devoted to public life.
The dangerous rivalry of the surrounding Italian States, and
afterwards of Carthage, demanded and secured a constant
vigilance. Roman education was skilfully designed to elicit
heroic patriotism, and the great men of the past became
the ideal figures of the imagination. Religion hallowed
the local feeling by rites and legends, instituted many useful
and domestic habits, taught men the sanctity of oaths,
and, by fostering a continual sense of a superintending
Providence, gave a depth and solemnity to the whole
character.

Such were the chief influences by which the national type
of virtue had been formed, but nearly all of these were cor-
roded or perverted by advancing civilisation. The domestic
and local religion lost its ascendancy amid the increase of
scepticism and the invasion of a crowd of foreign superstitions.
The simplicity of manners, which sumptuary laws and the
institution of the censorship had long maintained, was replaced
by the extravagances of a Babylonian luxury. The aris-

tocratic dignity perished with the privileges on which it reposed. The patriotic energy and enthusiasm died away in a universal empire which embraced all varieties of language, custom, and nationality.

But although the virtues of a poor and struggling community necessarily disappear before increasing luxury, they are in a normal condition of society replaced by virtues of a different stamp. Gentler manners and enlarged benevolence follow in the train of civilisation, greater intellectual activity and more extended industrial enterprise give a new importance to the moral qualities which each of these require, the circle of political interests expands, and if the virtues that spring from privilege diminish, the virtues that spring from equality increase.

In Rome, however, there were three great causes which impeded the normal development—the Imperial system, the institution of slavery, and the gladiatorial shows. Each of these exercised an influence of the widest and most pernicious character on the morals of the people. To trace those influences in all their ramifications would lead me far beyond the limits I have assigned to the present work, but I shall endeavour to give a concise view of their nature and general character.

The theory of the Roman Empire was that of a representative despotism. The various offices of the Republic were not annihilated, but they were gradually concentrated in a single man. The senate was still ostensibly the depository of supreme power, but it was made in fact the mere creature of the Emperor, whose power was virtually uncontrolled. Political spies and private accusers, who in the latter days of the Republic had been encouraged to denounce plots against the State, began under Augustus to denounce plots against the Emperor ; and the class being enormously increased under Tiberius, and stimulated by the promise of part of the confiscated property, they menaced every leading politician and even every wealthy man. The nobles were gradually depressed, ruined, or driven by the dangers of public life into orgies of private luxury. The poor were conciliated, not by any increase of liberty or even of permanent prosperity, but by gratuitous distributions of corn and by public games, while, in order to invest themselves with a sacred character, the emperors adopted the religious device of an apotheosis.

This last superstition, of which some traces may still be found in the titles appropriated to royalty, was not wholly a suggestion of politicians. Deified men had long occupied a prominent place in ancient belief, and the founders of cities had been very frequently worshipped by the inhabitants.[1] Although to more educated minds the ascription of divinity to a sovereign was simply an unmeaning flattery, although it in no degree prevented either innumerable plots against his life, or an unsparing criticism of his memory, yet the popular reverence not unfrequently anticipated politicians in representing the emperor as in some special way under the protection of Providence. Around Augustus a whole constellation of miraculous stories soon clustered. An oracle, it was said, had declared his native city destined to produce a ruler of the world. When a child, he had been borne by invisible hands from his cradle, and placed on a lofty tower, where he was found with his face turned to the rising sun. He rebuked the frogs that croaked around his grandfather's home, and they became silent for ever. An eagle snatched a piece of bread from his hand, soared into the air, and then, descending, presented it to him again. Another eagle dropped at his feet a chicken, bearing a laurel-branch in its beak. When his body was burnt, his image was seen rising to heaven above the flames. When another man tried to sleep in the bed in which the Emperor had been born, the profane intruder was

---

[1] Many examples of this are given by Coulanges, *La Cité antique,* pp. 177–178.

dragged forth by an unseen hand. A patrician named Lætorius, having been condemned for adultery, pleaded in mitigation of the sentence that he was the happy possessor of the spot of ground on which Augustus was born.[1] An Asiatic town, named Cyzicus, was deprived of its freedom by Tiberius, chiefly because it had neglected the worship of Augustus.[2] Partly, no doubt, by policy, but partly also by that spontaneous process by which in a superstitious age conspicuous characters so often become the nuclei of legends,[3] each emperor was surrounded by a supernatural aureole. Every usurpation, every break in the ordinary line of succession, was adumbrated by a series of miracles; and signs, both in heaven and earth, were manifested whenever an emperor was about to die.

Of the emperors themselves, a great majority, no doubt, accepted their divine honours as an empty pageant, and more than one exhibited beneath the purple a simplicity of tastes and character which the boasted heroes of the Republic had never surpassed. It is related of Vespasian that, when dying, he jested mournfully on his approaching dignity, observing, as he felt his strength ebbing away, 'I think I am becoming a god.'[4] Alexander Severus and Julian refused to accept the ordinary language of adulation, and of those who did not reject it we know that many looked upon it as a modern sovereign looks upon the phraseology of petitions or the ceremonies of the Court. Even Nero was so far from being intoxicated with his Imperial dignity that he continually sought triumphs as a singer or an actor, and it was his artistic skill, not his divine prerogatives, that excited his vanity.[5] Caligula, however, who appears to have been literally deranged,[6]

---

[1] All this is related by Suetonius, *August.*

[2] Tacit. *Annal.* iv. 36.

[3] See, e g., the sentiments of the people about Julius Cæsar, Sueton. *J. C.* lxxxviii.

[4] Sueton. *Vesp.* xxiii.

[5] 'Qualis artifex pereo' were his dying words.

[6] See Sueton. *Calig.* 1.

is said to have accepted his divinity as a serious fact, to have substituted his own head for that of Jupiter on many of the statues,[1] and to have once started furiously from his seat during a thunderstorm that had interrupted a gladiatorial show, shouting with frantic gestures his imprecations against Heaven, and declaring that the divided empire was indeed intolerable, that either Jupiter or himself must speedily succumb.[2] Heliogabalus, if we may give any credence to his biographer, confounded all things, human and divine, in hideous and blasphemous orgies, and designed to unite all forms of religion in the worship of himself.

A curious consequence of this apotheosis was that the images of the emperors were invested with a sacred character like those of the gods. They were the recognised refuge of the slave or the oppressed,[4] and the smallest disrespect to them was resented as a heinous crime. Under Tiberius, slaves and criminals were accustomed to hold in their hands an image of the emperor, and, being thus protected, to pour with impunity a torrent of defiant insolence upon their masters or judges.[5] Under the same emperor, a man having, when drunk, accidentally touched a nameless domestic utensil with a ring on which the head of the emperor was carved, he was immediately denounced by a spy.[6] A man in this reign was accused of high treason for having sold an image of the emperor with a garden.[7] It was made a capital offence to beat a slave, or to undress, near a statue of Augustus, or to enter a brothel with a piece of money on which his head was engraved,[8] and at a later period a woman, it is said, was ac-

---

[1] Sueton. *Calig.* xxii. A statue of Jupiter is said to have burst out laughing just before the death of this emperor.

[2] Seneca, *De Ira*, i. 46; Sueton. *Calig.* xxii.

[3] Lampridius, *Heliogab.*

[4] Senec. *De Clemen.* i. 18.

[5] Tacit. *Annal.* iii. 36.

[6] Senec. *De Benefic.* iii. 26.

[7] Tacit. *Annal.* i. 73. Tiberius refused to allow this case to be proceeded with. See, too, Philost. *Apollonius of Tyana*, i. 15.

[8] Suet. *Tiber.* lviii.

tually executed for undressing before the statue of Domitian.[1]

It may easily be conceived that men who had been raised to this pinnacle of arrogance and power, men who exercised uncontrolled authority in the midst of a society in a state of profound corruption, were often guilty of the most atrocious extravagances. In the first period of the Empire more especially, when traditions were not yet formed, and when experience had not yet shown the dangers of the throne, the brains of some of its occupants reeled at their elevation, and a kind of moral insanity ensued. The pages of Suetonius remain as an eternal witness of the abysses of depravity, the hideous, intolerable cruelty, the hitherto unimagined extravagances of nameless lust that were then manifested on the Palatine, and while they cast a fearful light upon the moral chaos into which pagan society had sunk, they furnish ample evidence of the demoralising influences of the empire. The throne was, it is true, occupied by some of the best as well as by some of the worst men who have ever lived; but the evil, though checked and mitigated, was never abolished. The corruption of a Court, the formation of a profession of spies, the encouragement given to luxury, the distributions of corn, and the multiplication of games, were evils which varied greatly in their degrees of intensity, but the very existence of the empire prevented the creation of those habits of political life which formed the moral type of the great republics of antiquity. Liberty, which is often very unfavourable to theological systems, is almost always in the end favourable to morals : for the most effectual method that has been devised for diverting men from vice is to give free scope to a higher ambition. This scope was absolutely wanting in the Roman Empire, and the moral condition, in the absence of lasting political habits, fluctuated greatly with the character of the Emperors.

---

[1] 'Mulier quædam, quod semel uerat ante statuam Domitiani, damnata et interfecta est.'—Xiphilin, lxvii. 12.

The results of the institution of slavery were probably even more serious. In addition to its manifest effect in encouraging a tyrannical and ferocious spirit in the masters, it cast a stigma upon all labour, and at once degraded and impoverished the free poor. In modern societies the formation of an influential and numerous middle class, trained in the sober and regular habits of industrial life, is the chief guarantee of national morality, and where such a class exists, the disorders of the upper ranks, though undoubtedly injurious, are never fatal to society. The influence of great outbursts of fashionable depravity, such as that which followed the Restoration in England, is rarely more than superficial. The aristocracy may revel in every excess of ostentatious vice, but the great mass of the people, at the loom, the counter, or the plough, continue unaffected by their example, and the habits of life into which they are forced by the condition of their trades preserve them from gross depravity. It was the most frightful feature of the corruption of ancient Rome that it extended through every class of the community. In the absence of all but the simplest machinery, manufactures, with the vast industrial life they beget, were unknown. The poor citizen found almost all the spheres in which an honourable livelihood might be obtained wholly or at least in a very great degree preoccupied by slaves, while he had learnt to regard trade with an invincible repugnance. Hence followed the immense increase of corrupt and corrupting professions, as actors, pantomimes, hired gladiators, political spies, ministers to passion, astrologers, religious charlatans, pseudo-philosophers, which gave the free classes a precarious and occasional subsistence, and hence, too, the gigantic dimensions of the system of clientage. Every rich man was surrounded by a train of dependants, who lived in a great measure at his expense, and spent their lives in ministering to his passions and flattering his vanity. And, above all, the public distribution of corn, and occasionally of money, was carried on to such an extent, that, so far as the first necessaries of life were concerned, the whole poor free population of Rome was supported gratuitously by the Government. To effect this distribution promptly and lavishly was the main object of the Imperial policy, and its consequences were worse than could have resulted from the most extravagant poor-laws or the most excessive charity. The mass of the people were supported in absolute idleness by corn, which was given without any reference to desert, and was received, not as a favour, but as a right, while gratuitous public amusements still further diverted them from labour.

Under these influences the population rapidly dwindled away. Productive enterprise was almost extinct in Italy, and an unexampled concurrence of causes made a vicious celibacy the habitual condition. Already in the days of Augustus the evil was apparent, and the dangers which in later reigns drove the patricians still more generally from public life, drove them more and more into every extravagance of sensuality. Greece, since the destruction of her liberty, and also the leading cities of Asia Minor and of Egypt, had become centres of the wildest corruption, and Greek and Oriental captives were innumerable in Rome. Ionian slaves of a surpassing beauty, Alexandrian slaves, famous for their subtle skill in stimulating the jaded senses of the confirmed and sated libertine, became the ornaments of every patrician house, the companions and the instructors of the young. The disinclination to marriage was so general, that men who spent their lives in endeavouring by flatteries to secure the inheritance of wealthy bachelors became a numerous and a notorious class. The slave population was itself a hotbed of vice, and it contaminated all with which it came in contact; while the attractions of the games, and especially of the public baths, which became the habitual resort of the idle, combined with the charms of the Italian climate, and with the miserable domestic architecture that was general, to draw the poor

citizens from indoor life.  Idleness, amusements, and a pare
subsistence were alone desired, and the general practice of
abortion among the rich, and of infanticide and exposition in
all classes, still further checked the population.

The destruction of all public spirit in a population so
situated was complete and inevitable.  In the days of the
Republic a consul had once advocated the admission of a brave
Italian people to the right of Roman citizenship, on the
ground that 'those who thought only of liberty deserved to
be Romans.'[1]  In the Empire all liberty was cheerfully bartered for games and corn, and the worst tyrant could by
these means be secure of popularity.  In the Republic, when
Marius threw open the houses of those he had proscribed, to
be plundered, the people, by a noble abstinence, rebuked the
act, for no Roman could be found to avail himself of the
permission.[2]  In the Empire, when the armies of Vitellius
and Vespasian were disputing the possession of the city, the
degenerate Romans gathered with delight to the spectacle as
to a gladiatorial show, plundered the deserted houses, encouraged either army by their reckless plaudits, dragged out
the fugitives to be slain, and converted into a festival the
calamity of their country.[3]  The degradation of the national
character was permanent.  Neither the teaching of the
Stoics, nor the government of the Antonines, nor the triumph
of Christianity could restore it.  Indifferent to liberty, the
Roman now, as then, asks only for an idle subsistence and
for public spectacles, and countless monasteries and ecclesiastical pageants occupy in modern Rome the same place as
did the distributions of corn and the games of the amphitheatre in the Rome of the Cæsars.

It must be remembered, too, that while public spirit had

---

[1] ' Eos demum, qui nihil præter-
quam de libertate cogitent, dignos
esse, qui Romani fiant.'—Livy, viii.
21.

[2] Valerius Maximus, iv. 3, § 14.
[3] See the picture of this scene
in Tacitus, *Hist.* iii. 83.

thus decayed in the capital of the empire, there existed no
independent or rival power to reanimate by its example the
smouldering flame. The existence in modern Europe of
many distinct nations on the same level of civilisation, but
with different forms of government and conditions of national
life, secures the permanence of some measure of patriotism
and liberty. If these perish in one nation, they survive in
another, and each people affects those about it by its rivalry
or example. But an empire which comprised all the civilised
globe could know nothing of this political interaction. In
religious, social, intellectual, and moral life, foreign ideas
were very discernible, but the enslaved provinces could have
no influence in rekindling political life in the centre, and
those which rivalled Italy in their civilisation, even surpassed
it in their corruption and their servility.

In reviewing, however, the conditions upon which the
moral state of the empire depended, there are still two very
important centres or seed-plots of virtue to which it is
necessary to advert. I mean the pursuit of agriculture and
the discipline of the army. A very early tradition, which
was attributed to Romulus, had declared that warfare and
agriculture were the only honourable occupations for a
citizen,[1] and it would be difficult to overrate the influence of
the last in forming temperate and virtuous habits among the
people. It is the subject of the only extant work of the
elder Cato. Virgil had adorned it with the lustre of his
poetry. A very large part of the Roman religion was intended to symbolise its stages or consecrate its operations.
Varro expressed an eminently Roman sentiment in that
beautiful sentence which Cowper has introduced into English
poetry, 'Divine Providence made the country, but human
art the town.'[2] The reforms of Vespasian consisted chiefly

---

[1] Dion. Halicarnass.
[2] 'Divina Natura dedit agros; ars humana ædificavit urbes.'

19

of the elevation to high positions of the agriculturists of the
provinces.   Antoninus, who was probably the most perfect
of all the Roman emperors, was through his whole reign a
zealous farmer.

As far as the distant provinces were concerned, it is probable that the Imperial system was on the whole a good.
The scandalous rapacity of the provincial governors, which
disgraced the closing years of the Republic, and which is immortalised by the indignant eloquence of Cicero, appears to
have ceased, or at least greatly diminished, under the supervision of the emperors.   Ample municipal freedom, good
roads, and for the most part wise and temperate rulers,
secured for the distant sections of the empire a large measure
of prosperity.   But in Italy itself, agriculture, with the
habits of life that attended it, speedily and fatally decayed.
The peasant proprietor soon glided hopelessly into debt.   The
immense advantages which slavery gave the rich gradually
threw nearly all the Italian soil into their hands.   The
peasant who ceased to be proprietor found himself excluded
by slave labour from the position of a hired cultivator, while
the gratuitous distributions of corn drew him readily to the
metropolis.   The gigantic scale of these distributions induced
the rulers to obtain their corn in the form of a tribute from
distant countries, chiefly from Africa and Sicily, and it almost
ceased to be cultivated in Italy.   The land fell to waste, or
was cultivated by slaves or converted into pasture, and over
vast tracts the race of free peasants entirely disappeared.

This great revolution, which profoundly affected the
moral condition of Italy, had long been impending.   The
debts of the poor peasants, and the tendency of the patricians
to monopolise the conquered territory, had occasioned some
of the fiercest contests of the Republic, and in the earliest
days of the Empire the blight that seemed to have fallen on
the Italian soil was continually and pathetically lamented.
Livy, Varro, Columella, and Pliny have noticed it in the

most emphatic terms,[1] and Tacitus observed that as early as the reign of Claudius, Italy, which had once supplied the distant provinces with corn, had become dependent for the very necessaries of life upon the winds and the waves.[2] The evil was indeed of an almost hopeless kind. Adverse winds, or any other accidental interruption of the convoys of corn, occasioned severe distress in the capital; but the prospect of the calamities that would ensue if any misfortune detached the great corn-growing countries from the empire, might well have appalled the politician. Yet the combined influence of slavery, and of the gratuitous distributions of corn, acting in the manner I have described, rendered every effort to revive Italian agriculture abortive, and slavery had taken such deep root that it would have been impossible to abolish it, while no emperor dared to encounter the calamities and rebellion that would follow a suspension or even a restriction of the distributions.[3] Many serious efforts were made to remedy the evil.[4] Alexander Severus advanced money to the poor to buy portions of land, and accepted a gradual payment without interest from the produce of the soil. Pertinax settled poor men as proprietors on deserted land, on the sole condition that they should cultivate it. Marcus Aurelius began, and Aurelian and Valentinian continued, the system of settling great numbers of barbarian captives upon the Italian soil, and compelling them as slaves to till it. The introduction

---

[1] See a collection of passages from these writers in Wallon, *Hist. de l'Esclavage*, tome ii. pp. 378–379. Pliny, in the first century, noticed (*Hist. Nat.* xviii. 7) that the *latifundia*, or system of large properties, was ruining both Italy and the provinces, and that six landlords whom Nero killed were the possessors of half Roman Africa.

[2] Tacit. *Annal.* xii. 43. The same complaint had been made still earlier by Tiberius, in a letter to the Senate. (*Annal.* iii. 54.)

[3] Augustus, for a time, contemplated abolishing the distributions, but soon gave up the idea. (Suet. *Aug.* xlii.) He noticed that it had the effect of causing the fields to be neglected.

[4] M. Wallon has carefully traced this history. (*Hist. de l'Esclav.* tome iii. pp. 294–297.)

of this large foreign element into the heart of Italy was eventually one of the causes of the downfall of the empire, and it is also about this time that we first dimly trace the condition of serfdom or servitude to the soil into which slavery afterwards faded, and which was for some centuries the general condition of the European poor. But the economical and moral causes that were destroying agriculture in Italy were too strong to be resisted, and the simple habits of life which agricultural pursuits promote had little or no place in the later empire.

A somewhat less rapid but in the end not less complete decadence had taken place in military life. The Roman army was at first recruited exclusively from the upper classes, and the service, which lasted only during actual warfare, was gratuitous. Before the close of the Republic, however, these conditions had disappeared. Military pay is said to have been instituted at the time of the siege of Veii.[1] Some Spaniards who were enrolled during the rivalry of Rome and Carthage were the first example of the employment of foreign mercenaries by the former.[2] Marius abolished the property qualification of the recruits.[3] In long residences in Spain and in the Asiatic provinces discipline gradually relaxed, and the historian who traced the progress of Oriental luxury in Rome dwelt with a just emphasis upon the ominous fact that it had first been introduced into the city by soldiers.[4] The civil wars contributed to the destruction of the old military traditions, but being conducted by able generals it is probable that they had more effect upon the patriotism than upon the discipline of the army. Augustus reorganised the whole military system, establishing a body of soldiers known as the Prætorian guard, and dignified with some special privileges, permanently in Rome, while the

---

[1] Livy, iv. 59–60. Florus, i. 12.      [3] Sallust, *Bell. Jugurth.* 84–86.
[2] Livy, xxiv. 49.      [4] Livy, xxxix. 6.

other legions were chiefly mustered upon the frontiers.
During his long reign, and during that of Tiberius, both
sections were quiescent, but the murder of Caligula by his
soldiers opened a considerable period of insubordination.
Claudius, it was observed, first set the fatal example of pur-
chasing his safety from his soldiers by bribes.[1] The armies
of the provinces soon discovered that it was possible to elect
an emperor outside Rome, and Galba, Otho, Vitellius, and
Vespasian were all the creatures of revolt. The evil was,
however, not yet past recovery. Vespasian and Trajan enforced discipline with great stringency and success. The
emperors began more frequently to visit the camps. The
number of the soldiers was small, and for some time the
turbulence subsided. The history of the worst period of the
Empire, it has been truly observed, is full of instances of brave
soldiers trying, under circumstances of extreme difficulty,
simply to do their duty. But the historian had soon occasion
to notice again the profound influence of the voluptuous
Asiatic cities upon the legions.[2] Removed for many years
from Italy, they lost all national pride, their allegiance was
transferred from the sovereign to the general, and when the
Imperial sceptre fell into the hands of a succession of incom-
petent rulers, they habitually urged their commanders to
revolt, and at last reduced the empire to a condition of military anarchy. A remedy was found for this evil, though
not for the luxurious habits that had been acquired, in the
division of the empire, which placed each army under the
direct supervision of an emperor, and it is probable that at a
later period Christianity diminished the insubordination,
though it may have also diminished the military fire, of the
soldiers.[3] But other and still more powerful causes were in

[1] 'Primus Cæsarum fidem mi-
litis etiam præmio pigneratus.'—
Suet. *Claud.* x.
[2] See Tacitus, *Annal.* xiii. 35;
*Hist.* ii. 69.

[3] M. Sismondi thinks that the
influence of Christianity in sub-
duing the spirit of revolt, if not in
the army, at least in the people,
was very great. He says: 'Il est

operation preparing the military downfall of Rome. The habits of inactivity which the Imperial policy had produced, and which, through a desire for popularity, most emperors laboured to encourage, led to a profound disinclination for the hardships of military life. Even the Prætorian guard, which was long exclusively Italian, was selected after Septimus Severus from the legions on the frontiers,[1] while, Italy being relieved from the regular conscription, these were recruited solely in the provinces, and innumerable barbarians were subsidised. The political and military consequences of this change are sufficiently obvious. In an age when, artillery being unknown, the military superiority of civilised nations over barbarians was far less than at present, the Italians had become absolutely unaccustomed to real war, and had acquired habits that were beyond all others incompatible with military discipline, while many of the barbarians who menaced and at last subverted the empire had been actually trained by Roman generals. The moral consequence is equally plain—military discipline, like agricultural labour, ceased to have any part among the moral influences of Italy.

To those who have duly estimated the considerations I have enumerated, the downfall and moral debasement of the empire can cause no surprise, though they may justly wonder that its agony should have been so protracted, that it should have produced a multitude of good and great men, both

---

remarquable qu'en cinq ans, sept prétendans au trône, tous bien supérieurs à Honorius en courage, en talens et en vertus, furent successivement envoyés captifs à Ravenne ou punis de mort, que le peuple applaudit toujours à ces jugemens et ne se sépara point de l'autorité légitime, tant la doctrine du droit divin des rois que les évêques avoient commencé à prêcher sous Théodose avoit fait de progrès,

et tant le monde romain sembloit déterminé à périr avec un monarque imbécile plutôt que tenté de se donner un sauveur.'—*Hist. de la Chute de l'Empire romain*, tome i. p. 221.

[1] See Gibbon, ch. v.; Merivale's *Hist. of Rome*, ch. lxvii. It was thought that troops thus selected would be less likely to revolt. Constantine abolished the Prætorians.

pagan and Christian, and that these should have exercised
so wide an influence as they unquestionably did. Almost
every institution or pursuit by which virtuous habits would
naturally have been formed had been tainted or destroyed,
while agencies of terrific power were impelling the people to
vice. The rich, excluded from most honourable paths of ambition, and surrounded by countless parasites who inflamed
their every passion, found themselves absolute masters of innumerable slaves who were their willing ministers, and often
their teachers, in vice. The poor, hating industry and destitute of all intellectual resources, lived in habitual idleness,
and looked upon abject servility as the normal road to
fortune. But the picture becomes truly appalling when we
remember that the main amusement of both classes was the
spectacle of bloodshed, of the death, and sometimes of the
torture, of men.

The gladiatorial games form, indeed, the one feature of
Roman society which to a modern mind is almost inconceivable in its atrocity. That not only men, but women, in an
advanced period of civilisation—men and women who not
only professed but very frequently acted upon a high code of
morals—should have made the carnage of men their habitual
amusement, that all this should have continued for centuries,
with scarcely a protest, is one of the most startling facts in
moral history. It is, however, perfectly normal, and in no
degree inconsistent with the doctrine of natural moral perceptions, while it opens out fields of ethical enquiry of a very
deep though painful interest.

These games, which long eclipsed, both in interest and in
influence, every other form of public amusement at Rome,[1]

---

[1] The gladiatorial shows are
treated incidentally by most Roman
historians, but the three works from
which I have derived most assistance in this part of my subject are
the *Saturnalia* of Justus Lipsius,
Magnin, *Origines du Théâtre* (an
extremely learned and interesting
book, which was unhappily never
completed), and Friedlænder's

were originally religious ceremonies celebrated at the tombs
of the great, and intended as human sacrifices to appease the
Manes of the dead.[1]    They were afterwards defended as a
means of sustaining the military spirit by the constant spectacle of courageous death,[2] and with this object it was
customary to give a gladiatorial show to soldiers before their
departure to a war.[3]    In addition to these functions they had
a considerable political importance, for at a time when all
the regular organs of liberty were paralysed or abolished, the
ruler was accustomed in the arena to meet tens of thousands
of his subjects, who availed themselves of the opportunity to
present their petitions, to declare their grievances, and to
censure freely the sovereign or his ministers.[4]    The games

---

*Roman Manners from Augustus to
the Antonines* (the second volume of
the French translation). M. Wallon
has also compressed into a few
pages (*Hist. de l'Esclavage*, tome ii.
pp. 129-139) much information on
the subject.

[1] Hence the old name of *bus-
tuarii* (from *bustum*, a funeral pile)
given to gladiators (Nieupoort, *De
Ritibus Romanorum*, p. 514).    According to Pliny (*Hist. Nat.* xxx. 3),
'regular human sacrifices were only
abolished in Rome by a decree of
the senate, B.C. 97,' and there are
some instances of them at a still
later period.    Much information
about them is collected by Sir
C. Lewis, *Credibility of Roman
History*, vol. ii. p. 430; Merivale,
*Conversion of the Roman Empire*,
pp. 230-233; Legendre, *Traité de
l'Opinion*, vol. i. pp. 229-231.    Porphyry, in his *De Abstinentia Carnis*,
devoted considerable research to
this matter.    Games were habitually celebrated by wealthy private
individuals, during the early part of
the empire, at the funerals of their
relatives, but their mortuary cha-

racter gradually ceased, and after
Marcus Aurelius they had become
mere public spectacles, and were
rarely celebrated at Rome by private men.    (See Wallon, *Hist. de
l'Esclav.* tome ii. pp. 135-136.)
The games had then really passed
into their purely secular stage,
though they were still nominally
dedicated to Mars and Diana, and
though an altar of Jupiter Latiaris
stood in the centre of the arena.
(Nieupoort, p. 365.)

[2] Cicero, *Tusc.* lib. ii.

[3] Capitolinus, *Maximus et Bal-
binus.*    Capitolinus says this is the
most probable origin of the custom,
though others regarded it as a sacrifice to appease Nemesis by an offering of blood.

[4] Much curious information on
this subject may be found in Friedländer, *Mœurs romaines*, liv. vi. ch.
i.    Very few Roman emperors ventured to disregard or to repress
these outcries, and they led to the
fall of several of the most powerful
ministers of the empire.    On the
whole these games represent the
strangest and most ghastly form

are said to have been of Etruscan origin; they were first
introduced into Rome, B.C. 264, when the two sons of a man
named Brutus compelled three pair of gladiators to fight at
the funeral of their father,[1] and before the close of the
Republic they were common on great public occasions, and,
what appears even more horrible, at the banquets of the
nobles.[2] The rivalry of Cæsar and Pompey greatly multiplied them, for each sought by this means to ingratiate himself with the people. Pompey introduced a new form of
combat between men and animals.[3] Cæsar abolished the old
custom of restricting the mortuary games to the funerals of
men, and his daughter was the first Roman lady whose tomb
was desecrated by human blood.[4] Besides this innovation,
Cæsar replaced the temporary edifices in which the games
had hitherto been held by a permanent wooden amphitheatre,
shaded the spectators by an awning of precious silk, compelled
the condemned persons on one occasion to fight with silver
lances,[5] and drew so many gladiators into the city that the
Senate was obliged to issue an enactment restricting their
number.[6] In the earliest years of the Empire, Statilius
Taurus erected the first amphitheatre of stone.[7] Augustus

---

political liberty has ever assumed.
On the other hand, the people
readily bartered all genuine freedom
for abundant games.

[1] Valer. Maximus, ii. 4, § 7.

[2] On the gladiators at banquets,
see J. Lipsius, *Saturnalia,* lib. i., c.
vi., Magnin; *Origines du Théâtre,*
pp. 380–385. This was originally
an Etruscan custom, and it was
also very common at Capua. As
Silius Italicus says:—

'Exhilarare viris convivia cæde
Mos olim, et miscere epulis spec-
tacula dira.'

Verus, the colleague of Marcus
Aurelius, was especially addicted to
this kind of entertainment. (Capi-

tolinus, *Verus.*) See, too, Athenæus,
iv. 40, 41.

[3] Senec. *De Brevit. Vit.* c. xiii.

[4] Sueton. *J. Cæsar,* xxvi. Pliny
(*Ep.* vi. 34) commends a friend for
having given a show in memory of
his departed wife.

[5] Pliny, *Hist. Nat.* xxxiii. 16.

[6] Sueton. *Cæsar,* x.; Dion Cassius, xliii. 24.

[7] Sueton. *Aug.* xxix. The history of the amphitheatres is given
very minutely by Friedlænder, who,
like nearly all other antiquaries,
believes this to have been the first
of stone. Pliny mentions the existence, at an earlier period, of two
connected wooden theatres, which

ordered that not more than 120 men should fight on a single occasion, and that no prætor should give more than two spectacles in a single year,[1] and Tiberius again fixed the maximum of combatants,[2] but notwithstanding these attempts to limit them the games soon acquired the most gigantic proportions. They were celebrated habitually by great men in honour of their dead relatives, by officials on coming into office, by conquerors to secure popularity, and on every occasion of public rejoicing, and by rich tradesmen who were desirous of acquiring a social position.[3] They were also among the attractions of the public baths. Schools of gladiators—often the private property of rich citizens—existed in every leading city of Italy, and, besides slaves and criminals, they were thronged with freemen, who voluntarily hired themselves for a term of years. In the eyes of multitudes, the large sums that were paid to the victor, the patronage of nobles and often of emperors, and still more the delirium of popular enthusiasm that centred upon the successful gladiator, outweighed all the dangers of the profession. A complete recklessness of life was soon engendered both in the spectators and the combatants. The 'lanistæ,' or purveyors of gladiators, became an important profession. Wandering bands of gladiators traversed Italy, hiring themselves for the provincial amphitheatres. The influence of the games gradually pervaded the whole texture of Roman life. They became the common-place of conversation.[4] The children imitated them in their play.[5] The philosophers drew from

---

swung round on hinges and formed an amphitheatre. (*Hist. Nat.* xxxvi. 24.)

[1] Dion Cassius, liv. 2. It appears, however, from an inscription, that 10,000 gladiators fought in the reign and by the command of Augustus. Wallon, *Hist. de l'Esclavage*, tome, ii. p. 133.

[2] Sueton. *Tiber.* xxxiv. Nero

made another slight restriction (Tacit. *Annal.* xiii. 31), which appears to have been little observed.

[3] Martial notices (*Ep.* iii. 59) and ridicules a spectacle given by a shoemaker at Bologna, and by a fuller at Modena.

[4] Epictetus, *Enchir.* xxxiii. § 2.

[5] Arrian, iii. 15.

them their metaphors and illustrations. The artists pourtrayed them in every variety of ornament.[1] The vestal virgins had a seat of honour in the arena.[2] The Colosseum, which is said to have been capable of containing more than 80,000 spectators, eclipsed every other monument of Imperial splendour, and is even now at once the most imposing and the most characteristic relic of pagan Rome.

In the provinces the same passion was displayed. From Gaul to Syria, wherever the Roman influence extended, the spectacles of blood were introduced, and the gigantic remains of amphitheatres in many lands still attest by their ruined grandeur the scale on which they were pursued. In the reign of Tiberius, more than 20,000 persons are said to have perished by the fall of the amphitheatre at the suburban town of Fidenæ.[3] Under Nero, the Syracusans obtained, as a special favour, an exemption from the law which limited the number of gladiators.[4] Of the vast train of prisoners brought by Titus from Judea, a large proportion were destined by the conqueror for the provincial games.[5] In Syria, where they were introduced by Antiochus Epiphanes, they at first produced rather terror than pleasure ; but the effeminate Syrians soon learned to contemplate them with a passionate enjoyment,[6] and on a single occasion Agrippa caused 1,400 men to fight in the amphitheatre at Berytus.[7] Greece alone was in

---

[1] See these points minutely proved in Friedlænder.

[2] Suet. *Aug.* xliv. This was noticed before by Cicero. The Christian poet Prudentius dwelt on this aspect of the games in some forcible lines :—

Virgo modesta jubet converso pollice rumpi
Ne lateat pars ulla animæ vitalibus imis
Altius impresso dum palpitat ense secutor.'

[3] Sueton. *Tiberius*, xl. Tacitus, who gives a graphic description of the disaster (*Annal.* iv. 62–63), says 50,000 persons were killed or wounded.

[4] Tacit. *Annal.* xiii. 49.

[5] Joseph. *Bell. Jud.* vi. 9.

[6] See the very curious picture which Livy has given (xli. 20) of the growth of the fascination.

[7] Joseph. *Antiq. Jud.* xix. 7

some degree an exception. When an attempt was made to introduce the spectacle into Athens, the cynic philosopher Demonax appealed successfully to the better feelings of the people by exclaiming, 'You must first overthrow the altar of Pity.'[1] The games are said to have afterwards penetrated to Athens, and to have been suppressed by Apollonius of Tyana;[2] but with the exception of Corinth, where a very large foreign population existed, Greece never appears to have shared the general enthusiasm.[3]

One of the first consequences of this taste was to render the people absolutely unfit for those tranquil and refined amusements which usually accompany civilisation. To men who were accustomed to witness the fierce vicissitudes of deadly combat, any spectacle that did not elicit the strongest excitement was insipid. The only amusements that at all rivalled the spectacles of the amphitheatre and the circus were those which appealed strongly to the sensual passions, such as the games of Flora, the postures of the pantomimes, and the ballet.[4] Roman comedy, indeed, flourished for a short period, but only by throwing itself into the same career. The pander and the courtesan are the leading characters of Plautus, and the more modest Terence never attained an equal popularity. The different forms of vice have a continual tendency to act and react upon one another, and the intense craving after excitement which the amphitheatre must necessarily have produced, had probably no

---

[1] Lucian, *Demonax.*

[2] Philost. *Apoll.* iv. 22.

[3] Friedlænder, tome ii. pp. 95–96. There are, however, several extant Greek inscriptions relating to gladiators, and proving the existence of the shows in Greece. Pompeii, which was a Greek colony, had a vast amphitheatre, which we may still admire; and, under Nero, games were prohibited at Pompeii

for ten years, in consequence of a riot that broke out during a gladiatorial show. (Tacit. *Annal.* xiv. 17.) After the defeat of Perseus, Paulus Emilius celebrated a show in Macedonia. (Livy, xli. 20.)

[4] These are fully discussed by Magnin and Friedlænder. There is a very beautiful description of a ballet, representing the 'Judgment of Paris,' in Apuleius, *Metamorph.* x.

small influence in stimulating the orgies of sensuality which Tacitus and Suetonius describe.

But if comedy could to a certain extent flourish with the gladiatorial games, it was not so with tragedy. It is, indeed, true that the tragic actor can exhibit displays of more intense agony and of a grander heroism than were ever witnessed in the arena. His mission is not to paint nature as it exists in the light of day, but nature as it exists in the heart of man. His gestures, his tones, his looks, are such as would never have been exhibited by the person he represents, but they display to the audience the full intensity of the emotions which that person would have felt, but which he would have been unable adequately to reveal. But to those who were habituated to the intense realism of the amphitheatre, the idealised suffering of the stage was unimpressive. All the genius of a Siddons or a Ristori would fail to move an audience who had continually seen living men fall bleeding and mangled at their feet. One of the first functions of the stage is to raise to the highest point the susceptibility to disgust. When Horace said that Medea should not kill her children upon the stage, he enunciated not a mere arbitrary rule, but one which grows necessarily out of the development of the drama. It is an essential characteristic of a refined and cultivated taste to be shocked and offended at the spectacle of bloodshed; and the theatre, which somewhat dangerously dissociates sentiment from action, and causes men to waste their compassion on ideal sufferings, is at least a barrier against the extreme forms of cruelty by developing this susceptibility to the highest degree. The gladiatorial games, on the other hand, destroyed all sense of disgust, and therefore all refinement of taste, and they rendered the permanent triumph of the drama impossible.[1]

---

[1] Pacuvius and Accius were the founders of Roman tragedy. The abridger, Velleius Paterculus, who is the only Roman historian who pays any attention to literary history, boasts that the latter might

It is abundantly evident, both from history and from present experience, that the instinctive shock, or natural feeling of disgust, caused by the sight of the sufferings of men is not generically different from that which is caused by the sight of the sufferings of animals. The latter, to those who are not accustomed to it, is intensely painful. The former continually becomes by use a matter of absolute indifference. If the repugnance which is felt in the one case appears greater than in the other, it is not on account of any innate sentiment which commands us to reverence our species, but simply because our imagination finds less difficulty in realising human than animal suffering, and also because education has strengthened our feelings in the one case much more than in the other. There is, however, no fact more clearly established than that when men have regarded it as not a crime to kill some class of their fellow-men, they have soon learnt to do so with no more natural compunction or hesitation than they would exhibit in killing a wild animal. This is the normal condition of savage men. Colonists and Red Indians even now often shoot each other with precisely the same indifference as they shoot beasts of prey, and the whole history of warfare—especially when warfare was conducted on more savage principles than at present—is an illustration of the fact. Startling, therefore, as it may now appear, it is in no degree unnatural that Roman spectators should have contemplated with perfect equanimity the slaughter of men. The Spaniard, who is brought in infancy to the bull-ring, soon learns to gaze with indifference or with pleasure upon sights before which the unpractised eye of the stranger quails with horror, and the same process would be equally efficacious had the spectacle been the sufferings of men.

We now look back with indignation upon this indifference;

---

rank honourably with the best Greek tragedians. He adds, 'ut in illis [the Greeks] limæ, in hoc pœne plus videatur fuisse sanguinis.'— *Hist. Rom.* ii. 9.

but yet, although it may be hard to realise, it is probably true that there is scarcely a human being who might not by custom be so indurated as to share it. Had the most benevolent person lived in a country in which the innocence of these games was deemed axiomatic, had he been taken to them in his very childhood, and accustomed to associate them with his earliest dreams of romance, and had he then been left simply to the play of the emotions, the first paroxysm of horror would have soon subsided, the shrinking repugnance that followed would have grown weaker and weaker, the feeling of interest would have been aroused, and the time would probably come in which it would reign alone. But even this absolute indifference to the sight of human suffering does not represent the full evil resulting from the gladiatorial games. That some men are so constituted as to be capable of taking a real and lively pleasure in the simple contemplation of suffering as suffering, and without any reference to their own interests, is a proposition which has been strenuously denied by those in whose eyes vice is nothing more than a displacement, or exaggeration, of lawful self-regarding feelings, and others, who have admitted the reality of the phenomenon, have treated it as a very rare and exceptional disease.[1] That it is so—at least in its extreme forms—in the present condition of society, may reasonably be hoped, though I imagine that few persons who have watched the habits of boys would question that to take pleasure in giving at least some degree of pain is sufficiently common, and though it is not quite certain that all the sports of adult men would be entered into with exactly the same zest if their victims were not sentient beings. But in every society in which atrocious punishments have been common, this side of human nature

---

[1] Thus, e.g., Hobbes: 'Alienæ calamitatis contemptus nominatur crudelitas, proceditque a propriæ securitatis opinione. Nam ut ali- quis sibi placeat in malis alienis sine alio fine, videtur mihi impossibile.'—*Leviathan*, pars i. c. vi.

has acquired an undoubted prominence. It is related of
Claudius that his special delight at the gladiatorial shows
was in watching the countenances of the dying, for he had
learnt to take an artistic pleasure in observing the variations
of their agony.[1] When the gladiator lay prostrate it was
customary for the spectators to give the sign with their
thumbs, indicating whether they desired him to be spared or
slain, and the giver of the show reaped most popularity
when, in the latter case, he permitted no consideration of
economy to make him hesitate to sanction the popular
award.[2]

Besides this, the mere desire for novelty impelled the
people to every excess or refinement of barbarity.[3] The
simple combat became at last insipid, and every variety of
atrocity was devised to stimulate the flagging interest. At
one time a bear and a bull, chained together, rolled in fierce
contest along the sand ; at another, criminals dressed in the
skins of wild beasts were thrown to bulls, which were mad-
dened by red-hot irons, or by darts tipped with burning
pitch. Four hundred bears were killed on a single day under
Caligula ; three hundred on another day under Claudius.
Under Nero, four hundred tigers fought with bulls and elephants ; four hundred bears and three hundred lions were
slaughtered by his soldiers. In a single day, at the dedication
of the Colosseum by Titus, five thousand animals perished.
Under Trajan, the games continued for one hundred and
twenty-three successive days.[4] Lions, tigers, elephants, rhi-

---

[1] Sueton. *Claudius*, xxxiv.

[2] 'Et verso pollice vulgi
Quemlibet occidunt populariter.'—
Juvenal, *Sat.* iii. 36–37.

[3] Besides the many incidental
notices scattered through the Roman historians, and through the
writings of Seneca, Plutarch, Juvenal and Pliny, we have a curious

little book, *De Spectaculis*, by
Martial—a book which is not more
horrible from the atrocities it recounts than from the perfect absence of all feeling of repulsion or
compassion it everywhere displays.

[4] These are but a few of the many
examples given by Magnin, who
has collected a vast array of authorities on the subject. (*Origines*

noceroses, hippopotami, giraffes, bulls, stags, even crocodiles
and serpents, were employed to give novelty to the spectacle
Nor was any form of human suffering wanting. The first
Gordian, when edile, gave twelve spectacles, in each of which
from one hundred and fifty to five hundred pair of gladiators
appeared.[1] Eight hundred pair fought at the triumph of
Aurelian.[2] Ten thousand men fought during the games of
Trajan.[3] Nero illumined his gardens during the night by
Christians burning in their pitchy shirts.[4] Under Domitian,
an army of feeble dwarfs was compelled to fight,[5] and, more
than once, female gladiators descended to perish in the arena.[6]
A criminal personating a fictitious character was nailed to a
cross, and there torn by a bear.[7] Another, representing
Scævola, was compelled to hold his hand in a real flame.[8] A
third, as Hercules, was burnt alive upon the pile.[9] So intense

du Théâtre, pp. 445–453.) M.
Mongez has devoted an interesting
memoir to ' Les animaux promenés
ou tués dans le cirque.' (Mém. de
l'Acad. des Inscrip. et Belles-lettres,
tome x.) See, too, Friedlænder. Pliny
rarely gives an account of any wild
animal without accompanying it by
statistics about its appearances in
the arena. The first instance of a
wild beast hunt in the amphitheatre
is said to be that recorded by Livy
(xxxix. 22), which took place about
80 B.C.
[1] Capitolinus, Gordiani.
[2] Vopiscus, Aurelian.
[3] Xiphilin, lxviii. 15.
[4] Tacit. Annal. xv. 44.
[5] Xiphilin, lxvii. 8; Statius,
Sylv. i. 6.
[6] During the Republic, a rich
man ordered in his will that
some women he had purchased for
the purpose should fight in the
funeral games to his memory, but
the people annulled the clause.
(Athenæus, iv. 39.) Under Nero

and Domitian, female gladiators
seem to have been not uncommon.
See Statius, Sylv. i. 6; Sueton.
Domitian, iv.; Xiphilin, lxvii. 8.
Juvenal describes the enthusiasm
with which Roman ladies practised
with the gladiatorial weapons (Sat.
vi. 248, &c.), and Martial (De
Spectac. vi.) mentions the combats
of women with wild beasts. One,
he says, killed a lion. A combat
of female gladiators, under Severus,
created some tumult, and it was
decreed that they should no longer
be permitted. (Xiphilin, lxxv. 16.)
See Magnin, pp. 434–435.
[7] Martial, De Spectac. vii.
[8] Ibid. Ep. viii. 30.
[9] Tertullian, Ad Nation. i. 10.
One of the most ghastly features
of the games was the comic aspect
they sometimes assumed. This was
the case in the combats of dwarfs.
There were also combats by blind-
folded men. Petronius (Satyricon,
c. xlv.) has given us a horrible description of the maimed and feeble

was the craving for blood, that a prince was less unpopular if
he neglected the distribution of corn than if he neglected the
games ; and Nero himself, on account of his munificence in
this respect, was probably the sovereign who was most
beloved by the Roman multitude.  Heliogabalus and Galerius
are reported, when dining, to have regaled themselves with
the sight of criminals torn by wild beasts.  It was said of the
latter that 'he never supped without human blood.'[1]

It is well for us to look steadily on such facts as these.
They display more vividly than any mere philosophical disquisition the abyss of depravity into which it is possible for
human nature to sink.  They furnish us with striking proofs
of the reality of the moral progress we have attained, and
they enable us in some degree to estimate the regenerating
influence that Christianity has exercised in the world.  For
the destruction of the gladiatorial games is all its work.
Philosophers, indeed, might deplore them, gentle natures
might shrink from their contagion, but to the multitude they
possessed a fascination which nothing but the new religion
could overcome.

Nor was this fascination surprising, for no pageant has
ever combined more powerful elements of attraction.  The
magnificent circus, the gorgeous dresses of the assembled
Court, the contagion of a passionate enthusiasm thrilling
almost visibly through the mighty throng, the breathless
silence of expectation, the wild cheers bursting simultaneously
from eighty thousand tongues, and echoing to the farthest
outskirts of the city, the rapid alternations of the fray, the

---

men who were sometimes compelled to fight.    People afflicted
with epilepsy were accustomed to
drink the blood of the wounded
gladiators, which they believed to
be a sovereign remedy.  (Pliny,
*Hist. Nat.* xxviii. 2; Tertul.
*Apol.* ix.)

[1] 'Nec unquam sine humano
cruore cœnabat.'—Lactan. *De Mort.
Persec.*  Much the same thing is
told of the Christian emperor Justinian II., who lived at the end of
the seventh century.  (Sismondi,
*Hist. de la Chute de l'Empire
Romain,* tome ii. p. 85.)

deeds of splendid courage that were manifested, were all well fitted to entrance the imagination. The crimes and servitude of the gladiator were for a time forgotten in the blaze of glory that surrounded him. Representing to the highest degree that courage which the Romans deemed the first of virtues, the cynosure of countless eyes, the chief object of conversation in the metropolis of the universe, destined, if victorious, to be immortalised in the mosaic and the sculpture,[1] he not unfrequently rose to heroic grandeur. The gladiator Spartacus for three years defied the bravest armies of Rome. The greatest of Roman generals had chosen gladiators for his body-guard.[2] A band of gladiators, faithful even to death, followed the fortunes of the fallen Antony, when all besides had deserted him.[3] Beautiful eyes, trembling with passion, looked down upon the fight, and the noblest ladies in Rome, even the empress herself, had been known to crave the victor's love.[4] We read of gladiators lamenting that the games occurred so seldom,[5] complaining bitterly if they were not permitted to descend into the arena,[6] scorning to fight except with the most powerful antagonists,[7] laughing aloud as their wounds were dressed,[8] and at last, when prostrate in the dust, calmly turning their throats to the sword of the conqueror.[9] The enthusiasm that gathered round them was so intense that special laws were found necessary, and were sometimes insufficient to prevent patricians from enlisting in their ranks,[10] while the tranquil

---

[1] Winckelmann says the statue called 'The Dying Gladiator' does not represent a gladiator. At a later period, however, statues of gladiators were not uncommon, and Pliny notices (*Hist. Nat.* xxxv. 33) paintings of them. A fine specimen of mosaic portraits of gladiators is now in the Lateran Museum.

[2] Plutarch's *Life of Cæsar.*

[3] Dion Cassius, li. 7.

[4] Faustina, the wife of Marcus Aurelius, was especially accused of this weakness. (Capitolinus, *Marcus Aurelius.*)

[5] Seneca, *De Provident.* iv.

[6] Arrian's *Epictetus*, i. 29.

[7] Seneca, *De Provident.* iii.

[8] Aulus Gellius, xii. 5.

[9] Cicero, *Tusc.* lib. ii.

[10] Some Equites fought under Julius Cæsar, and a senator named

courage with which they never failed to die supplied the
philosopher with his most striking examples.[1] The severe
continence that was required before the combat, contrasting
vividly with the licentiousness of Roman life, had even
invested them with something of a moral dignity; and it is
a singularly suggestive fact that of all pagan characters the
gladiator was selected by the Fathers as the closest approxi-
mation to a Christian model.[2] St. Augustine tells us how
one of his friends, being drawn to the spectacle, endeavoured
by closing his eyes to guard against a fascination he knew to
be sinful. A sudden cry caused him to break his resolution,
and he never could withdraw his gaze again.[3]

And while the influences of the amphitheatre gained a
complete ascendancy over the populace, the Roman was not
without excuses that could lull his moral feelings to repose.
The games, as I have said, were originally human sacrifices—
religious rites sacred to the dead—and it was argued that the
death of the gladiator was both more honourable and more

---

Fulvius Setinus wished to fight,
but Cæsar prevented him. (Suet.
*Cæsar*, xxxix.; Dion Cassius, xliii.
23.) Nero, according to Suetonius,
compelled men of the highest rank
to fight. Laws prohibiting patricians from fighting were several
times made and violated. (Friedlænder, pp. 39–41.) Commodus is
said to have been himself passionately fond of fighting as a gladiator. Much, however, of what
Lampridius relates on this point is
perfectly incredible. On the other
hand, the profession of the gladiator was constantly spoken of as
infamous; but this oscillation between extreme admiration and contempt will surprise no one who
has noticed the tone continually
adopted about prize-fighters in
England, and about the members
of some other professions on the

Continent. Juvenal dwells (*Sat.*
viii. 197–210) with great indignation on an instance of a patrician
fighting,

[1] 'Quis mediocris gladiator in-
gemuit, quis vultum mutavit unquam?'—Cic. *Tusc. Quæst.* lib. ii.

[2] E.g. Clem. Alex. *Strom.* iii.
There is a well-known passage of
this kind in Horace, *Ars Poet.* 412–
415. The comparison of the good
man to an athlete or gladiator,
which St. Paul employed, occurs also
in Seneca and Epictetus, from which
some have inferred that they must
have known the writings of the
Apostle. M. Denis, however, has
shown (*Idées morales dans l'Antiquité,* tome ii. p. 240) that the
same comparison had been used,
before the rise of Christianity, by
Plato, Æschines, and Cicero.

[3] *Confess.* vi. 8.

merciful than that of the passive victim, who, in the Homeric
age, was sacrificed at the tomb. The combatants were either
professional gladiators, slaves, criminals, or military captives.
The lot of the first was voluntary. The second had for
a long time been regarded as almost beneath or beyond a
freeman's care; but when the enlarging circle of sympathy
had made the Romans regard their slaves as 'a kind of
second human nature,' [1] they perceived the atrocity of exposing them in the games, and an edict of the emperor forbade
it. [2] The third had been condemned to death, and as the
victorious gladiator was at least sometimes pardoned, [3] a
permission to fight was regarded as an act of mercy. The
fate of the fourth could not strike the early Roman with the
horror it would now inspire, for the right of the conquerors
to massacre their prisoners was almost universally admitted. [4]
But, beyond the point of desiring the games to be in some
degree restricted, extremely few of the moralists of the
Roman Empire ever advanced. That it was a horrible and
demoralising thing to make the spectacle of the deaths, even
of guilty men, a form of popular amusement, was a position
which no Roman school had attained, and which was only
reached by a very few individuals. Cicero observes, 'that
the gladiatorial spectacles appear to some cruel and inhuman,'
and, he adds, 'I know not whether as they are now conducted it is not so, but when guilty men are compelled to
fight, no better discipline against suffering and death can be

---

[1] '[Servi] etsi per fortunam in
omnia obnoxii, tamen quasi secun-
dum hominum genus sunt.'—
Florus, Hist. iii. 20.

[2] Macrinus, however, punished
fugitive slaves by compelling them
to fight as gladiators. (Capitolinus, Macrinus.)

[3] Tacit. Annal. xii. 56. According to Friedländer, however,
there were two classes of criminals.

One class were condemned only to
fight, and pardoned if they conquered; the others were condemned
to fight till death, and this was
considered an aggravation of capital
punishment.

[4] 'Ad conciliandum plebis fa-
vorem effusa largitio, quum spectaculis indulget, supplicia quondam
hostium artem facit.'—Florus, iii.
12.

presented to the eye. [1]  Seneca, it is true, adopts a far nobler
language.   He denounced the games with a passionate
eloquence.   He refuted indignantly the argument derived
from the guilt of the combatants, and declared that under
every form and modification these amusements were brutalising, savage, and detestable. [2]  Plutarch went even farther,
and condemned the combats of wild beasts on the ground
that we should have a bond of sympathy with all sentient
beings, and that the sight of blood and of suffering is necessarily and essentially depraving. [3]  To these instances we
may add Petronius, who condemned the shows in his poem
on the civil war; Junius Mauricus, who refused to permit
the inhabitants of Vienne to celebrate them, and replied to
the remonstrances of the emperor, ' Would to Heaven it were
possible to abolish such spectacles, even at Rome!' [4] and,
above all, Marcus Aurelius, who, by compelling the gladiators
to fight with blunted swords, rendered them for a time comparatively harmless. [5]  But these, with the Athenian remonstrances I have already noticed, are almost the only instances
now remaining of pagan protests against the most conspicuous
as well as the most atrocious feature of the age.   Juvenal,
whose unsparing satire has traversed the whole field of
Roman manners, and who denounces fiercely all cruelty to
slaves, has repeatedly noticed the gladiatorial shows, but on
no single occasion does he intimate that they were inconsistent
with humanity.   Of all the great historians who recorded
them, not one seems to have been conscious that he was
recording a barbarity, not one appears to have seen in them

---

[1] *Tusc. Quæst.* ii. 17.
[2] See his magnificent letter on
the subject.  (*Ep.* vii.)
[3] In his two treatises *De Esu
Carnium.*
[4] Pliny, *Ep.* iv. 22.
[5] Xiphilin, lxxi. 29. Capitolinus,
*M. Aurelius.*  The emperor also

once carried off the gladiators to a
war with his army, much to the
indignation of the people. (Capit.)
He has himself noticed the extreme
weariness he felt at the public
amusements he was obliged to
attend. (vii. 3.)

any greater evils than an increasing tendency to pleasure and the excessive multiplication of a dangerous class. The Roman sought to make men brave and fearless, rather than gentle and humane, and in his eyes that spectacle was to be applauded which steeled the heart against the fear of death, even at the sacrifice of the affections. Titus and Trajan, in whose reigns, probably, the greatest number of shows were compressed into a short time, were both men of conspicuous clemency, and no Roman seems to have imagined that the fact of 3,000 men having been compelled to fight under the one, and 10,000 under the other, cast the faintest shadow upon their characters. Suetonius mentions, as an instance of the amiability of Titus, that he was accustomed to jest with the people during the combats of the gladiators,[1] and Pliny especially eulogised Trajan because he did not patronise spectacles that enervate the character, but rather those which impel men 'to noble wounds and to the contempt of death.'[2] The same writer, who was himself in many ways conspicuous for his gentleness and charity, having warmly commended a friend for acceding to a petition of the people of Verona, who desired a spectacle, adds this startling sentence: 'After so general a request, to have refused would not have been firmness—it would have been cruelty.'[3] Even in the closing years of the fourth century, the præfect Symmachus, who was regarded as one of the most estimable pagans of his age, collected some Saxon prisoners to fight in honour of his son. They strangled themselves in prison, and Symmachus lamented the misfortune that had befallen him from their 'impious hands,' but endeavoured to calm his feelings by recalling the patience of Socrates and the precepts of philosophy.[4]

---

[1] Sueton. *Titus*, viii.

[2] 'Visum est spectaculum inde non enerve nec fluxum, nec quod animos vircrum molliret et frangeret, sed quod ad pulchra vulnera contemptumque mortis accenderet.'

— Pliny, *Paneg.* xxxiii.

[3] 'Præterea tanto consensu rogabaris, ut negare non constans sed durum videretur.'—Plin. *Epist.* vi. 34.

[4] Symmach. *Epist.* ii. 46.

While, however, I have no desire to disguise or palliate
the extreme atrocity of this aspect of Roman life, there are
certain very natural exaggerations, against which it is necessary for us to guard.    There are in human nature, and more
especially in the exercise of the benevolent affections, inequalities, inconsistencies, and anomalies, of which theorists
do not always take account.    We should be altogether in
error if we supposed that a man who took pleasure in a
gladiatorial combat in ancient Rome was necessarily as inhuman as a modern would be who took pleasure in a similar
spectacle.    A man who falls but a little below the standard
of his own merciful age is often in reality far worse than a
man who had conformed to the standard of a much more
barbarous age, even though the latter will do some things
with perfect equanimity from which the other would recoil
with horror.    We have a much greater power than is sometimes supposed of localising both our benevolent and malevolent feelings.    If a man is very kind, or very harsh to some
particular class, this is usually, and on the whole justly, regarded as an index of his general disposition, but the
inference is not infallible, and it may easily be pushed too
far.    There are some who appear to expend all their kindly
feelings on a single class, and to treat with perfect indifference all outside it.    There are others who regard a certain
class as quite outside the pale of their sympathies, while in
other spheres their affections prove lively and constant.
There are many who would accede without the faintest re-
luctance to a barbarous custom, but would be quite incapable
of an equally barbarous act which custom had not consecrated.    Our affections are so capricious in their nature that
it is continually necessary to correct by detailed experience
the most plausible deductions.    Thus, for example, it is a
very unquestionable and a very important truth that cruelty
to animals naturally indicates and promotes a habit of mind
which leads to cruelty to men; and that, on the other hand,

an affectionate and merciful disposition to animals commonly implies a gentle and amiable nature. But, if we adopted this principle as an infallible criterion of humanity, we should soon find ourselves at fault. To the somewhat too hackneyed anecdote of Domitian gratifying his savage propensities by killing flies,[1] we might oppose Spinoza, one of the purest, most gentle, most benevolent of mankind, of whom it is related that almost the only amusement of his life was putting flies into spiders' webs and watching their struggles and their deaths.[2] It has been observed that a very large proportion of the men who during the French Revolution proved themselves most absolutely indifferent to human suffering were deeply attached to animals. Fournier was devoted to a squirrel, Couthon to a spaniel, Panis to two gold pheasants, Chaumette to an aviary, Marat kept doves.[3] Bacon has noticed that the Turks, who are a cruel people, are nevertheless conspicuous for their kindness to animals, and he mentions the instance of a Christian boy who was nearly stoned to death for gagging a long-billed fowl.[4] In Egypt there are hospitals for superannuated cats, and the most loathsome insects are regarded with tenderness; but human life is treated as if it were of no account, and human suffering scarcely elicits a care.[5] The same contrast appears more or

---

[1] Sueton. *Domitian.* iii. It is very curious that the same emperor, about the same time (the beginning of his reign), had such a horror of bloodshed that he resolved to prohibit the sacrifice of oxen. (Suet. *Dom.* ix.)

[2] ' Pendant qu'il restait au logis, il n'était incommode à personne; il y passait la meilleure partie de son temps tranquillement dans sa chambre. . . . Il se divertissait aussi quelquefois à fumer une pipe de tabac ; ou bien lorsqu'il voulait se relâcher l'esprit un peu plus longtemps, il cherchait des arai-

gnées qu'il faisait battre ensemble, ou des mouches qu'il jetait dans la toile d'araignée, et regardait ensuite cette bataille avec tant de plaisir qu'il éclatait quelquefois de rire.'—Colerus, *Vie de Spinoza.*

[3] This is noticed by George Duval in a curious passage of his *Souvenirs de la Terreur,* quoted by Lord Lytton in a note to his *Zanoni.*

[4] *Essay on Goodness.*

[5] This contrast has been noticed by Archbishop Whately in a lecture on Egypt. See, too, Legendre, *Traité de l'Opinion,* tome ii. p. 374.

less in all Eastern nations. On the other hand, travellers are unanimous in declaring that in Spain an intense passion for the bull-fight is quite compatible with the most active benevolence and the most amiable disposition. Again, to pass to another sphere, it is not uncommon to find conquerors, who will sacrifice with perfect callousness great masses of men to their ambition, but who, in their dealings with isolated individuals, are distinguished by an invariable clemency. Anomalies of this kind continually appear in the Roman population. The very men who looked down with delight when the sand of the arena was reddened with human blood, made the theatre ring with applause when Terence, in his famous line, proclaimed the universal brotherhood of man. When the senate, being unable to discover the murderer of a patrician, resolved to put his four hundred slaves to death, the people rose in open rebellion against the sentence.[1] A knight named Erixo, who in the days of Augustus had so scourged his son that he died of the effects, was nearly torn to pieces by the indignant population.[2] The elder Cato deprived a senator of his rank, because he had fixed an execution at such an hour that his mistress could enjoy the spectacle.[3] Even in the amphitheatre there were certain traces of a milder spirit. Drusus, the people complained, took too visible a pleasure at the sight of blood;[4] Caligula was too curious in watching death;[5] Caracalla, when a boy, won enthusiastic plaudits by shedding tears at the execution of criminals.[6] Among the most popular spectacles at Rome was rope-dancing, and then, as now, the cord being stretched at a great height above the ground, the apparent, and indeed

---

[1] Tacit. *Annal.* xiv. 45.
[2] Senec. *De Clemen.* i. 14.
[3] Val. Max. ii. 9. This writer speaks of 'the eyes of a mistress delighting in human blood' with as much horror as if the gladiatorial games were unknown. Livy gives a rather different version of this story.
[4] Tacit. *Annal.* i. 76.
[5] Sueton. *Calig.* xi.
[6] Spartian. *Caracalla.* Tertullian mentions that his nurse was a Christian.

real, danger added an evil zest to the performances. In the
reign of Marcus Aurelius an accident had occurred, and the
emperor, with his usual sensitive humanity, ordered that no
rope-dancer should perform without a net or a mattress being
spread out below.  It is a singularly curious fact that this
precaution, which no Christian nation has adopted, continued
in force during more than a century of the worst period of
the Roman Empire, when the blood of captives was poured
out like water in the Colosseum.[1]  The standard of humanity
was very low, but the sentiment was still manifest, though
its displays were capricious and inconsistent.

The sketch I have now drawn will, I think, be sufficient
to display the broad chasm that existed between the Roman
moralists and the Roman people.  On the one hand we find
a system of ethics, of which when we consider the range and
beauty of its precepts, the sublimity of the motives to which
it appealed, and its perfect freedom from superstitious elements, it is not too much to say that though it may have
been equalled, it has never been surpassed.  On the other
hand, we find a society almost absolutely destitute of moralising institutions, occupations, or beliefs, existing under an
economical and political system which inevitably led to
general depravity, and passionately addicted to the most
brutalising amusements.  The moral code, while it expanded
in theoretical catholicity, had contracted in practical application.  The early Romans had a very narrow and imperfect
standard of duty, but their patriotism, their military system,
and their enforced simplicity of life had made that standard
essentially popular.  The later Romans had attained a very
high and spiritual conception of duty, but the philosopher

---

[1] Capitolinus, *Marcus Aurelius.*
Capitolinus, who wrote under Diocletian, says that in his time the
custom of spreading a net under
the rope-dancer still continued.  I
do not know when it ceased at
Rome, but St. Chrysostom mentions that in his time it had been
abolished in the East.— Jortin's
*Remarks on Ecclesiastical History,*
ii. 71 (ed. 1846).

with his group of disciples, or the writer with his few readers, had scarcely any point of contact with the people. The great practical problem of the ancient philosophers was how they could act upon the masses. Simply to tell men what is virtue, and to extol its beauty, is insufficient. Something more must be done if the characters of nations are to be moulded and inveterate vices eradicated.

This problem the Roman Stoics were incapable of meeting, but they did what lay in their power, and their efforts, though altogether inadequate to the disease, were by no means contemptible. In the first place they raised up many great and good rulers who exerted all the influence of their position in the cause of virtue. In most cases these reforms were abolished on the accession of the first bad emperor, but there were at least some that remained. It has been observed that the luxury of the table, which had acquired the most extravagant proportions during the period that elapsed between the battle of Actium and the reign of Galba, began from this period to decline, and the change is chiefly attributed to Vespasian, who had in a measure reformed the Roman aristocracy by the introduction of many provincials, and who made his court an example of the strictest frugality.[1] The period from the accession of Nerva to the death of Marcus Aurelius, comprising no less than eighty-four years, exhibits a uniformity of good government which no other despotic monarchy has equalled. Each of the five emperors who then reigned deserves to be placed among the best rulers who have ever lived. Trajan and Hadrian, whose personal characters were most defective, were men of great and conspicuous genius. Antoninus and Marcus Aurelius, though less distinguished as politicians, were among the most perfectly virtuous men who have ever sat on a throne. During forty years of this period, perfect, unbroken peace reigned

---

[1] Tacit. *Ann.* iii. 55.

over the entire civilised globe. The barbarian encroach-
ments had not yet begun. The distinct nationalities that
composed the Empire, gratified by perfect municipal and by
perfect intellectual freedom, had lost all care for political
liberty, and little more than three hundred thousand soldiers
guarded a territory which is now protected by much more
than three millions.[1]

In creating this condition of affairs, Stoicism, as the chief
moral agent of the Empire, had a considerable though not a
preponderating influence. In other ways its influence was
more evident and exclusive. It was a fundamental maxim
of the sect, 'that the sage should take part in public life,'[2]
and it was therefore impossible that Stoicism should flourish
without producing a resuscitation of patriotism. The same
moral impulse which transformed the Neoplatonist into a
dreaming mystic and the Catholic into a useless hermit,
impelled the Stoic to the foremost post of danger in the
service of his country. While landmark after landmark of
Roman virtue was submerged, while luxury and scepticism
and foreign habits and foreign creeds were corroding the
whole framework of the national life, amid the last paroxysms of expiring liberty, amid the hideous carnival of
vice that soon followed upon its fall, the Stoic remained unchanged, the representative and the sustainer of the past.
A party which had acquired the noble title of the Party of
Virtue, guided by such men as Cato or Thrasea or Helvidius
or Burrhus, upheld the banner of Roman virtue and Roman
liberty in the darkest hours of despotism and of apostasy.
Like all men who carry an intense religious fervour into
politics, they were often narrow-minded and intolerant, blind
to the inevitable changes of society, incapable of compromise,
turbulent and inopportune in their demands,[3] but they more

---

[1] Champagny, *Les Antonins*,
tome ii. pp. 179–200.

[2] πολιτεύεσθαι τον σόφον.—Diog.
Laërt. *Zeno*.

[3] Thus Tigellinus spoke of
'Stoicorum arrogantia sectaque quæ
turbidos et negotiorum appetentes
faciat.'—Tacit. *Ann.* xiv. 57. The

than redeemed their errors by their noble constancy and
courage.  The austere purity of their lives, and the heroic
grandeur of their deaths, kept alive the tradition of Roman
liberty even under a Nero or a Domitian.  While such men
existed it was felt that all was not lost.  There was still a
rallying point of freedom, a seed of virtue that might germi-
nate anew, a living protest against the despotism and the
corruption of the Empire.

A third and still more important service which Stoicism
rendered to popular morals was in the formation of Roman
jurisprudence.[1]  Of all the many forms of intellectual exertion in which Greece and Rome struggled for the mastery
this is perhaps the only one in which the superiority of the
latter is indisputable.  'To rule the nations' was justly pronounced by the Roman poet the supreme glory of his
countrymen, and their administrative genius is even now unrivalled in history.  A deep reverence for law was long one
of their chief moral characteristics, and in order that it
might be inculcated from the earliest years it was a part of
the Roman system of education to oblige the children to

---

accusation does not appear to have
been quite untrue, for Vespasian,
who was a very moderate emperor,
thought it necessary to banish
nearly all the philosophers from
Rome on account of their factious-
ness.  Sometimes the Stoics showed
their independence by a rather
gratuitous insolence  Dion Cassius relates that, when Nero was
thinking of writing a poem in 400
books, he asked the advice of the
Stoic Cornutus, who said, that
no one would read so long a work.
'But,' answered Nero, 'your favourite Chrysippus wrote still more
numerous books.'  'True,' rejoined
Cornutus, 'but then they were of
use to humanity.'  On the other

hand, Seneca is justly accused of
condescending too much to the
vices of Nero in his efforts to mitigate their effects.

[1] The influence of Stoicism on
Roman law has been often exa-
mined.  See, especially, Degerando,
*Hist. de la Philosophie* (2nd ed.),
tome iii. pp. 202–204 ; Laferrière,
*De l'Influence du Stoïcisme sur les
Jurisconsultes romains* ; Denis,
*Théories et Idées morales dans
l'Antiquité*, tome ii. pp. 187–217 ;
Troplong, *Influence du Christianisme
sur le Droit civil des Romains* ;
Merivale, *Conversion of the Roman
Empire*, lec. iv. ; and the great work
of Gravina, *De Ortu et Progressu
Juris civilis*.

repeat by rote the code of the decemvirs.[1] The laws of the
Republic, however, being an expression of the contracted,
local, military, and sacerdotal spirit that dominated among
the people, were necessarily unfit for the political and intellectual expansion of the Empire, and the process of renova-
tion which was begun under Augustus by the Stoic Labeo,[2]
was continued with great zeal under Hadrian and Alexander
Severus, and issued in the famous compilations of Theodosius
and Justinian. In this movement we have to observe two
parts. There were certain general rules of guidance laid
down by the great Roman lawyers which constituted what
may be called the ideal of the jurisconsults—the ends to
which their special enactments tended—the principles of
equity to guide the judge when the law was silent or ambiguous. There were also definite enactments to meet specific
cases. The first part was simply borrowed from the Stoics,
whose doctrines and method thus passed from the narrow
circle of a philosophical academy and became the avowed
moral beacons of the civilised globe. The fundamental difference between Stoicism and early Roman thought was that
the former maintained the existence of a bond of unity
among mankind which transcended or annihilated all class
or national limitations. The essential characteristic of the
Stoical method was the assertion of the existence of a certain
law of nature to which it was the end of philosophy to conform. These tenets were laid down in the most unqualified
language by the Roman lawyers. ' As far as natural law is
concerned,' said Ulpian, ' all men are equal.'[3] ' Nature,'
said Paul, ' has established among us a certain relationship.'[4]
' By natural law,' Ulpian declared, ' all men are born free.'[5]

---

[1] Cic. *De Legib.* ii. 4, 23.

[2] There were two rival schools,
that of Labeo and that of Capito.
The first was remarkable for its
strict adherence to the letter of
the law—the second for the latitude of interpretation it admitted.

[3] *Dig.* lib. i. tit. 17–32.

[4] Ibid. i. tit. 1–3.

[5] Ibid. i. tit. 1–4.

'Slavery was defined by Florentinus as 'a custom of the law of nations, by which one man, contrary to the law of nature, is subjected to the dominion of another.'[1]  In accordance with these principles it became a maxim among the Roman lawyers that in every doubtful case where the alternative of slavery or freedom was at issue, the decision of the judge should be towards the latter.[2]

The Roman legislation was in a twofold manner the child of philosophy.  It was in the first place itself formed upon the philosophical model, for, instead of being a mere empirical system adjusted to the existing requirements of society, it laid down abstract principles of right to which it endeavoured to conform;[3] and, in the next place, these principles were borrowed directly from Stoicism.  The prominence the sect had acquired among Roman moralists, its active intervention in public affairs, and also the precision and brevity of its phraseology, had recommended it to the lawyers,[4] and the

---

[1] *Dig.* lib. i. tit. 4–5.

[2] Laferrière, p. 32.  Wallon, *Hist. de l'Esclavage dans l'Antiquité,* tome iii. pp. 71–80.  M. Wallon gives many curious instances of legal decisions on this point.

[3] To prove that this is the correct conception of law was the main object of Cicero's treatise *De Legibus.*  Ulpian defined jurisprudence as 'divinarum atque humanarum rerum notitia, justi atque injusti scientia.'—*Dig.* lib. i. tit. 1–10.  So Paul 'Id quod semper æquum ac bonum est jus dicitur ut est jus naturale.'—*Dig.* lib. i. tit. 1–11.  And Gaius, ' Quod vero naturalis ratio inter omnes homines constituit . . . vocatur jus gentium.'—*Dig.* lib. i. tit. 1–9.  The Stoics had defined true wisdom as 'rerum divinarum atque humanarum scientia.'—Cic. *De Offic.* i. 43.

[4] Cicero compares the phraseo-

logy of the Stoics with that of the Peripatetics, maintaining that the precision of the former is well adapted to legal discussions, and the redundancy of the latter to oratory.  'Omnes fere Stoici prudentissimi in disserendo sint et id arte faciant, sintque architecti pene verborum ; iidem traducti a disputando ad dicendum, inopes reperiantur: unum excipio Catonem. . . . . Peripateticorum institutis commodius fingeretur oratio . . . . nam ut Stoicorum astrictior est oratio, aliquantoque contractior quam aures populi requirunt: sic illorum liberior et latior quam patitur consuetudo judiciorum et fori.'—*De Claris Oratoribus.*  A very judicious historian of philosophy observes: ' En général à Rome le petit nombre d'hommes livrés à la méditation et à l'enthousiasme préférèrent Pythagore et

union then effected between the legal and philosophical spirit is felt to the present day. To the Stoics and the Roman lawyers is mainly due the clear recognition of the existence of a law of nature above and beyond all human enactments which has been the basis of the best moral and of the most influential though most chimerical political speculation of later ages, and the renewed study of Roman law was an important element in the revival that preceded the Reformation.

It is not necessary for my present purpose to follow into very minute detail the application of these principles to practical legislation. It is sufficient to say, that there were few departments into which the catholic and humane principles of Stoicism were not in some degree carried. In the political world, as we have already seen, the right of Roman citizenship, with the protection and the legal privileges attached to it, from being the monopoly of a small class, was gradually but very widely diffused. In the domestic sphere, the power which the old laws had given to the father of the family, though not destroyed, was greatly abridged, and an important innovation, which is well worthy of a brief notice, was thus introduced into the social system of the Empire.

It is probable that in the chronology of morals, domestic virtue takes the precedence of all others; but in its earliest phase it consists of a single article—the duty of absolute submission to the head of the household. It is only at a later period, and when the affections have been in some degree evoked, that the reciprocity of duty is felt, and the whole tendency of civilisation is to diminish the disparity between the different members of the family. The process by which the wife from a simple slave becomes the companion and

Platon; les hommes du monde et ceux qui cultivaient les sciences naturelles s'attachèrent à Épicure; les orateurs et les hommes d'État à la nouvelle Académie; les jurisconsultes au Portique.' — Degerando, *Hist. de la Philos.* tome iii. p. 196.

equal of her husband, I shall endeavour to trace in a future chapter. The relations of the father to his children are profoundly modified by the new position the affections assume in education, which in a rude nation rests chiefly upon authority, but in a civilised community upon sympathy. In Rome the absolute authority of the head of the family was the centre and archetype of that whole system of discipline and subordination which it was the object of the legislator to sustain. Filial reverence was enforced as the first of duties. It is the one virtue which Virgil attributed in any remarkable degree to the founder of the race. The marks of external respect paid to old men were scarcely less than in Sparta.[1] It was the boast of the lawyers that in no other nation had the parent so great an authority over his children.[2] The child was indeed the absolute slave of his father, who had a right at any time to take away his life and dispose of his entire property. He could look to no time during the life of his father in which he would be freed from the thraldom. The man of fifty, the consul, the general, or the tribune, was in this respect in the same position as the infant, and might at any moment be deprived of all the earnings of his labour, driven to the most menial employments, or even put to death, by the paternal command.[3]

There can, I think, be little question that this law, at least in the latter period of its existence, defeated its own

[1] See a very remarkable passage in Aulus Gellius, *Noct.* ii. 15.

[2] 'Fere enim nulli alii sunt homines qui talem in filios suos habeant potestatem qualem nos habemus.'—Gaius.

[3] A full statement of these laws is given by Dion. Halicarn. ii. 4. It was provided that if a father sold his son and if the son was afterwards enfranchised by the purchaser, he became again the slave of his father, who might sell him a second, and, if manumission again ensued, a third time. It was only on the third sale that he passed for ever out of the parental control. A more merciful law, attributed to Numa, provided that when the son married (if that marriage was with the consent of the father), the father lost the power of selling him. In no other way, however, was his authority even then abridged.

object. There are few errors of education to which more unhappy homes may be traced than this—that parents have sought to command the obedience, before they have sought to win the confidence, of their children. This was the path which the Roman legislator indicated to the parent, and its natural consequence was to chill the sympathies and arouse the resentment of the young. Of all the forms of virtue filial affection is perhaps that which appears most rarely in Roman history. In the plays of Plautus it is treated much as conjugal fidelity was treated in England by the playwriters of the Restoration. An historian of the reign of Tiberius has remarked that the civil wars were equally remarkable for the many examples they supplied of the devotion of wives to their husbands, of the devotion of slaves to their masters, and of the treachery or indifference of sons to their fathers.[1]

The reforms that were effected during the pagan empire did not reconstruct the family, but they at least greatly mitigated its despotism. The profound change of feeling that had taken place on the subject is shown by the contrast between the respectful, though somewhat shrinking, acquiescence, with which the ancient Romans regarded parents who had put their children to death,[2] and the indignation excited under Augustus by the act of Erixo. Hadrian, apparently by a stretch of despotic power, banished a man who had assassinated his son.[3] Infanticide was forbidden, though

---

[1] Velleius Paterculus, ii. 67. A great increase of parricide was noticed during the Empire (Senec. *De Clem.* i. 23). At first, it is said, there was no law against parricide, for the crime was believed to be too atrocious to be possible.

[2] Numerous instances of these executions are collected by Livy, Val. Maximus, &c.; their history is fully given by Cornelius van Bynkershoek, 'De Jure occidendi, vendendi, et exponendi liberos apud veteres Romanos,' in his works (Cologne, 1761).

[3] This proceeding of Hadrian, which is related by the lawyer Marcian, is doubly remarkable, because the father had surprised his son in adultery with his stepmother. Now a Roman had originally not only absolute authority over the life of his son, but also the right of killing any one whom he found committing adultery with his wife. Yet Marcian praises the severity

not seriously repressed, but the right of putting to death an adult child had long been obsolete, when Alexander Severus formally withdrew it from the father. The property of children was also in some slight degree protected. A few instances are recorded of wills that were annulled because they had disinherited legitimate sons,[1] and Hadrian, following a policy that had been feebly initiated by his two predecessors, gave the son an absolute possession of whatever he might gain in the military service. Diocletian rendered the sale of children by the fathers, in all cases, illegal.[2]

In the field of slavery the legislative reforms were more important. This institution, indeed, is one that meets us at every turn of the moral history of Rome, and on two separate occasions in the present chapter I have already had occasion to notice it. I have shown that the great prominence of the slave element in Roman life was one of the causes of the enlargement of sympathies that characterises the philosophy of the Empire, and also that slavery was in a very high degree, and in several distinct ways, a cause of the corruption of the free classes. In considering the condition of the slaves themselves, we may distinguish, I think, three periods. In the earlier and simpler days of the Republic, the head of the family was absolute master of his slaves, but circumstances in a great measure mitigated the evil of the despotism. The slaves were very few in number. Each Roman proprietor had commonly one or two who assisted him in cultivating the soil, and superintended his property when he was absent in the army. In the frugal habits of the time, the master was brought into the most intimate connection with his

---

of Hadrian, 'Nam patria potestas in pietate debet, non atrocitate, consistere.'—*Digest.* lib. xlviii. tit. 9, § 5.

[1] Valer. Max. vii. 7.

[2] See, on all this subject, Gibbon, *Decline and Fall,* ch. xliv.; Trop-long, *Influence du Christianisme sur le Droit,* ch. ix.; Denis, *Hist. des Idées morales,* tome ii. pp. 107–120; Laferrière, *Influence du Stoïcisme sur les Jurisconsultes,* pp. 37–44.

slaves. He shared their labours and their food, and the control he exercised over them, in most cases probably differed little from that which he exercised over his sons. Under such circumstances, great barbarity to slaves, though always possible, was not likely to be common, and the protection of religion was added to the force of habit. Hercules, the god of labour, was the special patron of slaves. There was a legend that Sparta had once been nearly destroyed by an earthquake sent by Neptune to avenge the treacherous murder of some Helots.[1] In Rome, it was said, Jupiter had once in a dream commissioned a man to express to the senate the divine anger at the cruel treatment of a slave during the public games.[2] By the pontifical law, slaves were exempted from field labours on the religious festivals.[3] The Saturnalia and Matronalia, which were especially intended for their benefit, were the most popular holidays in Rome, and on these occasions the slaves were accustomed to sit at the same table with their masters.[4]

Even at this time, however, it is probable that great atrocities were occasionally committed. Everything was permitted by law, although it is probable that the censor in cases of extreme abuse might interfere, and the aristocratic feelings of the early Roman, though corrected in a measure by the associations of daily labour, sometimes broke out in a fierce scorn for all classes but his own. The elder Cato, who may be regarded as a type of the Romans of the earlier period, speaks of slaves simply as instruments for obtaining wealth, and he encouraged masters, both by his precept and his example, to sell them as useless when aged and infirm.[5]

---

Ælian, *Hist. Var.* vi. 7.
[2] Livy, ii. 36 ; Cicero, *De Divin.* ii. 26.
[3] Cicero, *De Legibus,* ii. 8–12. Cato, however, maintained that slaves might on those days be employed on work which did not require oxen. — Wallon, *Hist. de l'Esclavage,* tome ii. p. 215.
[4] See the *Saturnalia* of Macrobius.
[5] See his *Life* by Plutarch, and his book on agriculture.

In the second period, the condition of slaves had greatly
deteriorated.   The victories of Rome, especially in the East,
had introduced into the city innumerable slaves [1] and the
wildest luxury, and the despotism of the master remained
unqualified by law, while the habits of life that had originally
mitigated it had disappeared.   The religious sentiments of
the people were at the same time fatally impaired, and many
new causes conspired to aggravate the evil.   The passion for
gladiatorial shows had begun, and it continually produced a
savage indifference to the infliction of pain.   The servile wars
of Sicily, and the still more formidable revolt of Spartacus,
had shaken Italy to the centre, and the shock was felt in
every household.   'As many enemies as slaves,' had become
a Roman proverb.   The fierce struggles of barbarian captives
were repaid by fearful punishments, and many thousands of
revolted slaves perished on the cross.   An atrocious law,
intended to secure the safety of the citizens, provided that if
a master were murdered, all the slaves in his house, who
were not in chains or absolutely helpless through illness,
should be put to death. [2]

Numerous acts of the most odious barbarity were committed.   The well-known anecdotes of Flaminius ordering a
slave to be killed to gratify, by the spectacle, the curiosity of

[1] The number of the Roman
slaves has been a matter of much
controversy. M. Dureau de la
Malle (*Econ. politique des Romains*)
has restricted it more than any
other writer.  Gibbon (*Decline and
Fall*, chap. ii.) has collected many
statistics on the subject, but the
fullest examination is in M. Wallon's admirable *Hist. de l'Esclavage*.
On the contrast between the character of the slaves of the Republic
and those of the Empire, see Tac.
*Ann.* xiv. 44.

[2] Tacit. *Annal.* xiii. 32; xiv.
42-45.  Wallon, *Hist. de l'Esclav.*

ii. 293.  I have already noticed the
indignant rising of the people
caused by the proposal to execute
the 400 slaves of the murdered
Pedanius. Their interposition was
however (as Tacitus informs us),
unavailing, and the slaves, guarded
against rescue by a strong band of
soldiers, were executed.   It was
proposed to banish the freedmen
who were in the house, but Nero
interposed and prevented it.  Pliny
notices (*Ep.* viii. 14) the banishment of the freedmen of a murdered
man.

a guest; of Vedius Pollio feeding his fish on the flesh of slaves; and of Augustus sentencing a slave, who had killed and eaten a favourite quail, to crucifixion, are the extreme examples that are recorded; for we need not regard as an historical fact the famous picture in Juvenal of a Roman lady, in a moment of caprice, ordering her unoffending servant to be crucified. We have, however, many other very horrible glimpses of slave life at the close of the Republic and in the early days of the Empire. The marriage of slaves was entirely unrecognised by law, and in their case the words adultery, incest, or polygamy had no legal meaning. Their testimony was in general only received in the law-courts when they were under torture. When executed for a crime, their deaths were of a most hideous kind. The ergastula, or private prisons, of the masters were frequently their only sleeping-places. Old and infirm slaves were constantly exposed to perish on an island of the Tiber. We read of slaves chained as porters to the doors, and cultivating the fields in chains. Ovid and Juvenal describe the fierce Roman ladies tearing their servants' faces, and thrusting the long pins of their brooches into their flesh. The master, at the close of the Republic, had full power to sell his slave as a gladiator, or as a combatant with wild beasts.[1]

All this is very horrible, but it must not be forgotten that there was another side to the picture. It is the custom of many ecclesiastical writers to paint the pagan society of the Empire as a kind of pandemonium, and with this object they collect the facts I have cited, which are for the most part narrated by Roman satirists or historians, as examples of the most extreme and revolting cruelty; they represent them as fair specimens of the ordinary treatment of the servile class, and they simply exclude from their con-

[1] See all this fully illustrated in Wallon. The plays of Plautus and the Roman writers on agriculture contain numerous allusions to the condition of slaves.

sideration the many qualifying facts that might be alleged
Although the marriage of a slave was not legally recognised,
it was sanctioned by custom, and it does not appear to have
been common to separate his family.[1] Two customs to which
I have already referred distinguish ancient slavery broadly
from that of modern times. The peculium, or private property of slaves, was freely recognised by masters, to whom,
however, after the death of the slave, part or all of it usually
reverted,[2] though some masters permitted their slaves to
dispose of it by will.[3] The enfranchisement of slaves was
also carried on to such an extent as seriously to affect the
population of the city. It appears from a passage in Cicero
that an industrious and well-conducted captive might commonly look forward to his freedom in six years.[4] Isolated
acts of great cruelty undoubtedly occurred; but public
opinion strongly reprehended them, and Seneca assures us
that masters who ill-treated their slaves were pointed at and
insulted in the streets.[5] The slave was not necessarily the
degraded being he has since appeared. The physician who
tended the Roman in his sickness, the tutor to whom he
confided the education of his son, the artists whose works
commanded the admiration of the city, were usually slaves.
Slaves sometimes mixed with their masters in the family, ate
habitually with them at the same table,[6] and were regarded
by them with the warmest affection. Tiro, the slave and
afterwards the freedman of Cicero, compiled his master's
letters, and has preserved some in which Cicero addressed

---

[1] Wallon, tome ii. pp. 209–210,
357. There were no laws till the
time of the Christian emperors
against separating the families of
slaves, but it was a maxim of the
jurisconsults that in forced sales
they should not be separated.
(Wallon, tome iii. pp. 55–56.)

[2] Ibid. tome ii. pp. 211–213.

[3] Plin. *Epist.* viii. 16. It was
customary to allow the public or
State slaves to dispose of half their
goods by will. (Wallon, tome iii.
p. 59.)

[4] Wallon, tome ii. p. 419. This
appears from an allusion of Cicero,
*Philip.* viii. 11.

[5] Senec. *De Clem.* i. 18.

[6] Ibid. *Ep.* xlvii.

him in terms of the most sincere and delicate friendship.
I have already referred to the letter in which the younger
Pliny poured out his deep sorrow for the death of some of his
slaves, and endeavoured to console himself with the thought
that as he had emancipated them before their death, at least
they had died free.[1] Epictetus passed at once from slavery
to the friendship of an emperor.[2] The great multiplication
of slaves, though it removed them from the sympathy of their
masters, must at least have in most cases alleviated their
burdens. The application of torture to slave witnesses,
horrible as it was, was a matter of rare occurrence, and was
carefully restricted by law.[3] Much vice was undoubtedly
fostered, but yet the annals of the civil wars and of the
Empire are crowded with the most splendid instances of the
fidelity of slaves. In many cases they refused the boon of
liberty and defied the most horrible tortures rather than
betray their masters, accompanied them in their flight when
all others had abandoned them, displayed undaunted courage
and untiring ingenuity in rescuing them from danger, and in
some cases saved the lives of their owners by the deliberate
sacrifice of their own.[4] This was, indeed, for some time the
pre-eminent virtue of Rome, and it proves conclusively that
the masters were not so tyrannical, and that the slaves were
not so degraded, as is sometimes alleged.

The duty of humanity to slaves had been at all times one

---

[1] Pliny, *Ep.* viii. 16.

[2] Spartianus, *Hadrianus.*

[3] Compare Wallon, tome ii. p.
186; tome iii. pp. 65–66. Slaves
were only to be called as witnesses in cases of incest, adultery,
murder, and high treason, and
where it was impossible to establish the crime without their evidence. Hadrian considered that
the reality of the crime must have
already acquired a strong probability, and the jurisconsult Paul

laid down that at least two free
witnesses should be heard before
slaves were submitted to torture,
and that the offer of an accused
person to have his slaves tortured
that they might attest his innocence
should not be accepted.

[4] Numerous and very noble in-
stances of slave fidelity are given by
Seneca, *De Benefic.* iii. 19–27; Val.
Max. vi. 8; and in Appian's *His-
tory of the Civil Wars.* See, too,
Tacit. *Hist.* i. 3.

of those which the philosophers had most ardently inculcated. Plato and Aristotle, Zeno and Epicurus, were, on
this point, substantially agreed.[1] The Roman Stoics gave
the duty a similar prominence in their teaching, and Seneca
especially has filled pages with exhortations to masters to
remember that the accident of position in no degree affects
the real dignity of men, that the slave may be free by virtue
while the master may be a slave by vice, and that it is the
duty of a good man to abstain not only from all cruelty, but
even from all feeling of contempt towards his slaves.[2] But
these exhortations, in which some have imagined that they
have discovered the influence of Christianity, were, in
fact, simply an echo of the teaching of ancient Greece, and
especially of Zeno, the founder of Stoicism, who had laid down,
long before the dawn of Christianity, the broad principles
that ' all men are by nature equal, and that virtue alone establishes a difference between them.'[3] The softening influence
of the peace of the Antonines assisted this movement of
humanity, and the slaves derived a certain incidental benefit
from one of the worst features of the despotism of the
Cæsars. The emperors, who continually apprehended plots
against their lives or power, encouraged numerous spies
around the more important of their subjects, and the facility
with which slaves could discover the proceedings of their
masters inclined the Government in their favour.

Under all these influences many laws were promulgated

---

[1] Aristotle had, it is true, declared slavery to be part of the law
of nature—an opinion which, he
said, was rejected by some of his
contemporaries ; but he advocated
humanity to slaves quite as emphatically as the other philosophers
(Economics, i. 5). Epicurus was
conspicuous even among Greek
philosophers for his kindness to
slaves, and he associated some of

his own with his philosophical labours. (Diog. Laërt. Epicurus.)

[2] De Benef. iii. 18–28 ; De Vita
Beata, xxiv. ; De Clem. i. 18, and
especially Ep. xlvii. Epictetus, as
might be expected from his history,
frequently recurs to the duty. Plutarch writes very beautifully upon
it in his treatise De Cohibenda Ira,

[3] Diog. Laërt. Zeno.

which profoundly altered the legal position of the slaves, and opened what may be termed the third period of Roman slavery. The Petronian law, which was issued by Augustus, or, more probably, by Nero, forbade the master to condemn his slave to combat with wild beasts without a sentence from a judge.[1] Under Claudius, some citizens exposed their sick slaves on the island of Æsculapius in the Tiber, to avoid the trouble of tending them, and the emperor decreed that if the slave so exposed recovered from his sickness he should become free, and also, that masters who killed their slaves instead of exposing them should be punished as murderers.[2] It is possible that succour was afforded to the abandoned slave in the temple of Æsculapius,[3] and it would appear from these laws that the wanton slaughter of a slave was already illegal. About this time the statue of the emperor had become an asylum for slaves.[4] Under Nero, a judge was appointed to hear their complaints, and was instructed to punish masters who treated them with barbarity, made them the instruments of lust, or withheld from them a sufficient quantity of the necessaries of life.[5] A considerable pause appears to have ensued; but Domitian made a law, which was afterwards reiterated, forbidding the Oriental custom of mutilating slaves for sensual purposes, and the reforms were renewed with great energy in the period of the Antonines. Hadrian and his two successors formally deprived masters of the right of killing their slaves; forbade them to sell slaves to the lanistæ, or speculators in gladiators; destroyed the ergastula, or private prisons; ordered that, when a master was murdered, those slaves only should be

---

[1] Bodin thinks it was promulgated by Nero, and he has been followed by Troplong and Mr. Merivale. Champagny (*Les Antonins*, tome ii. p. 115) thinks that no law after Tiberius was called *lex*.

[2] Sueton. *Claud.* xxv.; Dion Cass. lx. 29.

[3] See Dumas, *Secours publics chez les Anciens* (Paris, 1813), pp. 125–130.

[4] Senec. *De Clem.* i. 18.

[5] Senec. *De Benef.* iii. 22.

tortured who were within hearing;[1] appointed officers through
all the provinces to hear the complaints of slaves; enjoined
that no master should treat his slaves with excessive severity;
and commanded that, when such severity was proved, the
master should be compelled to sell the slave he had ill-
treated.[2] When we add to these laws the broad maxims of
equity asserting the essential equality of the human race,
which the jurists had borrowed from the Stoics, and which
supplied the principles to guide the judges in their decisions,
it must be admitted that the slave code of Imperial Rome
compares not unfavourably with those of some Christian
nations.

While a considerable portion of the principles, and even
much of the phraseology, of Stoicism passed into the system
of public law, the Roman philosophers had other more direct
means of acting on the people. On occasions of family
bereavement, when the mind is most susceptible of impressions, they were habitually called in to console the survivors.
Dying men asked their comfort and support in the last hours
of their life. They became the directors of conscience to
numbers who resorted to them for a solution of perplexing
cases of practical morals, or under the influence of despondency or remorse.[3] They had their special exhortations

---

[1] Spartian. *Hadrianus.* Hadrian
exiled a Roman lady for five years
for treating her slaves with atrocious cruelty. (*Digest.* lib. i. tit. 6,
§ 2.)

[2] See these laws fully examined
by Wallon, tome iii. pp. 51–92,
and also Laferrière, *Sur l'Influence
du Stoïcisme sur le Droit.* The
jurisconsults gave a very wide scope
to their definitions of cruelty. A
master who degraded a literary
slave, or a slave musician, to some
coarse manual employment, such
as a porter, was decided to have

ill-treated him. (Wallon, tome iii.
p. 62.)

[3] Thus, e.g., Livia called in the
Stoic Areus to console her after
the death of Drusus (Senec. *Ad
Marc.*). Many of the letters of
Seneca and Plutarch are written
to console the suffering. Cato,
Thrasea, and many others appear
to have fortified their last hours
by conversation with philosophers.
The whole of this aspect of Stoicism
has been admirably treated by M.
Martha (*Les Moralistes de l'Empire
Romain*).

for every vice, and their remedies adapted to every variety of character. Many cases were cited of the conversion of the vicious or the careless, who had been sought out and fasci nated by the philosopher,[1] and who, under his guidance, had passed through a long course of moral discipline, and had at last attained a high degree of virtue. Education fell in a great degree into their hands. Many great families kept a philosopher among them in what in modern language might be termed the capacity of a domestic chaplain,[2] while a system of popular preaching was created and widely diffused.

Of these preachers there were two classes who differed greatly in their characters and their methods. The first, who have been very happily termed the ' monks of Stoicism,'[3] were the Cynics, who appear to have assumed among the later moralists of the Pagan empire a position somewhat resembling that of the mendicant orders in Catholicism. In a singularly curious dissertation of Epictetus,[4] we have a picture of the ideal at which a Cynic should aim, and it is impossible in reading it not to be struck by the resemblance it bears to the missionary friar. The Cynic should be a man devoting his entire life to the instruction of mankind. He must be unmarried, for he must have no family affections to divert or to dilute his energies. He must wear the meanest dress, sleep upon the bare ground, feed upon the simplest food, abstain from all earthly pleasures, and yet exhibit to the world the example of uniform cheerfulness and content. No one, under pain of provoking the Divine anger, should embrace such a career, unless he believes himself to be called

---

[1] We have a pleasing picture of the affection philosophers and their disciples sometimes bore to one another in the lines of Persius (*Sat.* v.) to his master Cornutus.

[2] Grant's *Aristotle*, vol. i. pp. 277-278.

[3] Champagny, *Les Antonins*, tome i. p. 405.

[4] Arrian, iii. 22. Julian has also painted the character of the true Cynic, and contrasted it with that of the impostors who assumed the garb. See Neander's *Life of Julian* (London, 1850), p. 94.

and assisted by Jupiter. It is his mission to go among men
as the ambassador of God, rebuking, in season and out of
season, their frivolity, their cowardice, and their vice. He
must stop the rich man in the market-place. He must
preach to the populace in the highway. He must know no
respect and no fear. He must look upon all men as his sons,
and upon all women as his daughters. In the midst of a
jeeling crowd, he must exhibit such a placid calm that men
may imagine him to be of stone. Ill-treatment, and exile,
and death must have no terror in his eyes, for the discipline
of his life should emancipate him from every earthly tie; and,
when he is beaten, 'he should love those who beat him, for
he is at once the father and the brother of all men.'

A curious contrast to the Cynic was the philosophic
rhetorician, who gathered around his chair all that was most
brilliant in Roman or Athenian society. The passion for
oratory which the free institutions of Greece had formed, had
survived the causes that produced it, and given rise to a very
singular but a very influential profession; which, though
excluded from the Roman Republic, acquired a great development after the destruction of political liberty. The rhetoricians were a kind of itinerant lecturers, who went about
from city to city, delivering harangues that were often received with the keenest interest. For the most part, neither
their characters nor their talents appear to have deserved
much respect. Numerous anecdotes are recorded of their
vanity and rapacity, and their success was a striking proof of
the decadence of public taste.[1]  They had cultivated the his-

[1] Seneca the rhetorician (father
of the philosopher) collected many
of the sayings of the rhetoricians of
his time.  At a later period, Philostratus wrote the lives of eminent
rhetoricians, Quintilian discussed
their rules of oratory, and Aulus
Gellius painted the whole society in
which they moved.  On their injurious influence upon eloquence, see
Petronius, *Satyricon*, i. 2.  Much
curious information about the rhetoricians is collected in Martha,
*Moralistes de l'Empire Romain*, and
in Nisard, *Etudes sur les Poëtes
Latins de la Décadence*, art. Juvenal

trionic part of oratory with the most minute attention. The arrangement of their hair, the folds of their dresses, all their postures and gestures were studied with artistic care. They had determined the different kinds of action that are appropriate for each branch of a discourse and for each form of eloquence. Sometimes they personated characters in Homer or in ancient Greek history, and delivered speeches which those characters might have delivered in certain conjunctures of their lives. Sometimes they awakened the admiration of their audience by making a fly, a cockroach, dust, smoke, a mouse, or a parrot the subject of their eloquent eulogy.[1] Others, again, exercised their ingenuity in defending some glaring paradox or sophism, or in debating some intricate case of law or morals, or they delivered literary lectures remarkable for a minute but captious and fastidious criticism. Some of the rhetoricians recited only harangues prepared with the most elaborate care, others were ready debaters, and they travelled from city to city, challenging opponents to discuss some subtle and usually frivolous question. The poet Juvenal and the satirist Lucian had both for a time followed this profession. Many of the most eminent acquired immense wealth, travelled with a splendid retinue, and excited transports of enthusiasm in the cities they visited. They were often charged by cities to appear before the emperor to plead for a remission of taxes, or of the punishment due for some offence. They became in a great measure the educators of the people and contributed very largely to form and direct their taste.

---

[1] 'Cependant ces orateurs n'étaient jamais plus admirés que lorsqu'ils avaient le bonheur de trouver un sujet où la louange fut un tour de force. . . . Lucien a fait l'éloge de la mouche; Fronton de la poussière, de la fumée, de la négligence; Dion Chrysostome de la chevelure, du perroquet, etc. Au cinquième siècle, Synésius, qui fut un grand évêque, fera le panégyrique de la calvitie, long ouvrage où toutes les sciences sont mises à contribution pour apprendre aux hommes ce qu'il y a non-seulement de bonheur mais aussi de mérite à être chauve.'—Martha, *Moralistes de l'Empire Romain* (ed. 1865), p. 275.

It had been from the first the custom of some philosophers
to adopt this profession, and to expound in the form of rhetorical lectures the principles of their school. In the Flavian
period and in the age of the Antonines, this alliance of philosophy, and especially of Stoical philosophy, with rhetoric
became more marked, and the foundation of liberally
endowed chairs of rhetoric and philosophy by Vespasian,
Hadrian, and Marcus Aurelius contributed to sustain it.
Discourses of the Platonist Maximus of Tyre, and of the
Stoic Dion Chrysostom, have come down to us, and they are
both of a high order of intrinsic merit. The first turn
chiefly on such subjects as the comparative excellence of
active and contemplative life, the pure and noble conceptions
of the Divine nature which underlie the fables or allegories
of Homer, the dæmon of Socrates, the Platonic notions of
the Divinity, the duty of prayer, the end of philosophy, and
the ethics of love.[1]  Dion Chrysostom, in his orations,
expounded the noblest and purest theism, examined the
place which images should occupy in worship, advocated
humanity to slaves, and was, perhaps, the earliest writer in
the Roman Empire who denounced hereditary slavery as
illegitimate.[2]  His life was very eventful and very noble.
He had become famous as a sophist and rhetorician, skilled
in the laborious frivolities of the profession. Calamity,
however, and the writings of Plato induced him to abandon
them and devote himself exclusively to the improvement of
mankind.  Having defended with a generous rashness a man
who had been proscribed by the tyranny of Domitian, he
was compelled to fly from Rome in the garb of a beggar ; and,
carrying with him only a work of Plato and a speech of
Demosthenes, he travelled to the most distant frontiers of
the empire.  He gained his livelihood by the work of his

[1] There is a good review of the
teaching of Maximus in Champagny, Les Antonins, tome ii. pp.
207–215.

[2] Orat. xv. ; De Servitute.

hands, for he refused to receive money for his discourses; but he taught and captivated the Greek colonists who were scattered among the barbarians, and even the barbarians themselves. Upon the assassination of Domitian, when the legions hesitated to give their allegiance to Nerva, the eloquence of Dion Chrysostom overcame their irresolution. By the same eloquence he more than once appeased seditions in Alexandria and the Greek cities of Asia Minor. He preached before Trajan on the duties of royalty, taking a line of Homer for his text. He electrified the vast and polished audience assembled at Athens for the Olympic games as he had before done the rude barbarians of Scythia. Though his taste was by no means untainted by the frivolities of the rhetorician, he was skilled in all the arts that awaken curiosity and attention, and his eloquence commanded the most various audiences in the most distant lands. His special mission, however, was to popularise Stoicism by diffusing its principles through the masses of mankind.[1]

The names, and in some cases a few fragments, of the writings of many other rhetorical philosophers, such as Herod Atticus, Favorinus, Fronto, Taurus, Fabianus, and Julianus, have come down to us, and each was the centre of a group of passionate admirers, and contributed to form a literary society in the great cities of the empire. We have a vivid picture of this movement in the ' Attic Nights ' of Aulus Gellius—a work which is, I think, one of the most curious and instructive in Latin literature, and which bears to the literary society of the period of the Antonines much the same relation as the writings of Helvétius bear to the Parisian society on the eve of the Revolution. Helvétius, it is said, collected the materials for his great work on ' Mind ' chiefly from the conversation of the drawing-rooms of Paris at a time when that conversation had attained a degree of

---

[1] See the singularly charming essay on Dion Chrysostom, in M. Martha's book.

perfection which even Frenchmen had never before equalled. He wrote in the age of the 'Encyclopædia,' when the social and political convulsions of the Revolution were as yet unfelt; when the first dazzling gleams of intellectual freedom had flashed upon a society long clouded by superstition and aristocratic pride; when the genius of Voltaire and the peerless conversational powers of Diderot, irradiating the bold philosophies of Bacon and Locke, had kindled an intellectual enthusiasm through all the ranks of fashion;[1] and when the contempt for the wisdom and the methods of the past was only equalled by the prevailing confidence in the future. Brilliant, graceful, versatile, and superficial, with easy eloquence and lax morals, with a profound disbelief in moral excellence, and an intense appreciation of intellectual beauty, disdaining all pedantry, superstition, and mystery, and with an almost fanatical persuasion of the omnipotence of analysis, he embodied the principles of his contemporaries in a philosophy which represents all virtue and heroism as but disguised self-interest; he illustrated every argument, not by the pedantic learning of the schools, but by the sparkling anecdotes and acute literary criticisms of the drawing-room, and he thus produced a work which, besides its intrinsic merits, was the most perfect mirror of the society from which it sprang.[2] Very different, both in form, subject, and tendency, but no less truly representative, was the work of Aulus Gellius. It is the journal, or common-place book, or miscellany of a scholar moving in the centre of the literary society of both Rome and Athens during the latter period of

---

[1] Mr. Buckle, in his admirable chapter on the 'Proximate Causes of the French Revolution' (*Hist. of Civilisation*, vol. i.), has painted this fashionable enthusiasm for knowledge with great power, and illustrated it with ample learning.

[2] The saying of Mme. Dudeffand

about Helvétius is well known: 'C'est un homme qui a dit le secret de tout le monde.' How truly Helvétius represented this fashionable society appears very plainly from the vivid portrait of it in the *Nouvelle Héloïse*, part ii. letter xvii., a masterpiece of its kind.

the Antonines, profoundly imbued with its spirit, and devoting his leisure to painting its leading figures, and compiling the substance of their teaching. Few books exhibit a more curious picture of the combination of intense child-like literary and moral enthusiasm with the most hopeless intellectual degeneracy. Each prominent philosopher was surrounded by a train of enthusiastic disciples, who made the lecture-room resound with their app'ause,[1] and accepted him as their monitor in all the affairs of life. He rebuked publicly every instance of vice or of affectation he had observed in their conduct, received them at his own table, became their friend and confidant in their troubles, and sometimes assisted them by his advice in their professional duties.[2] Taurus, Favorinus, Fronto, and Atticus were the most prominent figures, and each seems to have formed, in the centre of a corrupt society, a little company of young men devoted with the simplest and most ardent earnestness to the cultivation of intellectual and moral excellence. Yet this society was singularly puerile. The age of genius had closed, and the age of pedantry had succeeded it. Minute, curious, and fastidious verbal criticism of the great writers of the past was the chief occupation of the scholar, and the whole tone of his mind had become retrospective and even archaic. Ennius was esteemed a greater poet than Virgil, and Cato a greater prose writer than Cicero. It was the affectation of some to tesselate their conversation with antiquated and obsolete words.[3] The study of etymologies had risen into great favour, and curious questions of grammar and pro-

---

[1] Musonius tried to stop this custom of applauding the lecturer. (Aul. Gell. *Noct.* v. i.) The habits that were formed in the schools of the rhetoricians were sometimes carried into the churches, and we have notices of preachers (especially St. Chrysostom) being vocife- rously applauded.

[2] Thus Gellius himself consulted Favorinus about a perplexing case which he had, in his capacity of magistrate, to determine, and received from his master a long dissertation on the duties of a judge (xiv. 2).

[3] i. 10.

nunciation were ardently debated. Logic, as in most ages
of intellectual poverty, was greatly studied and prized.
Bold speculations and original thought had almost ceased,
but it was the delight of the philosophers to throw the
arguments of great writers into the form of syllogisms, and
to debate them according to the rules of the schools. The
very amusements of the scholars took the form of a whim-
sical and puerile pedantry. Gellius recalls, with a thrill of
emotion, those enchanting evenings when, their more serious
studies being terminated, the disciples of Taurus assembled
at the table of their master to pass the happy hours in discussing such questions as when a man can be said to die,
whether in the last moment of life or in the first moment of
death ; or when he can be said to get up, whether when he is
still on his bed or when he has just left it.[1] Sometimes they
proposed to one another literary questions, as what old
writer had employed some common word in a sense that had
since become obsolete ; or they discussed such syllogisms as
these :—' You have what you have not lost ; you have not
lost horns, therefore you have horns.' ' You are not what I
am. I am a man ; therefore you are not a man.'[2] As
moralists, they exhibited a very genuine love of moral excellence, but the same pedantic and retrospective character.
They were continually dilating on the regulations of the
censors and the customs of the earliest period of the Republic.
They acquired the habit of never enforcing the simplest
lesson without illustrating it by a profusion of ancient
examples and by detached sentences from some philosopher,
which they employed much as texts of Scripture are often
employed in the writings of the Puritans.[3] Above all, they

---

[1] Noct. Att. vi. 13. They called
these questions symposiacæ, as being well fitted to stimulate minds
already mellowed by wine.
[2] xviii. 2.

[3] We have a curious example of
this in a letter of Marcus Aurelius
preserved by Gallicanus in his
Life of Avidius Cassius.

delighted in cases of conscience, which they discussed with the subtilty of the schoolmen.

Lactantius has remarked that the Stoics were especially noted for the popular or democratic character of their teaching.[1] To their success in this respect their alliance with the rhetoricians probably largely contributed; but in other ways it hastened the downfall of the school. The useless speculations, refinements, and paradoxes which the subtle genius of Chrysippus had connected with the simple morals of Stoicism, had been for the most part thrown into the background by the early Roman Stoics; but in the teaching of the rhetoricians they became supreme. The endowments given by the Antonines to philosophers attracted a multitude of impostors, who wore long beards and the dress of the philosopher, but whose lives were notoriously immoral. The Cynics especially, professing to reject the ordinary conventionalities of society, and being under none of that discipline or superintendence which in the worst period has secured at least external morality among the mendicant monks, continually threw off every vestige of virtue and of decency. Instead of moulding great characters and inspiring heroic actions, Stoicism became a school of the idlest casuistry, or the cloak for manifest imposture.[2] The very generation which saw Marcus Aurelius on the throne, saw also the extinction of the influence of his sect.

The internal causes of the decadence of Stoicism, though very powerful, are insufficient to explain this complete

---

[1] 'Senserunt hoc Stoici qui servis et mulieribus philosophandum esse dixerunt.'—Lact. *Nat. Div.* iii. 25. Zeno was often reproached for gathering the poorest and most sordid around him when he lectured. (Diog. Laërt. *Zeno.*)

[2] This decadence was noticed and rebuked by some of the leading philosophers. See the language of Epictetus in Arrian, ii. 19, iv. 8, and of Herod Atticus in Aul. Gell. i. 2, ix. 2. St. Augustine speaks of the Cynics as having in his time sunk into universal contempt. See much evidence on this subject in Friedlænder, *Hist. des Mœurs Romaines*, tome iv. 378–385.

eclipse.  The chief cause must be found in the fact that the
minds of men had taken a new turn, and their enthusiasm
was flowing rapidly in the direction of Oriental religions,
and, under the guidance of Plotinus, Porphyry, Iamblichus,
and Proclus, of a mythical philosophy which was partly
Egyptian and partly Platonic.  It remains for me, in concluding this review of the Pagan empire, to indicate and explain this last transformation of Pagan morals.

It was in the first place a very natural reaction against
the extreme aridity of the Stoical casuistry, and also against
the scepticism which Sextus Empiricus had revived, and in
this respect it represents a law of the human mind which
has been more than once illustrated in later times.  Thus,
the captious, unsatisfying, intellectual subtleties of the
schoolmen were met by the purely emotional and mystical
school of St. Bonaventura, and afterwards of Tauler, and
thus the adoration of the human intellect, that was general
in the philosophy of the last century, prepared the way
for the complete denial of its competency by De Maistre and
by Lamennais.

In the next place, mysticism was a normal continuation
of the spiritualising movement which had long been advancing.  We have already seen that the strong tendency of
ethics, from Cato to Marcus Aurelius, was to enlarge the
prominence of the emotions in the type of virtue.  The formation of a gentle, a spiritual, and, in a word, a religious
character had become a prominent part of moral culture, and
it was regarded not simply as a means, but as an end.  Still,
both Marcus Aurelius and Cato were Stoics.  They both
represented the same general cast or conception of virtue,
although in Marcus Aurelius the type had been profoundly
modified.  But the time was soon to come when the balance
between the practical and the emotional parts of virtue,
which had been steadily changing, should be decisively turned

in favour of the latter, and the type of Stoicism was then necessarily discarded.

A concurrence of political and commercial causes had arisen, very favourable to the propagation of Oriental beliefs. Commerce had produced a constant intercourse between Egypt and Italy. Great numbers of Oriental slaves, passionately devoted to their national religions, existed in Rome; and Alexandria, which combined a great intellectual development with a geographical and commercial position exceedingly favourable to a fusion of many doctrines, soon created a school of thought which acted powerfully upon the world. Four great systems of eclecticism arose; Aristobulus and Philo tinctured Judaism with Greek and Egyptian philosophy. The Gnostics and the Alexandrian fathers united, though in very different proportions, Christian doctrines with the same elements; while Neoplatonism, at least in its later forms, represented a fusion of the Greek and Egyptian mind. A great analogy was discovered between the ideal philosophy of Plato and the mystical philosophy that was indigenous to the East, and the two systems readily blended.[1]

But the most powerful cause of the movement was the intense desire for positive religious belief, which had long been growing in the Empire. The period when Roman incredulity reached its extreme point had been the century that preceded and the half century that followed the birth of Christ. The sudden dissolution of the old habits of the Republic effected through political causes, the first comparison of the multitudinous religions of the Empire and also the writings of Euhemerus had produced an absolute religious disbelief which Epicureanism represented and encouraged. This belief, however, as I have already noticed, co-existed with numerous magical and astrological superstitions, and

---

[1] This movement is well treated by Vacherot, *Hist. de l'École d'Alexandrie.*

the ignorance of physical science was so great, and the conception of general laws so faint, that the materials for a great revival of superstition still remained. From the middle of the first century, a more believing and reverent spirit began to arise. The worship of Isis and Serapis forced its way into Rome in spite of the opposition of the rulers. Apollonius of Tyana, at the close of the Flavian period, had endeavoured to unite moral teaching with religious practices; the oracles, which had long ceased, were partially restored under the Antonines; the calamities and visible decline of the Empire withdrew the minds of men from that proud patriotic worship of Roman greatness, which was long a substitute for religious feeling; and the frightful pestilence that swept over the land in the reigns of Marcus Aurelius and his successor was followed by a blind, feverish, and spasmodic superstition. Besides this, men have never acquiesced for any considerable time in a neglect of the great problems of the origin, nature, and destinies of the soul, or dispensed with some form of religious worship and aspiration. That religious instincts are as truly a part of our nature as are our appetites and our nerves, is a fact which all history establishes, and which forms one of the strongest proofs of the reality of that unseen world to which the soul of man continually tends. Early Roman Stoicism, which in this respect somewhat resembled the modern positive school, diverted for the most part its votaries from the great problems of religion, and attempted to evolve its entire system of ethics out of existing human nature, without appealing to any external supernatural sanction. But the Platonic school, and the Egyptian school which connected itself with the name of Pythagoras, were both essentially religious. The first aspired to the Deity as the source and model of virtue, admitted dæmons or subordinate spiritual agents acting upon mankind, and explained and purified, in no hostile spirit, the popular religions. The latter made the state of ecstasy or quietism its ideal condition, and sought to purify the mind by theurgy or special religious rites. Both philosophies conspired to effect a great religious reformation, in which the Greek spirit usually represented the rational, and the Egyptian the mystical, element.

Of the first, Plutarch was the head. He taught the supreme authority of reason. He argued elaborately that superstition is worse than atheism, for it calumniates the character of the Deity, and its evils are not negative, but positive. At the same time, he is far from regarding the Mythology as a tissue of fables. Some things he denies. Others he explains away. Others he frankly accepts. He teaches for the most part a pure monotheism, which he reconciles with the common belief, partly by describing the different divinities as simply popular personifications of Divine attributes, and partly by the usual explanation of dæmons. He discarded most of the fables of the poets, applying to them with fearless severity the tests of human morality, and rejecting indignantly those which attribute to the Deity cruel or immoral actions. He denounces all religious terrorism, and draws a broad line of distinction between both the superstitious and idolatrous conception of the Deity on the one hand, and the philosophical conception on the other. ' The superstitious man believes in the gods, but he has a false idea of their nature. Those good beings whose providence watches over us with so much care, those beings so ready to forget our faults, he represents as ferocious and cruel tyrants, taking pleasure in tormenting us. He believes the founders of brass, the sculptors of stone, the moulders of wax ; he attributes to the gods a human form ; he adorns and worships the image he has made, and he listens not to the philosophers, and men of knowledge who associate the Divine image, not with bodily beauty, but with grandeur and majesty, with gentleness and goodness.' [1] On the other hand,

---

[1] *De Superstitione.*

Plutarch believed that there was undoubtedly a certain supernatural basis in the Pagan creed; he believed in oracles; he
defended, in a very ingenious essay, hereditary punishment,
and the doctrine of a special Providence; he admitted a
future retribution, though he repudiated the notion of
physical torment; and he brought into clear relief the moral
teaching conveyed in some of the fables of the poets.

The position which Plutarch occupied under Trajan,
Maximus of Tyre occupied in the next generation. Like
Plutarch, but with a greater consistency, he maintained a
pure monotheistic doctrine, declaring that 'Zeus is that most
ancient and guiding mind that begot all things—Athene is
prudence—Apollo is the sun.'[1] Like Plutarch, he developed
the Platonic doctrine of dæmons as an explanation of much
of the mythology, and he applied an allegorical interpretation
with great freedom to the fables of Homer, which formed the
text-book or the Bible of Paganism. By these means he
endeavoured to clarify the popular creed from all elements
inconsistent with a pure monotheism, and from all legends
of doubtful morality, while he sublimated the popular worship
into a harmless symbolism. 'The gods,' he assures us, 'themselves need no images,' but the infirmity of human nature requires visible signs 'on which to rest.' 'Those who possess
such faculties, that with a steady mind they can rise to
heaven, and to God, are in no need of statues. But such men
are very rare.' He then proceeds to recount the different
ways by which men have endeavoured to represent or
symbolise the Divine nature, as the statues of Greece, the
animals of Egypt, or the sacred flame of Persia. 'The God,'
he continues, 'the Father and the Founder of all that exists,
older than the sun, older than the sky, greater than all time,
than every age, and than all the works of nature, whom no
words can express, whom no eye can see . . . What can we

---

[1] *Dissertations*, x. § 8 (ed. Davis, London, 1740). In some editions
this is *Diss.* xxix.

say concerning his images? Only let men understand that there is but one Divine nature; but whether the art of Phidias chiefly preserves his memory among the Greeks, or the worship of animals among the Egyptians, a river among these, or a flame among those, I do not blame the variety of the representations—only let men understand that there is but one; only let them love one, let them preserve one in their memory.'[1]

A third writer who, nearly at the same time as Maximus of Tyre, made some efforts in the same direction, was Apuleius, who, however, both as a moral teacher, and in his freedom from superstition, was far inferior to the preceding. The religion he most admired was the Egyptian; but in his philosophy he was a Platonist, and in that capacity, besides an exposition of the Platonic code of morals, he has left us a singularly clear and striking disquisition on the doctrine of dæmons. 'These dæmons,' he says, 'are the bearers of blessings and prayers between the inhabitants of earth and heaven, carrying prayers from the one and assistance from the other . . . By them also, as Plato maintained in his "Banquet," all revelations, all the various miracles of magicians, all kinds of omens, are ruled. They have their several tasks to perform, their different departments to govern; some directing dreams, others the disposition of the entrails, others the flight of birds . . . The supreme deities do not descend to these things—they leave them to the intermediate divinities.'[2] But these intermediate spirits are not simply the agents of supernatural phenomena—they are also the guardians of our virtue and the recorders of our actions. 'Each man has in life witnesses and guards of his deeds, visible to no one, but always present, witnessing not only every act but every thought. When life has ended and we must return whence we came, the same genius who had

---

[1] *Dissert.* xxxviii.  [2] *De Dæmone Socratis.*

charge over us, takes us away and hurries us in his custody to judgment, and then assists us in pleading our cause. If any thing is falsely asserted he corrects it—if true, he substantiates it, and according to his witness our sentence is determined.'[1]

There are many aspects in which these attempts at religious reform are both interesting and important. They are interesting, because the doctrine of dæmons, mingled, it is true, with the theory of Euhemerus about the origin of the deities, was universally accepted by the Fathers as the true explanation of the Pagan theology, because the notion and, after the third century, even the artistic type of the guardian genius reappeared in that of the guardian angel, and because the transition from polytheism to the conception of a single deity acting by the delegation or ministration of an army of subsidiary spirits, was manifestly fitted to prepare the way for the reception of Christianity. They are interesting, too, as showing the anxiety of the human mind to sublimate its religious creed to the level of the moral and intellectual standard it had attained, and to make religious ordinances in some degree the instruments of moral improvement. But they are interesting above all, because the Greek and Egyptian methods of reform represent with typical distinctness the two great tendencies of religious thought in all succeeding periods. The Greek spirit was essentially rationalistic and eclectic; the Egyptian spirit was essentially mystical and devotional. The Greek sat in judgment upon his religion. He modified, curtailed, refined, allegorised, or selected. He treated its inconsistencies or absurdities, or immoralities, with precisely the same freedom of criticism as those he encountered in ordinary life. The Egyptian, on the other hand, bowed low before the Divine presence.

---

[1] *De Dæmone Socratis.* See, on the office of dæmons or genii, Arrian i. 14, and a curious chapter in Ammianus Marcell. xxi. 14. See, too, Plotinus, 3rd *Enn.* lib. iv.

He veiled his eyes, he humbled his reason, he represented the introduction of a new element into the moral life of Europe, the spirit of religious reverence and awe.

'The Egyptian deities,' it was observed by Apuleius, 'were chiefly honoured by lamentations, and the Greek divinities by dances.'[1] The truth of the last part of this very significant remark appears in every page of Greek history. No nation had a richer collection of games and festivals growing out of its religious system; in none did a light, sportive, and often licentious fancy play more fearlessly around the popular creed, in none was religious terrorism more rare. The Divinity was seldom looked upon as holier than man, and a due observance of certain rites and ceremonies was deemed an ample tribute to pay to him. In the Egyptian system the religious ceremonies were veiled in mystery and allegory. Chastity, abstinence from animal food, ablutions, long and mysterious ceremonies of preparation or initiation, were the most prominent features of worship. The deities representing the great forces of nature, and shrouded by mysterious symbols, excited a degree of awe which no other ancient religion approached.

The speculative philosophy, and the conceptions of morals, that accompanied the inroad of Oriental religions, were of a kindred nature. The most prominent characteristic of the first was its tendency to supersede the deductions of the reason by the intuitions of ecstasy. Neoplatonism, and the philosophies that were allied to it, were fundamentally pantheistic,[2] but they differed widely from the pantheism of the Stoics. The Stoics identified man with God, for the purpose of glorifying man—the Neoplatonists for the purpose of aggrandising God. In the conception of the first, man, independent, self controlled, and participating in the highest

---

[1] De Dæmone Socratis.

[2] I should except Plotinus, however, who was faithful in this point to Plato, and was in consequence much praised by the Christian Fathers.

nature of the universe, has no superior in creation. According to the latter, man is almost a passive being, swayed and permeated by a divine impulse. Yet he is not altogether divine. The divinity is latent in his soul, but dulled, dimmed, and crushed by the tyranny of the body. 'To bring the God that is in us into conformity with the God that is in the universe,' to elicit the ideas that are graven in the mind, but obscured and hidden by the passions of the flesh—above all, to subdue the body, which is the sole obstacle to our complete fruition of the Deity—was the main object of life. Porphyry described all philosophy as an anticipation of death—not in the Stoical sense of teaching us to look calmly on our end, but because death realises the ideal of philosophy, the complete separation of soul and body. Hence followed an ascetic morality, and a supersensual philosophy. 'The greatest of all evils,' we are told, 'is pleasure; because by it the soul is nailed or riveted to the body, and thinks that true which the body persuades it, and is thus deprived of the sense of divine things.'[1] 'Justice, beauty, and goodness, and all things that are formed by them, no eye has ever seen, no bodily sense can apprehend. Philosophy must be pursued by pure and unmingled reason and with deadened senses; for the body disturbs the mind, so that it cannot follow after wisdom. As long as it is lost and mingled in the clay, we shall never sufficiently possess the truth we desire.'[2]

But the reason which is thus extolled as the revealer of truth must not be confounded with the process of reasoning. It is something quite different from criticism, analysis, comparison, or deduction. It is essentially intuitive, but it only acquires its power of transcendental intuition after a

---

[1] 'Omnium malorum maximum voluptas, qua tanquam clavo et fibula anima corpori nectitur; putatque vera quæ et corpus suadet, et ita spoliatur rerum divinarum aspectu.' — Iamblichus, *De Secta Pythagor.* (Romæ, 1556), p. 33. Plotinus, 1st *Enn.* vi. 6.

[2] *De Sect. Pyth.* pp. 36, 37.

long process of discipline. When a man passes from the daylight into a room which is almost dark, he is at first absolutely unable to see the objects around him ; but gradu-ally his eye grows accustomed to the feeble light, the outline of the room becomes dimly visible, object after object emerges into sight, until at last, by intently gazing, he acquires the power of seeing around him with tolerable distinctness. In this fact we have a partial image of the Neoplatonic doctrine of the knowledge of divine things. Our soul is a dark chamber, darkened by contact with the flesh, but in it there are graven divine ideas, there exists a living divine element. The eye of reason, by long and steady introspection, can learn to deci-pher these characters ; the will, aided by an appointed course of discipline, can evoke this divine element, and cause it to blend with the universal spirit from which it sprang. The powers of mental concentration, and of metaphysical abstrac-tion, are therefore the highest intellectual gifts ; and quietism, or the absorption of our nature in God, is the last stage of virtue. ' The end of man,' said Pythagoras, ' is God.' The mysterious ' One,' the metaphysical abstraction without attributes and without form which constitutes the First Person of the Alex-andrian Trinity, is the acme of human thought, and the condition of ecstasy is the acme of moral perfection. Plotinus, it was said, had several times attained it. Porphyry, after years of discipline, once, and but once.[1] The process of reasoning is here not only useless, but pernicious. ' An innate knowledge of the gods is implanted in our minds prior to all reasoning.'[2] In divine things the task of man is not to create or to acquire, but to educe. His means of perfection are not dialectics or research, but long and patient meditation, silence, abstinence from the distractions and occupations of life, the subjugation of the flesh, a life of continual discipline, a constant attendance on those mysterious rites which detach

---

[1] Porphyry, *Life of Plotinus.*        [2] Iamblichus, *De Mysteriis,* 1.

him from material objects, overawe and elevate his mind, and quicken his realisation of the Divine presence.[1]

The system of Neoplatonism represents a mode of thought which in many forms, and under many names, may be traced through the most various ages and creeds. Mysticism, transcendentalism, inspiration, and grace, are all words expressing the deep-seated belief that we possess fountains of knowledge apart from all the acquisitions of the senses; that there are certain states of mind, certain flashes of moral and intellectual illumination, which cannot be accounted for by any play or combination of our ordinary faculties. For the sobriety, the timidity, the fluctuations of the reasoning spirit, Neoplatonism substituted the transports of the imagination; and, though it cultivated the power of abstraction, every other intellectual gift was sacrificed to the discipline of asceticism. It made men credulous, because it suppressed that critical spirit which is the sole barrier to the ever-encroaching imagination; because it represented superstitious rites as especially conducive to that state of ecstasy which was the condition of revelation; because it formed a nervous, diseased, expectant temperament, ever prone to hallucinations, ever agitated by vague and uncertain feelings that were readily attributed to inspiration. As a moral system it carried, indeed, the purification of the feelings and imagination to a higher perfection than any preceding school, but it had the deadly fault of separating sentiment from action. In this respect it was well fitted to be the close, the final suicide, of Roman philosophy. Cicero assigned a place of happiness in the future world to all who faithfully served the State.[2] The Stoics had taught that all virtue was vain that did not issue in action. Even Epictetus, in his portrait of the

---

[1] See, on this doctrine of ecstasy, Vacherot, *Hist. de l'École d'Alex-andrie*, tome i. p. 576, &c.

[2] 'Sic habeto, omnibus qui patriam conservaverint, adjuverint, auxerint, certum esse in cœlo ac definitum locum ubi beati ævo sempiterno fruantur.'— Cic. *Somn. Scip.*

ascetic cynic—even Marcus Aurelius, in his minute self-examination—had never forgotten the outer world. The early Platonists, though they dwelt very strongly on mental discipline, were equally practical. Plutarch reminds us that the same word is used for light, and for man,[1] for the duty of man is to be the light of the world; and he shrewdly remarked that Hesiod exhorted the husbandman to pray for the harvest, but to do so with his hand upon the plough. Apuleius, expounding Plato, taught 'that he who is inspired by nature to seek after good must not deem himself born for himself alone, but for all mankind, though with diverse kinds and degrees of obligation, for he is formed first of all for his country, then for his relations, then for those with whom he is joined by occupation or knowledge.' Maximus of Tyre devoted two noble essays to showing the vanity of all virtue which exhausts itself in mental transports without radiating in action among mankind. 'What use,' he asked, 'is there in knowledge unless we do those things for which knowledge is profitable? What use is there in the skill of the physician unless by that skill he heals the sick, or in the art of Phidias unless he chisels the ivory or the gold. . . . Hercules was a wise man, but not for himself, but that by his wisdom he might diffuse benefits over every land and sea. . . Had he preferred to lead a life apart from men, and to follow an idle wisdom, Hercules would indeed have been a Sophist, and no one would call him the son of Zeus. For God himself is never idle; were He to rest, the sky would cease to move, and the earth to produce, and the rivers to flow into the ocean, and the seasons to pursue their appointed course.'[2] But the Neoplatonists, though they sometimes spoke of civic

---

[1] Φῶς, which, according to Plutarch (who here confuses two distinct words), is poetically used for man (*De Latenter Vivendo*). A similar thought occurs in M.

Aurelius, who speaks of the good man as light which only ceases to shine when it ceases to be.
[2] *Diss.* xxi. § 6.

virtues, regarded the condition of ecstasy as not only tran·
scending, but including all, and that condition could only be
arrived at by a passive life.  The saying of Anaxagoras, that
his mission was  to contemplate the sun, the stars, and the
course of nature, and that this contemplation was wisdom,'
was accepted as an epitome of their philosophy.[1]  A senator
named Rogantianus, who had followed the teaching of
Plotinus, acquired so intense a disgust for the things of life,
that he left all his property, refused to fulfil the duties of a
prætor, abandoned his senatorial functions, and withdrew
himself from every form of business and pleasure.  Plotinus,
instead of reproaching him, overwhelmed him with eulogy,
selected him as his favourite disciple, and continually represented him as the model of a philosopher.[2]

The two characteristics I have noticed—the abandonment of civic duties, and the discouragement of the critical
spirit—had from a very early period been manifest in the
Pythagorean school.[3]  In the blending philosophies of the
third and fourth centuries, they became continually more
apparent.  Plotinus was still an independent philosopher,
inheriting the traditions of Greek thought, though not the
traditions of Greek life, building his system avowedly by a
rational method, and altogether rejecting theurgy or religious
magic.  His disciple, Porphyry, first made Neoplatonism
anti-Christian, and, in his violent antipathy to the new faith,
began to convert it into a religious system.  Iamblichus,
who was himself an Egyptian priest, completed the trans-

---

[1] Iamblichus, *De Sect. Pythagoræ*, p. 35.

[2] Porphyry, *Life of Plotinus*, cap. vii.; Plotinus, 1st *Enn.* iv. 7.  See on this subject Degerando, *Hist. de la Philos.* iii. p. 383.

[3] Thus it was said of Apollonius that in his teaching at Ephesus he did not speak after the manner of the followers of Socrates, but en-deavoured to detach his disciples from all occupation other than phi-losophy.—*Philostr. Apoll. of Tyana*, iv. 2.  Cicero notices the aversion the Pythagoreans of his time dis-played to argument: 'Quum ex iis quæreretur quare ita esset, re-spondere solitos, Ipse dixit ; ipse autem erat Pythagoras.'—*De Nat Deor.* i. 5.

formation,[1] resolved all moral discipline into theurgy, **and**
sacrificed all reasoning to faith.[2]   Julian attempted to realise
the conception of a revived Paganism, blending with and
purified by philosophy.   In every form the appetite for
miracles and for belief was displayed.   The theory of
dæmons completely superseded the old Stoical naturalism,
which regarded the different Pagan divinities as allegories or
personifications of the Divine attributes.   The Platonic
ethics were again, for the most part, in the ascendant, but
they were deeply tinctured by a foreign element.   Thus,
suicide was condemned by the Neoplatonists, not merely on
the principle of Plato, that it is an abandonment of the post
of duty to which the Deity has called us, but also on the
quietist ground, that perturbation is necessarily a pollution
of the soul, and that, as mental perturbation accompanies
the act, the soul of the suicide departs polluted from the
body.[3]   The belief in a future world, which was the common
glory of the schools of Pythagoras and of Plato, had become
universal.   As Roman greatness, in which men had long
seen the reward of virtue, faded rapidly away, the conception of 'a city of God' began to grow more clearly in the
minds of men, and the countless slaves who were among the
chief propagators of Oriental faiths, and who had begun to exercise an unprecedented influence in Roman life, turned with a
natural and a touching eagerness towards a happier and a freer
world.[4]   The incredulity of Lucretius, Cæsar, and Pliny had

---

[1] See Vacherot, tome ii. p. 66.
[2] See Degerando, *Hist. de la Philosophie*, tome iii. pp. 400, 401.
[3] Plotinus, 1st *Enn.* ix.
[4] See a strong passage, on the universality of this belief, in Plotinus, 1st *Enn.* i. 12, and Origen, *Cont. Cels.* vii.   A very old tradition represented the Egyptians as the first people who held the doctrine of the immortality of the soul.

Cicero (*Tusc. Quæst.*) says that the Syrian Pherecydes, master of Pythagoras, first taught it.   Maximus of Tyre attributes its origin to Pythagoras, and his slave Zamolxis was said to have introduced it into Greece.   Others say that Thales first taught it.   None of these assertions have any real historical value.

disappeared. Above all, a fusion had been effected between moral discipline and religion, and the moralist sought his chief means of purification in the ceremonies of the temple.

I have now completed the long and complicated task to which the present chapter has been devoted. I have endeavoured to exhibit, so far as can be done, by a description of general tendencies, and by a selection of quotations, the spirit of the long series of Pagan moralists who taught at Rome during the period that elapsed between the rise of Roman philosophy and the triumph of Christianity. My object has not been to classify these writers with minute accuracy, according to their speculative tenets, but rather, as I had proposed, to exhibit the origin, the nature, and the fortunes of the general notion or type of virtue which each moralist had regarded as supremely good. History is not a mere succession of events connected only by chronology. It is a chain of causes and effects. There is a great natural difference of degree and direction in both the moral and intellectual capacities of individuals, but it is not probable that the general average of natural morals in great bodies of men materially varies. When we find a society very virtuous or very vicious —when some particular virtue or vice occupies a peculiar prominence, or when important changes pass over the moral conceptions or standard of the people—we have to trace in these things simply the action of the circumstances that were dominant. The history of Roman ethics represents a steady and uniform current, guided by the general conditions of society, and its progress may be marked by the successive ascendancy of the Roman, the Greek, and the Egyptian spirit.

In the age of Cato and Cicero the character of the ideal was wholly Roman, although the philosophical expression of that character was derived from the Greek Stoics. It exhibited all the force, the grandeur, the hardness, the practical tendency which Roman circumstances had early created, combined with that catholicity of spirit which resulted from very recent political and intellectual changes. In the course of time, the Greek element, which represented the gentler and more humane spirit of antiquity, gained an ascendancy. It did so by simple propagandism, aided by the long peace of the Antonines, by the effeminate habits produced by the increasing luxury, by the attractions of the metropolis, which had drawn multitudes of Greeks to Rome, by the patronage of the Emperors, and also by the increasing realisation of the doctrine of universal brotherhood, which Panætius and Cicero had asserted, but of which the full consequences were only perceived by their successors. The change in the type of virtue was shown in the influence of eclectic, and for the most part Platonic, moralists, whose special assaults were directed against the Stoical condemnation of the emotions, and in the gradual softening of the Stoical type. In Seneca the hardness of the sect, though very apparent, is broken by precepts of a real and extensive benevolence, though that benevolence springs rather from a sense of duty than from tenderness of feeling. In Dion Chrysostom the practical benevolence is not less prominent, but there is less both of pride and of callousness. Epictetus embodied the sternest Stoicism in his Manual, but his dissertations exhibit a deep religious feeling and a wide range of sympathies. In Marcus Aurelius the emotional elements had greatly increased, and the amiable qualities began to predominate over the heroic ones. We find at the same time a new stress laid upon purity of thought and imagination, a growing feeling of reverence, and an earnest desire to reform the popular religion.

This second stage exhibits a happy combination of the Roman and Greek spirits. Disinterested, strictly practical, averse to the speculative subtilties of the Greek intellect, Stoicism was still the religion of a people who were the rulers and the organisers of the world, whose enthusiasm was essentially patriotic, and who had learnt to sacrifice everything but pride to the sense of duty. It had, however, become amiable, gentle, and spiritual. It had gained much in beauty, while it had lost something in force. In the world of morals, as in the world of physics, strength is nearly allied to hardness. He who feels keenly is easily moved, and a sensitive sympathy which lies at the root of an amiable character is in consequence a principle of weakness. The race of great Roman Stoics, which had never ceased during the tyranny of Nero or Domitian, began to fail. In the very moment when the ideal of the sect had attained its supreme perfection, a new movement appeared, the philosophy sank into disrepute, and the last act of the drama began.

In this, as in the preceding ones, all was normal and regular. The long continuance of despotic government had gradually destroyed the active public spirit of which Stoicism was the expression. The predominance of the subtile intellect of Greece, and the multiplication of rhetoricians, had converted the philosophy into a school of disputation and of casuistry. The increasing cultivation of the emotions continued, till what may be termed the moral centre was changed, and the development of feeling was deemed more important than the regulation of actions. This cultivation of the emotions predisposed men to religion. A reaction, intensified by many minor causes, set in against the scepticism of the preceding generation, and Alexandria gradually became the moral capital of the empire. The Roman type speedily disappeared. A union was effected between superstitious rites and philosophy, and the worship of Egyptian deities prepared the way for the teaching of the Neoplatonists, who combined the most visionary part of the speculations of Plato with the ancient philosophies of the East. In Plotinus we find most of the first; in Iamblichus most of the second. The minds of men, under their influence, grew introspective, credulous, and superstitious, and found their ideal states in the hallucinations of ecstasy and the calm of an unpractical mysticism.

Such were the influences which acted in turn upon a society which, by despotism, by slavery, and by atrocious

amusements, had been debased and corrupted to the very
core.   Each sect which successively arose contributed something to remedy the evil.   Stoicism placed beyond cavil the
great distinctions between right and wrong.   It inculcated
the doctrine of universal brotherhood, it created a noble literature and a noble legislation, and it associated its moral
system with the patriotic spirit which was then the animating
spirit of Roman life.   The early Platonists of the Empire corrected the exaggerations of Stoicism, gave free scope to the
amiable qualities, and supplied a theory of right and wrong,
suited not merely for heroic characters and for extreme emer-
gencies, but also for the characters and the circumstances of
common life.   The Pythagorean and Neoplatonic schools revived the feeling of religious reverence, inculcated humility,
prayerfulness, and purity of thought, and accustomed men to
associate their moral ideals with the Deity, rather than with
themselves.

The moral improvement of society was now to pass into
other hands.   A religion which had long been increasing in
obscurity began to emerge into the light.   By the beauty
of its moral precepts, by the systematic skill with which it
governed the imagination and habits of its worshippers, by
the strong religious motives to which it could appeal, by its
admirable ecclesiastical organisation, and, it must be added,
by its unsparing use of the arm of power, Christianity soon
eclipsed or destroyed all other sects, and became for many
centuries the supreme ruler of the moral world.   Combining
the Stoical doctrine of universal brotherhood, the Greek predilection for the amiable qualities, and the Egyptian spirit
of reverence and religious awe, it acquired from the first an
intensity and universality of influence which none of the philosophies it had superseded had approached.   I have now to
examine the moral causes that governed the rise of this religion in Rome, the ideal of virtue it presented, the degree and
manner in which it stamped its image upon the character of
nations, and the perversions and distortions it underwent.

# CHAPTER III.

## THE CONVERSION OF ROME.

THERE is no fact in the history of the human mind more remarkable than the complete unconsciousness of the importance and the destinies of Christianity, manifested by the Pagan writers before the accession of Constantine. So large an amount of attention has been bestowed on the ten or twelve allusions to it they furnish, that we are sometimes apt to forget how few and meagre those allusions are, and how utterly impossible it is to construct from them, with any degree of certainty, a history of the early Church. Plutarch and the elder Pliny, who probably surpass all other writers of their time in the range of their illustrations, and Seneca, who was certainly the most illustrious moralist of his age, never even mention it. Epictetus and Marcus Aurelius have each adverted to it with a passing and contemptuous censure. Tacitus describes in detail the persecution by Nero, but treats the suffering religion merely as 'an execrable superstition;' while Suetonius, employing the same expression, reckons the persecution among the acts of the tyrant that were either laudable or indifferent. Our most important document is the famous letter of the younger Pliny. Lucian throws some light both on the extent of Christian charity, and on the aspect in which Christians were regarded by the religious jugglers of their age, and the long series of Pagans who wrote the lives of the Emperors in that most critical period from the accession of Hadrian, almost to the eve of the triumph of the Church, among a crowd of details concerning the dresses, games, vices, and follies of the Court, supply us with six or seven short notices of the religion that was transforming the world.

The general silence of the Pagan writers on this subject did not arise from any restrictions imposed upon them by authority, for in this field the widest latitude was conceded, nor yet from the notions of the dignity of history, or the importance of individual exertions, which have induced some historians to resolve their task into a catalogue of the achievements of kings, statesmen, and generals. The conception of history, as the record and explanation of moral revolutions, though of course not developed to the same prominence as among some modern writers, was by no means unknown in antiquity,[1] and in many branches our knowledge of the social changes of the Roman Empire is extremely copious. The dissolution of old beliefs, the decomposition of the entire social and moral system that had arisen under the Republic, engaged in the very highest degree the attention of the literary classes, and they displayed the most commendable diligence in tracing its stages. It is very curious and instructive to contrast the ample information they have furnished us concerning the growth of Roman luxury, with their almost absolute silence concerning the growth of Christianity. The moral importance of the former movement they clearly recognised, and they have accordingly preserved so full a record of all the changes in dress, banquets, buildings, and spectacles, that it would be possible to write with the most minute detail the whole history of Roman luxury, from the day when a censor deprived an elector of his vote because his garden was negli-

---

[1] We have a remarkable instance of the clearness with which some even of the most insignificant historians recognised the folly of confining history to the biographies of the Emperors, in the opening chapter of Capitolinus, *Life of Macrinus.* —Tacitus is full of beautiful episodes, describing the manners and religion of the people.

gently cultivated, to the orgies of Nero or Heliogabalus.
The moral importance of the other movement they altogether
overlooked, and their oversight leaves a chasm in history
which can never be supplied.

That the greatest religious change in the history of man
kind should have taken place under the eyes of a brilliant
galaxy of philosophers and historians, who were profoundly
conscious of the decomposition around them, that all of these
writers should have utterly failed to predict the issue of the
movement they were observing, and that, during the space
of three centuries, they should have treated as simply contemptible an agency which all men must now admit to have
been, for good or for evil, the most powerful moral lever that
has ever been applied to the affairs of man, are facts well
worthy of meditation in every period of religious transition.
The explanation is to be found in that broad separation between the spheres of morals and of positive religion we have
considered in the last chapter.   In modern times, men who
were examining the probable moral future of the world, would
naturally, and in the first place, direct their attention to the
relative positions and the probable destinies of religious institutions.   In the Stoical period of the Roman Empire,
positive religion had come to be regarded as merely an art
for obtaining preternatural assistance in the affairs of life,
and the moral amelioration of mankind was deemed altogether external to its sphere.   Philosophy had become to the
educated most literally a religion.   It was the rule of life, the
exposition of the Divine nature, the source of devotional feeling   The numerous Oriental superstitions that had deluged
the city were regarded as peculiarly pernicious and contemptible, and of these none was less likely to attract the favour
of the philosophers than that of the Jews,[1] who were noto-

---

[1] The passages relating to the
Jews in Roman literature are collected in Aubertin's *Rapports supposes entre Sénèque et St. Paul.*
Champagny, *Rome et Judée,* tome i.
pp. 134–137.

rious as the most sordid, the most turbulent,[1] and the most unsocial[2] of the Oriental colonists. Of the ignorance of their tenets, displayed even by the most eminent Romans, we have a striking illustration in the long series of grotesque fables concerning their belief, probably derived from some satirical pamphlet, which Tacitus has gravely inserted in his history.[3] Christianity, in the eyes of the philosopher, was simply a sect of Judaism.

Although I am anxious in the present work to avoid, as far as possible, all questions that are purely theological, and to consider Christianity merely in its aspect as a moral agent, it will be necessary to bestow a few preliminary pages upon its triumph in the Roman Empire, in order to ascertain how far that triumph was due to moral causes, and what were its relations to the prevailing philosophy. There are some writers who have been so struck with the conformity between some of the doctrines of the later Stoics and those of Christianity that they have imagined that Christianity had early obtained a decisive influence over philosophy, and that the leading teachers of Rome had been in some measure its disciples. There are others who reduce the conversion of the Roman Empire to a mere question of evidences, to the overwhelming proofs the Christian teachers produced of the authenticity of the Gospel narratives. There are others, again, who deem the triumph of Christianity simply miraculous. Everything, they tell us, was against it. The course of the Church was like that of a ship sailing rapidly and steadily to the goal, in direct defiance of both wind and tide, and the conversion of the Empire was as literally supernatural as the raising of the dead, or the sudden quelling of the storm.

On the first of these theories it will not, I think, be

---

[1] Cicero, *pro Flacco*, 28 ; Sueton. *Claudius*, 25.

[2] Juvenal, *Sat.* xiv.

[3] *Hist.* v.

necessary, after the last chapter, to expatiate at length. It is
admitted that the greatest moralists of the Roman Empire
either never mentioned Christianity, or mentioned it with
contempt; that they habitually disregarded the many religions which had arisen among the ignorant; and that we
have no direct evidence of the slightest value of their ever
having come in contact with or favoured the Christians.
The supposition that they were influenced by Christianity
rests mainly upon their enforcement of the Christian duty of
self-examination, upon their strong assertion of the universal
brotherhood of mankind, and upon the delicate and expansive
humanity they at last evinced. But although on all these
points the later Stoics approximated much to Christianity,
we have already seen that it is easy to discover in each case
the cause of the tendency. The duty of self-examination was
simply a Pythagorean precept, enforced in that school long
before the rise of Christianity, introduced into Stoicism when
Pythagoreanism became popular in Rome, and confessedly
borrowed from this source. The doctrine of the universal
brotherhood of mankind was the manifest expression of those
political and social changes which reduced the whole civilised
globe to one great empire, threw open to the most distant
tribes the right of Roman citizenship, and subverted all
those class divisions around which moral theories had been
formed. Cicero asserted it as emphatically as Seneca. The
theory of pantheism, representing the entire creation as one
great body, pervaded by one Divine soul, harmonised with it;
and it is a curious fact that the very phraseology concerning
the fellow-membership of all things in God, which has been
most confidently adduced by some modern writers as proving
the connection between Seneca and Christianity, was selected
by Lactantius as the clearest illustration of the pantheism of
Stoicism.[1]   The humane character of the later Stoical teach-

---

[1] Lact. *Inst. Div.* vii. 3.

ing was obviously due to the infusion of the Greek element
into Roman life, which began before the foundation of the
Empire, and received a new impulse in the reign of Hadrian,
and also to the softening influence of a luxurious civilisation,
and of the long peace of the Antonines.    While far inferior
to the Greeks in practical and realised humanity, the Romans
never surpassed their masters in theoretical humanity except
in one respect.    The humanity of the Greeks, though very
earnest, was confined within a narrow circle.    The social and
political circumstances of the Roman Empire destroyed the
barrier.

The only case in which any plausible arguments have been
urged in favour of the notion that the writings of the Stoics
were influenced by the New Testament is that of Seneca.
This philosopher was regarded by all the mediæval writers
as a Christian, on the ground of a correspondence with St.
Paul, which formed part of a forged account of the martyrdom of St. Peter and St. Paul, attributed to St. Linus.
These letters, which were absolutely unnoticed during the
first three centuries, and are first mentioned by St. Jerome,
are now almost universally abandoned as forgeries; [1] but
many curious coincidences of phraseology have been pointed
out between the writings of Seneca and the epistles of St.
Paul ; and the presumption derived from them has been
strengthened by the facts that the brother of Seneca was that
Gallio who refused to hear the disputes between St. Paul and
the Jews, and that Burrhus, who was the friend and colleague of Seneca, was the officer to whose custody St. Paul
had been entrusted at Rome.    Into the minute verbal critic-

---

[1] See their history fully investigated in Aubertin.    Augustine
followed Jerome in mentioning the
letters, but neither of these writers
asserted their genuineness.    Lactantius, nearly at the same time
(*Inst. Div.* vi. 24), distinctly spoke
of Seneca as a Pagan, as Tertullian
(*Apol.* 50) had done before.    The
immense number of forged documents is one of the most disgraceful
features of the Church history of
the first few centuries.

ism to which this question had given rise,[1] it is not necessary for me to enter. It has been shown that much of what was deemed Christian phraseology grew out of the pantheistic notion of one great body including, and one Divine mind animating and guiding, all existing things; and many other of the pretended coincidences are so slight as to be altogether worthless as an argument. Still I think most persons who review what has been written on the subject will conclude that it is probable some fragments at least of Christian language had come to the ears of Seneca. But to suppose that his system of morals is in any degree formed after the model or under the influence of Christianity, is to be blind to the most obvious characteristics of both Christianity and Stoicism; for no other moralist could be so aptly selected as representing their extreme divergence. Reverence and humility, a constant sense of the supreme majesty of God and of the weakness and sinfulness of man, and a perpetual reference to another world, were the essential characteristics of Christianity, the source of all its power, the basis of its distinctive type. Of all these, the teaching of Seneca is the direct antithesis. Careless of the future world, and profoundly convinced of the supreme majesty of man, he laboured to emancipate his disciples 'from every fear of God and man;' and the proud language in which he claimed for the sage an equality with the gods represents, perhaps, the highest point to which philosophic arrogance has been carried. The Jews, with whom the Christians were then universally identified, he emphatically describes as 'an accursed race.'[2] One man, indeed, there was

---

[1] Fleury has written an elaborate work maintaining the connection between the apostle and the philosopher. Troplong (*Influence du Christianisme sur le Droit*) has adopted the same view. Aubertin, in the work I have already cited, has maintained the opposite view (which is that of all or nearly all English critics) with masterly skill and learning. The Abbé Dourif (*Rapports du Stoïcisme et du Christianisme*) has placed side by side the passages from each writer which are most alike.

[2] Quoted by St. Augustine.— *De Civ. Dei*, vi. 11.

among the later Stoics who had almost realised the Christian type, and in whose pure and gentle nature the arrogance of his school can be scarcely traced; but Marcus Aurelius, who of all the Pagan world, if we argued by internal evidence alone, would have been most readily identified with Christianity, was a persecutor of the faith, and he has left on record in his ' Meditations ' his contempt for the Christian martyrs.[1]

The relation between the Pagan philosophers and the Christian religion was a subject of much discussion and of profound difference of opinion in the early Church.[2] While the writers of one school apologised for the murder of Socrates, described the martyred Greek as the ' buffoon of Athens,'[3] and attributed his inspiration to diabolical influence;[4] while they designated the writings of the philosophers as ' the schools of heretics,' and collected with a malicious assiduity all the calumnies that had been heaped upon their memory— there were others who made it a leading object to establish a close affinity between Pagan philosophy and the Christian revelation. Imbued in many instances, almost from childhood, with the noble teaching of Plato, and keenly alive to the analogies between his philosophy and their new faith, these writers found the exhibition of this resemblance at once deeply grateful to themselves and the most successful way of dispelling the prejudices of their Pagan neighbours. The success that had attended the Christian prophecies attributed to the Sibyls and the oracles, the passion for eclecticism, which the social and commercial position of Alexandria had generated, and also the example of the Jew Aristobulus, who had some time before contended that the Jewish

---

[1] xi. 3.

[2] The history of the two schools has been elaborately traced by Ritter, Pressense, and many other writers. I would especially refer to the fourth volume of Degerando's most fascinating *His-* *toire de la Philosophie.*

[3] 'Scurra Atticus,' Min. Felix, *Octav.* This term is said by Cicero to have been given to Socrates by Zeno. (Cic. *De Nat. Deor.* i. 34.)

[4] Tertull. *De Anima,* 39.

writings had been translated into Greek, and had been the
source of much of the Pagan wisdom, encouraged them in
their course. The most conciliatory, and at the same time
the most philosophical school, was the earliest in the Church.
Justin Martyr—the first of the Fathers whose writings possess any general philosophical interest—cordially recognises
the excellence of many parts of the Pagan philosophy, and
even attributes it to a Divine inspiration, to the action of
the generative or 'seminal Logos,' which from the earliest
times had existed in the world, had inspired teachers like
Socrates and Musonius, who had been persecuted by the
dæmons, and had received in Christianity its final and perfect
manifestation.[1]    The same generous and expansive apprecia
tion may be traced in the writings of several later Fathers,
although the school was speedily disfigured by some grotesque
extravagances. Clement of Alexandria—a writer of wide
sympathies, considerable originality, very extensive learning,
but of a feeble and fantastic judgment—who immediately
succeeded Justin Martyr, attributed all the wisdom of antiquity to two sources. The first source was tradition; for
the angels, who had been fascinated by the antediluvian
ladies, had endeavoured to ingratiate themselves with their
fair companions by giving them an abstract of the metaphysical and other learning which was then current in heaven,
and the substance of these conversations, being transmitted
by tradition, supplied the Pagan philosophers with their
leading notions.    The angels did not know everything, and
therefore the Greek philosophy was imperfect; but this event
formed the first great epoch in literary history.    The second
and most important source of Pagan wisdom was the Old
Testament,[2] the influence of which many of the early Christians traced in every department of ancient wisdom.  Plato had

---

[1] See especially his *Apol.* ii. 8,
12, 13. He speaks of the σπερματικὸς
λόγος.

[2] See, on all this, Clem. Alex.
*Strom.* v., and also i. 22.

borrowed from it all his philosophy, Homer the noblest conceptions of his poetry, Demosthenes the finest touches of his eloquence. Even Miltiades owed his military skill to an assiduous study of the Pentateuch, and the ambuscade by which he won the battle of Marathon was imitated from the strategy of Moses.[1] Pythagoras, moreover, had been himself a circumcised Jew.[2] Plato had been instructed in Egypt by the prophet Jeremiah. The god Serapis was no other than the patriarch Joseph, his Egyptian name being manifestly derived from his great-grandmother Sarah.[3]

Absurdities of this kind, of which I have given extreme but by no means the only examples, were usually primarily intended to repel arguments against Christianity, and they are illustrations of the tendency which has always existed in an uncritical age to invent, without a shadow of foundation, the most elaborate theories of explanation rather than recognise the smallest force in an objection. Thus, when the Pagans attempted to reduce Christianity to a normal product of the human mind, by pointing to the very numerous Pagan legends which were precisely parallel to the Jewish histories,

---

[1] St. Clement repeats this twice (*Strom.* i. 24, v. 14). The writings of this Father are full of curious, and sometimes ingenious, attempts to trace different phrases of the great philosophers, orators, and poets to Moses. A vast amount of learning and ingenuity has been expended in the same cause by Eusebius. (*Præp. Evan.* xii. xiii.) The tradition of the derivation of Pagan philosophy from the Old Testament found in general little favour among the Latin writers. There is some curious information on this subject in Waterland's 'Charge to the Clergy of Middlesex, to prove that the wisdom of the ancients was borrowed from revelation; delivered in 1731.' It is in the 8th volume of Waterland's works (ed. 1731).

[2] St. Clement (*Strom.* i.) mentions that some think him to have been Ezekiel, an opinion which St. Clement himself does not hold. See, on the patristic notions about Pythagoras, Legendre, *Traité de l'Opinion,* tome i. p. 164.

[3] This was the opinion of Julius Firmicus Maternus, a Latin writer of the age of Constantine, 'Nam quia Saræ pronepos fuerat . . . Serapis dictus est Græco sermone, hoc est Σαρâς ἄπο.'—Julius Firmicus Maternus, *De Errore Profanarum Religionum,* cap. xiv.

24

it was answered that the dæmons were careful students of prophecy, that they foresaw with terror the advent of their Divine Conqueror, and that, in order to prevent men believing in him, they had invented, by anticipation, a series of legends resembling the events which were foretold.[1] More frequently, however, the early Christians retorted the accusations of plagiarism, and by forged writings attributed to Pagan authors, or, by pointing out alleged traces of Jewish influence in genuine Pagan writings, they endeavoured to trace through the past the footsteps of their faith. But this method of assimilation, which culminated in the Gnostics, the Neoplatonists, and especially in Origen, was directed not to the later Stoics of the Empire, but to the great philosophers who had preceded Christianity. It was in the writings of Plato, not in those of Epictetus or Marcus Aurelius, that the Fathers of the first three centuries found the influence of the Jewish Scriptures, and at the time when the passion for discovering these connections was most extravagant, the notion of Seneca and his followers being inspired by the Christians was unknown.

Dismissing then, as altogether groundless, the notion that Christianity had obtained a complete or even a partial influence over the philosophic classes during the period of Stoical ascendancy, we come to the opinion of those who suppose that the Roman Empire was converted by a system of evidences—by the miraculous proofs of the divinity of Christianity, submitted to the adjudication of the people. To estimate this view aright, we have to consider both the capacity of the men of that age for judging miracles, and also—which is a different question—the extent to which such evidence would weigh upon their minds. To treat this subject satis-

---

[1] Justin Martyr, *Apol.* i. 54; Trypho, 69–70. There is a very curious collection of Pagan legends that were parallel to Jewish incidents, in La Mothe le Vayer, let. xciii.

factorily, it may be advisable to enter at some little length into the broad question of the evidence of the miraculous.

With the exception of a small minority of the priests of the Catholic Church, a general incredulity on the subject of miracles now underlies the opinions of almost all educated men. Nearly every one, however cordially he may admit some one particular class of miracles, as a general rule regards the accounts of such events, which are so frequent in all old historians, as false and incredible, even when he fully believes the natural events that are authenticated by the same testimony. The reason of this incredulity is not altogether the impossibility or even extreme natural improbability of miracles; for, whatever may be the case with some, there is at least one class or conception of them which is perfectly free from logical difficulty. There is no contradiction involved in the belief that spiritual beings, of power and wisdom immeasurably transcending our own, exist, or that, existing, they might, by the normal exercise of their powers, perform feats as far surpassing the understanding of the most gifted of mankind, as the electric telegraph and the prediction of an eclipse surpass the faculties of a savage. Nor does the incredulity arise, I think, as is commonly asserted, from the want of that amount and kind of evidence which in other departments is deemed sufficient. Very few of the minor facts of history are authenticated by as much evidence as the Stigmata of St. Francis, or the miracle of the holy thorn, or those which were said to have been wrought at the tomb of the Abbé Paris. We believe, with tolerable assurance, a crowd of historical events on the testimony of one or two Roman historians; but when Tacitus and Suetonius describe how Vespasian restored a blind man to sight, and a cripple to strength,[1] their deliberate

---

[1] Suet. *Vesp.* 7; Tacit. *Hist.* iv. 81. There is a slight difference between the two historians about the second miracle. Suetonius

assertions do not even beget in our minds a suspicion that
the narrative may possibly be true.    We are quite certain
that miracles were not ordinary occurrences in classical or
mediæval times, but nearly all the contemporary writers from
whom we derive our knowledge of those periods were convinced that they were.

If, then, I have correctly interpreted the opinions of
ordinary educated people on this subject, it appears that the
common attitude towards miracles is not that of doubt, of
hesitation, of discontent with the existing evidence, but
rather of absolute, derisive, and even unexamining incredulity.    Such a fact, when we consider that the antecedent
possibility of at least some miracles is usually admitted, and
in the face of the vast mass of tradition that may be adduced
in their favour, appears at first sight a striking anomaly, and
the more so because it can be shown that the belief in miracles had in most cases not been reasoned down, but had
simply faded away.

In order to ascertain the process by which this state of
mind has been attained, we may take an example in a sphere
which is happily removed from controversy.    There are very
few persons with whom the fictitious character of fairy tales
has not ceased to be a question, or who would hesitate to
disbelieve or even to ridicule any anecdote of this nature
which was told them, without the very smallest examination
of its evidence.    Yet, if we ask in what respect the existence
of fairies is naturally contradictory or absurd, it would be
difficult to answer the question.    A fairy is simply a being

---

says it was the leg, Tacitus that it
was the hand, that was diseased.
The god Serapis was said to have
revealed to the patients that they
would be cured by the emperor.
Tacitus says that Vespasian did
not believe in his own power; that
it was only after much persuasion
he was induced to try the experiment; that the blind man was
well known in Alexandria, where
the event occurred, and that eye-
witnesses who had no motive to
lie still attested the miracle.

possessing a moderate share of human intelligence, with little
or no moral faculty, with a body pellucid, winged, and
volatile, like that of an insect, with a passion for dancing,
and, perhaps, with an extraordinary knowledge of the properties of different plants.   That such beings should exist, or
that, existing, they should be able to do many things beyond
human power, are propositions which do not present the
smallest difficulty.   For many centuries their existence was
almost universally believed.   There is not a country, not a
province, scarcely a parish, in which traditions of their
appearance were not long preserved.   So great a weight of
tradition, so many independent trains of evidence attesting
statements perfectly free from intrinsic absurdity, or even
improbability, might appear sufficient, if not to establish conviction, at least to supply a very strong *primâ facie* case,
and ensure a patient and respectful investigation of the
subject.

It has not done so, and the reason is sufficiently plain.
The question of the credibility of fairy tales has not been
resolved by an examination of evidence, but by an observation
of the laws of historic development.   Wherever we find an
ignorant and rustic population, the belief in fairies is found
to exist, and circumstantial accounts of their apparitions are
circulated.   But invariably with increased education this
belief passes away.   It is not that the fairy tales are refuted
or explained away, or even narrowly scrutinised.   It is that
the fairies cease to appear.   From the uniformity of this
decline, we infer that fairy tales are the normal product of
a certain condition of the imagination; and this position is
raised to a moral certainty when we find that the decadence
of fairy tales is but one of a long series of similar transformations.

When the savage looks around upon the world and begins
to form his theories of existence, he falls at once into three
great errors, which become the first principles of his subse-

quent opinions.  He believes that this earth is the centre of
the universe, and that all the bodies encircling it are intended
for its use; that the disturbances and dislocations it presents,
and especially the master curse of death, are connected with
some event in his history, and also that the numerous phenomena and natural vicissitudes he sees around him are due
to direct and isolated volitions, either of spirits presiding
over, or of intelligences inherent in, matter.  Around these
leading conceptions a crowd of particular legends speedily
cluster.  If a stone falls beside him, he naturally infers that
some one has thrown it.  If it be an aërolite, it is attributed to some celestial being.  Believing that each comet,
tempest, or pestilence results from a direct and isolated act,
he proceeds to make theories regarding the motives that
have induced his spiritual persecutors to assail him, and the
methods by which he may assuage their anger.  Finding
numerous distinct trains or series of phenomena, he invents
for each appropriate presiding spirits.  Miracles are to him
neither strange events nor violations of natural law, but
simply the unveiling or manifestation of the ordinary government of the world.

With these broad intellectual conceptions several minor
influences concur.  A latent fetichism, which is betrayed in
that love of direct personification, or of applying epithets
derived from sentient beings to inanimate nature, which
appears so largely in all poetry and eloquence, and especially
in those of an early period of society, is the root of a great
part of our opinions.  If—to employ a very familiar illustration—the most civilised and rational of mankind will
observe his own emotions, when by some accident he has
struck his head violently against a door-post, he will probably
find that his first exclamation was not merely of pain but of
anger, and of anger directed against the wood.  In a moment
reason checks the emotion ; but if he observes carefully his
own feelings, he may easily convince himself of the uncon

scious fetichism which is latent in his mind, and which, in the case of a child or a savage, displays itself without reserve. Man instinctively ascribes volition to whatever powerfully affects him. The feebleness of his imagination conspires with other causes to prevent an uncivilised man from rising above the conception of an anthropomorphic Deity, and the capricious or isolated acts of such a being form his exact notion of miracles. The same feebleness of imagination makes him clothe all intellectual tendencies, all conflicting emotions, all forces, passions, or fancies, in material forms. His mind naturally translates the conflict between opposing feelings into a history of the combat between rival spirits. A vast accumulation of myths is spontaneously formed—each legend being merely the material expression of a moral fact. The simple love of the wonderful, and the complete absence of all critical spirit, aid the formation.

In this manner we find that in certain stages of society, and under the action of the influences I have stated, an accretion of miraculous legends is naturally formed around prominent personages or institutions. We look for them as we look for showers in April, or for harvest in autumn. We can very rarely show with any confidence the precise manner in which a particular legend is created or the nucleus of truth it contains, but we can analyse the general causes that have impelled men towards the miraculous; we can show that these causes have never failed to produce the effect, and we can trace the gradual alteration of mental conditions invariably accompanying the decline of the belief. When men are destitute of critical spirit, when the notion of uniform law is yet unborn, and when their imaginations are still incapable of rising to abstract ideas, histories of miracles are always formed and always believed, and they continue to flourish and to multiply until these conditions have altered. Miracles cease when men cease to believe and to expect them. In periods that are equally credulous, they multiply or

diminish in proportion to the intensity with which the imagination is directed to theological topics. A comparison of the
histories of the most different nations shows the mythical
period to have been common to all; and we may trace in
many quarters substantially the same miracles, though varied
by national characteristics, and with a certain local cast and
colouring. As among the Alps the same shower falls as rain
in the sunny valleys, and as snow among the lofty peaks, so
the same intellectual conceptions which in one moral latitude
take the form of nymphs, or fairies, or sportive legends, appear in another as dæmons or appalling apparitions. Sometimes we can discover the precise natural fact which the
superstition had misread. Thus, epilepsy, the phenomenon
of nightmare, and that form of madness which leads men
to imagine themselves transformed into some animal, are,
doubtless, the explanation of many tales of demoniacal possession, of incubi, and of lycanthropy. In other cases we may
detect a single error, such as the notion that the sky is close
to the earth, or that the sun revolves around the globe, which
had suggested the legend. But more frequently we can give
only a general explanation, enabling us to assign these legends
to their place, as the normal expression of a certain stage of
knowledge or intellectual power; and this explanation is
their refutation. We do not say that they are impossible, or
even that they are not authenticated by as much evidence as
many facts we believe. We only say that, in certain conditions of society, illusions of the kind inevitably appear. No
one can prove that there are no such things as ghosts; but if
a man whose brain is reeling with fever declares that he has
seen one, we have no great difficulty in forming an opinion
about his assertion.

The gradual decadence of miraculous narratives which
accompanies advancing civilisation may be chiefly traced to
three causes. The first is that general accuracy of observation
and of statement which all education tends more or less to

produce, which checks the amplifications of the undisciplined imagination, and is speedily followed by a much stronger moral feeling on the subject of truth than ever exists in ι r de civilisation. The second is an increased power of abstraction, which is likewise a result of general education, and which, by correcting the early habit of personifying all phenomena, destroys one of the most prolific sources of legends, and closes the mythical period of history. The third is the progress of physical science, which gradually dispels that conception of a universe governed by perpetual and arbitrary interference, from which, for the most part, these legends originally sprang. The whole history of physical science is one continued revelation of the reign of law. The same law that governs the motions of a grain of dust, or the light of the glowworm's lamp, is shown to preside over the march of the most majestic planet or the fire of the most distant sun. Countless phenomena, which were for centuries universally believed to be the results of spiritual agency, portents of calamity, or acts of Divine vengeance, have been one by one explained, have been shown to rise from blind physical causes, to be capable of prediction, or amenable to human remedies. Forms of madness which were for ages supposed to result from possession, are treated successfully in our hospitals. The advent of the comet is predicted. The wire invented by the sceptic Franklin defends the crosses on our churches from the lightning stroke of heaven. Whether we examine the course of the planets or the world of the animalculæ; to whatever field of physical nature our research is turned, the uniform, invariable result of scientific enquiry is to show that even the most apparently irregular and surprising phenomena are governed by natural antecedents, and are parts of one great connected system. From this vast concurrence of evidence, from this uniformity of experience in so many spheres, there arises in the minds of scientific men a conviction, amounting to absolute moral certainty, that the whole course of physical

nature is governed by law, that the notion of the perpetual
interference of the Deity with some particular classes of its
phenomena is false and unscientific, and that the theological
habit of interpreting the catastrophes of nature as Divine
warnings or punishments, or disciplines, is a baseless and a
pernicious superstition.

The effects of these discoveries upon miraculous legends are
of various kinds. In the first place, a vast number which
have clustered around the notion of the irregularity of some
phenomenon which is proved to be regular—such as the
innumerable accounts collected by the ancients to corroborate
their opinion of the portentous nature of comets—are directly
overthrown. In the next place, the revelation of the inter-
dependence of phenomena greatly increases the improbability
of some legends which it does not actually disprove. Thus,
when men believed the sun to be simply a lamp revolving
around and lighting our world, they had no great difficulty
in believing that it was one day literally arrested in its
course, to illuminate an army which was engaged in mas-
sacring its enemies; but the case became different when it
was perceived that the sun was the centre of a vast system
of worlds, which a suspension of the earth's motion must have
reduced to chaos, without a miracle extending through it all.
Thus, again, the old belief that some animals became for the
first time carnivorous in consequence of the sin of Adam, appeared tolerably simple so long as this revolution was supposed to be only a change of habits or of tastes; but it
became more difficult of belief when it was shown to involve
a change of teeth; and the difficulty was, I suppose, still
further aggravated when it was proved that, every animal
having digestive organs specially adapted to its food, these
also must have been changed.

In the last place, physical science exercises a still wider
influence by destroying what I have called the centre ideas
out of which countless particular theories were evolved, of

which they were the natural expression, and upon which their permanence depends. Proving that our world is not the centre of the universe, but is a simple planet, revolving with many others around a common sun; proving that the disturbances and sufferings of the world do not result from an event which occurred but 6,000 years ago; that long before that period the earth was dislocated by the most fearful convulsions; that countless generations of sentient animals, and also, as recent discoveries appear conclusively to show, of men, not only lived but died; proving, by an immense accumulation of evidence, that the notion of a universe governed by isolated acts of special intervention is untrue—physical science had given new directions to the currents of the imagination, supplied the judgment with new measures of probability, and thus affected the whole circle of our beliefs.

With most men, however, the transition is as yet but imperfectly accomplished, and that part of physical nature which science has hitherto failed to explain is regarded as a sphere of special interposition. Thus, multitudes who recognise the fact that the celestial phenomena are subject to inflexible law, imagine that the dispensation of rain is in some sense the result of arbitrary interpositions, determined by the conduct of mankind. Near the equator, it is true, it is tolerably constant and capable of prediction; but in proportion as we recede from the equator, the rainfall becomes more variable, and consequently, in the eyes of some, supernatural, and although no scientific man has the faintest doubt that it is governed by laws as inflexible as those which determine the motions of the planets, yet because, owing to the great complexity of the determining causes, we are unable fully to explain them, it is still customary to speak of 'plagues of rain and water' sent on account of our sins, and of 'scarcity and dearth, which we most justly suffer for our iniquity.' Corresponding language is employed about the forms of

disease and death which science has but imperfectly ex
plained.    If men are employed in some profession which
compels them to inhale steel filings or noxious vapours, or if
they live in a pestilential marsh, the diseases that result
from these conditions are not regarded as a judgment or a
discipline, for the natural cause is obvious and decisive.    But
if the conditions that produced the disease are very subtle
and very complicated; if physicians are incapable of tracing
with certainty its nature or its effects; if, above all, it
assumes the character of an epidemic, it is continually treated
as a Divine judgment.    The presumption against this view
arises not only from the fact that, in exact proportion as
medical science advances, diseases are proved to be the necessary consequence of physical conditions, but also from many
characteristics of unexplained disease which unequivocally
prove it to be natural.    Thus, cholera, which is frequently
treated according to the theological method, varies with the
conditions of temperature, is engendered by particular forms
of diet, follows the course of rivers, yields in some measure to
medical treatment, can be aggravated or mitigated by courses
of conduct that have no relation to vice or virtue, takes its
victims indiscriminately from all grades of morals or opinion.
Usually, when definite causes are assigned for a supposed
judgment, they lead to consequences of the most grotesque
absurdity.    Thus, when a deadly and mysterious disease fell
upon the cattle of England, some divines, not content with
treating it as a judgment, proceeded to trace it to certain
popular writings containing what were deemed heterodox
opinions about the Pentateuch, or about the eternity of punishment.    It may be true that the disease was imported from
a country where such speculations are unknown; that the
authors objected to had no cattle; that the farmers, who
chiefly suffered by the disease, were for the most part absolutely unconscious of the existence of these books, and if they

knew them would have indignantly repudiated them ; that the town populations, who chiefly read them, were only affected indirectly by a rise in the price of food, which falls with perfect impartiality upon the orthodox and upon the heterodox ; that particular counties were peculiarly sufferers, without being at all conspicuous for their scepticism ; that similar writings appeared in former periods, without cattle being in any respect the worse ; and that, at the very period at which the plague was raging, other countries, in which far more audacious speculations were rife, enjoyed an absolute immunity. In the face of all these consequences, the theory has been confidently urged and warmly applauded.

It is not, I think, sufficiently observed how large a proportion of such questions are capable of a strictly inductive method of discussion. If it is said that plagues or pestilences are sent as a punishment of error or of vice, the assertion must be tested by a comprehensive examination of the history of plagues on the one hand, and of periods of great vice and heterodoxy on the other. If it be said that an influence more powerful than any military agency directs the course of battles, the action of this force must be detected as we would detect electricity, or any other force, by experiment. If the attribute of infallibility be ascribed to a particular Church, an inductive reasoner will not be content with enquiring how far an infallible Church would be a desirable thing, or how far certain ancient words may be construed as a prediction of its appearance ; he will examine, by a wide and careful survey of ecclesiastical history, whether this Church has actually been immutable and consistent in its teaching, whether it has never been affected by the ignorance or the passion of the age ; whether its influence has uniformly been exerted on the side which proved to be true ; whether it has never supported by its authority scientific views which were afterwards demonstrated to be false, or countenanced and consolidated popular errors, or thrown obstacles in the path of those who were afterwards recognised as the enlighteners of mankind. If ecclesiastical deliberations are said to be specially inspired or directed by an illuminating and supernatural power, we should examine whether the councils and convocations of clergymen exhibit a degree and harmony of wisdom that cannot reasonably be accounted for by the play of our unassisted faculties. If institutions are said to owe their growth to special supernatural agencies, distinct from the ordinary system of natural laws, we must examine whether their courses are so striking and so peculiar that natural laws fail to explain them. Whenever, as in the case of a battle, very many influences concur to the result, it will frequently happen that that result will baffle our predictions. It will also happen that strange coincidences, such as the frequent recurrence of the same number in a game of chance, will occur. But there are limits to these variations from what we regard as probable. If, in throwing the dice, we uniformly attained the same number, or if in war the army which was most destitute of all military advantages was uniformly victorious, we should readily infer that some special cause was operating to produce the result. We must remember, too, that in every great historical crisis the prevalence of either side will bring with it a long train of consequences, and that we only see one side of the picture. If Hannibal, after his victory at Cannæ, had captured and burnt Rome, the vast series of results that have followed from the ascendancy of the Roman Empire would never have taken place, but the supremacy of a maritime, commercial, and comparatively pacific power would have produced an entirely different series, which would have formed the basis and been the essential condition of all the subsequent progress; a civilisation, the type and character of which it is now impossible to conjecture, would have arisen, and its theologians would probably have regarded the career of Hannibal as one of the most manifest instances of special interposition on record.

If we would form sound opinions on these matters, we must take a very wide and impartial survey of the phenomena of history. We must examine whether events have tended in a given direction with a uniformity or a persistence that is not naturally explicable. We must examine not only the facts that corroborate our theory, but also those which oppose it.

That such a method is not ordinarily adopted must be manifest to all. As Bacon said, men 'mark the hits, but not the misses;' they collect industriously the examples in which many, and sometimes improbable, circumstances have converged to a result which they consider good, and they simply leave out of their consideration the circumstances that tend in the opposite direction. They expatiate with triumph upon the careers of emperors who have been the unconscious pioneers or agents in some great movement of human progress, but they do not dwell upon those whose genius was expended in a hopeless resistance, or upon those who, like Bajazet or Tamerlane, having inflicted incalculable evils upon mankind, passed away, leaving no enduring fruit behind them. A hundred missionaries start upon an enterprise, the success of which appears exceedingly improbable. Ninety-nine perish and are forgotten. One missionary succeeds, and his success is attributed to supernatural interference, because the probabilities were so greatly against him. It is observed that a long train of political or military events ensured the triumph of Protestantism in certain nations and periods. It is forgotten that another train of events destroyed the same faith in other lands, and paralysed the efforts of its noblest martyrs. We are told of showers of rain that followed public prayer; but we are not told how often prayers for rain proved abortive, or how much longer than usual the dry weather had already continued when they were

offered.[1]   As the old philosopher observed, the votive tablets
of those who escaped are suspended in the temple, while those
who were shipwrecked are forgotten.

Unfortunately, these inconsistencies do not arise simply
from intellectual causes.   A feeling which was intended to
be religious, but which was in truth deeply the reverse, once
led men to shrink from examining the causes of some of the
more terrible of physical phenomena, because it was thought
that these should be deemed special instances of Divine interference, and should, therefore, be regarded as too sacred for
investigation.[2]   In the world of physical science this mode
of thought has almost vanished, but a corresponding sentiment
may be often detected in the common judgments of history.
Very many well-meaning men—censuring the pursuit of
truth in the name of the God of Truth—while they regard
it as commendable and religious to collect facts illustrating

---

[1] The following is a good specimen of the language which may
still be uttered, apparently without exciting any protest, from the
pulpit in one of the great centres
of English learning: 'But we
have prayed, and not been heard,
at least in this present visitation.
Have we deserved to be heard?
In former visitations it was observed commonly how the cholera
lessened from the day of the public
humiliation.   When we dreaded
famine   from   long - continued
drought, on the morning of our
prayers the heaven over our head
was of brass; the clear burning
sky showed no token of change.
Men looked with awe at its unmitigated clearness.   In the evening was the cloud like a man's
hand; the relief was come.'  (And
then the author adds, in a note):
'This describes what I myself
saw on the Sunday morning in

Oxford, on returning from the
early communion at St. Mary's at
eight. There was no visible change
till the evening.'—Pusey's *Miracles
of Prayer*, preached at Oxford,
1866.

[2] E.g.: 'A master of philosophy,
travelling with others on the way,
when a fearful thunderstorm arose,
checked the fear of his fellows, and
discoursed to them of the natural
reasons of that uproar in the clouds,
and those sudden flashes where-
with they seemed (out of the ignorance of causes) to be too much
affrighted: in the midst of his
philosophical discourse he was
struck dead with the dreadful
eruption which he slighted. What
could this be but the finger of that
God who will have his works
rather entertained with wonder and
trembling than with curious scan-
ning?'—Bishop Hall, *The Invisible World*, § vi.

or corroborating the theological theory of life, consider it
irreverent and wrong to apply to those facts, and to that
theory, the ordinary severity of inductive reasoning.

What I have written is not in any degree inconsistent
with the belief that, by the dispensation of Providence, moral
causes have a natural and often overwhelming influence upon
happiness and upon success, nor yet with the belief that our
moral nature enters into a very real, constant, and immediate
contact with a higher power. Nor does it at all disprove the
possibility of Divine interference with the order even of
physical nature. A world governed by special acts of intervention, such as that which mediæval theologians imagined,
is perfectly conceivable, though it is probable that most impartial enquirers will convince themselves that this is not the
system of the planet we inhabit ; and if any instance of such
interference be sufficiently attested, it should not be rejected
as intrinsically impossible. It is, however, the fundamental
error of most writers on miracles, that they confine their
attention to two points—the possibility of the fact, and the
nature of the evidence. There is a third element, which in
these questions is of capital importance : the predisposition
of men in certain stages of society towards the miraculous,
which is so strong that miraculous stories are then invariably
circulated and credited, and which makes an amount of
evidence that would be quite sufficient to establish a natural
fact, altogether inadequate to establish a supernatural one.
The positions for which I have been contending are that a
perpetual interference of the Deity with the natural course
of events is the earliest and simplest notion of miracles, and
that this notion, which is implied in so many systems of belief, arose in part from an ignorance of the laws of nature,
and in part also from an incapacity for inductive reasoning,
which led men merely to collect facts coinciding with their
preconceived opinions, without attending to those that were
inconsistent with them. By this method there is no super-

25

stition that could not be defended.   Volumes have been
written giving perfectly authentic histories of wars, famines,
and pestilences that followed the appearance of comets.  There
is not an cmen, not a prognostic, however childish, that has
not in the infinite variety of events, been occasionally verified, and to minds that are under the influence of a superstitious imagination these occasional verifications more than
outweigh all the instances of error.   Simple knowledge is
wholly insufficient to correct the disease.   No one is so firmly
convinced of the reality of lucky and unlucky days, and of
supernatural portents, as the sailor, who has spent his life in
watching the deep, and has learnt to read with almost un-
erring skill the promise of the clouds.   No one is more persuaded of the superstitions about fortune than the habitual
gambler.   Sooner than abandon his theory, there is no extravagance of hypothesis to which the superstitious man will
not resort.   The ancients were convinced that dreams were
usually supernatural.   If the dream was verified, this was
plainly a prophecy.   If the event was the exact opposite of
what the dream foreshadowed, the latter was still supernatural,
for it was a recognised principle that dreams should sometimes be interpreted by contraries.   If the dream bore no
relation to subsequent events, unless it were transformed
into a fantastic allegory, it was still supernatural, for allegory
was one of the most ordinary forms of revelation.   If no ingenuity of interpretation could find a prophetic meaning in
a dream, its supernatural character was even then not necessarily destroyed ; for Homer said there was a special portal
through which deceptive visions passed into the mind, and
the Fathers declared that it was one of the occupations of
the dæmons to perplex and bewilder us with unmeaning
dreams.

     To estimate aright the force of the predisposition to the
miraculous should be one of the first tasks of the enquirer into
its reality ; and no one, I think, can examine the subject with

impartiality without arriving at the conclusion that in many
periods of history it has been so strong as to accumulate
around pure delusions an amount of evidence far greater than
would be sufficient to establish even improbable natural
facts. Through the entire duration of Pagan Rome, it was
regarded as an unquestionable truth, established by the most
ample experience, that prodigies of various kinds announced
every memorable event, and that sacrifices had the power of
mitigating or arresting calamity. In the Republic, the Senate
itself officially verified and explained the prodigies.[1] In the
Empire there is not an historian, from Tacitus down to the
meanest writer in the Augustan history, who was not convinced that numerous prodigies foreshadowed the accession
and death of every sovereign, and every great catastrophe
that fell upon the people. Cicero could say with truth that
there was not a single nation of antiquity, from the polished
Greek to the rudest savage, which did not admit the existence
of a real art enabling men to foretell the future, and that the
splendid temples of the oracles, which for so many centuries
commanded the reverence of mankind, sufficiently attested
the intensity of the belief.[2] The reality of the witch miracles
was established by a critical tribunal, which, however imperfect, was at least the most searching then existing in the
world, by the judicial decisions of the law courts of every
European country, supported by the unanimous voice of
public opinion, and corroborated by the investigation of some
of the ablest men during several centuries. The belief that
the king's touch can cure scrofula flourished in the most
brilliant periods of English history.[3] It was unshaken by

[1] Sir C. Lewis *On the Credibility
of Roman Hist.* vol. i. p. 50.
[2] Cic. *De Divin.* lib. i. c. 1.
[3] 'The days on which the
miracle [of the king's touch] was
to be wrought were fixed at sittings
of the Privy Council, and were
solemnly notified by the clergy
to all the parish churches of the
realm. When the appointed time
came, several divines in full canoni-
cals stood round the canopy of
state. The surgeon of the royal
household introduced the sick. A

the most numerous and public experiments. It was asserted by the privy council, by the bishops of two religions, by the general voice of the clergy in the palmiest days of the English Church, by the University of Oxford, and by the enthusiastic assent of the people. It survived the ages of the Reformation, of Bacon, of Milton, and of Hobbes. It was by no means extinct in the age of Locke, and would probably have lasted still longer, had not the change of dynasty at the Revolution assisted the tardy scepticism.[1] Yet there is now

---

passage of Mark xvi. was read. When the words "They shall lay their hands on the sick and they shall recover,"had been pronounced, there was a pause and one of the sick was brought to the king. His Majesty stroked the ulcers. . . . Then came the Epistle, &c. The Service may still be found in the Prayer Books of the reign of Anne. Indeed, it was not until some time after the accession of George I. that the University of Oxford ceased to reprint the office of healing, together with the Liturgy. Theologians of eminent learning, ability, and virtue gave the sanction of their authority to this mummery, and, what is stranger still, medical men of high note believed, or affected to believe, it. . . . Charles II., in the course of his reign, touched near 100,000 persons. . . . In 1682 he performed the rite 8,500 times. In 1684 the throng was such that six or seven of the sick were trampled to death. James, in one of his progresses, touched 800 persons in the choir of the cathedral of Chester.'—Macaulay's *History of England*, c. xiv.

[1] One of the surgeons of Charles II. named John Brown, whose official duty it was to superintend the ceremony, and who assures us that he has witnessed many thousands touched, has written an extremely curious account of it, called *Charisma Basilicon* (London, 1684). This miraculous power existed exclusively in the English and French royal families, being derived, in the first, from Edward the Confessor, in the second, from St. Lewis. A surgeon attested the reality of the disease before the miracle was performed. The king hung a riband with a gold coin round the neck of the person touched; but Brown thinks the gold, though possessing great virtue, was not essential to the cure. He had known cases where the cured person had sold, or ceased to wear, the medal, and his disease returned. The gift was unimpaired by the Reformation, and an obdurate Catholic was converted on finding that Elizabeth, after the Pope's excommunication, could cure his scrofula. Francis I. cured many persons when prisoner in Spain. Charles I., when a prisoner, cured a man by his simple benediction, the Puritans not permitting him to touch him. His blood had the same efficacy; and Charles II., when an exile in the Netherlands, still retained it. There were, how-

scarcely an educated man who will defend these miracles. Considered abstractedly, indeed, it is perfectly conceivable that Providence might have announced coming events by prodigies, or imparted to some one a miraculous power, or permitted evil spirits to exist among mankind and assist them in their enterprises. The evidence establishing these miracles is cumulative, and it is immeasurably greater than the evidence of many natural facts, such as the earthquakes at Antioch, which no one would dream of questioning. We disbelieve the miracles, because an overwhelming experience proves that in certain intellectual conditions, and under the influence of certain errors which we are enabled to trace, superstitions of this order invariably appear and flourish, and that, when these intellectual conditions have passed, the prodigies as invariably cease, and the whole fabric of superstition melts silently away.

It is extremely difficult for an ordinary man, who is little conversant with the writings of the past, and who unconsciously transfers to other ages the critical spirit of his own, to realise the fact that histories of the most grotesquely extravagant nature could, during the space of many centuries, be continually propounded without either provoking the smallest question or possessing the smallest truth. We may, however, understand something of this credulity when we remember the diversion of the ancient mind from physical science to speculative

ever, some 'Atheists, Sadducees, and ill-conditioned Pharisees' who even then disbelieved it; and Brown gives the letter of one who went, a complete sceptic, to satisfy his friends, and came away cured and converted. It was popularly, but Brown says erroneously, believed that the touch was peculiarly efficacious on Good Friday. An official register was kept, for every month in the reign of Charles II., of the persons touched, but two years and a half appear to be wanting. The smallest number touched in one year was 2,983 (in 1669); the total, in the whole reign, 92,107. Brown gives numbers of specific cases with great detail. Shakspeare has noticed the power (*Macbeth*, Act iv. Scene 3). Dr. Johnson, when a boy, was touched by Queen Anne; but at that time few persons, except Jacobites, believed the miracle.

philosophy; the want of the many checks upon error which printing affords; the complete absence of that habit of cautious, experimental research which Bacon and his contemporaries infused into modern philosophy; and, in Christian times, the theological notion that the spirit of belief is a virtue, and the spirit of scepticism a sin. We must remember, too, that before men had found the key to the motions of the heavenly bodies—before the false theory of the vortices and the true theory of gravitation—when the multitude of apparently capricious phenomena was very great, the notion that the world was governed by distinct and isolated influences was that which appeared most probable even to the most rational intellect. In such a condition of knowledge—which was that of the most enlightened days of the Roman Empire— the hypothesis of universal law was justly regarded as a rash and premature generalisation. Every enquirer was confronted with innumerable phenomena that were deemed plainly miraculous. When Lucretius sought to banish the supernatural from the universe, he was compelled to employ much ingenuity in endeavouring to explain, by a natural law, why a miraculous fountain near the temple of Jupiter Ammon was hot by night and cold by day, and why the temperature of wells was higher in winter than in summer.[1] Eclipses were supposed by the populace to foreshadow calamity; but the Roman soldiers believed that by beating drums and cymbals they could cause the moon's disc to regain its brightness.[2]    In obedience to dreams, the great Emperor

[1] Lucretius, lib. vi. The poet says there are certain seeds of fire in the earth, around the water, which the sun attracts to itself, but which the cold of the night represses, and forces back upon the water.

The fountain of Jupiter Ammon, and many others that were deemed miraculous, are noticed by Pliny, *Hist. Nat.* ii. 106.

'Fly not yet; the fount that played
In times of old through Ammon's shade,
Though icy cold by day it ran,
Yet still, like souls of mirth, began
To burn when night was near.'—
    Moore's *Melodies.*

[2] Tacit. *Annal.* i. 28. Long afterwards, the people of Turin were accustomed to greet every

Augustus went begging money through the streets of Rome,[1] and the historian who records the act himself wrote to Pliny, entreating the postponement of a trial.[2] The stroke of the lightning was an augury,[3] and its menace was directed especially against the great, who cowered in abject terror during a thunder-storm. Augustus used to guard himself against thunder by wearing the skin of a sea-calf.[4] Tiberius, who professed to be a complete freethinker, had greater faith in laurel leaves.[5] Caligula was accustomed during a thunder-storm to creep beneath his bed.[6] During the games in honour of Julius Cæsar, a comet appearing for seven days in the sky, the people believed it to be the soul of the dead,[7] and a temple was erected in its honour.[8] Sometimes we find this credulity broken by curious inconsistencies of belief, or semi-rationalistic explanations. Livy, who relates with perfect faith innumerable prodigies, has observed, never-

---

eclipse with loud cries, and St. Maximus of Turin energetically combated their superstition. (Ceillier, *Hist. des Auteurs sacrés*, tome xiv. p. 607.)

[1] Suet. *Aug.* xci.

[2] See the answer of the younger Pliny (*Ep.* i. 18), suggesting that dreams should often be interpreted by contraries. A great many instances of dreams that were believed to have been verified are given in Cic. (*De Divinatione*, lib. i.) and Valerius Maximus (lib. i. c. vii.). Marcus Aurelius (Capitolinus) was said to have appeared to many persons after his death in dreams, and predicted the future.

[3] The augurs had noted eleven kinds of lightning with different significations. (Pliny, *Hist. Nat.* ii. 53.) Pliny says all nations agree in clapping their hands when it lightens (xxviii. 5). Cicero very shrewdly remarked that the

Roman considered lightning a good omen when it shone upon his left, while the Greeks and barbarians believed it to be auspicious when it was upon the right. (Cic. *De Divinat.* ii. 39.) When Constantine prohibited all other forms of magic, he especially authorised that which was intended to avert hail and lightning. (*Cod. Theod.* lib. ix. tit. xvi. l. 3.)

[4] Suet. *Aug.* xc.

[5] Ibid. *Tiber.* lxix. The virtue of laurel leaves, and of the skin of a sea-calf, as preservatives against lightning, are noticed by Pliny (*Hist. Nat.* ii. 56), who also says (xv. 40) that the laurel leaf is believed to have a natural antipathy to fire, which it shows by its angry crackling when in contact with that element.

[6] Suet. *Calig.* ii.

[7] Suet. *Jul. Cæs.* lxxxviii.

[8] Plin. *Hist. Nat.* ii. 23.

theless, that the more prodigies are believed, the more they are announced.[1] Those who admitted most fully the reality of the oracles occasionally represented them as natural, contending that a prophetic faculty was innate in all men, though dormant in most; that it might be quickened into action by sleep, by a pure and ascetic life, or in the prostration that precedes death, or in the delirium produced by certain vapours; and that the gradual enfeebling of the last was the cause of the cessation of the oracles.[2]    Earthquakes

---

[1] 'Prodigia eo anno multa nuntiata sunt, quæ quo magis credebant simplices ac religiosi homines eo plura nuntiabantur' (xxiv. 10). Compare with this the remark of Cicero on the oracles: 'Quando autem illa vis evanuit? An postquam homines minus creduli esse cœperunt?' (*De Div.* ii. 57.)

[2] This theory, which is developed at length by the Stoic, in the first book of the *De Divinatione* of Cicero, grew out of the pantheistic notion that the human soul is a part of the Deity, and therefore by nature a participator in the Divine attribute of prescience. The soul, however, was crushed by the weight of the body; and there were two ways of evoking its prescience—the ascetic way, which attenuates the body, and the magical way, which stimulates the soul. Apollonius declared that his power of prophecy was not due to magic, but solely to his abstinence from animal food. (Philost. *Ap. of Tyana,* viii. 5.) Among those who believed the oracles, there were two theories. The first was that they were inspired by dæmons or spirits of a degree lower than the gods. The second was, that they were due to the action of certain vapours which emanated from the taverns beneath the

temples, and which, by throwing the priestess into a state of delirium, evoked her prophetic powers. The first theory was that of the Platonists, and it was adopted by the Christians, who, however, changed the signification of the word dæmon. The second theory, which appears to be due to Aristotle (Baltus, *Réponse à l'Histoire des Oracles,* p. 132), is noticed by Cic. *De Div.* i. 19; Plin. *H. N.* ii. 95; and others. It is closely allied to the modern belief in clairvoyance. Plutarch, in his treatise on the decline of the oracles, attributes that decline sometimes to the death of the dæmons (who were believed to be mortal), and sometimes to the exhaustion of the vapours. The oracles themselves, according to Porphyry (Fontenelle, *Hist. des Oracles,* pp. 220–222, first ed.), attributed it to the second cause. Iamblichus (*De Myst.* § iii. c. xi.) combines both theories, and both are very clearly stated in the following curious passage: 'Quamquam Platoni credam inter deos atque homines, natura et loco medias quasdam divorum potestates intersitas, easque divinationes cunctas et magorum miracula gubernare. Quin et illud mecum reputo, posse animum humanum, præsertim, puerilem et simplicem,

were believed to result from supernatural interpositions, and
to call for expiatory sacrifices, but at the same time they
had direct natural antecedents. The Greeks believed that
they were caused by subterranean waters, and they accordingly sacrificed to Poseidon. The Romans were uncertain as
to their physical antecedents, and therefore inscribed no
name on the altar of expiation.[1] Pythagoras is said to have
attributed them to the strugglings of the dead.[2] Pliny,
after a long discussion, decided that they were produced by
air forcing itself through fissures of the earth, but he immediately proceeds to assert that they are invariably the
precursors of calamity.[3] The same writer, having recounted
the triumph of astronomers in predicting and explaining
eclipses, bursts into an eloquent apostrophe to those great
men who had thus reclaimed man from the dominion of
superstition, and in high and enthusiastic terms urges them
to pursue still further their labour in breaking the thraldom
of ignorance.[4] A few chapters later he professes his unhesi-
tating belief in the ominous character of comets.[5] The
notions, too, of magic and astrology, were detached from all
theological belief, and might be found among many who were
absolute atheists.[6]

These few examples will be sufficient to show how fully
the Roman soil was prepared for the reception of miraculous
histories, even after the writings of Cicero and Seneca, in the

seu carminum avocamento, sive
odorum delenimento, soporari, et
ad oblivionem præsentium exter-
nari : et paulisper remota corporis
memoria, redigi ac redire ad na-
turam suam, quæ est immortalis
scilicet et divina ; atque ita veluti
quodam sopore futura rerum præ-
sagire.'—Apuleius, *Apolog.*
    [1] Aul. Gell. *Noct.* ii. 28. Florus,
however (*Hist.* i. 19), mentions a
Roman general appeasing the goddess Earth on the occasion of an

earthquake that occurred during a
battle.
    [2] Ælian, *Hist. Var.* iv. 17.
    [3] *Hist. Nat.* ii. 81–86.
    [4] Ibid. ii. 9.
    [5] Ibid. ii. 23.
    [6] I have referred in the last
chapter to a striking passage of
Am. Marcellinus on this combination. The reader may find some
curious instances of the superstitions of Roman sceptics in Cham
pagry, *Les Antonins*, tome iii. p. 46.

brilliant days of Augustus and the Antonines. The feebleness of the uncultivated mind, which cannot rise above
material conceptions, had indeed passed away, the legends of
the popular theology had lost all power over the educated,
but at the same time an absolute ignorance of physical science
and of inductive reasoning remained. The facility of belief
that was manifested by some of the most eminent men,
even on matters that were not deemed supernatural, can only
be realised by those who have an intimate acquaintance with
their works. Thus, to give but a few examples, that great
naturalist whom I have so often cited tells us with the utmost gravity how the fiercest lion trembles at the crowing of
a cock ; [1] how elephants celebrate their religious ceremonies ; [2]
how the stag draws serpents by its breath from their holes,
and then tramples them to death ; [3] how the salamander is
so deadly that the food cooked in water, or the fruit grown
on trees it has touched, are fatal to man ; [4] how, when a ship
is flying before so fierce a tempest that no anchors or chains
can hold it, if only the remora or echinus fastens on its keel,
it is arrested in its course, and remains motionless and rooted
among the waves. [5] On matters that would appear the most
easily verified, he is equally confident. Thus, the human
saliva, he assures us, has many mysterious properties. If a
man, especially when fasting, spits into the throat of a ser-
pent, it is said that the animal speedily dies. [6] It is certain
that to anoint the eyes with spittle is a sovereign remedy
against ophthalmia. [7] If a pugilist, having struck his adver-
sary, spits into his own hand, the pain he caused instantly

---

[1] viii. 19. This is also mentioned by Lucretius.

[2] viii. 1.

[3] viii. 50. This was one of the
reasons why the early Christians
sometimes adopted the stag as a
symbol of Christ.

[4] xxix. 23.

[5] xxxii. 1.

[6] vii. 2.

[7] xxviii. 7. The blind man
restored to sight by Vespasian was
cured by anointing his eyes with
spittle. (Suet. *Vesp.* 7; Tacit.
*Hist.* iv. 81.)

ceases. If he spits into his hand before striking, the blow is the more severe.[1] Aristotle, the greatest naturalist of Greece, had observed that it was a curious fact that on the sea-shore no animal ever dies except during the ebbing of the tide. Several centuries later, Pliny, the greatest naturalist of an empire that was washed by many tidal seas, directed his attention to this statement. He declared that, after careful observations which had been made in Gaul, it had been found to be inaccurate, for what Aristotle stated of all animals was in fact only true of man.[2] It was in 1727 and the two following years, that scientific observations made at Rochefort and at Brest finally dissipated the delusion.[3]

Volumes might be filled with illustrations of how readily, in the most enlightened days of the Roman Empire, strange, and especially miraculous, tales were believed, even under circumstances that would appear to give every facility for the detection of the imposture. In the field of the supernatural, however, it should be remembered that a movement, which I have traced in the last chapter, had produced a very exceptional amount of credulity during the century and a half that preceded the conversion of Constantine. Neither the writings of Cicero and Seneca, nor even those of Pliny and Plutarch, can be regarded as fair samples of the belief of the educated. The Epicurean philosophy which rejected, the Academic philosophy which doubted, and the Stoic philosophy which simplified and sublimated superstition, had alike disappeared. The 'Meditations' of Marcus Aurelius closed the period of Stoical influence, and the 'Dialogues' of Lucian were the last solitary protest of expiring scepticism.[4] The aim of the philosophy of Cicero had been to ascertain truth

---

[1] Ibid. The custom of spitting in the hand before striking still exists among pugilists.

[2] ii. 101.

[3] Legendre, Traité de l'Opinion, tome ii. p. 17. The superstition is, however, said still to linger in many sea-coast towns.

[4] Lucian is believed to have died about two years before Marcus Aurelius.

by the free exercise of the critical powers. The aim of the Pythagorean philosophy was to attain the state of ecstasy, and to purify the mind by religious rites. Every philosopher soon plunged into magical practices, and was encircled, in the eyes of his disciples, with a halo of legend. Apollonius of Tyana, whom the Pagans opposed to Christ, had raised the dead, healed the sick, cast out devils, freed a young man from a lamia or vampire with whom he was enamoured, prophesied, seen in one country events that were occurring in another, and filled the world with the fame of his miracles and of his sanctity.[1] A similar power, notwithstanding his own disclaimer, was popularly attributed to the Platonist Apuleius.[2]

---

[1] See his very curious Life by Philostratus. This Life was written at the request of Julia Domna, the wife of Septimus Severus, whether or not with the intention of opposing the Gospel narrative is a question still fiercely discussed. Among the most recent Church historians, Pressensé maintains the affirmative, and Neander the negative. Apollonius was born at nearly the same time as Christ, but outlived Domitian. The traces of his influence are widely spread through the literature of the empire. Eunapius calls him ''Aπολλώνιος ὁ ἐκ Τυάνων, οὐκέτι φιλόσοφος ἀλλ' ἦν τι θεῶν τε καὶ ἀνθρώπου μέσον.' —*Lives of the Sophists.* Xiphilin relates (lxvii. 18) the story, told also by Philostratus, how Apollonius, being at Ephesus, saw the assassination of Domitian at Rome. Alexander Severus placed (*Lampridius Severus*) the statue of Apollonius with those of Orpheus, Abraham, and Christ, for worship in his oratory. Aurelian was reported to have been diverted from his intention of destroying Tyana by the ghost of the philosopher,

who appeared in his tent, rebuked him, and saved the city (Vopiscus, *Aurelian*); and, lastly, the Pagan philosopher Hierocles wrote a book opposing Apollonius to Christ, which was answered by Eusebius. The Fathers of the fourth century always spoke of him as a great magician. Some curious passages on the subject are collected by M. Chassang, in the introduction to his French translation of the work of Philostratus.

[2] See his defence against the charge of magic. Apuleius, who was at once a brilliant rhetorician, the writer of an extremely curious novel (*The Metamorphoses, or Golden Ass*), and of many other works, and an indefatigable student of the religious mysteries of his time, lived through the reigns of Hadrian and his two successors. After his death his fame was for about a century apparently eclipsed; and it has been noticed as very remarkable that Tertullian, who lived a generation after Apuleius, and who, like him, was a Carthaginian, has never even mentioned him. During the fourth century his reputation re-

Lucian has left us a detailed account of the impostures by
which the philosopher Alexander endeavoured to acquire the
fame of a miracle-worker.[1]   When a magician plotted against
Plotinus, his spells recoiled miraculously against himself; and
when an Egyptian priest endeavoured by incantations to evoke
the guardian dæmon of the philosopher, instead of a dæmon
the temple of Isis was irradiated by the presence of a god.[2]
Porphyry was said to have expelled an evil dæmon from a
bath.[3]   It was reported among his disciples that when Iamblichus prayed he was raised (like the saints of another creed)
ten cubits from the ground, and that his body and his dress
assumed a golden hue.[4]   It was well known that he had at
Gadara drawn forth from the waters of two fountains their
guardian spirits, and exhibited them in bodily form to his
disciples.[5]   A woman named Sospitra had been visited by two
spirits under the form of aged Chaldeans, and had been endowed with a transcendent beauty and with a superhuman
knowledge.   Raised above all human frailties, save only love
and death, she was able to see at once the deeds which were
done in every land, and the people, dazzled by her beauty and
her wisdom, ascribed to her a share of the omnipresence of
the Deity.[6]

Christianity floated into the Roman Empire on the wave
of credulity that brought with it this long train of Oriental

vived, and Lactantius, St. Jerome,
and St. Augustine relate that many
miracles were attributed to him,
and that he was placed by the
Pagans on a level with Christ, and
regarded by some as even a greater
magician.   See the sketch of his
life by M. Bétolaud prefixed to the
Panckoucke edition of his works.
[1] *Life of Alexander*.   There is
an extremely curious picture of the
religious jugglers, who were wandering about the Empire, in the
eighth and ninth books of the

*Metamorphoses* of Apuleius.   See,
too, Juvenal, *Sat.* vi. 510–585.
[2] Porphyry's *Life of Plotinus*.
[3] Eunapius, *Porph.*
[4] Ibid. *Iamb.*   Iamblichus himself only laughed at the report.
[5] Eunapius, *Iamb.*
[6] See her life in Eunapius,
*Œdescus.*   Ælian and the rhetorician Aristides are also full of the
wildest prodigies.   There is an interesting dissertation on this subject in Friedlænder (*Trad. Franc.*
tome iv. p. 177–186).

superstitions and legends.   In its moral aspect it was broadly
distinguished from the systems around it, but its miracles
were accepted by both friend and foe as the ordinary accom-
paniments of religious teaching.   The Jews, in the eyes of
the Pagans, had long been proverbial for their credulity,[1] and
the Christians inherited a double measure of their reputation.
Nor is it possible to deny that in the matter of the miraculous the reputation was deserved.   Among the Pagans the
theory of Euhemerus, who believed the gods to be but deified
men, had been the stronghold of the Sceptics, while the
Platonic notion of dæmons was adopted by the more believing
philosophers.   The Christian teachers combined both theories,
maintaining that deceased kings had originally supplied the
names of the deities, but that malevolent dæmons had taken
their places; and without a single exception the Fathers
maintained the reality of the Pagan miracles as fully as their
own.[2]   The oracles, as we have seen, had been ridiculed and
rejected by numbers of the philosophers, but the Christians
unanimously admitted their reality.   They appealed to a long
series of oracles as predictions of their faith; and there is, I
believe, no example of the denial of their supernatural character in the Christian Church till 1696, when a Dutch
Anabaptist minister named Van Dale, in a remarkable book,[3]

---

[1] 'Credat Judæus Apella.'—
Hor. *Sat.* v. 100.

[2] This appears from all the
writings of the Fathers.   There
were, however, two forms of Pagan
miracles about which there was
some hesitation in the early Church
—the beneficent miracle of healing and the miracle of prophecy.
Concerning the first, the common
opinion was that the dæmons only
cured diseases they had themselves
caused, or that, at least, if they ever
(in order to enthral men more effectually) cured purely natural dis-

eases, they did it by natural means,
which their superior knowledge
and power placed at their disposal.
Concerning prophecy, it was the
opinion of some of the Fathers that
intuitive prescience was a Divine
prerogative, and that the prescience
of the dæmons was only acquired
by observation.   Their immense
knowledge enabled them to forecast
events to a degree far transcending human faculties, and they employed this power in the oracles.

[3] *De Origine ac Progressu Idola-*
*triæ* (Amsterdam).

which was abridged and translated by Fontenelle, asserted, in opposition to the unanimous voice of ecclesiastical authority, that they were simple impostures—a theory which is now almost universally accepted. To suppose that men who held these opinions were capable, in the second or third centuries, of ascertaining with any degree of just confidence whether miracles had taken place in Judæa in the first century, is grossly absurd; nor would the conviction of their reality have made any great impression on their minds at a time when miracles were supposed to be so abundantly diffused.

In truth, the question of the reality of the Jewish miracles must be carefully distinguished from that of the conversion of the Roman Empire. With the light that is furnished to us by modern investigations and habits of thought, we weigh the testimony of the Jewish writers; but most of the more judicious of modern apologists, considering the extreme credulity of the Jewish people, decline to make the question simply one of evidence, and occupy themselves chiefly in endeavouring to show that miracles are possible, that those recorded in the Biblical narratives are related in such a manner, and are so interwoven with the texture of a simple and artless narrative, as to carry with them an internal proof of their reality; that they differ in kind from later miracles, and especially that the character and destinies of Christianity are such as to render its miraculous origin antecedently probable. But in the ages when the Roman Empire was chiefly converted, all sound and discriminating historical investigation of the evidence of the early miracles was impossible, nor was any large use made of those miracles as proofs of the religion. The rhetorician Arnobius is probably the only one of the early apologists who gives, among the evidences of the faith, any prominent place to the miracles of Christ.[1] When

---

[1] This characteristic of early Christian apology is forcibly ex-hibited by Pressensé, *Hist. des trois premiers Siècles*, 2me série, tome ii.

evidential reasoning was employed, it was usually an appeal
not to miracles, but to prophecy.    But here again the opinions
of the patristic age must be pronounced absolutely worthless.
To prove that events had taken place in Judæa, accurately
corresponding with the prophecies, or that the prophecies
were themselves genuine, were both tasks far transcending
the critical powers of the Roman converts.    The wild extravagance of fantastic allegory, commonly connected with
Origen, but which appears at a much earlier date in the
writings of Justin Martyr and Irenæus, had thrown the interpretation of prophecy into hopeless confusion, while the
deliberate and apparently perfectly unscrupulous forgery of a
whole literature, destined to further the propagation either
of Christianity as a whole, or of some particular class of
tenets that had arisen within its border,[1] made criticism at
once pre-eminently difficult and necessary.    A long series of
oracles were cited, predicting in detail the sufferings of Christ.
The prophecies forged by the Christians, and attributed by
them to the heathen Sibyls, were accepted as genuine by the
entire Church, and were continually appealed to as among
the most powerful evidences of the faith.    Justin Martyr
declared that it was by the instigation of dæmons that it had
been made a capital offence to read them.[2]    Clement of
Alexandria preserved the tradition that St. Paul had urged
the brethren to study them.[3]    Celsus designated the Christians
Sibyllists, on account of the pertinacity with which they in-
sisted upon them.[4]    Constantine the Great adduced them in
a solemn speech before the Council of Nice.[5]    St. Augustine
notices that the Greek word for a fish, which, containing the
initial letters of the name and titles of Christ, had been

---

[1] The immense number of these
forged writings is noticed by all
candid historians, and there is, I
believe, only one instance of any
attempt being made to prevent
this pious fraud.    A priest was degraded for having forged some
voyages of St. Paul and St. Thecla.
(Tert. *De Baptismo,* 17.)

[2] *Apol.* i.    [3] *Strom.* vi. c. 5.
[4] Origen, *Cont. Cels.* v.
[5] *Oratio* (apud Euseb.) xviii.

adopted by the Early Church as its sacred symbol, contains also the initial letters of some prophetic lines ascribed to the Sibyl of Erythra.[1] The Pagans, it is true, accused their opponents of having forged or interpolated these prophecies;[2] but there was not a single Christian writer of the patristic period who disputed their authority, and there were very few even of the most illustrious who did not appeal to them. Unanimously admitted by the Church of the Fathers, they were unanimously admitted during the middle ages, and an allusion to them passed into the most beautiful lyric of the Missal. It was only at the period of the Reformation that the great but unhappy Castellio pointed out many passages in them which could not possibly be genuine. He was followed, in the first years of the seventeenth century, by a Jesuit named Possevin, who observed that the Sibyls were known to have lived at a later period than Moses, and that many passages in the Sibylline books purported to have been written before Moses. Those passages, therefore, he said, were interpolated; and he added, with a characteristic sagacity, that they had doubtless been inserted by Satan, for the purpose of throwing suspicion upon the books.[3] It was in 1649 that a French Protestant minister, named Blondel, ventured for the first time in the Christian Church to denounce these writings as deliberate and clumsy forgeries, and after much angry controversy his sentiment has acquired an almost undisputed ascendancy in criticism.

But although the opinion of the Roman converts was extremely worthless, when dealing with past history or with literary criticism, there was one branch of miracles concerning which their position was somewhat different. Contem-

---

[1] *De Civ. Dei*, xviii. 23.

[2] Constantine, *Oratio* xix. 'His testimoniis quidam revicti solent eo confugere ut aiant non esse illa carmina Sibyllina, sed a nostris conficta atque composita.'—Lactant. *Div. Inst.* iv. 15.

[3] Antonius Possevinus, *Apparatus Sacer* (1606), verb. ' Sibylla.'

porary miracles, often of the most extraordinary character,
but usually of the nature of visions, exorcisms, or healing the
sick, were from the time of Justin Martyr uniformly represented by the Fathers as existing among them,[1] and they continue steadily along the path of history, till in the pages of
Evagrius and Theodoret, in the Lives of Hilarion and Paul,
by St. Jerome, of Antony, by St. Athanasius, and of Gregory
Thaumaturgus, by his namesake of Nyssa, and in the Dialogues of St. Gregory the Great, they attain as grotesque an
extravagance as the wildest mediæval legends.    Few things
are more striking than the assertions hazarded on this matter
by some of the ablest of the Fathers.    Thus, St. Irenæus
assures us that all Christians possessed the power of working
miracles; that they prophesied, cast out devils, healed the
sick, and sometimes even raised the dead; that some who had
been thus resuscitated lived for many years among them, and
that it would be impossible to reckon the wonderful acts that
were daily performed.[2]    St. Epiphanius tells us that some
rivers and fountains were annually transformed into wine, in
attestation of the miracle of Cana; and he adds that he had
himself drunk of one of these fountains, and his brethren of
another.[3]    St. Augustine notices that miracles were less
frequent and less widely known than formerly, but that many
still occurred, and some of them he had himself witnessed.
Whenever a miracle was reported, he ordered that a special
examination into its circumstances should be made, and that
the depositions of the witnesses should be read publicly to
the people.    He tells us, besides many other miracles, that
Gamaliel in a dream revealed to a priest named Lucianus the
place where the bones of St. Stephen were buried; that those
bones, being thus discovered, were brought to Hippo, the
diocese of which St. Augustine was bishop; that they raised

[1] This subject is fully treated
by Middleton in his *Free Enquiry*,
whom I have closely followed.

[2] Irenæus, *Contr. Hæres.* ii. 32.
[3] Epiphan. *Adv. Hæres.* ii. 30.

five dead persons to life; and that, although only a portion of the miraculous cures they effected had been registered, the certificates drawn up in two years in the diocese, and by the orders of the saint, were nearly seventy. In the adjoining diocese of Calama they were incomparably more numerous.[1] In the height of the great conflict between St. Ambrose and the Arian Empress Justina, the saint declared that it had been revealed to him by an irresistible presentiment—or, as St. Augustine, who was present on the occasion, says, in a dream—that relics were buried in a spot which he indicated. The earth being removed, a tomb was found filled with blood, and containing two gigantic skeletons, with their heads severed from their bodies, which were pronounced to be those of St. Gervasius and St. Protasius, two martyrs of remarkable physical dimensions, who were said to have suffered about 300 years before. To prove that they were genuine relics, the bones were brought in contact with a blind man, who was restored to sight, and with demoniacs, who were cured; the dæmons, however, in the first place, acknowledging that the relics were genuine; that St. Ambrose was the deadly enemy of the powers of hell; that the Trinitarian doctrine was true; and that those who rejected it would infallibly be damned. The next day St. Ambrose delivered an invective against all who questioned the miracle. St. Augustine recorded it in his works, and spread the worship of the saints through Africa. The transport of enthusiasm with which the miracles were greeted at Milan enabled St. Ambrose to overcome every obstacle; but the Arians treated them with a derisive incredulity, and declared that the pretended demoniacs had been bribed by the saint.[2]

Statements of this kind, which are selected from very

---

St. Aug. *De Civ. Dei*, xxii. 8.
[2] This history is related by St. Ambrose in a letter to his sister Marcellina; by St. Paulinus of Nola, in his *Life of Ambrose;* and by St. Augustine, *De Civ. Dei*, xxii. 8; *Confess.* ix. 7.

many that are equally positive, though not equally precise, suggest veins of thought of obvious interest and importance. We are now, however, only concerned with the fact, that, with the exception of one or two isolated miracles, such as the last I have noticed, and of one class of miracles which I shall proceed to describe, these prodigies, whether true or false, were wrought for the exclusive edification of confirmed believers. The exceptional miracles were those of exorcism, which occupied a very singular position in the early Church. The belief that certain diseases were inflicted by Divine agency was familiar to the ancients, but among the early Greeks the notion of diabolical possession appears to have been unknown. A dæmon, in the philosophy of Plato, though inferior to a deity, was not an evil spirit, and it is extremely doubtful whether the existence of evil dæmons was known either to the Greeks or Romans till about the time of the advent of Christ.[1] The belief was introduced with the Oriental superstitions which then poured into Rome, and it brought in its train the notions of possession and exorcism. The Jews, who in their own country appear to have regarded it as a most ordinary occurrence to meet men walking about visibly possessed by devils, and who professed to have learnt from Solomon the means of expelling them, soon became the principal exorcists, accomplishing their feats partly by adjuration, and partly by means of a certain miraculous root named Baaras. Josephus assures us that he had himself, in the reign of Vespasian, seen a Jew named Eleazar drawing by these means a dæmon through the nostrils of a possessed person, who fell to the ground on the accomplishment of the miracle; while, upon the command of the magician, the

---

[1] Plutarch thought they were known by Plato, but this opinion has been much questioned. See a very learned discussion on the subject in Farmer's *Dissertation on* *Miracles*, pp. 129–140; and Fontenelle, *Hist. des Oracles*, pp. 26, 27. Porphyry speaks much of evil dæmons.

devil, to prove that it had really left his victim, threw down a cup of water which had been placed at a distance.[1] The growth of Neoplatonism and kindred philosophies greatly strengthened the belief, and some of the later philosophers, as well as many religious charlatans, practised exorcism. But, of all classes, the Christians became in this respect the most famous. From the time of Justin Martyr, for about two centuries, there is, I believe, not a single Christian writer who does not solemnly and explicitly assert the reality and frequent employment of this power; [2] and although, after the Council of Laodicea, the instances became less numerous, they by no means ceased. The Christians fully recognised the supernatural power possessed by the Jewish and Gentile exorcists, but they claimed to be in many respects their superiors. By the simple sign of the cross, or by repeating the name of their Master, they professed to be able to cast out devils which had resisted all the enchantments of Pagan

---

[1] Josephus, *Antiq.* viii. 2, § 5.

[2] This very curious subject is fully treated by Baltus (*Réponse à l'Histoire des Oracles*, Strasburg, 1707, published anonymously in reply to Van Dale and Fontenelle), who believed, in the reality of the Pagan as well as the patristic miracles; by Bingham (*Antiquities of the Christian Church*, vol. i. pp. 316–324), who thinks the Pagan and Jewish exorcists were impostors, but not the Christians; and by Middleton (*Free Enquiry*, pp. 80–93), who disbelieves in all the exorcists after the apostolic times. It has also been the subject of a special controversy in England, carried on by Dodwell, Church, Farmer, and others. Archdeacon Church says: ' If we cannot vindicate them [the Fathers of the first three centuries]

on this article, their credit must be lost for ever; and we must be obliged to decline all further defence of them. It is impossible for any words more strongly to express a claim to this miracle than those used by all the best writers of the second and third centuries.' — *Vindication of the Miracles of the First Three Centuries*, p. 199. So, also, Baltus: ' De tous les anciens auteurs ecclésiastiques, n'y en ayant pas un qui n'ait parlé de ce pouvoir admirable que les Chrétiens avoient de chasser les démons' (p. 296). Gregory of Tours describes exorcism as sufficiently common in his time, and mentions having himself seen a monk named Julian cure by his words a possessed person. (*Hist.* iv. 32.)

exorcists, to silence the oracles, to compel the dæmons to con
fess the truth of the Christian faith.  Sometimes their power
extended still further.  Dæmons, we are told, were accustomed to enter into animals, and these also were expelled by
the Christian adjuration.  St. Jerome, in his ' Life of St.
Hilarion,' has given us a graphic account of the courage with
which that saint confronted, and the success with which
he relieved, a possessed camel.[1]  In the reign of Julian, the
very bones of the martyr Babylas were sufficient to silence
the oracle of Daphne ; and when, amid the triumphant
chants of the Christians, the relics, by the command of
Julian, were removed, the lightning descended from heaven
and consumed the temple.[2]  St. Gregory Thaumaturgus
having expelled the dæmons from an idol temple, the priest,
finding his means of subsistence destroyed, came to the saint,
imploring him to permit the oracles to be renewed.  St.
Gregory, who was then on his journey, wrote a note containing the words ' Satan, return,' which was immediately obeyed,
and the priest, awe-struck by the miracle, was converted to
Christianity.[3]  Tertullian, writing to the Pagans in a time
of persecution, in language of the most deliberate earnestness,
challenges his opponents to bring forth any person who is

---

[1] *Vit. Hilar.*  Origen notices
that cattle were sometimes possessed by devils.  See Middleton's
*Free Enquiry,* pp. 88, 89.

[2] The miracle of St. Babylas
is the subject of a homily by St.
Chrysostom, and is related at
length by Theodoret, Sozomen,
and Socrates.  Libanius mentions
that, by command of Julian, the
bones of St. Babylas were removed from the temple.  The
Christians said the temple was destroyed by lightning ; the Pagans
declared it was burnt by the Christians, and Julian ordered measures
of reprisal to be taken.  Amm.
Marcellinus, however, mentions a

report that the fire was caused
accidentally by one of the numerous candles employed in the ceremony.  The people of Antioch
defied the emperor by chanting,
as they removed the relics, ' Confounded be all they that trust in
graven images.'

[3] See the *Life of Gregory
Thaumaturgus,* by Gregory of
Nyssa.  St. Gregory the Great
assures us (*Dial.* iii. 10) that
Sabinus, Bishop of Placentia, wrote
a letter to the river Po, which had
overflowed its banks and flooded
some church lands.  When the
letter was thrown into the stream
the waters at once subsided.

possessed by a dæmon or any of those virgins or prophets who are supposed to be inspired by a divinity. He asserts that, in reply to the interrogation of any Christian, the dæmons will be compelled to confess their diabolical character; he invites the Pagans, if it be otherwise, to put the Christian immediately to death; and he proposes this as at once the simplest and most decisive demonstration of the faith.[1] Justin Martyr,[2] Origen,[3] Lactantius,[4] Athanasius,[5] and Minucius Felix,[6] all in language equally solemn and explicit, call upon the Pagans to form their opinions from the confessions wrung from their own gods. We hear from them, that when a Christian began to pray, to make the sign of the cross, or to utter the name of his Master in the presence of a possessed or inspired person, the latter, by screams and frightful contortions, exhibited the torture that was inflicted, and by this torture the evil spirit was compelled to avow its nature. Several of the Christian writers declare that this was generally known to the Pagans. In one respect, it was observed, the miracle of exorcism was especially available for evidential purposes; for, as dæmons would not expel dæmons, it was the only miracle which was necessarily divine.

It would be curious to examine the manner in which the challenge was received by the Pagan writers; but unhappily, the writings which were directed against the faith having been destroyed by the Christian emperors, our means of information on this point are very scanty. Some information,

---

[1] 'Edatur hic aliquis sub tribunalibus vestris, quem dæmone agi constet. Jussus a quolibet Christiano loqui spiritus ille, tam se dæmonem confitebitur de vero, quam alibi deum de falso. Æque producatur aliquis ex iis qui de deo pati existimantur, qui aris inhalantes numen de nidore concipiunt . . . nisi se dæmones confessi fuerint, Christiano mentiri non audentes, ibidem illius Christiani procacissimi sanguinem fundite. Quid isto opere manifestius? quid hæc probatione fidelius?'— Tert. Apol. xxiii.

[2] Apol. i.; Trypho
[3] Cont. Cels. vii.
[4] Inst. Div. iv. 27
[5] Life of Antony.
[6] Octavius.

however, we possess, and it would appear to show that, among the educated classes at least, these phenomena did not extort any great admiration. The eloquent silence about diabolical possession observed by the early philosophers, when discussing such questions as the nature of the soul and of the spiritual world, decisively show that in their time possession had not assumed any great prominence or acquired any general credence. Plutarch, who admitted the reality of evil dæmons, and who was the most strenuous defender of the oracles, treats the whole class of superstitions to which exorcism belongs with much contempt.[1] Marcus Aurelius, in recounting the benefits he had received from different persons with whom he had been connected, acknowledges his debt of gratitude to the philosopher Diognetus for having taught him to give no credence to magicians, jugglers, and expellers of dæmons.[2] Lucian declares that every cunning juggler could make his fortune by going over to the Christians and preying upon their simplicity.[3] Celsus described the Christians as jugglers performing their tricks among the young and the credulous.[4] The most decisive evidence, however, we possess, is a law of Ulpian, directed, it is thought, against the Christians, which condemns those ‘who use incantations or imprecations, or (to employ the common word of impostors) exorcisms.’[5] Modern criticism has noted a few facts which may throw some light upon this obscure subject. It has been observed that the

[1] De Superstitione.

[2] i. 6.

[3] De Mort. Peregrin.

[4] Origen, Adv. Cels. vi. Compare the curious letter which Vopiscus (Saturninus) attributes to Hadrian, ‘Nemo illic [i.e. in Egypt] archisynagogus Judæorum, nemo Samarites, nemo Christianorum presbyter, non mathematicus, non aruspex, non aliptes.’

[5] ‘Si incantavit, si imprecatus est, si (ut vulgari verbo impostorum utor) exorcizavit.’—Bingham, Antiquities of the Christian Church (Oxf., 1855), vol. i. p. 318. This law is believed to have been directed specially against the Christians, because these were very prominent as exorcists, and because Lactantius (Inst. Div. v. 11) says that Ulpian had collected the laws against them.

symptoms of possession were for the most part identical with those of lunacy or epilepsy ; that it is quite possible that the excitement of an imposing religious ceremony might produce or suspend the disorder ; that leading questions might in these cases be followed by the desired answers; and that some passages from the Fathers show that the exorcisms were not always successful, or the cures always permanent.    It has been observed, too, that at first the power of exorcism was open to all Christians without restraint; that this licence, in an age when religious jugglers were very common, and in a Church whose members were very credulous, gave great facilities to impostors ; that when the Laodicean Council, in the fourth century, forbade any one to exorcise, except those who were duly authorised by the bishop, these miracles speedily declined ; and that, in the very beginning of the fifth century, a physician named Posidonius denied the existence of possession.[1]

To sum up this whole subject, we may conclude that what is called the evidential system had no prominent place in effecting the conversion of the Roman Empire.    Historical criticisms were far too imperfect to make appeals to the miracles of former days of any value, and the notion of the wide diffusion of miraculous or magical powers, as well as the generally private character of the alleged miracles of the Patristic age, made contemporary wonders very unimpressive. The prophecies attributed to the Sibyls, and the practice of exorcism, had, however, a certain weight; for the first were connected with a religious authority, long and deeply revered at Rome, and the second had been forced by several circumstances into great prominence.    But the effect even of these may be safely regarded as altogether subsidiary, and the main causes of the conversion must be looked for in another and a wider sphere.

---

[1] Philostorgius, *Hist. Eccl.* viii. 10.

These causes were the general tendencies of the age. They are to be found in that vast movement of mingled scepticism and credulity, in that amalgamation or dissolution of many creeds, in that profound transformation of habits, of feelings, and of ideals, which I have attempted to paint in the last chapter. Under circumstances more favourable to religious proselytism than the world had ever before known, with the path cleared by a long course of destructive criticism, the religions and philosophies of mankind were struggling for the mastery in that great metropolis where all were amply represented, and in which alone the destinies of the world could be decided. Among the educated a frigid Stoicism, teaching a majestic but unattainable grandeur, and scorning the support of the affections, the hope of another world, and the consolations of worship, had for a time been in the ascendant, and it only terminated its noble and most fruitful career when it had become manifestly inadequate to the religious wants of the age. Among other classes, religion after religion ran its conquering course. The Jews, although a number of causes had made them the most hated of all the Roman subjects, and although their religion, from its intensely national character, seemed peculiarly unsuited for proselytism, had yet, by the force of their monotheism, their charity, and their exorcisms, spread the creed of Moses far and wide. The Empress Poppæa is said to have been a proselyte. The passion of Roman women for Jewish rites was one of the complaints of Juvenal. The Sabbath and the Jewish fasts became familiar facts in all the great cities, and the antiquity of the Jewish law the subject of eager discussion. Other Oriental religions were even more successful. The worship of Mithra, and, above all, of the Egyptian divinities, attracted their thousands, and during more than three centuries the Roman writings are crowded with allusions to their progress. The mysteries of the Bona Dea,[1] the

---

[1] See Juvenal, *Sat.* vi. 314–335.

solemn worship of Isis, the expiatory rites that cleansed the guilty soul, excited a very delirium of enthusiasm. Juvenal describes the Roman women, at the dawn of the winter day, breaking the ice of the Tiber to plunge three times into its sacred stream, dragging themselves on bleeding knees in penance around the field of Tarquin, offering to undertake pilgrimages to Egypt to seek the holy water for the shrine of Isis, fondly dreaming that they had heard the voice of the goddess.[1] Apuleius has drawn a graphic picture of the solemn majesty of her processions, and the spell they cast upon the most licentious and the most sceptical.[2] Commodus, Caracalla, and Heliogabalus were passionately devoted to them.[3] The temples of Isis and Serapis, and the statues of Mithra, are among the last prominent works of Roman art. In all other forms the same credulity was manifested. The oracles that had been silent were heard again; the astrologers swarmed in every city; the philosophers were surrounded with an atmosphere of legend; the Pythagorean school had raised credulity into a system. On all sides, and to a degree unparalleled in history, we find men who were no longer satisfied with their old local religion, thirsting for belief, passionately and restlessly seeking for a new faith.

In the midst of this movement, Christianity gained its ascendancy, and we can be at no loss to discover the cause of its triumph. No other religion, under such circumstances, had ever combined so many distinct elements of power and attraction. Unlike the Jewish religion, it was bound by no local ties, and was equally adapted for every nation and for every class. Unlike Stoicism, it appealed in the strongest manner to the affections, and offered all the charm of a sympathetic worship. Unlike the Egyptian religions, it united with its distinctive teaching a pure and noble system of

---

See Juvenal, *Sat.* vi. 520–530.  
[2] *Metamorphoses*, book x.  
[3] See their *Lives*, by Lampridius and Spartianus.

ethics, and proved itself capable of realising it in action. It proclaimed, amid a vast movement of social and national amalgamation, the universal brotherhood of mankind. Amid the softening influence of philosophy and civilisation, it taught the supreme sanctity of love. To the slave, who had never before exercised so large an influence over Roman religious life, it was the religion of the suffering and the oppressed. To the philosopher it was at once the echo of the highest ethics of the later Stoics, and the expansion of the best teaching of the school of Plato. To a world thirsting for prodigy, it offered a history replete with wonders more strange that those of Apollonius; while the Jew and the Chaldean could scarcely rival its exorcists, and the legends of continual miracles circulated among its followers. To a world deeply conscious of political dissolution, and prying eagerly and anxiously into the future, it proclaimed with a thrilling power the immediate destruction of the globe—the glory of all its friends, and the damnation of all its foes. To a world that had grown very weary gazing on the cold and passionless grandeur which Cato realised, and which Lucan sung, it presented an ideal of compassion and of love—a Teacher who could weep by the sepulchre of His friend, who was touched with the feeling of our infirmities. To a world, in fine, distracted by hostile creeds and colliding philosophies, it taught its doctrines, not as a human speculation, but as a Divine revelation, authenticated much less by reason than by faith. 'With the heart man believeth unto righteousness;' 'He that doeth the will of my Father will know the doctrine, whether it be of God;' 'Unless you believe you cannot understand;' 'A heart naturally Christian;' 'The heart makes the theologian,' are the phrases which best express the first action of Christianity upon the world. Like all great religions, it was more concerned with modes of feeling than with modes of thought. The chief cause of its success was the congruity of its teaching with the spiritual

nature ot mankind. It was because it was true to the moral
sentiments of the age, because it represented faithfully the
supreme type of excellence to which men were then tending,
because it corresponded with their religious wants, aims, and
emotions, because the whole spiritual being could then expand and expatiate under its influence, that it planted its
roots so deeply in the hearts of men.

To all these ⸱lements of attraction, others of a different
order must be added. Christianity was not merely a moral
influence, or a system of opinions, or an historical record, or
a collection of wonder-working men; it was also an institution definitely, elaborately, and skilfully organised, possessing a weight and a stability which isolated or undisciplined
teachers could never rival, and evoking, to a degree before
unexampled in the world, an enthusiastic devotion to its
corporate welfare, analogous to that of the patriot to his
country. The many forms of Pagan worship were pliant in
their nature. Each offered certain advantages or spiritual
gratifications; but there was no reason why all should not
exist together, and participation in one by no means implied
disrespect to the others. But Christianity was emphatically
exclusive; its adherent was bound to detest and abjure the
faiths around him as the workmanship of dæmons, and to
consider himself placed in the world to destroy them. Hence
there sprang a stern, aggressive, and at the same time disciplined enthusiasm, wholly unlike any other that had been
witnessed upon earth. The duties of public worship; the
sacraments, which were represented as the oaths of the
Christian warrior; the fasts and penances and commemorative
days, which strengthened the Church feeling; the intervention of religion in the most solemn epochs of life, conspired
to sustain it. Above all, the doctrine of salvation by belief,
which then for the first time flashed upon the world; the
persuasion, realised with all the vividness of novelty, that
Christianity opened out to its votaries eternal happiness,

while all beyond its pale were doomed to an eternity of torture, supplied a motive of action as powerful as it is perhaps possible to conceive. It struck alike the coarsest chords of hope and fear, and the finest chords of compassion and love. The polytheist, admitting that Christianity might possibly be true, was led by a mere calculation of prudence to embrace it, and the fervent Christian would shrink from no suffering to draw those whom he loved within its pale. Nor were other inducements wanting. To the confessor was granted in the Church a great and venerable authority, such as the bishop could scarcely claim.[1] To the martyr, besides the fruition of heaven, belonged the highest glory on earth. By winning that bloodstained crown, the meanest Christian slave might gain a reputation as glorious as that of a Decius or a Regulus. His body was laid to rest with a sumptuous splendour;[2] his relics, embalmed or shrined, were venerated with an almost idolatrous homage. The anniversary of his birth into another life was commemorated in the Church, and before the great assembly of the saints his heroic sufferings were recounted.[3] How, indeed, should he not be envied? He had passed away into eternal bliss. He had left upon earth an abiding name. By the 'baptism of blood' the sins of a life had been in a moment effaced.

Those who are accustomed to recognise heroic enthusiasm as a normal product of certain natural conditions, will have no difficulty in understanding that, under such circumstances

---

[1] The conflict between St. Cyprian and the confessors, concerning the power of remitting penances claimed by the latter, though it ended in the defeat of the confessors, shows clearly the influence they had obtained.

[2] 'Thura plane non emimus; si Arabiæ queruntur scient Sabæi pluris et carioris suas merces Christianis sepeliendis profligari

quam diis fumigandis.'—*Apol.* 42. Sometimes the Pagans burnt the bodies of the martyrs, in order to prevent the Christians venerating their relics.

[3] Many interesting particulars about these commemorative festivals are collected in Cave's *Primitive Christianity*, part i. c. vii. The anniversaries were called ' Natalia, or birth-days.

as I have described, a transcendent courage should have been evoked. Men seemed indeed to be in love with death. Believing, with St. Ignatius, that they were 'the wheat of God,' they panted for the day when they should be 'ground by the teeth of wild beasts into the pure bread of Christ!' Beneath this one burning enthusiasm all the ties of earthly love were snapt in twain. Origen, when a boy, being restrained by force from going forth to deliver himself up to the persecutors, wrote to his imprisoned father, imploring him not to let any thought of his family intervene to quench his resolution or to deter him from sealing his faith with his blood. St. Perpetua, an only daughter, a young mother of twenty-two, had embraced the Christian creed, confessed it before her judges, and declared herself ready to endure for it the martyr's death. Again and again her father came to her in a paroxysm of agony, entreating her not to deprive him of the joy and the consolation of his closing years. He appealed to her by the memory of all the tenderness he had lavished upon her — by her infant child — by his own gray hairs, that were soon to be brought down in sorrow to the grave. Forgetting in his deep anguish all the dignity of a parent, he fell upon his knees before his child, covered her hands with kisses, and, with tears streaming from his eyes, implored her to have mercy upon him. But she was unshaken though not untouched; she saw her father, frenzied with grief, dragged from before the tribunal; she saw him tearing his white beard, and lying prostrate and broken-hearted on the prison floor; she went forth to die for a faith she loved more dearly—for a faith that told her that her father would be lost for ever.[1] The desire for martyrdom became at times a form of absolute madness, a kind of epidemic of suicide, and the leading minds of the Church found it necessary to exert all their authority to prevent their followers

---

[1] See her acts in Ruinart.

from thrusting themselves into the hands of the persecutors.[1]
Tertullian mentions how, in a little Asiatic town, the entire
population once flocked to the proconsul, declaring themselves
to be Christians, and imploring him to execute the decree of
the emperor and grant them the privilege of martyrdom.
The bewildered functionary asked them whether, if they were
so weary of life, there were no precipices or ropes by which
they could end their days; and he put to death a small number of the suppliants, and dismissed the others.[2] Two illustrious Pagan moralists and one profane Pagan satirist have
noticed this passion with a most unpleasing scorn. 'There
are some,' said Epictetus, 'whom madness, there are others,
like the Galilæans, whom custom, makes indifferent to
death.'[3] 'What mind,' said Marcus Aurelius, 'is prepared,
if need be, to go forth from the body, whether it be to be
extinguished, or to be dispersed, or to endure?—prepared by
deliberate reflection, and not by pure obstinacy, as is the
custom of the Christians.'[4] 'These wretches,' said Lucian,
speaking of the Christians, 'persuade themselves that they
are going to be altogether immortal, and to live for ever;
wherefore they despise death, and many of their own accord
give themselves up to be slain.'[5]

'I send against you men who are as greedy of death as
you are of pleasures,' were the words which, in after days, the

---

[1] St. Clem. Alex. *Strom.* iv. 10.
There are other passages of the
same kind in other Fathers.

[2] *Ad Scapul.* v. Eusebius (*Martyrs
of Palestine*, ch. iii.) has given a detailed account of six young men,
who in the very height of the Ga-
lerian persecution, at a time when
the most hideous tortures were applied to the Christians, voluntarily
gave themselves up as believers.
Sulp. Severus (*Hist.* ii. 32), speaking of the voluntary martyrs under
Diocletian, says that Christians

then 'longed for death as they now
long for bishoprics.' 'Cogi qui
potest, nescit mori,' was the noble
maxim of the Christians.

[3] Arrian, iv. 7. It is not certain,
however, that this passage alludes
to the Christians. The followers
of Judas of Galilee were called
Galilæans, and they were famous
for their indifference to death. See
Joseph. *Antiq.* xviii. 1.

[4] xi. 3.

[5] *Peregrinus.*

Mohametan chief addressed to the degenerate Christians of
Syria, and which were at once the presage and the explanation of his triumph. Such words might with equal
propriety have been employed by the early Christian leaders
to their Pagan adversaries. The zeal of the Christians and
of the Pagans differed alike in degree and in kind. When
Constantine made Christianity the religion of the State, it is
probable that its adherents were but a minority in Rome.
Even in the days of Theodosius the senate was still wedded
to Paganism;[1] yet the measures of Constantine were both
natural and necessary. The majority were without inflexible belief, without moral enthusiasm, without definite
organisation, without any of those principles that inspire the
heroism either of resistance or aggression. The minority
formed a serried phalanx, animated by every motive that
could purify, discipline, and sustain their zeal. When once
the Christians had acquired a considerable position, the
question of their destiny was a simple one. They must either
be crushed or they must reign. The failure of the persecution of Diocletian conducted them inevitably to the
throne.

It may indeed be confidently asserted that the conversion
of the Roman Empire is so far from being of the nature of a
miracle or suspension of the ordinary principles of human
nature, that there is scarcely any other great movement on
record in which the causes and effects so manifestly correspond.
The apparent anomalies of history are not inconsiderable, but
they must be sought for in other quarters. That within the
narrow limits and scanty population of the Greek States
should have arisen men who, in almost every conceivable form
of genius, in philosophy, in epic, dramatic and lyric poetry,
in written and spoken eloquence, in statesmanship, in sculpture, in painting, and probably also in music, should have

---

[1] Zosimus.

27

attained almost or altogether the highest limits of human
perfection—that the creed of Mohamet should have preserved
its pure monotheism and its freedom from all idolatrous
tendencies, when adopted by vast populations in that intellectual condition in which, under all other creeds, a gross and
material worship has proved inevitable, both these are facts
which we can only very imperfectly explain.   Considerations
of climate, and still more of political, social, and intellectual
customs and institutions, may palliate the first difficulty, and
the attitude Mohamet assumed to art may supply us with a
partial explanation of the second ; but I suppose that, after
all has been said, most persons will feel that they are in
presence of phenomena very exceptional and astonishing.
The first rise of Christianity in Judæa is a subject wholly
apart from this book.   We are examining only the subsequent
movement in the Roman Empire.   Of this movement it may
be boldly asserted that the assumption of a moral or intellectual miracle is utterly gratuitous.   Never before was a
religious transformation so manifestly inevitable.   No other
religion ever combined so many forms of attraction as
Christianity, both from its intrinsic excellence, and from its
manifest adaptation to the special wants of the time.   One
great cause of its success was that it produced more heroic
actions and formed more upright men than any other creed ;
but that it should do so was precisely what might have been
expected.

To these reasonings, however, those who maintain that
the triumph of Christianity in Rome is naturally inexplicable,
reply by pointing to the persecutions which Christianity had
to encounter.   As this subject is one on which many misconceptions exist, and as it is of extreme importance on
account of its connection with later persecutions, it will be
necessary briefly to discuss it.

It is manifest that the reasons that may induce a ruler to
suppress by force some forms of religious worship or opinion,

are very various. He may do so on moral grounds, because they directly or indirectly produce immorality; or on religious grounds, because he believes them to be offensive to the Deity; or on political grounds, because they are injurious either to the State or to the Government; or on corrupt grounds, because he desires to gratify some vindictive or avaricious passion. From the simple fact, therefore, of a religious persecution we cannot at once infer the principles of the persecutor, but must examine in detail by which of the above motives, or by what combination of them, he has been actuated.

Now, the persecution which has taken place at the instigation of the Christian priests differs in some respects broadly from all others. It has been far more sustained, systematic, and unflinching. It has been directed not merely against acts of worship, but also against speculative opinions. It has been supported not merely as a right, but also as a duty. It has been advocated in a whole literature of theology, by the classes that are especially devout, and by the most opposing sects, and it has invariably declined in conjunction with a large portion of theological dogmas.

I have elsewhere examined in great detail the history of persecutions by Christians, and have endeavoured to show that, while exceptional causes have undoubtedly occasionally occurred, they were, in the overwhelming majority of cases, simply the natural, legitimate, and inevitable consequence of a certain portion of the received theology. That portion is the doctrine that correct theological opinions are essential to salvation, and that theological error necessarily involves guilt. To these two opinions may be distinctly traced almost all the sufferings that Christian persecutors have caused, almost all the obstructions they have thrown in the path of human progress; and those sufferings have been so grievous that it may be reasonably questioned whether superstition has not often proved a greater curse than vice, and that obstruction was so pertinacious, that the contraction of theological influence has been at once the best measure, and the essential condition of intellectual advance. The notion that he might himself be possibly mistaken in his opinions, which alone could cause a man who was thoroughly imbued with these principles to shrink from persecuting, was excluded by the theological virtue of faith, which, whatever else it might involve, implied at least an absolute unbroken certainty, and led the devotee to regard all doubt, and therefore all action based upon doubt, as sin.

To this general cause of Christian persecution I have shown that two subsidiary influences may be joined. A large portion of theological ethics was derived from writings in which religious massacres, on the whole the most ruthless and sanguinary upon record, were said to have been directly enjoined by the Deity, in which the duty of suppressing idolatry by force was given a greater prominence than any article of the moral code, and in which the spirit of intolerance has found its most eloquent and most passionate expressions.[1] Besides this, the destiny theologians represented as awaiting the misbeliever was so ghastly and so appalling as to render it almost childish to lay any stress upon the earthly suffering that might be inflicted in the extirpation of error.

That these are the true causes of the great bulk of Christian persecution, I believe to be one of the most certain as well as one of the most important facts in history. For the detailed proof I can only refer to what I have elsewhere written; but I may here notice that that proof combines every conceivable kind of evidence that in such a question can be demanded. It can be shown that these principles would naturally lead men to persecute. It can be shown that from the time of Constantine to the time when the

---

[1] 'Do I not hate them, O Lord, that hate thee?—yea, I hate them with a perfect hatred.'

rationalistic spirit wrested the bloodstained sword from the priestly hand, persecution was uniformly defended upon them—defended in long, learned, and elaborate treatises, by the best and greatest men the Church had produced, by sects that differed on almost all other points, by multitudes who proved in every conceivable manner the purity of their zeal. It can be shown, too, that toleration began with the distinction between fundamental and non-fundamental doctrines, expanded in exact proportion to the growing latitudinarianism, and triumphed only when indifference to dogma had become a prevailing sentiment among legislators. It was only when the battle had been won—when the anti-dogmatic party, acting in opposition to the Church, had rendered persecution impossible—that the great body of theologians revised their arguments, and discovered that to punish men for their opinions was wholly at variance with their faith. With the merits of this pleasing though somewhat tardy conversion I am not now concerned; but few persons, I think, can follow the history of Christian persecution without a feeling of extreme astonishment that some modern writers, not content with maintaining that the doctrine of exclusive salvation *ought* not to have produced persecution, have ventured, in defiance of the unanimous testimony of the theologians of so many centuries, to dispute the plain historical fact that it *did* produce it. They argue that the Pagans, who did not believe in exclusive salvation, persecuted, and that therefore that doctrine cannot be the cause of persecution. The answer is that no sane man ever maintained that all the persecutions on record were from the same source. We can prove by the clearest evidence that Christian persecutions sprang chiefly from the causes I have alleged. The causes of Pagan persecutions, though different, are equally manifest, and I shall proceed shortly to indicate them.

They were partly political and partly religious. The Governments in most of the ancient States, in the earlier stages of their existence, undertook the complete education of the people; professed to control and regulate all the details of their social life, even to the dresses they wore, or the dishes that were served upon their tables; and, in a word, to mould their whole lives and characters into a uniform type. Hence, all organisations and corporations not connected with the State, and especially all that emanated from foreign countries, were looked upon with distrust or antipathy. But this antipathy was greatly strengthened by a religious consideration. No belief was more deeply rooted in the ancient mind than that good or bad fortune sprang from the intervention of spiritual beings, and that to neglect the sacred rites was to bring down calamity upon the city. In the diminutive Greek States, where the function of the Government was immensely enlarged, a strong intolerance existed, which extended for some time not merely to practices, but to writings and discourses. The well-known persecutions of Anaxagoras, Theodorus, Diagoras, Stilpo, and Socrates; the laws of Plato, which were as opposed to religious as to domestic freedom; and the existence in Athens of an inquisitorial tribunal,[1] sufficiently attested it. But long before the final ruin of Greece, speculative liberty had been fully attained. The Epicurean and the Sceptical schools developed unmolested, and even in the days of Socrates, Aristophanes was able to ridicule the gods upon the stage.

In the earlier days of Rome religion was looked upon as a function of the State; its chief object was to make the gods auspicious to the national policy,[2] and its principal ceremonies were performed at the direct command of the Senate. The national theory on religious matters was that the best religion

---

[1] See Renan's *Apôtres*, p. 314.

[2] M. Pressensé very truly says of the Romans, ' Leur religion était essentiellement un art—l'art de découvrir les desseins des dieux et d'agir sur eux par des rites variés.' —*Hist. des Trois premiers Siècles*, tome i. p. 192. Montesquieu has written an interesting essay on the political nature of the Roman religion.

is always that of a man's own country. At the same time,
the widest tolerance was granted to the religions of conquered
nations. The temples of every god were respected by the
Roman army. Before besieging a city, the Romans were
accustomed to supplicate the presiding deities of that city.
With the single exception of the Druids, whose human sacrifices it was thought a matter of humanity to suppress,[1] and
whose fierce rebellions it was thought necessary to crush, the
teachers of all national religions continued unmolested by the
conqueror.

This policy, however, applied specially to religious rites
practised in the countries in which they were indigenous.
The liberty to be granted to the vast confluence of strangers
attracted to Italy during the Empire was another question.
In the old Republican days, when the censors regulated with
the most despotic authority the minutest affairs of life, and
when the national religion was interwoven with every detail
of political and even domestic transactions, but little liberty
could be expected. When Carneades endeavoured to inculcate
his universal scepticism upon the Romans, by arguing alternately for and against the same proposition, Cato immediately
urged the Senate to expel him from the city, lest the people
should be corrupted by his teaching.[2] For a similar reason
all rhetoricians had been banished from the Republic.[3] The
most remarkable, however, and at the same time the extreme expression of Roman intolerance that has descended
to us, is the advice which Mæcenas is represented as having
given to Octavius Cæsar, before his accession to the throne.
' Always,' he said, ' and everywhere, worship the gods according to the rites of your country, and compel others to the
same worship. Pursue with your hatred and with punish-

---

[1] Sueton. *Claud.* xxv.
[2] Plin. *Hist. Nat.* vii. 31.
[3] Tacit. *De Orat.* xxxv.; Aul.
Gell. *Noct.* xv. 11. It would appear, from this last authority, that
the rhetoricians were twice expelled.

ments those who introduce foreign religions, not only for the sake of the gods—the despisers of whom can assuredly never do anything great—but also because they who introduce new divinities entice many to use foreign laws. Hence arise conspiracies, societies, and assemblies, things very unsuited to an homogeneous empire. Tolerate no despiser of the gods, and no religious juggler. Divination is necessary, and therefore let the aruspices and augurs by all means be sustained, and let those who will, consult them; but the magicians must be utterly prohibited, who, though they sometimes tell the truth, more frequently, by false promises, urge men on to conspiracies.' [1]

This striking passage exhibits very clearly the extent to which in some minds the intolerant spirit was carried in antiquity, and also the blending motives that produced it. We should be, however, widely mistaken if we regarded it as a picture of the actual religious policy of the Empire. In order to realise this, it will be necessary to notice separately liberty of speculation and liberty of worship.

When Asinius Pollio founded the first public library in Rome, he placed it in the Temple of Liberty. The lesson which was thus taught to the literary classes was never forgotten. It is probable that in no other period of the history of the world was speculative freedom so perfect as in the Roman Empire. The fearless scrutiny of all notions of popular belief, displayed in the writings of Cicero, Seneca, Lucretius, or Lucian, did not excite an effort of repression. Philosophers were, indeed, persecuted by Domitian and Vespasian for their ardent opposition to the despotism of the throne,[2] but on their own subjects they were wholly untram-

---

[1] Dion Cassius, lii. 36. Most historians believe that this speech represents the opinions, not of the Augustan age, but of the age of the writer who relates it.

[2] On the hostility of Vespasian to philosophers, see Xiphilin, lxvi. 13; on that of Domitian, the *Letters* of Pliny and the *Agricola* of Tacitus.

melled. The Greek writers consoled themselves for the extinction of the independence of their country by the reflection that in the sphere of intellect the meddling policy of the Greek States was replaced by an absolute and a majestic freedom.[1] The fierceness of the opposition of sects faded beneath its influence. Of all the speculative conflicts of antiquity, that which most nearly approached the virulence of later theological controversies was probably that between the Stoics and the Epicureans; but it is well worthy of notice that some of the most emphatic testimonies to the moral goodness of Epicurus have come from the writings of his opponents.

But the policy of the Roman rulers towards religious rites was very different from, and would at first sight appear to be in direct opposition to, their policy towards opinions. An old law, which Cicero mentions, expressly forbade the introduction of new religions,[2] and in the Republican days and the earliest days of the Empire there are many instances of its being enforced. Thus, in A.U.C. 326, a severe drought having led men to seek help from new gods, the Senate charged the ædiles to allow none but Roman deities to be worshipped.[3] Lutatius, soon after the first Punic war, was forbidden by the Senate to consult foreign gods, 'because,' said the historian, 'it was deemed right the Republic should be administered according to the national auspices, and not according to those of other lands.'[4] During the second Punic war, a severe edict of the Senate enjoined the suppression of certain recent innovations.[5] About A.U.C. 615 the prætor Hispalus exiled those who had introduced the worship of the Sabasian Jupiter.[6] The rites of Bacchus, being accompanied by gross and scandalous obscenity, were suppressed,

[1] See a remarkable passage in Dion Chrysostom, *Or.* lxxx. *De Libertate.*

[2] Cic. *De Legib.* ii. 11; Tertull. *Apol.* v.

[3] Livy, iv. 30.

[4] Val. Maximus, i. 3, § 1.

[5] Livy, xxv. 1.

[6] Val. Max. i. 3, § 2.

the consul, in a remarkable speech, calling upon the people **to** revive the religious policy of their ancestors.[1] The worship of Isis and Serapis only gained its footing after a long struggle, and no small amount of persecution. The gross immorality it sometimes favoured, its wild and abject superstition, so thoroughly alien to the whole character of Roman life and tradition, and also the organisation of its priesthood, rendered it peculiarly obnoxious to the Government. When the first edict of suppression was issued, the people hesitated to destroy a temple which seemed so venerable in their eyes, and the consul Æmilius Paulus dispelled their fears by seizing an axe and striking the first blow himself.[2] During the latter days of the Republic, edicts had commanded the destruction of the Egyptian temples. Octavius, however, in his younger days, favoured the new worship, but, soon after, it was again suppressed.[3] Under Tiberius it had once more crept in; but the priests of Isis having enabled a patrician named Mundus to disguise himself as the god Anubis, and win the favours of a devout worshipper, the temple, by order of the emperor, was destroyed, the images were thrown into the Tiber, the priests were crucified, and the seducer was banished.[4] Under the same emperor four thousand persons were exiled to Sardinia, as affected with Jewish and Egyptian superstitions. They were commissioned to repress robbers; but the Roman historian

---

[1] See the account of these proceedings, and of the very remarkable speech of Postumius, in Livy, xxxix. 8–19. Postumius notices the old prohibition of foreign rites, and thus explains it: — ' Judicabant enim prudentissimi viri omnis divini humanique juris, nihil æque dissolvendæ religionis esse, quam ubi non patrio sed externo ritu sacrificaretur.' The Senate, though suppressing these rites on account of the outrageous immoralities con-

nected with them, decreed, that if any one thought it a matter of religious duty to perform religious ceremonies to Bacchus, he should be allowed to do so on applying for permission to the Senate, provided there were not more than five assistants, no common purse, and no presiding priest.

[2] Val. Max. i. 3.

[3] See Dion Cassius, xl. 47 ; xlii. 26 ; xlvii. 15 ; liv. 6.

[4] Joseph. *Antiq.* xviii. 3.

observed, with a characteristic scorn, that if they died through the unhealthiness of the climate, it would be but a 'small loss.'[1]

These measures represent together a considerable amount of religious repression, but they were produced exclusively by notions of policy or discipline. They grew out of that intense national spirit which sacrificed every other interest to the State, and resisted every form of innovation, whether secular or religious, that could impair the unity of the national type, and dissolve the discipline which the predominance of the military spirit and the stern government of the Republic had formed. They were also, in some cases, the result of moral scandals. When, however, it became evident that the internal condition of the Republic was unsuited for the Empire, the rulers frankly acquiesced in the change, and from the time of Tiberius, with the single exception of the Christians, perfect liberty of worship seems to have been granted to the professors of all religions in Rome.[2] The old law upon the subject was not revoked, but it was not generally enforced. Sometimes the new creeds were expressly authorised. Sometimes they were tacitly permitted. With a single exception, all the religions of the world raised their heads unmolested in the ' Holy City.'[3]

The liberty, however, of professing and practising a foreign worship did not dispense the Roman from the obligation of performing also the sacrifices or other religious rites of his own land. It was here that whatever religious fanaticism mingled with Pagan persecutions was displayed. Eusebius tells us that religion was divided by the Romans

---

[1] Tacit. *Annal.* ii. 85.

[2] Tacitus relates (*Ann.* xi. 15) that under Claudius a senatus consultus ordered the pontiffs to take care that the old Roman (or, more properly, Etruscan) system of divination was observed, since the influx of foreign superstitions had led to its disuse; but it does not appear that this measure was intended to interfere with any other form of worship.

[3] 'Sacrosanctam istam civitatem accedo.'—Apuleius, *Metam.* lib. x. It is said that there were at one time no less than 420 ædes sacræ in Rome. Nieupoort, *De Ritibus Romanorum* (1716), p. 276

**into** three parts—the mythology, or legends that had descended from the poets; the interpretations or theories by
which the philosophers endeavoured to rationalise, filter, or
explain away these legends; and the ritual or official religious
observances. In the first two spheres perfect liberty was
accorded, but the ritual was placed under the control of the
Government, and was made a matter of compulsion.[1]    In
order to realise the strength of the feeling that supported it,
we must remember that the multitude firmly believed that
the prosperity and adversity of the Empire depended chiefly
upon the zeal or indifference that was shown in conciliating
the national divinities, and also that the philosophers, as I
have noticed in the last chapter, for the most part not only
practised, but warmly defended, the official observances.
The love of truth in many forms was exhibited among the
Pagan philosophers to a degree which has never been surpassed; but there was one form in which it was absolutely
unknown. The belief that it is wrong for a man in religious
matters to act a lie, to sanction by his presence and by his
example what he regards as baseless superstitions, had no
place in the ethics of antiquity. The religious flexibility
which polytheism had originally generated, the strong political feeling that pervaded all classes, and also the manifest
impossibility of making philosophy the creed of the ignorant,
had rendered nearly universal among philosophers a state of
feeling which is often exhibited, but rarely openly professed,
among ourselves.[2]    The religious opinions of men had but

---

[1] Euseb. *Præp. Evang.* iv. 1.
Fontenelle says very truly, 'Il y a
lieu de croire que chez les payens
la religion n'estoit qu'une pratique,
dont la spéculation estoit indiffé-
rente. Faites comme les autres et
croyez ce qu'il vous plaira.'—*Hist.
des Oracles*, p. 95. It was a saying
of Tiberius, that it is for the gods
to care for the injuries done to

them: 'Deorum injurias diis curæ.'
—Tacit. *Annal.* i. 73.
[2] The most melancholy modern
instance I remember is a letter
of Hume to a young man who was
thinking of taking orders, but who,
in the course of his studies, became
a complete sceptic. Hume strongly
advised him not to allow this consideration to interfere with his

little influence on their religious practices, and the sceptic considered it not merely lawful, but a duty, to attend the observances of his country. No one did more to scatter the ancient superstitions than Cicero, who was himself an augur, and who strongly asserted the duty of complying with the national rites.[1] Seneca, having recounted in the most derisive terms the absurdities of the popular worship, concludes his enumeration by declaring that 'the sage will observe all these things, not as pleasing to the Divinities, but as commanded by the law,' and that he should remember 'that his worship is due to custom, not to belief.'[2] Epictetus, whose austere creed rises to the purest monotheism, teaches as a fundamental religious maxim that every man in his devotions should 'conform to the customs of his country.'[3] The Jews and Christians, who alone refused to do so, were the representatives of a moral principle that was unknown to the Pagan world.

It should be remembered, too, that the Oriental custom of deifying emperors having been introduced into Rome, to burn incense before their statues had become a kind of test of loyalty. This adoration does not, it is true, appear to have implied any particular article of belief, and it was probably regarded by most men as we regard the application of the term 'Sacred Majesty' to a sovereign, and the custom of kneeling in his presence ; but it was esteemed inconsistent with Christianity, and the conscientious refusal of the Christians to comply with it aroused a feeling resembling that which was long produced in Christendom by the refusal of Quakers to comply with the usages of courts.

---

career (Burton, *Life of Hume*, vol. ii. pp. 187, 188.) The utilitarian principles of the philosopher were doubtless at the root of his judgment.

[1] *De Divinat.* ii. 33; *De Nat. Deor.* ii. 3.

[2] 'Quæ omnia sapiens servabit tanquam legibus jussa non tanquam diis grata. . . . Meminerimus cultum ejus magis ad morem quam ad rem pertinere.'—St. Aug. *De Civ. Dei*, vi. 10. St. Augustine denounces this view with great power. See, too, Lactantius *Inst. Div.* ii. 3

[3] *Enchirid.* xxxi.

The obligation to perform the sacred rites of an idolatrous worship, if rigidly enforced, would have amounted, in the case of the Jews and the Christians, to a complete proscription. It does not, however, appear that the Jews were ever persecuted on this ground. They formed a large and influential colony in Rome. They retained undiminished, in the midst of the Pagan population, their exclusive habits, refusing not merely all religious communion, but most social intercourse with the idolaters, occupying a separate quarter of the city, and sedulously practising their distinctive rites. Tiberius, as we have seen, appears to have involved them in his proscription of Egyptian superstitions; but they were usually perfectly unmolested, or were molested only when their riotous conduct had attracted the attention of the rulers. The Government was so far from compelling them to perform acts contrary to their religion, that Augustus expressly changed the day of the distribution of corn, in order that they might not be reduced to the alternative of forfeiting their share, or of breaking the Sabbath.[1]

It appears, then, that the old Republican intolerance had in the Empire been so modified as almost to have disappeared. The liberty of speculation and discussion was entirely unchecked. The liberty of practising foreign religious rites, though ostensibly limited by the law against unauthorised religions, was after Tiberius equally secure. The liberty of abstaining from the official national rites, though more precarious, was fully conceded to the Jews, whose jealousy of idolatry was in no degree inferior to that of the Christians. It remains, then, to examine what were the causes of the very exceptional fanaticism and animosity that were directed against the latter.

The first cause of the persecution of the Christians was the religious notion to which I have already referred. The

---

[1] This is noticed by Philo.

belief that our world is governed by isolated acts of Divine
intervention, and that, in consequence, every great calamity,
whether physical, or military, or political, may be regarded
as a punishment or a warning, was the basis of the whole
religious system of antiquity.[1] In the days of the Republic
every famine, pestilence, or drought was followed by a searching investigation of the sacred rites, to ascertain what
irregularity or neglect had caused the Divine anger, and two
instances are recorded in which vestal virgins were put to
death because their unchastity was believed to have provoked
a national calamity.[2] It might appear at first sight that the
fanaticism which this belief would naturally produce would
have been directed against the Jews as strongly as against
the Christians; but a moment's reflection is sufficient to explain the difference. The Jewish religion was essentially
conservative and unexpansive. Although, in the passion
for Oriental religions, many of the Romans had begun to
practise its ceremonies, there was no spirit of proselytism in
the sect; and it is probable that almost all who followed this
religion, to the exclusion of others, were of Hebrew nationality. The Christians, on the other hand, were ardent missionaries; they were, for the most part, Romans who had
thrown off the allegiance of their old gods, and their activity
was so great that from a very early period the temples were

---

[1] The ship in which the atheist
Diagoras sailed was once nearly
wrecked by a tempest, and the
sailors declared that it was a just
retribution from the gods because
they had received the philosopher
into their vessel. Diagoras, pointing to the other ships that were
tossed by the same storm, asked
whether they imagined there was
a Diagoras in each. (Cic. *De Nat.
Deor.* iii. 37.)

[2] The vestal Oppia was put to

death because the diviners attributed to her unchastity certain
'prodigies in the heavens,' that
had alarmed the people at the beginning of the war with Veii.
(Livy, ii. 42.) The vestal Urbinia
was buried alive on account of a
plague that had fallen upon the
Roman women, which was attributed to her incontinence, and
which is said to have ceased suddenly upon her execution. (Dion
Halicar. ix.)

in some districts almost deserted.[1] Besides this, the Jews simply abstained from and despised the religions around them. The Christians denounced them as the worship of dæmons, and lost no opportunity of insulting them. It is not, there-fore, surprising that the populace should have been firmly convinced that every great catastrophe that occurred was due to the presence of the enemies of the gods. 'If the Tiber ascends to the walls,' says Tertullian, 'or if the Nile does not overflow the fields, if the heaven refuses its rain, if the earth quakes, if famine and pestilence desolate the land, immediately the cry is raised, "The Christians to the lions!"'[2] 'There is no rain—the Christians are the cause,' had become a popular proverb in Rome.[3] Earthquakes, which, on ac-count of their peculiarly appalling, and, to ignorant men, mysterious nature, have played a very large part in the history of superstition, were frequent and terrible in the Asiatic provinces, and in three or four instances the persecu-tion of the Christians may be distinctly traced to the fanati-cism they produced.

There is no part of ecclesiastical history more curious than the effects of this belief in alternately assisting or impeding the progress of different Churches. In the first three centuries of Christian history, it was the cause of fear-ful sufferings to the faith; but even then the Christians usually accepted the theory of their adversaries, though they differed concerning its application. Tertullian and Cyprian strongly maintained, sometimes that the calamities were due to the anger of the Almighty against idolatry, sometimes that they were intended to avenge the persecution of the truth. A collection was early made of men who, having been hostile to the Christian faith, had died by some horrible

---

[1] Pliny, in his famous letter to Trajan about the Christians, notices that this had been the case in Bithynia.

[2] Tert. *Apol.* xl. See, too, Cyprian, *contra Demetrian.*, and Arnobius, *Apol.* lib. i.

[3] St. Aug. *De Civ. Dei*, ii. 3.

death, and their deaths were pronounced to be Divine punishments.[1] The victory which established the power of the first Christian emperor, and the sudden death of Arius, were afterwards accepted as decisive proofs of the truth of Christianity, and of the falsehood of Arianism.[2] But soon the manifest signs of the dissolution of the Empire revived the zeal of the Pagans, who began to reproach themselves for their ingratitude to their old gods, and who recognised in the calamities of their country the vengeance of an insulted Heaven. When the altar of Victory was removed contemptuously from the Senate, when the sacred college of the vestals was suppressed, when, above all, the armies of Alaric encircled the Imperial city, angry murmurs arose which disturbed the Christians in their triumph. The standing-point of the theologians was then somewhat altered. St. Ambrose dissected with the most unsparing rationalism the theory that ascribed the national decline to the suppression of the vestals, traced it to all its consequences, and exposed all its absurdities. Orosius wrote his history to prove that great misfortunes had befallen the Empire before its conversion. Salvian wrote his treatise on Providence to prove that the

---

[1] Instances of this kind are given by Tertullian *Ad Scapulam*, and the whole treatise *On the Deaths of the Persecutors*, attributed to Lactantius, is a development of the same theory. St. Cyprian's treatise against Demetrianus throws much light on the mode of thought of the Christians of his time. In the later historians, anecdotes of adversaries of the Church dying horrible deaths became very numerous. They were said especially to have been eaten by worms. Many examples of this kind are collected by Jortin. (*Remarks on Eccles. Hist.* vol. i. p. 432.)

[2] 'It is remarkable, in all the proclamations and documents which Eusebius assigns to Constantine, some even written by his own hand, how, almost exclusively, he dwells on this worldly superiority of the God adored by the Christians over those of the heathens, and the visible temporal advantages which attend on the worship of Christianity. His own victory, and the disasters of his enemies, are his conclusive evidences of Christianity.'— Milman, *Hist. of Early Christianity* (ed. 1867), vol. ii. p. 327. 'It was a standing argument of Athanasius, that the death of Arius was a sufficient refutation of his heresy.'— Ibid. p. 382.

barbarian invasions were a Divine judgment on the immorality of the Christians.   St. Augustine concentrated all his
genius on a great work, written under the impression of the
invasion of Alaric, and intended to prove that 'the city of
God' was not on earth, and that the downfall of the Empire
need therefore cause no disquietude to the Christians.   St.
Gregory the Great continually represented the calamities of
Italy as warnings foreboding the destruction of the world.
When Rome sank finally before the barbarian hosts, it would
seem as though the doctrine that temporal success was the
proof of Divine favour must be finally abandoned.   But the
Christian clergy disengaged their cause from that of the
ruined Empire, proclaimed its downfall to be a fulfilment of
prophecy and a Divine judgment, confronted the barbarian
conquerors in all the majesty of their sacred office, and
overawed them in the very moment of their victory.   In the
conversion of the uncivilised tribes, the doctrine of special
intervention occupied a commanding place.   The Burgundians,
when defeated by the Huns, resolved, as a last resource, to
place themselves under the protection of the Roman God
whom they vaguely believed to be the most powerful, and the
whole nation in consequence embraced Christianity.[1]   In a
critical moment of a great battle, Clovis invoked the assistance of the God of his wife.   The battle was won, and he,
with many thousands of Franks, was converted to the faith.[2]
In England, the conversion of Northumbria was partly, and
the conversion of Mercia was mainly, due to the belief that
the Divine interposition had secured the victory of a Christian
king.[3]   A Bulgarian prince was driven into the Church by
the terror of a pestilence, and he speedily effected the conversion of his subjects.[4]   The destruction of so many

---

Socrates, *Eccl. Hist.*, vii. 30.
[2] Greg. Tur. ii. 30. 31.   Clovis
wrote to St. Avitus, 'Your faith is
our victory.'

[3] Milman's *Latin Christianity*
(ed. 1867), vol. ii. pp. 236–245.
[4] Ibid. vol. iii. p. 248.

shrines, and the defeat of so many Christian armies, by
the followers of Mohamet; the disastrous and ignominious
overthrow of the Crusaders, who went forth protected by
all the blessings of the Church, were unable to impair the
belief. All through the middle ages, and for some centuries after the middle ages had passed, every startling catastrophe was regarded as a punishment, or a warning, or a
sign of the approaching termination of the world  Churches
and monasteries were built. Religious societies were
founded. Penances were performed. Jews were massacred,
and a long catalogue might be given of the theories by
which men attempted to connect every vicissitude of fortune,
and every convulsion of nature, with the wranglings of
theologians. Thus, to give but a few examples : St. Ambrose
confidently asserted that the death of Maximus was a consequence of the crime he had committed in compelling the
Christians to rebuild a Jewish synagogue they had destroyed.[1]
One of the laws in the Justinian code, directed against the
Jews, Samaritans, and Pagans, expressly attributes to them
the sterility of the soil, which in an earlier age the Pagans
had so often attributed to the Christians.[2] A volcanic eruption that broke out at the commencement of the iconoclastic
persecution was adduced as a clear proof that the Divine
anger was aroused, according to one party, by the hostility
of the emperor to the sacred images; according to the other
party, by his sinful hesitation in extirpating idolatry.[3] Bodin,
in a later age, considered that the early death of the sovereign

---

[1] *Ep.* xl.

[2] 'An diutius perferimus mutari
temporum vices, irata cœli tem-
perie ? Quæ Paganorum exacerbata
perfidia nescit naturæ libramenta
servare. Unde enim ver solitam
gratiam abjuravit ? unde æstas,
messe jejuna, laboriosum agrico-
lam in spe destituit aristarum ?

unde hyemis intemperata ferocitas
uberitatem terrarum penetrabili
frigore sterilitatis læsione damnavit ? nisi quod ad impietatis vin-
dictam transit lege sua naturæ
decretum.' — Novell. lii. Theodos.
*De Judæis, Samaritanis, et Hæreticis.*

[3] Milman's *Latin Christianity*
vol. ii. p. 354.

who commanded the massacre of St. Bartholomew was due
to what he deemed the master crime of that sovereign's reign.
He had spared the life of a famous sorcerer.[1]  In the struggles
that followed the Reformation, physical calamities were continually ascribed in one age to the toleration, in another to
the endowment, of either heresy or Popery.[2]  Sometimes,
however, they were traced to the theatre, and sometimes to
the writings of freethinkers.  But gradually, and almost insensibly, these notions faded away.  The old language is often
heard, but it is no longer realised and operative, and the
doctrine which played so large a part in the history of the
world has ceased to exercise any appreciable influence upon
the actions of mankind.

In addition to this religious motive, which acted chiefly
upon the vulgar, there was a political motive which rendered
Christianity obnoxious to the educated.  The Church constituted a vast, highly organised, and in many respects secret
society, and as such was not only distinctly illegal, but was
also in the very highest degree calculated to excite the appre-
hensions of the Government.  There was no principle in the
Imperial policy more stubbornly upheld than the suppression
of all corporations that might be made the nuclei of revolt.
The extent to which this policy was carried is strikingly
evinced by a letter from Trajan to Pliny, in which the
emperor forbade the formation even of a guild of firemen, on
the ground that they would constitute an association and
hold meetings.[3]  In such a state of feeling, the existence of a
vast association, governed by countless functionaries, shroud-
ing its meetings and some of its doctrines in impenetrable
obscurity, evoking a degree of attachment and devotion

---

*Démonomanie des Sorciers*, p.
152.
    [2] See a curious instance in
Bayle's *Dictionary*, art. ' Vergerius.'
    [3] Pliny, *Ep.* x. 43. Trajan noticed
that Nicomedia was peculiarly turbulent.  On the edict against the
hetæriæ, or associations see *Ep.*
x. 97.

greater than could be elicited by the State, ramifying through the whole extent of the empire, and restlessly extending its influence, would naturally arouse the strongest apprehension. That it did so is clearly recognised by the Christian apologists, who, however, justly retorted upon the objectors the impossibility of showing a single instance in which, in an age of continual conspiracies, the numerous and persecuted Christians had proved disloyal. Whatever we may think of their doctrine of passive obedience, it is impossible not to admire the constancy with which they clung to it, when all their interests were the other way. But yet the Pagans were not altogether wrong in regarding the new association as fatal to the greatness of the Empire. It consisted of men who regarded the Roman Empire as a manifestation of Antichrist, and who looked forward with passionate longing to its destruction. It substituted a new enthusiasm for that patriotism which was the very life-blood of the national existence. Many of the Christians deemed it wrong to fight for their country. All of them aspired to a type of character, and were actuated by hopes and motives, wholly inconsistent with that proud martial ardour by which the triumphs of Rome had been won, and by which alone her impending ruin could be averted.

The aims and principles of this association were very imperfectly understood. The greatest and best of the Pagans spoke of it as a hateful superstition, and the phrase they most frequently reiterated, when speaking of its members, was 'enemies' or 'haters of the human race.' Such a charge, directed persistently against men whose main principle was the supreme excellence of love, and whose charity unquestionably rose far above that of any other class, was probably due in the first place to the unsocial habits of the converts, who deemed it necessary to abstain from all the forms of public amusement, to refuse to illuminate their houses, or hang garlands from their portals in honour of the national

triumphs, and who somewhat ostentatiously exhibited themselves as separate and alien from their countrymen.  It may
also have arisen from a knowledge of the popular Christian
doctrine about the future destiny of Pagans.  When the
Roman learnt what fate the Christian assigned to the heroes
and sages of his nation, and to the immense mass of his living
fellow-countrymen, when he was told that the destruction of
the once glorious Empire to which he belonged was one of
the most fervent aspirations of the Church, his feelings were
very likely to clothe themselves in such language as I have
cited.

But, in addition to the general charges, specific accusations[1] of the grossest kind were directed against Christian
morals.  At a time when the moral standard was very low,
they were charged with deeds so atrocious as to scandalise the
most corrupt.  They were represented as habitually, in their
secret assemblies, celebrating the most licentious orgies,
feeding on human flesh, and then, the lights having been
extinguished, indulging in promiscuous, and especially in
incestuous, intercourse.  The persistence with which these
accusations were made is shown by the great prominence they
occupy, both in the writings of the apologists and in the
narrations of the persecutions.  That these charges were
absolutely false will now be questioned by no one.  The
Fathers were long able to challenge their adversaries to produce a single instance in which any other crime than his
faith was proved against a martyr, and they urged with a
just and noble pride that whatever doubt there might be of
the truth of the Christian doctrines, or of the Divine origin
of the Christian miracles, there was at least no doubt that
Christianity had transformed the characters of multitudes,
vivified the cold heart by a new enthusiasm, redeemed, re-

---

[1] All the apologists are full of
these charges.  The chief passages
have been collected in that very
useful and learned work, Kortholt,
*De Calumniis contra Christianos*
(Cologne, 1683.)

generated, and emancipated the most depraved of mankind. Noble lives, crowned by heroic deaths, were the best arguments of the infant Church.[1] Their enemies themselves not unfrequently acknowledged it. The love shown by the early Christians to their suffering brethren has never been more emphatically attested than by Lucian,[2] or the beautiful simplicity of their worship than by Pliny,[3] or their ardent charity than by Julian.[4] There was, it is true, another side to the picture ; but even when the moral standard of Christians was greatly lowered, it was lowered only to that of the community about them.

These calumnies were greatly encouraged by the ecclesiastical rule, which withheld from the unbaptised all knowledge of some of the more mysterious doctrines of the Church, and veiled, at least, one of its ceremonies in great obscurity. Vague rumours about the nature of that sacramental feast, to which none but the baptised Christian was suffered to penetrate, and which no ecclesiastic was permitted to explain either to the catechumens or to the world, were probably the origin of the charge of cannibalism ; while the Agapæ or love feasts, the ceremony of the kiss of love, and the peculiar and, to the Pagans, perhaps unintelligible, language in which the Christians proclaimed themselves one body and fellow-members in Christ, may have suggested the other charges. The eager credulity with which equally baseless accusations against the Jews were for centuries believed, illustrates the readiness with which they were accepted, and the extremely imperfect system of police which rendered the verification of secret crimes very difficult, had no doubt greatly enlarged the sphere of calumny. But, in addition to these considerations, the orthodox were in some respects exceedingly unfortunate. In the eyes of the Pagans they

---

[1] Justin Martyr tells us it was the brave deaths of the Christians that converted him. (*Apol.* ii. 12.)

[2] Peregrinus.

[3] *Ep.* x. 97

[4] *Ep.* ii.

were regarded as a sect of Jews; and the Jews, on account
of their continual riots, their inextinguishable hatred of the
Gentile world,[1] and the atrocities that frequently accompanied their rebellions, had early excited the anger and the
contempt of the Pagans. On the other hand, the Jew, who
deemed the abandonment of the law the most heinous of
crimes, and whose patriotism only shone with a fiercer flame
amid the calamities of his nation, regarded the Christian
with an implacable hostility. Scorned or hated by those
around him, his temple levelled with the dust, and the last
vestige of his independence destroyed, he clung with a
desperate tenacity to the hopes and privileges of his ancient
creed. In his eyes the Christians were at once apostates
and traitors. He could not forget that in the last dark hour
of his country's agony, when the armies of the Gentile
encompassed Jerusalem, and when the hosts of the faithful
flocked to its defence, the Christian Jews had abandoned the
fortunes of their race, and refused to bear any part in the
heroism and the sufferings of the closing scene. They had
proclaimed that the promised Messiah, who was to restore
the faded glories of Israel, had already come; that the privileges which were so long the monopoly of a single people had
passed to the Gentile world; that the race which was once
supremely blest was for all future time to be accursed among
mankind. It is not, therefore, surprising that there should
have arisen between the two creeds an animosity which
Paganism could never rival. While the Christians viewed
with too much exultation the calamities that fell upon the
prostrate people,[2] whose cup of bitterness they were destined

---

[1] Juvenal describes the popular
estimate of the Jews:—
'Tradidit arcano quodcunque
    volumine Moses;
Non monstrare vias, eadem nisi
    sacra colenti,

Quæsitum ad fontem solos dedu
    cere verpos.'
            Sat. xix. 102–105.
It is not true that the Mosaic law
contains these precepts.
[2] See Merivale's Hist. of Rome.
vol. viii. p. 176.

through long centuries to fill to the brim, the Jews laboured with unwearied hatred to foment by calumnies the passions of the Pagan multitude.[1] On the other hand, the Catholic Christians showed themselves extremely willing to draw down the sword of the persecutor upon the heretical sects. When the Pagans accused the Christians of indulging in orgies of gross licentiousness, the first apologist, while repudiating the charge, was careful to add, of the heretics, 'Whether or not these people commit those shameful and fabulous acts, the putting out the lights, indulging in promiscuous intercourse, and eating human flesh, I know not.'[2] In a few years the language of doubt and insinuation was exchanged for that of direct assertion; and, if we may believe St. Irenæus and St. Clement of Alexandria, the followers of Carpocrates, the Marcionites, and some other Gnostic sects, habitually indulged, in their secret meetings, in acts of impurity and licentiousness as hideous and as monstrous as can be conceived, and their conduct was one of the causes of the persecution of the orthodox.[3] Even the most extravagant charges of the Pagan populace were reiterated by the Fathers in their accusations of the Gnostics. St. Epiphanius, in the fourth century, assures us that some of their sects were accustomed to kill, to dress with spices, and to eat the children born of their promiscuous intercourse.[4] The

---

[1] See Justin Martyr, *Trypho*, xvii.

[2] Justin Martyr, *Apol.* i. 26.

[3] Eusebius expressly notices that the licentiousness of the sect of Carpocrates occasioned calumnies against the whole of the Christian body. (iv. 7.) A number of passages from the Fathers describing the immorality of these heretics are referred to by Cave, *Primitive Christianity*, part ii. ch. v.

[4] Epiphanius, *Adv. Hær.* lib. i. Hær. 26. The charge of murdering children, and especially infants, occupies a very prominent place among the recriminations of religionists. The Pagans, as we have seen, brought it against the Christians, and the orthodox against some of the early heretics. The Christians accused Julian of murdering infants for magical purposes, and the bed of the Orontes was said to have been choked with their bodies. The accusation was then commonly directed against the Jews, against the witches, and against the mid

heretics, in their turn, gladly accused the Catholics, [1] while
the Roman judge, in whose eyes Judaism, orthodox Christianity, and heresy were but slightly differing modifications of
one despicable superstition, doubtless found in this interchange
of accusations a corroboration of his prejudices.

Another cause of the peculiar animosity felt against the
Christians was the constant interference with domestic life,
arising from the great number of female conversions.  The
Christian teacher was early noted for his unrivalled skill in
playing on the chords of a woman's heart.[2]  The graphic
title of 'Earpicker of ladies,'[3] which was given to a seductive
pontiff of a somewhat later period, might have been applied to
many in the days of the persecution; and to the Roman, who
regarded the supreme authority of the head of the family, in

---

wives, who were supposed to be
in confederation with the witches.

[1] See an example in Eusebius,
iii. 32. After the triumph of
Christianity the Arian heretics
appear to have been accustomed
to bring accusations of immorality
against the Catholics. They procured the deposition of St. Eusta-
thius, Bishop of Antioch, by suborn-
ing a prostitute to accuse him of
being the father of her child. The
woman afterwards, on her death-
bed, confessed the imposture.
(Theodor. *Hist.* i. 21–22.) They
also accused St. Athanasius of
murder and unchastity, both of
which charges he most trium-
phantly repelled. (Ibid. i. 30.)

[2] The great exertions and success of the Christians in making
female converts is indignantly
noticed by Celsus (*Origen*) and by
the Pagan interlocutor in Minucius
Felix (*Octavius*), and a more minute
examination of ecclesiastical history
amply confirms their statements.

I shall have in a future chapter to
revert to this matter. Tertullian
graphically describes the anger of
a man he knew, at the conversion
of his wife, and declares he would
rather have had her 'a prostitute
than a Christian.' (*Ad Nationes*,
i. 4.) He also mentions a governor
of Cappadocia, named Herminianus,
whose motive for persecuting the
Christians was his anger at the
conversion of his wife, and who, in
consequence of his having persecuted, was devoured by worms. (*Ad
Scapul.* 3.)

[3] 'Matronarum Auriscalpius.'
The title was given to Pope St.
Damasus. See Jortin's *Remarks
on Ecclesiastical History*, vol. ii. p.
27. Ammianus Marcellinus notices
(xxvii. 3) the great wealth the
Roman bishops of his time had
acquired through the gifts of women.
Theodoret (*Hist. Eccl.* ii. 17) gives
a curious account of the energetic
proceedings of the Roman ladies
upon the exile of Pope Liberius.

all religious matters, as the very foundation of domestic morality, no character could appear more infamous or more revolting. 'A wife,' said Plutarch, expressing the deepest conviction of the Pagan world, 'should have no friends but those of her husband; and, as the gods are the first of friends, she should know no gods but those whom her husband adores. Let her shut the door, then, against idle religions and foreign superstitions. No god can take pleasure in sacrifices offered by a wife without the knowledge of her husband.'[1] But these principles, upon which the whole social system of Paganism had rested, were now disregarded. Wives in multitudes deserted their homes to frequent the nocturnal meetings[2] of a sect which was looked upon with the deepest suspicion, and was placed under the ban of the law. Again and again, the husband, as he laid his head on the pillow by his wife, had the bitterness of thinking that all her sympathies were withdrawn from him; that her affections belonged to an alien priesthood and to a foreign creed; that, though she might discharge her duties with a gentle and uncomplaining fidelity, he had for ever lost the power of touch-

---

[1] *Conj. Præcept.* This passage has been thought to refer to the Christians; if so, it is the single example of its kind in the writings of Plutarch.

[2] Pliny, in his letter on the Christians, notices that their assemblies were before daybreak. Tertullian and Minucius Felix speak frequently of the 'nocturnes convocationes,' or 'nocturnes congregationes' of the Christians. The following passage, which the last of these writers puts into the mouth of a Pagan, describes forcibly the popular feeling about the Christians: 'Qui de ultima fæce collectis imperitioribus et mulieribus credulis sexus sui facilitate labentibus, plebem profanæ conju-

rationis instituunt: quæ nocturnis congregationibus et jejuniis solennibus et inhumanis cibis non sacro quodam sed piaculo fœderantur, latebrosa et lucifugax natio, in publico muta, in angulis garrula; templa ut busta despiciunt, deos despuunt, rident sacra.'— *Octavius.* Tertullian, in exhorting the Christian women not to intermarry with Pagans, gives as one reason that they would not permit them to attend this 'nightly convocation.' (*Ad Uxorem*, ii. 4.) This whole chapter is a graphic but deeply painful picture of the utter impossibility of a Christian woman having any real community of feeling with a 'servant of the devil.'

ing her heart—he was to her only as an outcast, as a brand
prepared for the burning. Even to a Christian mind there
is a deep pathos in the picture which St. Augustine has drawn
of the broken-hearted husband imploring the assistance of
the gods, and receiving from the oracle the bitter answer:
' You may more easily write in enduring characters on the
wave, or fly with feathers through the air, than purge the
mind of a woman when once tainted by the superstition.' [1]

I have already noticed the prominence which the practice
of exorcism had acquired in the early Church, the contempt
with which it was regarded by the more philosophic Pagans,
and the law which had been directed against its professors.
It is not, however, probable that this practice, though it
lowered the Christians in the eyes of the educated as much
as it elevated them in the eyes of the populace, had any
appreciable influence in provoking persecution. In the crowd
of superstitions that were invading the Roman Empire,
exorcism had a prominent place; all such practices were
popular with the masses; the only form of magic which under
the Empire was seriously persecuted was political astrology
or divination with a view to discovering the successors to the
throne, and of this the Christians were never accused. [2] There
was, however, another form of what was deemed superstition
connected with the Church, which was regarded by Pagan
philosophers with a much deeper feeling of aversion. To
agitate the minds of men with religious terrorism, to fill the
unknown world with hideous images of suffering, to govern
the reason by alarming the imagination, was in the eyes of the
Pagan world one of the most heinous of crimes. [3] These fears

---

[1] *De Civ. Dei*, xix. 23.
[2] The policy of the Romans
with reference to magic has been
minutely traced by Maury, *Hist. de
la Magie*. Dr. Jeremie conjectures
that the exorcisms of the Christians may have excited the antipathy
of Marcus Aurelius, he, as I have
already noticed, being a disbeliever
on this subject. (Jeremie, *Hist. of
Church in the Second and Third
Cent.* p. 26.) But this is mere conjecture.
[3] See the picture of the senti

were to the ancients the very definition of superstition, and their destruction was a main object both of the Epicurean and of the Stoic. To men holding such sentiments, it is easy to perceive how obnoxious must have appeared religious teachers who maintained that an eternity of torture was reserved for the entire human race then existing in the world, beyond the range of their own community, and who made the assertion of this doctrine one of their main instruments of success.[1] Enquiry, among the early theologians, was much less valued than belief,[2] and reason was less appealed to than fear. In philosophy the most comprehensive, but in theology the most intolerant, system is naturally the strongest. To weak women, to the young, the ignorant, and the timid, to all, in a word, who were doubtful of their own judgment, the doctrine of exclusive salvation must have come with an appalling power; and, as no other religion professed it, it supplied the Church with an invaluable vantage-ground, and

---

ments of the Pagans on this matter, in Plutarch's noble *Treatise on Superstition*.

[1] Thus Justin Martyr: 'Since sensation remains in all men who have been in existence, and everlasting punishment is in store, do not hesitate to believe, and be convinced that what I say is true. . . This Gehenna is a place where all will be punished who live unrighteously, and who believe not that what God has taught through Christ will come to pass.'—*Apol.* l. 18-19. Arnobius has stated very forcibly the favourite argument of many later theologians: 'Cum ergo hæc sit conditio futurorum ut teneri et comprehendi nullius possint anticipationis attactu: nonne parior ratio est, ex duobus incertis et in ambigua expectatione pendentibus, id potius credere quod

aliquas spes ferat, quam omnino quod nullas? In illo enim periculi nihil est, si quod dicitur imminere cassum fiat et vacuum. In hoc damnum est maximum.'—*Adv. Gentes*, lib. i.

[2] The continual enforcement of the duty of belief, and the credulity of the Christians, were perpetually dwelt on by Celsus and Julian. According to the first, it was usual for them to say, 'Do not examine, but believe only.' According to the latter, 'the sum of their wisdom was comprised in this single precept, believe.' The apologists frequently notice this charge of credulity as brought against the Christians, and some famous sentences of Tertullian go far to justify it. See Middleton's *Free Enquiry*, Introd. pp. xcii. xciii.

doubtless drove multitudes into its pale. To this doctrine we
may also, in a great degree, ascribe the agony of terror that
was so often displayed by the apostate, whose flesh shrank
from the present torture, but who was convinced that the
weakness he could not overcome would be expiated by an
eternity of torment.[1]  To the indignation excited by such
teaching was probably due a law of Marcus Aurelius, which
decreed that 'if any one shall do anything whereby the weak
minds of any may be terrified by superstitious fear, the
offender shall be exiled into an island.'[2]

There can, indeed, be little doubt that a chief cause of the
hostility felt against the Christian Church was the intolerant
aspect it at that time displayed.  The Romans were prepared
to tolerate almost any form of religion that would tolerate
others.  The Jews, though quite as obstinate as the Christians
in refusing to sacrifice to the emperor, were rarely molested,
except in the periods immediately following their insurrections,
because Judaism, however exclusive and unsocial, was still
an unaggressive national faith.    But the Christian teachers
taught that all religions, except their own and that of the
Jews, were constructed by devils, and that all who dissented
from their Church must be lost.  It was impossible that
men strung to the very highest pitch of religious excitement,
and imagining they saw in every ceremony and oracle the
direct working of a present dæmon, could restrain their zeal

---

[1] See the graphic picture of the
agony of terror manifested by the
apostates as they tottered to the
altar at Alexandria, in the Decian
persecution, in Dionysius apud
Eusebius, vi. 41.   Miraculous
judgments (often, perhaps, the
natural consequence of this extreme
fear) were said to have frequently
fallen upon the apostates.  St.
Cyprian has preserved a number of
these in his treatise De Lapsis.

Persons, when excommunicated,
were also said to have been sometimes visibly possessed by devils.
See Church, On Miraculous Powers
in the First Three Centuries, pp.
52–54.

[2] 'Si quis aliquid fecerit, quo
leves hominum animi superstitione
numinis terrerentur, Divus Marcus
hujusmodi homines in insulam
relegari rescripsit.' Dig. xlviii.
tit. 19, l. 30.

or respect in any degree the feelings of others. Proselytising
with an untiring energy, pouring a fierce stream of invective
and ridicule upon the gods on whose favour the multitude
believed all national prosperity to depend, not unfrequently
insulting the worshippers, and defacing the idols,[1] they soon
stung the Pagan devotees to madness, and convinced them that
every calamity that fell upon the empire was the righteous
vengeance of the gods. Nor was the sceptical politician more
likely to regard with favour a religion whose development
was plainly incompatible with the whole religious policy of
the Empire. The new Church, as it was then organised,
must have appeared to him essentially, fundamentally, necessarily intolerant. To permit it to triumph was to permit the
extinction of religious liberty in an empire which comprised
all the leading nations of the world, and tolerated all their
creeds. It was indeed true that in the days of their distress
the apologists proclaimed, in high and eloquent language, the
iniquity of persecution, and the priceless value of a free
worship; but it needed no great sagacity to perceive that the
language of the dominant Church would be very different.
The Pagan philosopher could not foresee the ghastly histories
of the Inquisition, of the Albigenses, or of St. Bartholomew;
but he could scarcely doubt that the Christians, when in the
ascendant, would never tolerate rites which they believed to
be consecrated to devils, or restrain, in the season of their
power, a religious animosity which they scarcely bridled
when they were weak. It needed no prophetic inspiration

---

[1] A number of instances have
been recorded, in which the punishment of the Christians was due to
their having broken idols, over-
turned altars, or in other ways
insulted the Pagans at their worship. The reader may find many
examples of this collected in Cave's
*Primitive Christianity*, part i. c. v.;
Kortholt. *De Calumniis contra*
*Christianos*; Barbeyrac, *Morale des*
*Pères*, c. xvii.; Tillemont, *Mém.*
*ecclésiast.* tome vii. pp. 354-355;
Ceillier, *Hist. des Auteurs sacrés*,
tome iii. pp. 531-533. The Council
of Illiberis found it necessary to
make a canon refusing the title of
'martyr' to those who were executed for these offences.

to anticipate the time, that so speedily arrived, when, amid the wailings of the worshippers, the idols and the temples were shattered, and when all who practised the religious ceremonies of their forefathers were subject to the penalty of death.

There has probably never existed upon earth a community whose members were bound to one another by a deeper or a purer affection than the Christians, in the days of the persecution. There has probably never existed a community which exhibited in its dealings with crime a gentler or more judicious kindness, which combined more happily an unflinching opposition to sin with a boundless charity to the sinner, and which was in consequence more successful in reclaiming and transforming the most vicious of mankind. There has, however, also never existed a community which displayed more clearly the intolerance that would necessarily follow its triumph. Very early tradition has related three anecdotes of the apostle John which illustrate faithfully this triple aspect of the Church. It is said that when the assemblies of the Christians thronged around him to hear some exhortation from his lips, the only words he would utter were, ' My little children, love one another ;' for in this, he said, is comprised the entire law. It is said that a young man he had once confided to the charge of a bishop, having fallen into the ways of vice, and become the captain of a band of robbers, the apostle, on hearing of it, bitterly reproached the negligence of the pastor, and, though in extreme old age, betook himself to the mountains till he had been captured by the robbers, when, falling with tears on the neck of the chief, he restored him to the path of virtue. It is said that the same apostle, once seeing the heretic Cerinthus in an establishment of baths into which he had entered, immediately rushed forth, fearing lest the roof should fall because a heretic was beneath it.[1]   All that fierce hatred

---

[1] The first of these anecdotes is told by St. Jerome, the second by St. Clement of Alexandria, the third by St. Irenæus.

which during the Arian and Donatist controversies convulsed
the Empire, and which in later times has deluged the world
with blood, may be traced in the Church long before the
conversion of Constantine. Already, in the second century,
it was the rule that the orthodox Christian should hold no
conversation, should interchange none of the most ordinary
courtesies of life, with the excommunicated or the heretic.[1]
Common sufferings were impotent to assuage the animosity,
and the purest and fondest relations of life were polluted by
the new intolerance. The Decian persecution had scarcely
closed, when St. Cyprian wrote his treatise to maintain that
it is no more possible to be saved beyond the limits of the
Church, than it was during the deluge beyond the limits of the
ark; that martyrdom itself has no power to efface the guilt of
schism; and that the heretic, who for his master's cause
expired in tortures upon the earth, passed at once, by that
master's decree, into an eternity of torment in hell![2] Even

---

[1] The severe discipline of the
early Church on this point has
been amply treated in Marshall's
*Penitential Discipline of the Primi-
tive Church* (first published in 1714,
but reprinted in the library of
Anglo-Catholic theology), and in
Bingham's *Antiquities of the Christian Church*, vol. vi. (Oxford, 1855).
The later saints continually dwelt
upon this duty of separation. Thus,
' St. Théodore de Phermé disoit,
que quand une personne dont nous
étions amis estoit tombée dans la
fornication, nous devions luy donner
la main et faire notre possible pour
le relever; mais que s'il estoit
tombé dans quelque erreur contre
la foi, et qu'il ne voulust pas s'en
corriger après les premières remonstrances, il falloit l'abandonner
promptement et rompre toute
amitié avec lu   de peur qu'en
nous amusant à le vouloir retirer
de ce gouffre il ne nous y entraînast

nous-mêmes.' — Tillemont, *Mém.
Ecclés.* tome xii. p. 367.

[2] ' Habere jam non potest Deum
patrem qui ecclesiam non habet
matrem. Si potuit evadere quis-
quam qui extra arcam Noe fuit,
et qui extra ecclesiam foris fuerit
evadit . . . hanc unitatem qui non
tenet . . . vitam non tenet et salutem . . . esse martyr non potest
qui in ecclesia non est. . . . Cum
Deo manere non possunt qui esse
in ecclesia Dei unanimes noluerunt.
Ardeant licet flammis et ignibus
traditi, vel objecti bestiis animas
suas ponunt, non erit illa fidei
corona, sed pœna perfidiæ, nec
religiosæ virtutis exitus gloriosus
sed desperationis interitus. Occidi
talis potest, coronari non potest.
Sic se Christianum esse profitetur
quo modo et Christum diabolus
sæpe mentitur.'—Cyprian, *De Unit.
Eccles.*

2 Q

in the arena the Catholic martyrs withdrew from the Montanists, lest they should be mingled with the heretics in death.[1] At a later period St. Augustine relates that, when he was a Manichean, his mother for a time refused even to eat at the same table with her erring child.[2] When St. Ambrose not only defended the act of a Christian bishop, who had burnt down a synagogue of the Jews, but denounced as a deadly crime the decree of the Government which ordered it to be rebuilt;[3] when the same saint, in advocating the plunder of the vestal virgins, maintained the doctrine that it is criminal for a Christian State to grant any endowment to the ministers of any religion but his own,[4] which it has needed all the efforts of modern liberalism to efface from legislation, he was but following in the traces of those earlier Christians, who would not even wear a laurel crown,[5] or join in the most innocent civic festival, lest they should appear in some indirect way to be acquiescing in the Pagan worship. While the apologists were maintaining against the Pagan persecutors the duty of tolerance, the Sibylline books, which were the popular literature of the Christians, were filled with passionate anticipations of the violent destruction of the Pagan temples.[6] And no sooner had Christianity mounted the throne than the policy they foreshadowed became ascendant. The indifference or worldly sagacity of some of the rulers, and the imposing number of the Pagans, delayed, no doubt, the final consummation; but, from the time of Constantine, restrictive laws were put in force, the influence of the ecclesiastics was ceaselessly exerted in their favour, and no sagacious man could fail to anticipate the speedy and

---

[1] Eusebius, v. 16.
[2] *Confess.* iii. 11. She was afterwards permitted by a special revelation to sit at the same table with her son!
[3] *Ep.* xl.
[4] *Ep.* xviii.

[5] Tertull. *De Corona.*
[6] Milman's *Hist. of Christianity,* vol. ii. pp. 116-125. It is remarkable that the Serapeum of Alexandria was, in the Sibylline books, specially menaced with destruction.

absolute proscription of the Pagan worship. It is related of the philosopher Antoninus, the son of the Pagan prophetess Sospitra, that, standing one day with his disciples before that noble temple of Serapis, at Alexandria, which was one of the wonders of ancient art, and which was destined soon after to perish by the rude hands of the Christian monks, the prophetic spirit of his mother fell upon him. Like another prophet before another shrine, he appalled his hearers by the prediction of the approaching ruin. The time would come, he said, when the glorious edifice before them would be overthrown, the carved images would be defaced, the temples of the gods would be turned into the sepulchres of the dead, and a great darkness would fall upon mankind ! [1]

And, besides the liberty of worship, the liberty of thought and of expression, which was the supreme attainment of Roman civilisation, was in peril. The new religion, unlike that which was disappearing, claimed to dictate the opinions as well as the actions of men, and its teachers stigmatised as an atrocious crime the free expression of every opinion on religious matters diverging from their own. Of all the forms of liberty, it was this which lasted the longest, and was the most dearly prized. Even after Constantine, the Pagans Libanius, Themistius, Symmachus, and Sallust enforced their views with a freedom that contrasts remarkably with the restraints imposed upon their worship, and the beautiful friendships of St. Basil and Libanius, of Synesius and Hypatia, are among the most touching episodes of their time. But though the traditions of Pagan freedom, and the true catholicism of Justin Martyr and Origen, lingered long, it was inevitable that error, being deemed criminal, should be made penal.

---

[1] Eunapius, *Lives of the Sophists.* Eunapius gives an extremely pathetic account of the downfall of this temple. There is a Christian account in Theodoret (v. 22). Theophilus, Bishop of Alexandria, was the leader of the monks. The Pagans, under the guidance of a philosopher named Olympus, made a desperate effort to defend their temple. The whole story is very finely told by Dean Milman. (*Hist. of Christianity,* vol. iii. pp. 68–72.)

The dogmatism of Athanasius and Augustine, the increasing power of the clergy, and the fanaticism of the monks, hastened the end. The suppression of all religions but one by Theodosius, the murder of Hypatia at Alexandria by the monks of Cyril, and the closing by Justinian of the schools of Athens, are the three events which mark the decisive overthrow of intellectual freedom. A thousand years had rolled away before that freedom was in part restored.

The considerations I have briefly enumerated should not in the smallest degree detract from the admiration due to the surpassing courage, to the pure, touching, and sacred virtues of the Christian martyrs; but they in some degree palliate the conduct of the persecutors, among whom must be included one emperor, who was probably, on the whole, the best and most humane sovereign who has ever sat upon a throne, and at least two others, who were considerably above the average of virtue. When, combined with the indifference to human suffering, the thirst for blood, which the spectacles of the amphitheatre had engendered, they assuredly make the persecutions abundantly explicable. They show that if it can be proved that Christian persecutions sprang from the doctrine of exclusive salvation, the fact that the Roman Pagans, who did not hold that doctrine, also persecuted, need not cause the slightest perplexity. That the persecutions of Christianity by the Roman emperors, severe as they undoubtedly were, were not of such a continuous nature as wholly to counteract the vast moral, social, and intellectual agencies that were favourable to its spread, a few dates will show.

We have seen that when the Egyptian rites were introduced into Rome, they were met by prompt and energetic measures of repression; that these measures were again and again repeated, but that at last, when they proved ineffectual, the governors desisted from their opposition, and the new worship assumed a recognised place. The history of Christianity, in its relation to the Government, is the reverse of this. Its first introduction into Rome appears to have been altogether unopposed. Tertullian asserts that Tiberius, on the ground of a report from Pontius Pilate, desired to enrol Christ among the Roman gods, but that the Senate rejected the proposal; but this assertion, which is altogether unsupported by trustworthy evidence, and is, intrinsically, extremely improbable, is now generally recognised as false.[1] An isolated passage of Suetonius states that in the time of Claudius 'the Jews, being continually rioting, at the instigation of a certain Chrestus,'[2] were expelled from the city; but no Christian writer speaks of his co-religionists being disturbed in this reign, while all, with a perfect unanimity, and with great emphasis, describe Nero as the first persecutor. His persecution began at the close of A.D. 64.[3] It was directed against Christians, not ostensibly on the ground of their religion, but because they were falsely accused of having set fire to Rome, and it is very doubtful whether it extended beyond the city.[4] It had also this peculiarity, that, being

---

[1] *Apology*, v. The overwhelming difficulties attending this assertion are well stated by Gibbon, ch. xvi. Traces of this fable may be found in Justin Martyr. The freedom of the Christian worship at Rome appears not only from the unanimity with which Christian writers date their troubles from Nero, but also from the express statement in *Acts* xxviii. 31.

[2] 'Judæos, impulsore Chresto, assidue tumultuantes, Roma expulit.'—Sueton. *Claud.* xxv. This banishment of the Jews is mentioned in *Acts* xviii. 2, but is not there connected in any way with Christianity. A passage in Dion Cassius (lx. 6) is supposed to refer to the same transaction. Lactantius notices that the Pagans were accustomed to call Christus, *Chres-*

*tus*: 'Eum immutata litera Chrestum solent dicere.'—*Div. Inst.* iv. 7.

[3] This persecution is fully described by Tacitus (*Annal.* xv. 44), and briefly noticed by Suetonius (*Nero*, xvi.).

[4] This has been a matter of very great controversy. Looking at the question apart from direct testimony, it appears improbable that a persecution directed against the Christians on the charge of having burnt Rome, should have extended to Christians who did not live near Rome. On the other hand, it has been argued that Tacitus speaks of them as 'haud perinde in crimine incendii, quam odio humani generis convicti;' and it has been maintained that 'hatred of the human race' was treated as a crime, and punished in the pro-

directed against the Christians not as Christians, but as incendiaries, it was impossible to escape from it by apostasy. Within
the walls of Rome it raged with great fury. The Christians, who
had been for many years [1] proselytising without restraint in the
great confluence of nations, and amid the disintegration of
old beliefs, had become a formidable body. They were, we
learn from Tacitus, profoundly unpopular; but the hideous
tortures to which Nero subjected them, and the conviction
that, whatever other crimes they might have committed, they
were not guilty of setting fire to the city, awoke general pity.
Some of them, clad in skins of wild beasts, were torn by
dogs. Others, arrayed in shirts of pitch, were burnt alive in

vinces. But this is, I think, extremely far-fetched; and it is evident from the sequel that the
Christians at Rome were burnt
as incendiaries, and that it was
the conviction that they were not
guilty of that crime that extorted
the pity which Tacitus notices.
There is also no reference in
Tacitus to any persecution beyond
the walls. If we pass to the
Christian evidence, a Spanish inscription referring to the Neronian
persecution, which was once appealed to as decisive, is now unanimously admitted to be a forgery.
In the fourth century, however,
Sulp. Severus (lib. ii.) and Orosius
(Hist. vii. 7) declared that general
laws condemnatory of Christianity
were promulgated by Nero; but
the testimony of credulous historians who wrote so long after
the event is not of much value.
Rossi, however, imagines that a
fragment of an inscription found
at Pompeii indicates a general
law against Christians. See his
Bulletino d'Archeologia Cristiana
(Roma, Dec. 1865), which, however,
should be compared with the very

remarkable Compte rendu of M.
Aubé, Acad. des Inscrip. et Belles-
lettres, Juin 1866. These two papers
contain an almost complete discussion of the persecutions of Nero
and Domitian. Gibbon thinks it
quite certain the persecution was
confined to the city; Mosheim
(Eccl. Hist. i. p. 71) adopts the
opposite view, and appeals to the
passage in Tertullian (Ap. v.), in
which he speaks of ' leges istæ . . .
quas Trajanus ex parte frustratus
est, vitando inquiri Christianos,' as
implying the existence of special
laws against the Christians. This
passage, however, may merely
refer to the general law against
unauthorised religions, which Tertullian notices in this very chapter;
and Pliny, in his famous letter,
does not show any knowledge of
the existence of special legislation
about the Christians.

[1] Ecclesiastical historians maintain, but not on very strong evidence, that the Church of Rome
was founded by St. Peter, A.D. 42
or 44. St. Paul came to Rome
A.D. 61.

Nero's garden.[1]  Others were affixed to crosses.  Great multitudes perished.  The deep impression the persecution made
on the Christian mind is shown in the whole literature of the
Sibyls, which arose soon after, in which Nero is usually the
central figure, and by the belief, that lingered for centuries,
that the tyrant was yet alive, and would return once more
as the immediate precursor of Antichrist, to inflict the last
great persecution upon the Church.[2]

Nero died A.D. 68.  From that time, for at least twenty-
seven years, the Church enjoyed absolute repose.  There is
no credible evidence whatever of the smallest interference
with its freedom till the last year of the reign of Domitian ;
and a striking illustration of the fearlessness with which it
exhibited itself to the world has been lately furnished in the
discovery, near Rome, of a large and handsome porch leading
to a Christian catacomb, built above ground between the
reigns of Nero and Domitian, in the immediate neighbourhood
of one of the principal highways.[3]  The long reign of Domitian,
though it may have been surpassed in ferocity, was never
surpassed in the Roman annals in the skilfulness and the
persistence of its tyranny.  The Stoics and literary classes,
who upheld the traditions of political freedom, and who had

---

[1] On this horrible punishment
see Juvenal, *Sat.* i. 155–157.

[2] Lactantius, in the fourth century, speaks of this opinion as
still held by some 'madmen' (*De
Mort. Persec.* cap. ii.) ; but Sulp.
Severus (*Hist.* lib. ii.) speaks of it
as a common notion, and he says
that St. Martin, when asked about
the end of the world, answered,
' Neronem et Antichristum prius
esse venturos : Neronem in occi-
dentali plaga regibus subactis
decem, imperaturum, persecutionem
autem ab eo hactenus exercendam
ut idola gentium coli cogat.'—
*Dial.* ii.  Among the Pagans, the

notion that Nero was yet alive
lingered long, and twenty years
after his death an adventurer pre-
tending to be Nero was enthusiastically received by the Parthians.
(Sueton. *Nero,* lvii.)

[3] See the full description of it
in Rossi's *Bulletino d'Archeol.
Crist.* Dec. 1865. Eusebius (iii. 17)
and Tertullian (*Apol.* v.) have
expressly noticed the very remarkable fact that Vespasian, who was
a bitter enemy to the Jews, and
who exiled all the leading Stoical
philosophers except Musonius,
never troubled the Christians.

already suffered much at the hands of Vespasian, were persecuted with relentless animosity. Metius Modestus, Aru-
lenus Rusticus, Senecio, Helvidius, Dion Chrysostom, the
younger Priscus, Junius Mauricus, Artemidorus, Euphrates,
Epictetus, Arria, Fannia, and Gratilla were either killed or
banished.[1] No measures, however, appear to have been
taken against the Christians till A.D. 95, when a short and
apparently not very severe persecution, concerning which
our information is both scanty and conflicting, was directed
against them. Of the special cause that produced it we are
left in much doubt. Eusebius mentions, on the not very
trustworthy authority of Hegesippus, that the emperor,
having heard of the existence of the grandchildren of Judas,
the brother of Christ, ordered them to be brought before him,
as being of the family of David, and therefore possible pre-
tenders to the throne; but on finding that they were simple
peasants, and that the promised kingdom of which they spoke
was a spiritual one, he dismissed them in peace, and arrested
the persecution he had begun.[2] A Pagan historian states
that, the finances of the Empire being exhausted by lavish
expenditure in public games, Domitian, in order to replenish
his exchequer, resorted to a severe and special taxation of the
Jews; that some of these, in order to evade the impost,
concealed their worship, while others, who are supposed to
have been Christians, are described as following the Jewish
rites without being professed Jews.[3] Perhaps, however, the
simplest explanation is the truest, and the persecution may
be ascribed to the antipathy which a despot like Domitian

---

See a pathetic letter of Pliny,
lib. iii. *Ep.* xi. and also lib. i. *Ep.*
v. and the *Agricola* of Tacitus.

[2] Euseb. iii. 20.

[3] 'Præter cæteros Judaicus
fiscus acerbissime actus est. Ad
quem deferebantur, qui vel impro-
fessi Judaicam intra urbem vive-
rent vitam, vel dissimulata origine
imposita genti tributa non pepen-
dissent.'—Sueton. *Domit.* xii. Suetonius adds that, when a young
man, he saw an old man of ninety
examined before a large assembly
to ascertain whether he was circumcised.

must necessarily have felt to an institution which, though it did not, like Stoicism, resist his policy, at least exercised a vast influence altogether removed from his control. St. John, who was then a very old man, is said to have been at this time exiled to Patmos. Flavius Clemens, a consul, and a relative of the emperor, was put to death. His wife, or, according to another account, his niece Domitilla, was banished, according to one account, to the island of Pontia, according to another, to the island of Pandataria, and many others were compelled to accompany her into exile.[1] Numbers, we are told, 'accused of conversion to impiety or Jewish rites,' were condemned. Some were killed, and others deprived of their offices.[2] Of the cessation of the persecution there are two different versions. Tertullian[3] and Eusebius[4] say that the tyrant speedily revoked his edict, and restored those who had been banished; but according to Lactantius these measures were not taken till after the death of Domitian,[5] and

---

[1] Euseb. iii. 18.

[2] See the accounts of these transactions in Xiphilin, the abbreviator of Dion Cassius (lxvii. 14); Euseb. iii. 17–18. Suetonius notices (*Domit.* xv.) that Flavius Clemens (whom he calls a man 'contemptissimæ inertiæ') was killed 'ex tenuissima suspicione.' The language of Xiphilin, who says he was killed for 'impiety and Jewish rites;' the express assertion of Eusebius, that it was for Christianity; and the declaration of Tertullian, that Christians were persecuted at the close of this reign, leave, I think, little doubt that this execution was connected with Christianity, though some writers have questioned it. At the same time, it is very probable, as Mr. Merivale thinks (*Hist. of Rome,* vol vii. pp. 381–384), that though the pretext of the execution might have been religious, the real

motive was political jealousy. Domitian had already put to death the brother of Flavius Clemens on the charge of treason. His sons had been recognised as successors to the throne, and at the time of his execution another leading noble named Glabrio was accused of having fought in the arena. Some ecclesiastical historians have imagined that there may have been two Domitillas—the wife and niece of Flavius Clemens. The islands of Pontia and Pandataria were close to one another.

[3] 'Tentaverat et Domitianus, portio Neronis de crudelitate; sed qua et homo facile cœptum repressit, restitutis etiam quos relegaverat.' (*Apol.* 5.) It will be observed that Tertullian makes no mention of any punishment more severe than exile.

[4] Euseb. iii. 20.

[5] *De Mort. Persec.* iii.

this latter statement is corroborated by the assertion of Dion Cassius, that Nerva, upon his accession, 'absolved those who were accused of impiety, and recalled the exiles.'[1]

When we consider the very short time during which this persecution lasted, and the very slight notice that was taken of it, we may fairly, I think, conclude that it was not of a nature to check in any appreciable degree a strong religious movement like that of Christianity. The assassination of Domitian introduces us to the golden age of the Roman Empire. In the eyes of the Pagan historian, the period from the accession of Nerva, in A.D. 96, to the death of Marcus Aurelius, in A.D. 180, is memorable as a period of uniform good government, of rapidly advancing humanity, of great legislative reforms, and of a peace which was very rarely seriously broken. To the Christian historian it is still more remarkable, as one of the most critical periods in the history of his faith. The Church entered into it considerable indeed, as a sect, but not large enough to be reckoned an important power in the Empire. It emerged from it so increased in its numbers, and so extended in its ramifications, that it might fairly defy the most formidable assaults. It remains, therefore, to be seen whether the opposition against which, during these eighty-four years, it had so successfully struggled was of such a kind and intensity that the triumph must be regarded as a miracle.

Nearly at the close of this period, during the persecution of Marcus Aurelius, St. Melito, Bishop of Sardis, wrote a letter of expostulation to the emperor, in which he explicitly asserts that in Asia the persecution of the pious was an event which 'had never before occurred,' and was the result of 'new and strange decrees;' that the ancestors of the emperor were accustomed to honour the Christian faith

---

[1] Xiphilin, lxviii. 1. An annotator to Mosheim conjectures that the edict may have been issued just before the death of the emperor, but not acted on till after it.

'like other religions;' and that 'Nero and Domitian alone' had been hostile to it.[1]  Rather more than twenty years later, Tertullian asserted, in language equally distinct and emphatic, that the two persecutors of the Christians were Nero and Domitian, and that it would be impossible to name a single good sovereign who had molested them.  Marcus Aurelius himself, Tertullian refuses to number among the persecutors, and, even relying upon a letter which was falsely imputed to him, enrols him among the protectors of the Church.[2]  About a century later, Lactantius, reviewing the history of the persecutions, declared that the good sovereigns who followed Domitian abstained from persecuting, and passes at once from the persecution of Domitian to that of Decius.  Having noticed the measures of the former emperor, he proceeds : 'The acts of the tyrant being revoked, the Church was not only restored to its former state, but shone forth with a greater splendour and luxuriance ; and a period following in which many good sovereigns wielded the Imperial sceptre, it suffered no assaults from its enemies, but stretched out its hands to the east and to the west ; . . . but at last the long peace was broken.  After many years, that hateful monster Decius arose, who troubled the Church.'[3]

We have here three separate passages, from which we may conclusively infer that the normal and habitual condition of the Christians during the eighty-four years we are considering, and, if we accept the last two passages, during a much longer period, was a condition of peace, but that peace was not absolutely unbroken.  The Christian Church, which was at first regarded simply as a branch of Judaism, had begun to be recognised as a separate body, and the Roman law professedly tolerated only those religions which were

---

Euseb. iv. 26.  The whole of this apology has been recently recovered, and translated into Latin by M. Renan in the *Spici-* *legium Solesmense.*
[2] *Apol.* 5.
[3] Lactant. *De Mort. Persec.* 3-4.

expressly authorised. It is indeed true that with the extension of the Empire, and especially of the city, the theory, or at least the practice, of religious legislation had been profoundly modified. First of all, certain religions, of which the Jewish was one, were officially recognised, and then many others, without being expressly authorised, were tolerated. In this manner, all attempts to resist the torrent of Oriental superstitions proving vain, the legislator had desisted from his efforts, and every form of wild superstition was practised with publicity and impunity. Still the laws forbidding them were unrevoked, although they were suffered to remain for the most part obsolete, or were at least only put in action on the occasion of some special scandal, or of some real or apprehended political danger. The municipal and provincial independence under the Empire was, however, so large, that very much depended on the character of the local governor; and it continually happened that in one province the Christians were unmolested or favoured, while in the adjoining province they were severely persecuted.

As we have already seen, the Christians had for many reasons become profoundly obnoxious to the people. They shared the unpopularity of the Jews, with whom they were confounded, while the general credence given to the calumnies about the crimes said to have been perpetrated at their secret meetings, their abstinence from public amusements, and the belief that their hostility to the gods was the cause of every physical calamity, were special causes of antipathy. The history of the period of the Antonines continually manifests the desire of the populace to persecute, restrained by the humanity of the rulers. In the short reign of Nerva there appears to have been no persecution, and our knowledge of the official proceedings with reference to the religion is comprised in two sentences of a Pagan historian, who tells us that the emperor 'absolved those who had been convicted

of impiety,' and 'permitted no one to be convicted of impiety
or Jewish rites.' Under Trajan, however, some serious
though purely local disturbances took place. The emperor
himself, though one of the most sagacious, and in most
respects humane of Roman sovereigns, was nervously jealous
of any societies or associations among his subjects, and had
propounded a special edict against them; but the persecution
of the Christians appears to have been not so much political
as popular. If we may believe Eusebius, local persecutions,
apparently of the nature of riots, but sometimes countenanced
by provincial governors, broke out in several quarters of the
Empire. In Bithynia, Pliny the Younger was the governor,
and he wrote a very famous letter to Trajan, in which he
professed himself absolutely ignorant of the proceedings to be
taken against the Christians, who had already so multiplied
that the temples were deserted, and who were arraigned in
great numbers before his tribunal. He had, he says, released
those who consented to burn incense before the image of the
emperor, and to curse Christ, but had caused those to be
executed who persisted in their refusal, and who were not
Roman citizens, 'not doubting that a pertinacious obstinacy
deserved punishment.' He had questioned the prisoners as to
the nature of their faith, and had not hesitated to seek
revelations by torturing two maid-servants, but had 'discovered nothing but a base and immoderate superstition.'
He had asked the nature of their secret services, and had
been told that they assembled on a certain day before dawn
to sing a hymn to Christ as to a god; that they made a
vow to abstain from every crime, and that they then, before
parting, partook together of a harmless feast, which, however,
they had given up since the decree against associations. To
this letter Trajan answered that Christians, if brought before
the tribunals and convicted, should be punished, but that
they should not be sought for; that, if they consented to
sacrifice, no inquisition should be made into their past lives,

and that no anonymous accusations should be received against
them.[1]  In this reign there are two authentic instances of
martyrdom.[2]  Simeon, Bishop of Jerusalem, a man, it is said,
one hundred and twenty years old, having been accused by
the heretics, was tortured during several days, and at last
crucified.  Ignatius, the Bishop of Antioch, was arrested,
brought to Rome, and, by the order of Trajan himself, thrown
to wild beasts.  Of the cause of this last act of severity we
are left in ignorance, but it has been noticed that about this
time Antioch had been the scene of one of those violent
earthquakes which so frequently produced an outburst of
religious excitement,[3] and the character of Ignatius, who
was passionately desirous of martyrdom, may have very
probably led him to some act of exceptional zeal.  The letters of the martyr prove that at Rome the faith was openly
and fearlessly professed ; the Government during the nineteen years of this reign never appears to have taken any
initiative against the Christians, and, in spite of occasional
local tumults, there was nothing resembling a general persecution.

During the two following reigns, the Government was
more decidedly favourable to the Christians.  Hadrian,
having heard that the populace at the public games frequently called for their execution, issued an edict in which
he commanded that none should be punished simply in
obedience to the outcries against them, or without a
formal trial and a conviction of some offence against the
law, and he ordered that all false accusers should be
punished.[4]  His disposition towards the Christians was so
pacific as to give rise to a legend that he intended to

---

[1] Pliny, *Ep.* x. 97–98.
[2] Euseb. lib. iii.
[3] There is a description of this earthquake in Merivale's *Hist. of the Romans,* vol. viii. pp. 155–156.

Orosius (*Hist.* vii. 12) thought it was a judgment on account of the persecution of the Christians.
[4] Eusebius, iv. 8–9. See, too, Justin Martyr, *Apol.* i. 68–69.

enrol Christ among the gods;[1] but it is probable that, although curious on religious matters, he regarded Christianity with the indifference of a Roman freethinker ; and a letter is ascribed to him in which he confounded it with the worship of Serapis.[2] As far as the Government were con- cerned, the Christians appear to have been entirely unmo- lested ; but many of them suffered dreadful tortures at the hands of the Jewish insurgents, who in this reign, with a desperate but ill-fated heroism, made one last effort to regain their freedom.[3] The mutual hostility exhibited at this time by the Jews and Christians contributed to separate them in the eyes of the Pagans, and it is said that when Hadrian forbade the Jews ever again to enter Jerusalem, he recog- nised the distinction by granting a full permission to the Christians.[4]

Antoninus, who succeeded Hadrian, made new efforts to restrain the passions of the people against the Christians. He issued an edict commanding that they should not be molested, and when, as a consequence of some earthquakes in Asia Minor, the popular anger was fiercely roused, he commanded that their accusers should be punished.[5] If we except these riots, the twenty-three years of his reign appear to have been years of absolute peace, which seems also to have continued during several years of the reign of Marcus

---

[1] This is mentioned incidentally by Lampridius in his *Life of A. Severus.*

[2] See this very curious letter in Vopiscus, *Saturninus.*

[3] Justin Mart. *Ap.* i. 31. Euse- bius quotes a passage from Hege- sippus to the same effect. (iv. 8.)

[4] 'Præcepitque ne cui Judæo introeundi Hierosolymam esset li- centia, Christianis tantum civitate permissa.'—*Oros.* vii. 13.

[5] A letter which Eusebius gives at full (iv. 13), and ascribes to Antoninus Pius, has created a good deal of controversy. Justin Mart. (*Apol.* i. 71) and Tertullian (*Apol.* 5) ascribe it to Marcus Aurelius. It is now generally believed to be a forgery by a Christian hand, being more like a Christian apology than the letter of a Pagan emperor. St. Melito, however, writing to Marcus Aurelius, expressly states that Antoninus had written a letter forbidding the persecution of Chris- tians. (Euseb. iv. 26.)

Aurelius; but at last persecuting edicts, of the exact nature
of which we have no knowledge, were issued. Of the
reasons which induced one of the best men who have ever
reigned to persecute the Christians, we know little or
nothing. That it was not any ferocity of disposition or any
impatience of resistance may be confidently asserted of one
whose only fault was a somewhat excessive gentleness—who,
on the death of his wife, asked the Senate, as a single
favour, to console him by sparing the lives of those who had
rebelled against him. That it was not, as has been strangely
urged, a religious fanaticism resembling that which led St.
Lewis to persecute, is equally plain. St. Lewis persecuted
because he believed that to reject his religious opinions was
a heinous crime, and that heresy was the path to hell.
Marcus Aurelius had no such belief, and he, the first Roman
emperor who made the Stoical philosophy his religion and
his comfort, was also the first emperor who endowed the
professors of the philosophies that were most hostile to
his own. The fact that the Christian Church, existing
as a State within a State, with government, ideals, enthusiasms, and hopes wholly different from those of the nation,
was incompatible with the existing system of the Empire,
had become more evident as the Church increased. The
accusations of cannibalism and incestuous impurity had
acquired a greater consistency, and the latter are said to have
been justly applicable to the Carpocratian heretics, who had
recently arisen. The Stoicism of Marcus Aurelius may have
revolted from the practices of exorcism or the appeals to the
terrors of another world, and the philosophers who surrounded him probably stimulated his hostility, for his master
and friend Fronto had written a book against Christianity,[1]
while Justin Martyr is said to have perished by the machi-
nations of the Cynic Crescens.[2] It must be added, too, that,

---

[1] It is alluded to by Minucius Felix.    [2] Eusebius, iv. 16.

while it is impossible to acquit the emperor of having issued severe edicts against the Christians,[1] the atrocious details of the persecutions in his reign were due to the ferocity of the populace and the weakness of the governors in distant provinces ; and it is inconceivable that, if he had been a very bitter enemy of the Christians, Tertullian, writing little more than twenty years later, should have been so ignorant of the fact as to represent him as one of the most conspicuous of their protectors.

But, whatever may be thought on these points, there can, unhappily, be no question that in this reign Rome was stained by the blood of Justin Martyr, the first philosopher, and one of the purest and gentlest natures in the Church, and that persecution was widely extended. In two far distant quarters, at Smyrna and at Lyons, it far exceeded in atrocity any that Christianity had endured since Nero, and in each case a heroism of the most transcendent order was displayed by the martyrs. The persecution at Smyrna, in which St. Polycarp and many others most nobly died, took place on the occasion of the public games, and we may trace the influence of the Jews in stimulating it.[2] The persecution at Lyons, which was one of the most atrocious in the whole compass of ecclesiastical history, and which has supplied the martyrology with some of its grandest and most pathetic figures, derived its worst features from a combination of the fury of the populace and of the subserviency of the governor.[3] Certain servants of the Christians, terrified by the prospect of torture, accused their masters of all the crimes which popular report attributed to them, of incest, of infanticide, of cannibalism, of hideous impurity. A fearful outburst of

---

[1] St. Melito expressly states that the edicts of Marcus Aurelius produced the Asiatic persecution.

[2] Eusebius, iv. 15.

[3] See the most touching and horrible description of this persecution in a letter written by the Christians of Lyons, in Eusebius, v. 1.

ferocity ensued. Tortures almost too horrible to recount
were for hours and even days applied to the bodies of old
men and of weak women, who displayed amid their agonies
a nobler courage than has ever shone upon a battle-field, and
whose memories are immortal among mankind. Blandina
and Pothinus wrote in blood the first page of the glorious
history of the Church of France.[1] But although, during the
closing years of Marcus Aurelius, severe persecutions took
place in three or four provinces, there was no general and
organised effort to suppress Christianity throughout the
Empire.[2]

We may next consider, as a single period, the space of
time that elapsed from the death of Marcus Aurelius, in
A.D. 180, to the accession of Decius, A.D. 249. During all
this time Christianity was a great and powerful body, exercising an important influence, and during a great part of it
Christians filled high civil and military positions. The
hostility manifested towards them began now to assume a
more political complexion than it had previously done,

---

[1] Sulpicius Severus (who was
himself a Gaul) says of their martyrdom (*H. E.*, lib. ii.), 'Tum
primum intra Gallias Martyria
visa, serius trans Alpes Dei reli-
gione suscepta.' Tradition ascribes
Gallic Christianity to the apostles,
but the evidence of inscriptions
appears to confirm the account of
Severus. It is at least certain
that Christianity did not acquire a
great extension till later. The
earliest Christian inscriptions found
are (one in each year) of A.D. 334,
347, 377, 405, and 409. They do
not become common till the middle
of the fifth century. See a full
discussion of this in the preface of
M. Le Blant's admirable and indeed exhaustive work, *Inscriptions
chrétiennes de la Gaule*.

[2] It was alleged among the
Christians, that towards the close
of his reign Marcus Aurelius issued
an edict protecting the Christians,
on account of a Christian legion
having, in Germany, in a moment
of great distress, procured a shower
of rain by their prayers. (Tert.
*Apol.* 5.) The shower is mentioned
by Pagan as well as Christian
writers, and is pourtrayed on the
column of Antoninus. It was
'ascribed to the incantations of an
Egyptian magician, to the prayers
of a legion of Christians, or to the
favour of Jove towards the best of
mortals, according to the various
prejudices of different observers.
—Merivale's *Hist. of Rome*, vol.
viii. p. 338.

except perhaps in the later years of Marcus Aurelius. The existence of a vast and rapidly increasing corporation, very alien to the system of the Empire, confronted every ruler. Emperors like Commodus or Heliogabalus were usually too immersed in selfish pleasures to have any distinct policy; but sagacious sovereigns, sincerely desiring the well-being of the Empire, either, like Marcus Aurelius and Diocletian, endeavoured to repress the rising creed, or, like Alexander Severus, and at last Constantine, actively encouraged it. The measures Marcus Aurelius had taken against Christianity were arrested under Commodus, whose favourite mistress, Marcia, supplies one of the very few recorded instances of female influence, which has been the cause of so much persecution, being exerted in behalf of toleration;[1] yet a Christian philosopher named Apollonius, and at the same time, by a curious retribution, his accuser, were in this reign executed at Rome.[2] During the sixty-nine years we are considering, the general peace of the Church was only twice broken. The first occasion was in the reign of Septimus Severus, who was for some time very favourable to the Christians, but who, in A.D. 202 or 203, issued an edict, forbidding any Pagan to join the Christian or Jewish faith;[3] and this edict was followed by a sanguinary persecu-

---

[1] Xiphilin, lxxii. 4. The most atrocious of the Pagan persecutions was attributed, as we shall see, to the mother of Galerius, and in Christian times the Spanish Inquisition was founded by Isabella the Catholic; the massacre of St. Bartholomew was chiefly due to Catherine of Medicis, and the most horrible English persecution to Mary Tudor.

[2] Euseb. v. 21. The accuser, we learn from St. Jerome, was a slave. On the law condemning slaves who accused their masters,

compare Pressensé, *Hist. des Trois premiers Siècles* (2me série), tome i. pp. 182–183, and Jeremie's *Church History of Second and Third Centuries*, p. 29. Apollonius was of senatorial rank. It is said that some other martyrs died at the same time.

[3] 'Judæos fieri sub gravi pœna vetuit. Idem etiam de Christianis sanxit.'—Spartian. *S. Severus*. The persecution is described by Eusebius, lib. vi. Tertullian says Severus was favourable to the Christians, a Christian named Pro

tion in Africa and Syria, in which the father of Origen, and also St. Felicitas and St. Perpetua, perished. This persecution does not appear to have extended to the West, and was apparently rather the work of provincial governors, who interpreted the Imperial edict as a sign of hostility to the Christians, than the direct act of the emperor,[1] whose decree applied only to Christians actively proselytising. It is worthy of notice that Origen observed that previous to this time the number of Christian martyrs had been very small.[2] The second persecution was occasioned by the murder of Alexander Severus by Maximinus. The usurper pursued with great bitterness the leading courtiers of the deceased emperor, among whom were some Christian bishops,[3] and about the same time severe earthquakes in Pontus and Cappadocia produced the customary popular ebullitions. But with these exceptions the Christians were undisturbed. Caracalla, Macrinus, and Heliogabalus took no measures against them, while Alexander Severus, who reigned for thirteen years, warmly and steadily supported them. A Pagan historian assures us that this emperor intended to build temples in honour of Christ, but was dissuaded by the priests, who urged that all the other temples would be deserted. He venerated in his private oratory the statues of Apollonius of Tyana, Abraham, Orpheus, and Christ. He decreed that the provincial governors should not be appointed till the people had the opportunity of declaring any crime they had committed, borrowing this rule avowedly from the pro-

culus (whom he, in consequence, retained in the palace till his death) having cured him of an illness by the application of oil. (*Ad Scapul.* 4.)

[1] 'Of the persecution under Severus there are few, if any, traces in the West. It is confined to Syria, perhaps to Cappadocia, to Egypt, and to Africa, and in the latter provinces appears as the act of hostile governors proceeding upon the existing laws, rather than the consequence of any recent edict of the emperor.'—Milman's *Hist. of Christianity,* vol. ii. pp. 156-157.

[2] *Adv. Cels.* iii. See Gibbon ch. xvi.

[3] Eusebius, vi. 28.

cedure of the Jews and Christians in electing their clergy; he
ordered the precept 'Do not unto others what you would not
that they should do unto you' to be engraven on the palace
and other public buildings, and he decided a dispute concerning a piece of ground which the Christians had occupied,
and which the owners of certain eating-houses claimed, in
favour of the former, on the ground that the worship of a
god should be most considered.[1] Philip the Arab, who
reigned during the last five years of the period we are
considering, was so favourable to the Christians that he
was believed, though on no trustworthy evidence, to have
been baptised.

We have now reviewed the history of the persecutions to
the year A.D. 249, or about two hundred years after the
planting of Christianity in Rome. We have seen that, although during that period much suffering was occasionally
endured, and much heroism displayed, by the Christians, there
was, with the very doubtful exception of the Neronian persecution, no single attempt made to suppress Christianity
throughout the Empire. Local persecutions of great severity
had taken place at Smyrna and Lyons, under Marcus Aurelius; in Africa and some Asiatic provinces, under Severus;
popular tumults, arising in the excitement of the public
games, or produced by some earthquake or inundation, or by
some calumnious accusation, were not unfrequent; but there
was at no time that continuous, organised, and universal persecution by which, in later periods, ecclesiastical tribunals
have again and again suppressed opinions repugnant to their
own; and there was no part of the Empire in which whole
generations did not pass away absolutely undisturbed. No
martyr had fallen in Gaul or in great part of Asia Minor
till Marcus Aurelius. In Italy, after the death of Nero,

---

[1] Lampridius, *A. Severus*. The historian adds, 'Judæis privilegia
reservavit. Christianos esse passus est.'

with the exception of some slight troubles under Domitian
and Maximinus, probably due to causes altogether distinct
from religion, there were, during the whole period we are considering, only a few isclated instances of martyrdom. The
bishops, as the leaders of the Church, were the special objects
of hostility, and several in different parts of the world had
fallen; but it is extremely questionable whether any Roman
bishop perished after the apostolic age, till Fabianus was
martyred under Decius.[1] If Christianity was not formally
authorised, it was, like many other religions in a similar position, generally acquiesced in, and, during a great part of the
time we have reviewed, its professors appear to have found
no obstacles to their preferment in the Court or in the army.
The emperors were for the most part indifferent or favourable to them. The priests in the Pagan society had but little
influence, and do not appear to have taken any prominent
part in the persecution till near the time of Diocletian. With
the single exception of the Jews, no class held that doctrine of the criminality of error which has been the parent of
most modern persecutions; and although the belief that great
calamities were the result of neglecting or insulting the gods
furnished the Pagans with a religious motive for persecution,
this motive only acted on the occasion of some rare and exceptional catastrophe.[2] In Christian times, the first objects

[1] Compare Milman's *History of
Early Christianity* (1867), vol. ii.
p. 188, and his *History of Latin
Christianity* (1867), vol. i. pp. 26–
59. There are only two cases of
alleged martyrdom before this time
that can excite any reasonable
doubt. Irenæus distinctly asserts
that Telesphorus was martyred;
but his martyrdom is put in the
beginning of the reign of Antoninus
Pius (he had assumed the mitre
near the end of the reign of
Hadrian), and Antoninus is represented, by the general voice of the
Church, as perfectly free from the
stain of persecution. A tradition,
which is in itself sufficiently probable, states that Pontianus, having
been exiled by Maximinus, was
killed in banishment.

[2] Tacitus has a very ingenious
remark on this subject, which
illustrates happily the half-scepti-
cism of the Empire. After recounting a number of prodigies that were
said to have taken place in the reign
of Otho, he remarks that these

of the persecutor are to control education, to prevent the publication of any heterodox works, to institute such a minute police inspection as to render impossible the celebration of the worship he desires to suppress. But nothing of this kind was attempted, or indeed was possible, in the period we are considering. With the exception of the body-guard of the emperor, almost the whole army, which was of extremely moderate dimensions, was massed along the vast frontier of the Empire. The police force was of the scantiest kind, sufficient only to keep common order in the streets. The Government had done something to encourage, but absolutely nothing to control, education, and parents or societies were at perfect liberty to educate the young as they pleased. The expansion of literature, by reason of the facilities which slavery gave to transcription, was very great, and it was for the most part entirely uncontrolled.[1] Augustus, it is true, had caused some volumes of forged prophecies to be burnt,[2] and, under the tyranny of Tiberius and Domitian, political writers and historians who eulogised tyrannicide, or vehemently opposed the Empire, were persecuted; but the extreme indignation these acts elicited attests their rarity, and, on matters unconnected with politics, the liberty of

---

were things habitually noticed in the ages of ignorance, but now only noticed in periods of terror. 'Rudibus sæculis etiam in pace observata, quæ nunc tantum in metu audiuntur.'—*Hist.* i. 86.

[1] M. de Champagny has devoted an extremely beautiful chapter (*Les Antonins*, tome ii. pp. 179–200) to the liberty of the Roman Empire. See, too, the fifty-fourth chapter of Mr. Merivale's *History*. It is the custom of some of the apologists for modern Cæsarism to defend it by pointing to the Roman Empire as the happiest period in human history. No apology can be more

unfortunate. The first task of a modern despot is to centralise to the highest point, to bring every department of thought and action under a system of police regulation, and, above all, to impose his shackling tyranny upon the human mind. The very perfection of the Roman Empire was, that the municipal and personal liberty it admitted had never been surpassed, and the intellectual liberty had never been equalled.

[2] Sueton. *Aug.* xxxi. It appears from a passage in Livy (xxxix. 16) that books of oracles had been sometimes burnt in the Republic.

literature was absolute.[1] In a word, the Church proselytised in a society in which toleration was the rule, and at a time when municipal, provincial, and personal independence had reached the highest point, when the ruling classes were for the most part absolutely indifferent to religious opinions, and when an unprecedented concourse of influences facilitated its progress.

When we reflect that these were the circumstances of the Church till the middle of the third century, we may readily

---

[1] Tacitus has given us a very remarkable account of the trial of Cremutius Cordus, under Tiberius, for having published a history in which he had praised Brutus and called Cassius the last of Romans. (*Annal.* iv. 34–35.) He expressly terms this 'novo ac tunc primum audito crimine,' and he puts a speech in the mouth of the accused, describing the liberty previously accorded to writers. Cordus avoided execution by suicide. His daughter, Marcia, preserved some copies of his work, and published it in the reign and with the approbation of Caligula. (Senec. *Ad Marc.* 1; Suet. *Calig.* 16.) There are, however, some traces of an earlier persecution of letters. Under the sanction of a law of the decemvirs against libellers, Augustus exiled the satiric writer Cassius Severus, and he also destroyed the works of an historian named Labienus, on account of their seditious sentiments. These writings were republished with those of Cordus. Generally, however, Augustus was very magnanimous in his dealings with his assailants. He refused the request of Tiberius to punish them (Suet. *Aug.* 51), and only excluded from his palace Timagenes, who bitterly satirised both him and the empress, and proclaimed himself everywhere the enemy of the emperor. (Senec. *De Ira,* iii. 23.) A similar magnanimity was shown by most of the other emperors; among others, by Nero. (Suet. *Nero,* 39.) Under Vespasian, however, a poet, named Maternus, was obliged to retouch a tragedy on Cato (Tacit. *De Or.* 2–3), and Domitian allowed no writings opposed to his policy. (Tacit. *Agric.*) But no attempt appears to have been made in the Empire to control religious writings till the persecution of Diocletian, who ordered the Scriptures to be burnt. The example was speedily followed by the Christian emperors. The writings of Arius were burnt in A.D. 321, those of Porphyry in A.D. 388. Pope Gelasius, in A.D. 496 drew up a list of books which should not be read, and all liberty of publication speedily became extinct. See on this subject Peignot, *Essai historique sur la Liberté d'Écrire;* Villemain, *Études de Littér. ancienne;* Sir C. Lewis on the *Credibility of Roman Hist.* vol. i. p. 52; Nadal, *Mémoire sur la liberté qu'avoient les soldats romains de dire des vers satyriques contre ceux qui triomphoient* (Paris, 1725)

perceive the absurdity of maintaining that Christianity was propagated in the face of such a fierce and continuous persecution that no opinions could have survived it without a miracle, or of arguing from the history of the early Church that persecution never has any real efficacy in suppressing truth. When, in addition to the circumstances under wl ich it operated, we consider the unexampled means both of attraction and of intimidation that were possessed by the Church, we can have no difficulty in understanding that it should have acquired a magnitude that would enable it to defy the far more serious assaults it was still destined to endure. That it had acquired this extension we have abundant evidence. The language I have quoted from Lactantius is but a feeble echo of the emphatic statements of writers before the Decian persecution.[1] 'There is no race of men, whether Greek or barbarian,' said Justin Martyr, 'among whom prayers and thanks are not offered up in the name of the crucified.'[2] 'We are but of yesterday,' cried Tertullian. 'and we fill all your cities, islands, forts, councils, even the camps themselves, the tribes, the decuries, the palaces, the senate, and the forum.'[3] Eusebius has preserved a letter of Cornelius, Bishop of Rome, containing a catalogue of the officers of his Church at the time of the Decian persecution. It consisted of one bishop, forty-six presbyters, seven deacons, seven subdeacons, forty-two acolytes, fifty-two exorcists, readers, and janitors. The Church also supported more than fifteen hundred widows, and poor or suffering persons.[4]

The Decian persecution, which broke out in A.D. 249, and was probably begun in hopes of restoring the Empire to its ancient discipline, and eliminating from it all extraneous

---

[1] See a collection of passages on this point in Pressensé, *Hist. des Trois premiers Siècles* (2ᵐᵉ série), tome i. pp. 3–4.

[2] *Trypho.*

[3] *Apol.* xxxvii.

[4] Euseb. vi. 43

and unpatriotic influences,[1] is the first example of a deliberate
attempt, supported by the whole machinery of provincial
government, and extending over the entire surface of the
Empire, to extirpate Christianity from the world. It would
be difficult to find language too strong to paint its horrors
The ferocious instincts of the populace, that were long repressed, burst out anew, and they were not only permitted,
but encouraged by the rulers. Far worse than the deaths
which menaced those who shrank from the idolatrous sacrifices, were the hideous and prolonged tortures by which the
magistrates often sought to subdue the constancy of the
martyr, the nameless outrages that were sometimes inflicted
on the Christian virgin.[2] The Church, enervated by a long
peace, and deeply infected with the vices of the age, tottered
beneath the blow. It had long since arrived at the period
when men were Christians not by conviction, but through
family relationship; when the more opulent Christians vied
in luxury with the Pagans among whom they mixed, and
when even the bishops were, in many instances, worldly

---

[1] Eusebius, it is true, ascribes
this persecution (vi. 39) to the
hatred Decius bore to his predecessor Philip, who was very friendly
to the Christians. But although
such a motive might account for a
persecution like that of Maximin,
which was one of the most common
the bishops who had been about
the Court of Severus, it is insufficient to account for a persecution
so general and so severe as that of
Decius. It is remarkable that this
emperor is uniformly represented
by the Pagan historians as an eminently wise and humane sovereign.
See Dodwell, *De Paucitate Mar-
tyrum*, lii.

[2] St. Cyprian (*Ep.* vii.) and, at
a later period, St. Jerome (*Vit.*

*Pauli*), both notice that during this
persecution the desire of the persecutors was to subdue the constancy
of the Christians by torture, without gratifying their desire for
martyrdom. The consignment of
Christian virgins to houses of ill
fame was one of the most common
incidents in the later acts of martyrs which were invented in the
middle ages. Unhappily, however,
it must be acknowledged that there
are some undoubted traces of it at
an earlier date. Tertullian, in a
famous passage, speaks of the cry
'Ad Lenonem' as substituted for
that of 'Ad Leonem;' and St. Ambrose recounts some strange stories
on this subject in his treatise *De
Virginibus*.

aspirants after civil offices. It is not, therefore, surprising that the defection was very large. The Pagans marked with triumphant ridicule, and the Fathers with a burning indignation, the thousands who thronged to the altars at the very commencement of persecution, the sudden collapse of the most illustrious churches, the eagerness with which the offer of provincial governors to furnish certificates of apostasy, without exacting a compliance with the conditions which those certificates attested, was accepted by multitudes.[1] The question whether those who abandoned the faith should afterwards be readmitted to communion, became the chief question that divided the Novatians, and one of the questions that divided the Montanists from the Catholics, while the pretensions of the confessors to furnish indulgences, remitting the penances imposed by the bishops, led to a conflict which contributed very largely to establish the undisputed ascendancy of the episcopacy. But the Decian persecution, though it exhibits the Church in a somewhat less noble attitude than the persecutions which preceded and which followed it, was adorned by many examples of extreme courage and devotion, displayed in not a few cases by those who were physically among the frailest of mankind. It was of a kind eminently fitted to crush the Church. Had it taken place at an earlier period, had it been continued for a long succession of years, Christianity, without a miracle, must have perished. But the Decian persecution fell upon a Church which had existed for two centuries, and it lasted less than two years.[2] Its

---

[1] St. Cyprian has drawn a very highly coloured picture of this general corruption, and of the apostasy it produced, in his treatise *De Lapsis*, a most interesting picture of the society of his time See, too, the *Life of St. Gregory Thaumaturgus*, by Greg. of Nyssa.

[2] 'La persécution de Dèce ne dura qu'environ un an dans sa grande violence. Car S. Cyprien, dans les lettres écrites en 251, dès devant Pasque, et mesme dans quelques-unes écrites apparemment dès la fin de 250, témoigne que son église jouissoit déjà de quelque paix, mais d'une paix encore peu affermie, en sorte que le moindre accident eust pu renouveler le trouble et la persécution. Il semble

intensity varied much in different provinces. In Alexandria
and the neighbouring towns, where a popular tumult had
anticipated the menaces of the Government, it was extremely
horrible.[1] In Carthage, at first, the proconsul being absent,
no capital sentence was passed, but on the arrival of that
functionary the penalty of death, accompanied by dreadful
tortures, was substituted for that of exile or imprisonment.[2]
The rage of the people was especially directed against the
bishop St. Cyprian, who prudently retired till the storm had
passed.[3] In general, it was observed that the object of the
rulers was much less to slay than to vanquish the Christians.

---

mesme que l'on n'eust pas encore
la liberté d'y tenir les assemblées,
et néanmoins il paroist que tous
les confesseurs prisonniers à Carthage y avoient esté mis en liberté
dès ce temps-là.'—Tillemont, *Mém.
d'Hist. ecclésiastique,* tome iii. p.
324.

[1] Dionysius the bishop wrote a
full account of it, which Eusebius
has preserved (vi. 41–42). In
Alexandria, Dionysius says, the
persecution produced by popular
fanaticism preceded the edict of
Decius by an entire year. He has
preserved a particular catalogue of
all who were put to death in Alexandria during the entire Decian
persecution. They were seventeen
persons. Several of these were
killed by the mob, and their deaths
were in nearly all cases accompanied by circumstances of extreme
atrocity. Besides these, others (we
know not how many) had been put
to torture. Many, Dionysius says,
perished in other cities or villages
of Egypt.

[2] See St. Cyprian, *Ep.* viii.

[3] There was much controversy
at this time as to the propriety of
bishops evading persecution by

flight. The Montanists maintained
that such a conduct was equivalent to apostasy. Tertullian had
written a book, *De Fuga in Perse-
cutione,* maintaining this view;
and among the orthodox the conduct of St. Cyprian (who afterwards nobly attested his courage
by his death) did not escape animadversion. The more moderate
opinion prevailed, but the leading
bishops found it necessary to support their conduct by declaring
that they had received special
revelations exhorting them to fly.
St. Cyprian, who constantly appealed to his dreams to justify
him in his controversies (see some
curious instances collected in Middleton's *Free Enquiry,* pp. 101–
105), declared (*Ep.* ix.), and his
biographer and friend Pontius re-
asserted (*Vit. Cyprianis*), that his
flight was 'by the command of
God.' Dionysius, the Bishop of
Alexandria, asserts the same thing
of his own flight, and attests it by
an oath (see his own words in
Euseb. vi. 40); and the same
thing was afterwards related of St.
Gregory Thaumaturgus. (See his
*Life* by Gregory of Nyssa.)

Horrible tortures were continually employed to extort an apostasy, and, when those tortures proved vain, great numbers were ultimately released.

The Decian persecution is remarkable in Christian archæology as being, it is believed, the first occasion in which the Christian catacombs were violated. Those vast subterranean corridors, lined with tombs and expanding very frequently into small chapels adorned with paintings, often of no mean beauty, had for a long period been an inviolable asylum in seasons of persecution. The extreme sanctity which the Romans were accustomed to attach to the place of burial repelled the profane, and as early, it is said, as the very beginning of the third century, the catacombs were recognised as legal possessions of the Church.[1] The Roman legislators however unfavourable to the formation of guilds or associations, made an exception in favour of burial societies, or associations of men subscribing a certain sum to ensure to each member a decent burial in ground which belonged to the corporation. The Church is believed to have availed itself of this privilege, and to have attained, in this capacity, a legal existence. The tombs, which were originally the properties of distinct families, became in this manner an ecclesiastical domain, and the catacombs were, from perhaps the first, made something more than places of burial.[2] The chapels with which they abound, and which are of the smallest dimensions and utterly unfit for general worship, were probably mortuary chapels, and may have also been employed in the services commemorating the martyrs, while the ordinary worship was probably at first conducted in

---

[1] 'E veramente che almeno fino dal secolo terzo i fedeli abbiano posseduto cimiteri a nome commune, e che il loro possesso sia stato riconosciuto dagl' imperatori, è cosa impossibile a negare.'— Rossi, *Roma Sotterranea*, tomo i.
p. 103.

[2] This is all fully discussed by Rossi, *Roma Sotterranea*, tomo i. pp. 101–108. Rossi thinks the Church, in its capacity of burial society, was known by the name of 'ecclesia fratrum.'

the private houses of the Christians. The decision of
Alexander Severus, which I have already noticed, is the
earliest notice we possess of the existence of buildings specially
devoted to the Christian services; but we cannot tell how
long before this time they may have existed in Rome.[1] In
serious persecution, however, they would doubtless have to
be abandoned; and, as a last resort, the catacombs proved a
refuge from the persecutors.

The reign of Decius only lasted about two years, and
before its close the persecution had almost ceased.[2] On the
accession of his son Gallus, in the last month of A.D. 251,
there was for a short time perfect peace; but Gallus resumed
the persecution in the spring of the following year, and
although apparently not very severe, or very general, it seems
to have continued to his death, which took place a year
after.[3] Two Roman bishops, Cornelius, who had succeeded
the martyred Fabianus, and his successor Lucius, were at
this time put to death.[4] Valerian, who ascended the throne

---

[1] See, on the history of early
Christian Churches, Cave's *Primitive Christianity*, part i. c. vi.

[2] Dodwell (*De Paucit. Martyr.*
lvii.) has collected evidence of the
subsidence of the persecution in
the last year of the reign of Decius.

[3] This persecution is not noticed
by St. Jerome, Orosius, Sulpicius
Severus, or Lactantius. The very
little we know about it is derived
from the letters of St. Cyprian,
and from a short notice by Dionysius of Alexandria, in Eusebius,
vii. 1. Dionysius says, Gallus began the persecution when his reign
was advancing prosperously, and
his affairs succeeding, which probably means, after he had procured
the departure of the Goths from
the Illyrian province, early in A.D.
252 (see Gibbon, chap. x.). The
disastrous position into which

affairs had been thrown by the
defeat of Decius appears, at first,
to have engrossed his attention.

[4] Lucius was at first exiled and
then permitted to return, on which
occasion St. Cyprian wrote him a
letter of congratulation (*Ep.* lvii.).
He was, however, afterwards rearrested and slain, but it is not, I
think, clear whether it was under
Gallus or Valerian. St. Cyprian
speaks (*Ep.* lxvi.) of both Cornelius
and Lucius as martyred. The
emperors were probably at this
time beginning to realise the power
the Bishops of Rome possessed.
We know hardly anything of the
Decian persecution at Rome except
the execution of the bishop; and
St. Cyprian says (*Ep.* li.) that
Decius would have preferred a
pretender to the throne to a
Bishop of Rome.

A.D. 254, at first not only tolerated, but warmly patronised
the Christians, and attracted so many to his Court that his
house, in the language of a contemporary, appeared 'the
Church of the Lord.'[1] But after rather more than four years
his disposition changed. At the persuasion, it is said, of an
Egyptian magician, named Macrianus, he signed in A.D. 258
an edict of persecution condemning Christian ecclesiastics
and senators to death, and other Christians to exile, or to
the forfeiture of their property, and prohibiting them from
entering the catacombs.[2] A sanguinary and general persecution ensued. Among the victims were Sixtus, the Bishop
of Rome, who perished in the catacombs,[3] and Cyprian, who
was exiled, and afterwards beheaded, and was the first Bishop
of Carthage who suffered martyrdom.[4] At last, Valerian,
having been captured by the Persians, Gallienus, in A.D. 260,
ascended the throne, and immediately proclaimed a perfect
toleration of the Christians.[5]

The period from the accession of Decius, in A.D. 249, to
the accession of Gallienus, in A.D. 260, which I have now very
briefly noticed, was by far the most disastrous the Church
had yet endured. With the exception of about five years in
the reigns of Gallus and Valerian, the persecution was continuous, though it varied much in its intensity and its range.
During the first portion, if measured, not by the number of
deaths, but by the atrocity of the tortures inflicted, it was
probably as severe as any upon record. It was subsequently
directed chiefly against the leading clergy, and, as we have
seen, four Roman bishops perished. In addition to the
political reasons that inspired it, the popular fanaticism

---

[1] Dionysius, Archbishop of
Alexandria; see Euseb. vii. 10.
[2] Eusebius, vii. 10–12; Cyprian, *Ep.* lxxxi. Lactantius says
of Valerian, 'Multum quamvis
brevi tempore justi sanguinis fudit.'

—*De Mort. Persec.* c. v.
[3] Cyprian. *Ep.* lxxxi.
[4] See his *Life* by the deacon
Pontius, which is reproduced by
Gibbon.
[5] Eusebius, vii. 13.

caused by great calamities, which were ascribed to anger
of the gods at the neglect of their worship, had in this as in
former periods a great influence. Political disasters, which
foreshadowed clearly the approaching downfall of the Empire,
were followed by fearful and general famines and plagues.
St. Cyprian, in a treatise addressed to one of the persecutors
who was most confident in ascribing these things to the
Christians, presents us with an extremely curious picture
both of the general despondency that had fallen upon the
Empire, and of the manner in which these calamities were
regarded by the Christians. Like most of his co-religionists,
the saint was convinced that the closing scene of the earth
was at hand. The decrepitude of the world, he said, had
arrived, the forces of nature were almost exhausted, the sun
had no longer its old lustre, or the soil its old fertility, the
spring time had grown less lovely, and the autumn less boun-
teous, the energy of man had decayed, and all things were
moving rapidly to the end. Famines and plagues were the
precursors of the day of judgment. They were sent to warn
and punish a rebellious world, which, still bowing down
before idols, persecuted the believers in the truth. 'So true
is this, that the Christians are never persecuted without the
sky manifesting at once the Divine displeasure.' The conception of a converted Empire never appears to have flashed
across the mind of the saint;[1] the only triumph he predicted
for the Church was that of another world; and to the threats
of the persecutors he rejoined by fearful menaces. 'A burning, scorching fire will for ever torment those who are
condemned; there will be no respite or end to their torments.
We shall through eternity contemplate in their agonies those
who for a short time contemplated us in tortures, and for the

---

[1] Tertullian had before, in a
curious passage, spoken of the impossibility of Christian Cæsars.
'Sed et Cæsares credidissent super
Christo si aut Cæsares non essent
seculo necessarii, aut si et Christiani potuissent esse Cæsares.'—
*Apol.* xxi.

brief pleasure which the barbarity of our persecutors took in feasting their eyes upon an inhuman spectacle, they will be themselves exposed as an eternal spectacle of agony.' As a last warning, calamity after calamity broke upon the world, and, with the solemnity of one on whom the shadow of death had already fallen, St. Cyprian adjured the persecutors to repent and to be saved.[1]

The accession of Gallienus introduced the Church to a new period of perfect peace, which, with a single inconsiderable exception, continued for no less than forty years. The exception was furnished by Aurelian, who during nearly the whole of his reign had been exceedingly favourable to the Christians, and had even been appealed to by the orthodox bishops, who desired him to expel from Antioch a prelate they had excommunicated for heresy,[2] but who, at the close of his reign, intended to persecute. He was assassinated, however, according to one account, when he was just about to sign the decrees; according to another, before they had been sent through the provinces; and if any persecution actually took place, it was altogether inconsiderable.[3] Christianity, during all this time, was not only perfectly free, it was greatly honoured. Christians were appointed governors of the provinces, and were expressly exonerated from the duty of sacrificing. The bishops were treated by the civil authorities with profound respect. The palaces of the emperor were filled with Christian servants, who were authorised freely to profess their religion, and were greatly valued for their fidelity. The popular prejudice seems to have been lulled to rest; and it has been noticed that the rapid progress of the faith excited no tumult or hostility. Spacious churches

---

[1] *Contra Demetrianum.*

[2] Eusebius, vii. 30. Aurelian decided that the cathedral at Antioch should be given up to whoever was appointed by the bishops of Italy.

[3] Compare the accounts in Eusebius, vii. 30, and Lactantius, *De Mort.* c. vi.

were erected in every quarter, and they could scarcely contain the multitude of worshippers.[1] In Rome itself, before the outburst of the Diocletian persecution, there were no less than forty churches.[2] The Christians may still have been outnumbered by the Pagans; but when we consider their organisation, their zeal, and their rapid progress, a speedy triumph appeared inevitable.

But before that triumph was achieved a last and a terrific ordeal was to be undergone. Diocletian, whose name has been somewhat unjustly associated with a persecution, the responsibility of which belongs far more to his colleague Galerius, having left the Christians in perfect peace for nearly eighteen years, suffered himself to be persuaded to make one more effort to eradicate the foreign creed. This emperor, who had risen by his merits from the humblest position, exhibited in all the other actions of his reign a moderate, placable, and conspicuously humane nature, and, although he greatly magnified the Imperial authority, the simplicity of his private life, his voluntary abdication, and, above all, his singularly noble conduct during many years of retirement, displayed a rare magnanimity of character. As a politician, he deserves, I think, to rank very high. Antoninus and Marcus Aurelius had been too fascinated by the traditions of the Republic, and by the austere teaching and retrospective spirit of the Stoics, to realise the necessity of adapting institutions to the wants of a luxurious and highly civilised people, and they therefore had little permanent influence upon the destinies of the Empire. But Diocletian invariably exhibited in his legislation a far-seeing and comprehensive mind, well aware of the condition of the society he ruled, and provident of distant events. Perceiving that Roman corruption was incurable, he attempted to regenerate

---

[1] See the forcible and very candid description of Eusebius, viii. 1.

[2] This is noticed by Optatus.

the Empire by creating new centres of political life in the great and comparatively unperverted capitals of the provinces; and Nicomedia, which was his habitual residence, Carthage, Milan, and Ravenna, all received abundant tokens of his favour. He swept away or disregarded the obsolete and inefficient institutions of Republican liberty that still remained, and indeed gave his government a somewhat Oriental character; but, at the same time, by the bold, and, it must be admitted, very perilous measure of dividing the Empire into four sections, he abridged the power of each ruler, ensured the better supervision and increased authority of the provinces, and devised the first effectual check to those military revolts which had for some time been threatening the Empire with anarchy. With the same energetic statesmanship, we find him reorganising the whole system of taxation, and attempting, less wisely, to regulate commercial transactions. To such an emperor, the problem presented by the rapid progress and the profoundly anti-national character of Christianity must have been a matter of serious consideration, and the weaknesses of his character were most unfavourable to the Church; for Diocletian, with many noble qualities of heart and head, was yet superstitious, tortuous, nervous, and vacillating, and was too readily swayed by the rude and ferocious soldier, who was impetuously inciting him against the Christians.

The extreme passion which Galerius displayed on this subject is ascribed, in the first instance, to the influence of his mother, who was ardently devoted to the Pagan worship. He is himself painted in dark colours by the Christian writers as a man of boundless and unbridled sensuality, of an imperiousness that rose to fury at opposition, and of a cruelty which had long passed the stage of callousness, and become a fiendish delight, in the infliction and contemplation of suffering.[1] His strong attachment to Paganism made him at

_____

[1] See the vivid pictures in Lact. *De Mort. Persec.*

length the avowed representative of his party, which several causes had contributed to strengthen. The philosophy of the Empire had by this time fully passed into its Neoplatonic and Pythagorean phases, and was closely connected with religious observances. Hierocles and Porphyry, who were among its most eminent exponents, had both written books against Christianity, and the Oriental religions fostered much fanaticism among the people. Political interests united with superstition, for the Christians were now a very formidable body in the State. Their interests were supposed to be represented by the Cæsar Constantius Chlorus, and the religion was either adopted, or at least warmly favoured, by the wife and daughter of Diocletian (the latter of whom was married to Galerius[1]), and openly professed by some of the leading officials at the Court. A magnificent church crowned the hill facing the palace of the emperor at Nicomedia. The bishops were, in most cities, among the most active and influential citizens, and their influence was not always exercised for good. A few cases, in which an ill-considered zeal led Christians to insult the Pagan worship, one or two instances of Christians refusing to serve in the army, because they believed military life repugnant to their creed, a scandalous relaxation of morals, that had arisen during the long peace, and the fierce and notorious discord displayed by the leaders of the Church, contributed in different ways to accelerate the persecution.[2]

For a considerable time Diocletian resisted all the urgency of Galerius against the Christians, and the only measure taken was the dismissal by the latter sovereign of a number of Christian officers from the army. In A.D. 303, however, Diocletian yielded to the entreaties of his colleague, and a fearful persecution, which many circumstances conspired to stimulate, began. The priests, in one of the public ceremonies,

---

[1] Lactant. De Mort. Persec. 15.     [2] Eusebius, viii.

had declared that the presence of Christians prevented the entrails from showing the accustomed signs. The oracle of Apollo, at Miletus, being consulted by Diocletian, exhorted him to persecute the Christians. A fanatical Christian, who avowed his deed, and expiated it by a fearful death, tore down the first edict of persecution, and replaced it by a bitter taunt against the emperor. Twice, after the outburst of the persecution, the palace at Nicomedia, where Diocletian and Galerius were residing, was set on fire, and the act was ascribed, not without probability, to a Christian hand, as were also some slight disturbances that afterwards arose in Syria.[1] Edict after edict followed in rapid succession. The first ordered the destruction of all Christian churches and of all Bibles, menaced with death the Christians if they assembled in secret for Divine worship, and deprived them of all civil rights. A second edict ordered all ecclesiastics to be thrown into prison, while a third edict ordered that these prisoners, and a fourth edict that all Christians, should be compelled by torture to sacrifice. At first Diocletian refused to permit their lives to be taken, but after the fire at Nicomedia this restriction was removed. Many were burnt alive, and the tortures by which the persecutors sought to shake their resolution were so dreadful that even such a death seemed an act of mercy. The only province of the Empire where the Christians were at peace was Gaul, which had received its baptism of blood under Marcus Aurelius, but was now governed by Constantius Chlorus, who protected them from personal molestation, though he was compelled, in obedience to the emperor, to destroy their churches. In Spain, which was also under the government, but not under the direct inspection, of Constantius, the persecution was moderate, but in all other parts of the Empire it raged with

---

[1] These incidents are noticed by Eusebius in his *History*, and in his *Life of Constantine*, and by Lactantius, *De Mort. Persec.*

fierceness till the abdication of Diocletian in 305. **This**
event almost immediately restored peace to the Western provinces,[1] but greatly aggravated the misfortunes of the Eastern
Christians, who passed under the absolute rule of Galerius.
Horrible, varied, and prolonged tortures were employed to
quell their fortitude, and their final resistance was crowned
by the most dreadful of all deaths, roasting over a slow fire.
It was not till A.D. 311, eight years after the commencement
of the general persecution, ten years after the first measure
against the Christians, that the **Eastern** persecution ceased.
Galerius, the arch-enemy of the Christians, was struck down
by a fearful disease. His body, it is said, became a mass of
loathsome and fœtid sores—a living corpse, devoured by
countless worms, and exhaling the odour of the charnel-house.
He who had shed so much innocent blood, shrank himself
from a Roman death. In his extreme anguish he appealed in
turn to physician after physician, and to temple after temple.
At last he relented towards the Christians. He issued a
proclamation restoring them to liberty, permitting them to
rebuild their churches, and asking their prayers for his recovery.[2] The era of persecution now closed. One brief
spasm, indeed, due to the Cæsar Maximian, shot through the
long afflicted Church of Asia Minor;[3] but it was rapidly
allayed. The accession of Constantine, the proclamation of
Milan, A.D. 313, the defeat of Licinius, and the conversion of

---

[1] 'Italy. Sicily, Gaul, and whatever parts extend towards the West,
—Spain, Mauritania, and Africa.'—
Euseb. *Mart. Palest.* ch. xiii. But
in Gaul, as I have said, the persecution had not extended beyond
the destruction of churches; in
these provinces the persecution,
Eusebius says, lasted not quite two
years.

[2] The history of this persecution
is given by Eusebius, *Hist.* lib.
viii., in his work on the *Martyrs*

of *Palestine,* and in Lactantius,
*De Mort. Persec.* The persecution
in Palestine was not quite continuous: in A.D. 308 it had almost
ceased; it then revived fiercely,
but at the close of A.D. 309, and in
the beginning of A.D. 310, there
was again a short lull, apparently
due to political causes. See
Mosheim, *Eccles. Hist.* (edited by
Soames), vol. i. pp. 286-287.

[3] Eusebius.

the conqueror, speedily followed, and Christianity became the religion of the Empire.

Such, so far as we can trace it, is the outline of the last and most terrible persecution inflicted on the early Church. Unfortunately we can place little reliance on any information we possess about the number of its victims, the provocations that produced it, or the objects of its authors. The ecclesiastical account of these matters is absolutely unchecked by any Pagan statement, and it is derived almost exclusively from the history of Eusebius, and from the treatise 'On the Deaths of the Persecutors,' which is ascribed to Lactantius. Eusebius was a writer of great learning, and of critical abilities not below the very low level of his time, and he had personal knowledge of some of the events in Palestine which he has recorded; but he had no pretensions whatever to impartiality. He has frankly told us that his principle in writing history was to conceal the facts that were injurious to the reputation of the Church; [1] and although his practice was sometimes better than his principle, the portrait he has drawn of the saintly virtues of his patron Constantine, which we are able to correct from other sources, abundantly proves with how little scruple the courtly bishop could stray into the paths of fiction. The treatise of Lactantius, which has been well termed 'a party pamphlet,' is much more untrustworthy. It is a hymn of exultation over the disastrous ends of the persecutors, and especially of Galerius, written in a strain of the fiercest and most passionate invective, and bearing on every page unequivocal signs of inaccuracy and exaggeration. The whole history of the early persecution was soon enveloped in a thick cloud of falsehood. A notion, derived from prophecy, that ten great persecutions must precede the day of judgment, at an early period stimulated

---

[1] See two passages, which Gibbon justly calls remarkable. (*H. E.* viii. 2; *Martyrs of Palest.* ch. xii.)

the imagination of the Christians, who believed that day to
be imminent; and it was natural that as time rolled on men
should magnify the sufferings that had been endured,, and
that in credulous and uncritical ages a single real incident
should be often multiplied, diversified, and exaggerated in
many distinct narratives. Monstrous fictions, such as the
crucifixion of ten thousand Christians upon Mount Ararat
under Trajan, the letter of Tiberianus to Trajan, complaining
that he was weary of ceaselessly killing Christians in Palestine, and the Theban legion of six thousand men, said to
have been massacred by Maximilian, were boldly propagated
and readily believed.[1]   The virtue supposed to attach to the
bones of martyrs, and the custom, and, after a decree of the
second Council of Nice, in the eighth century, the obligation,
of placing saintly remains under every altar, led to an immense multiplication of spurious relics, and a corresponding
demand for legends.   Almost every hamlet soon required a
patron martyr and a local legend, which the nearest monas-
tery was usually ready to supply.   The monks occupied their
time in composing and disseminating innumerable acts of
martyrs, which purported to be strictly historical, but which
were, in fact, deliberate, though it was thought edifying,
forgeries; and pictures of hideous tortures, enlivened by fantastic miracles, soon became the favourite popular literature.
To discriminate accurately the genuine acts of martyrs from
the immense mass that were fabricated by the monks has been

---

[1] There is one instance of a
wholesale massacre which appears
to rest on good authority. Eusebius
asserts that, during the Diocletian
persecution, a village in Phrygia,
the name of which he does not
mention, being inhabited entirely
by Christians who refused to sacrifice, was attacked and burnt with
all that were in it by the Pagan
soldiery. Lactantius (*Inst. Div.* v.
11) confines the conflagration to a
church in which the entire population was burnt; and an early Latin
translation of Eusebius states that
the people were first summoned to
withdraw, but refused to do so.
Gibbon (ch. xvi.) thinks that this
tragedy took place when the decree
of Diocletian ordered the destruction of the churches.

attempted by Ruinart, but is perhaps impossible. Modern criticism has, however, done much to reduce the ancient persecutions to their true dimensions. The famous essay of Dodwell, which appeared towards the close of the seventeenth century, though written, I think, a little in the spirit of a special pleader, and not free from its own exaggerations, has had a great and abiding influence upon ecclesiastical history, and the still more famous chapter which Gibbon devoted to the subject rendered the conclusions of Dodwell familiar to the world.

Notwithstanding the great knowledge and critical acumen displayed in this chapter, few persons, I imagine, can rise from its perusal without a feeling both of repulsion and dissatisfaction. The complete absence of all sympathy with the heroic courage manifested by the martyrs, and the frigid and, in truth, most unphilosophical severity with which the historian has weighed the words and actions of men engaged in the agonies of a deadly struggle, must repel every generous nature, while the persistence with which he estimates persecutions by the number of deaths rather than by the amount of suffering, diverts the mind from the really distinctive atrocities of the Pagan persecutions. He has observed, that while the anger of the persecutors was at all times especially directed against the bishops, we know from Eusebius that only nine bishops were put to death in the entire Diocletian persecution, and that the particular enumeration, which the historian made on the spot, of all the martyrs who perished during this persecution in Palestine, which was under the government of Galerius, and was therefore exposed to the full fury of the storm, shows the entire number to have been ninety-two. Starting from this fact, Gibbon, by a well-known process of calculation, has estimated the probable number of martyrs in the whole Empire, during the Diocletian persecution, at about two thousand, which happens to be the number of persons burnt by the Spanish Inquisition during the

presidency of Torquemada alone,[1] and about one twenty-fifth
of the number who are said to have suffered for their religion
in the Netherlands in the reign of Charles V.[2] But although,
if measured by the number of martyrs, the persecutions inflicted by Pagans were less terrible than those inflicted by
Christians, there is one aspect in which the former appear by
far the more atrocious, and a truthful historian should suffer
no false delicacy to prevent him from unflinchingly stating it.
The conduct of the provincial governors, even when they
were compelled by the Imperial edicts to persecute, was
often conspicuously merciful.   The Christian records contain
several examples of rulers who refused to search out the
Christians, who discountenanced or even punished their accusers, who suggested ingenious evasions of the law, who
tried by earnest and patient kindness to overcome what they
regarded as insane obstinacy, and who, when their efforts had
proved vain, mitigated by their own authority the sentence
they were compelled to pronounce.   It was only on very rare
occasions that any, except conspicuous leaders of the Church,
and sometimes persons of a servile condition, were in danger;
the time that was conceded them before their trials gave
them great facilities for escaping, and, even when condemned,
Christian women had usually full permission to visit them in
their prisons, and to console them by their charity.   But, on
the other hand, Christian writings, which it is impossible to
dispute, continually record barbarities inflicted upon converts,
so ghastly and so hideous that the worst horrors of the In-

---

[1] Mariana (*De Rebus Hispaniæ*,
xxiv. 17). Llorento thought this
number perished in the single year
1482; but the expressions of
Mariana, though he speaks of 'this
beginning,' do not necessarily imply this restriction.   Besides these
martyrs, 17,000 persons in Spain
recanted, and endured punishments
less than death, while great numbers fled.   There does not appear
to have been, in this case, either
the provocation or the political
danger which stimulated the Diocletian persecution.

[2] This is according to the calculation of Sarpi.  Grotius estimates the victims at 100,000. —
Gibbon, ch. xvi.

quisition pale before them.  It is, indeed, true that burning
heretics by a slow fire was one of the accomplishments of the
Inquisitors, and that they were among the most consummate
masters of torture of their age.  It is true that in one Catholic
country they introduced the atrocious custom of making the
spectacle of men burnt alive for their religious opinions an
element in the public festivities.[1]  It is true, too, that the
immense majority of the acts of the martyrs are the transparent forgeries of lying monks; but it is also true that
among the authentic records of Pagan persecutions there are
histories which display, perhaps more vividly than any other,
both the depth of cruelty to which human nature may sink,
and the heroism of resistance it may attain.   There was a time
when it was the just boast of the Romans, that no refinements of cruelty, no prolongations of torture, were admitted
in their stern but simple penal code.   But all this was
changed.  Those hateful games, which made the spectacle of
human suffering and death the delight of all classes, had
spread their brutalising influence wherever the Roman name
was known, had rendered millions absolutely indifferent to
the sight of human suffering, had produced in many, in the
very centre of an advanced civilisation, a relish and a passion
for torture, a rapture and an exultation in watching the
spasms of extreme agony, such as an African or an American
savage alone can equal.   The most horrible recorded instances
of torture were usually inflicted, either by the populace, or in
their presence, in the arena.[2]  We read of Christians bound
in chairs of red-hot iron, while the stench of their half-con-
sumed flesh rose in a suffocating cloud to heaven; of others
who were torn to the very bone by shells, or hooks of iron;

---

[1] See some curious information
on this in Ticknor's *Hist. of
Spanish Literature* (3rd American
edition), vol. iii. pp. 236–237.

[2] This was the case in the persecutions at Lyons and Smyrna,
under Marcus Aurelius.  In the
Diocletian persecution at Alexandria the populace were allowed to
torture the Christians as they
pleased.  (*Eusebius*, viii. 10.)

of holy virgins given over to the lust of the gladiator, or to the mercies of the pander; of two hundred and twenty-se.en converts sent on one occasion to the mines, each with the sinews of one leg severed by a red-hot iron, and with an eye scooped from its socket; of fires so slow that the victims writhed for hours in their agonies; of bodies torn limb from limb, or sprinkled with burning lead; of mingled salt and vinegar poured over the flesh that was bleeding from the rack; of tortures prolonged and varied through entire days. For the love of their Divine Master, for the cause they believed to be true, men, and even weak girls, endured these things without flinching, when one word would have freed them from their sufferings. No opinion we may form of the proceedings of priests in a later age should impair the reverence with which we bend before the martyr's tomb.

(1)

END OF THE FIRST VOLUME.